The Women's Torah Commentary

Jewish Lights books by Rabbi Elyse Goldstein

ReVisions: Seeing Torah through a Feminist Lens

The Women's Haftarah Commentary: New Insights from Women Rabbis on the 54 Weekly Haftarah Portions, the 5 Megillot & Special Shabbatot

New Jewish Feminism: Probing the Past, Forging the Future

The Women's
Torah Commentary

*New Insights from Women Rabbis
on the 54 Weekly Torah Portions*

EDITED BY RABBI ELYSE GOLDSTEIN

JEWISH LIGHTS Publishing
Woodstock, Vermont

The Women's Torah Commentary:
New Insights from Women Rabbis on the 54 Weekly Torah Portions

2008 Quality Paperback Edition, First Printing
2006 Hardcover Edition, Fourth Printing
2003 Hardcover Edition, Third Printing
2001 Hardcover Edition, Second Printing
2000 Hardcover Edition, First Printing

Grateful acknowledgment is given for permission to reprint *Shechina Makor Hayenu* from *Kavanat Ha'Lev* © Israel Movement for Progressive Judaism.

Library of Congress Cataloging-in-Publication Data
Goldstein, Elyse.
The women's Torah commentary : new insights from women rabbis on the 54 weekly Torah portions / Elyse Goldstein.
     p.   cm.
Includes bibliographical references (p.).
ISBN-13: 978-1-58023-076-6 (Hardcover)
ISBN-10: 1-58023-076-8 (Hardcover)
1. Bible. O.T. Pentateuch—Commentaries. 2. Bible. O.T. Pentateuch—Feminist criticism. 3. Feminism—Religious aspects—Judaism. I. Title.
BS1225.3 .G578 2000
222'.107'082—dc21   00-008694
ISBN-13: 978-1-58023-370-5 (quality pbk.)
ISBN-10: 1-58023-370-8 (quality pbk.)

10 9 8 7 6 5 4 3 2 1

Manufactured in the United States of America
❀ Printed on recycled paper.

Cover Art: "Tree of Life" Torah mantle courtesy of Yael Lurie and
              Jean Pierre Larochette, Lurie-Larochette Tapestries
Cover Design: Stacey Hood, BigEyedea Visual Design

Published by Jewish Lights Publishing
A Division of LongHill Partners, Inc.
Sunset Farm Offices, Route 4, P.O. Box 237
Woodstock, VT 05091
Tel: (802) 457-4000   Fax: (802) 457-4004
www.jewishlights.com

Say to Wisdom, "You are my sister,"
and call Understanding a kinswoman.
—*Proverbs 7:4*

I am a slow unlearner. But I love my unteachers.
—*Ursula K. LeGuin*

CONTENTS

Bereshit/Genesis

Contents

Shmot/Exodus

Vayikra/Leviticus

Contents

Bamidbar/Numbers

Devarim/Deuteronomy

Index by Author

RABBI AMY EILBERG

Foreword

The Different Voice
of Jewish Women

IN RECENT YEARS, I have had the privilege of moving around the country, addressing a variety of groups of people in a variety of communities. It has been a wonderful experience, a chance to meet many lovely people, to extend the network of those concerned with Jewish feminist issues, and, most of all, to learn from the questions that others would raise. As I think back over the kinds of questions that I have been asked over the years, I realize that one question recurs, cropping up wherever I go, inevitably arising in different intonations and moods, sometimes in jest and sometimes in puzzlement—but it is always asked: "What do you call the husband of a woman rabbi?"

I answer the question differently in different contexts, depending on my understanding of what it is the questioner really wants to know. Sometimes it satisfies the questioner to know that this particular woman rabbi's husband carries his own academic title. Sometimes I respond with paradoxical humor of my own, repeating the answer of a friend in the Reform movement, saying, "Some say to just call him lucky." But it is obvious that this superficially silly inquiry expresses some very deep questions and anxieties about the reality of rabbinic leadership by women.

For some, I think, this question is a way of expressing shock about the profundity of the change in Jewish life that the woman rabbi represents. (This is such a new sort of leader; we do not even have a Yiddish word to describe her spouse.) For others, this jovial question conceals serious concerns about changes in the rabbinic family and its relationships to the community. That is, how can congregations continue to flourish without the ever available, nurturing presence of a *rebbetzin,* not to mention her counterparts in the laity? Undeniably, too, some people are using this bit of serious humor to ask the underlying questions, "What sort of rabbi are you? Can I respect you, trust you, depend on your care? After all, are you the real thing?"

Jewish Feminism—Past and Future

There is no question that the phenomenon of rabbinic leadership by women represents a profound change in Jewish life and in modern Jewish history. The fact that all of non-Orthodox Jewry has now shown itself capable of responding creatively to the feminist challenge has far-ranging consequences. The decision to ordain women, the ultimate symbol of women's equality, sends out important messages to the community. For women, it means that it is now possible to reconcile one's identities as Jew and modern woman, a reconciliation that has often seemed difficult. More broadly still, this decision communicates to the Jewish community at large that one may maintain both intellectual integrity and connection to one's ancestral community, both allegiance to modern modes of thought and loyalty to traditional religion. In short, we are witnessing a new phase in the continuing process by which Judaism adapts itself to modernity. At the same time, we can scarcely be surprised that there are those for whom these changes seem frightening and traumatic, for the pace has been very rapid.

A mere twenty-five years ago, the Jewish feminist movement was in its infancy. Jewish women were deprived of a position of equality in their communities, often facing a cruel choice of needing to reject either their womanhood or their Jewishness, in an age in which it was difficult to maintain both. At that stage, too, the Jewish community was deprived of many of the rich contributions that women could make to Jewish life. The community was able to tap only half of its resources, half of its creativity, half of its genius.

Jewish feminism first arose to battle this deprivation and, in retrospect, made great strides in a remarkably short period of time. At that period, most Jewish feminist thinkers and activists concerned themselves with issues of equality. The task at hand was to help women to achieve equal access to all sources of Jewish learning, to roles of liturgical leadership, and to the ultimate position of authority in Jewish life, the rabbinate. Twenty-five years later, the struggle for equal access has been won with only pockets of resistance remaining. The civil libertarian agenda of the Jewish feminist movement has been achieved. Equality for women is now a reality.

There are many, then, who say that the work of Jewish feminism is completed. Our community, they say with a sigh of relief, can put "the women's issue" behind it, finally able to move on to the tasks of "real importance." We women rabbis may simply go about our business, live our professional lives without ever again wrestling with the ways in which our womanhood affects our rabbinate.

I could not disagree with this position more strongly. I remember it well, for I too once longed for the end of "the women's issue," of the seemingly endless calls to lecture on "Women in Judaism," of the painful sense of differentness. But the longing to grow past the sense of women's uniqueness belonged to an earlier phase of my life and the life of my community. The task at hand in the early years was to demonstrate the legitimacy of women as members of the rabbinical seminary community. That meant showing the faculty, and all who would see, that women were a serious constituency. To do that, at that stage, we had to do what oppressed minorities must always do: play by the rules defined by the majority, and do better. We had to buy our sense of legitimacy, in our own eyes and in the eyes of the community, by doing just what men did academically and religiously, but doing it better, thus forcing the leadership to recognize us, in their own terms.

During this phase, of course, our uniqueness as women was worse than irrelevant; it was dangerous. After all, if our sisters aspiring to positions of leadership in the business world had talked openly about women's special gifts of nurturance and intimacy, their employers would simply have said, "Take your feminine gifts and apply them where they are most appropriate—in the home." So, too, we felt that we had to structure our Jewish lives precisely as men do in order to achieve equality in the (male-dominated) community.

But now, as equals, we are free to explore our special nature as women. No longer afraid that our womanhood will be used against us, we can rediscover some of women's particular gifts, and rejoice in them. Most importantly, we can begin to show our communities how valuable our contributions can be, if only we allow ourselves to function as women, if we do not force ourselves to imitate stereotypically male styles and standards in the quest for legitimacy.

It is time to shift our focus, as some pioneering thinkers have already done, from questions of what women can do to how they do it. The new agenda calls for an exploration of women's unique relationship to Jewish community and tradition. It asks how women view and live within a tradition created without women's direct input. It calls on women to reencounter the ancient tradition, to examine the basic texts and tenets of Judaism with their own eyes, through the lens of their own experience. Finally, the new Jewish feminism implores the community to listen to women's insights, to embark on a new phase of communal growth and encounter with Judaism, as women's particular insights and orientations finally come to be incorporated into our view of Judaism.

Women Rabbis—a Different Orientation

The process may at first be most apparent in the way in which we women rabbis carry ourselves, and the way we work out the relationship between our womanhood and our rabbinate. For women, as feminist literature has long acknowledged, the most difficult challenges lie in the realm of self-assertiveness, of courage to advocate principles even at the expense of cooperative relationship, and of the appropriate expressions of anger and authority. For men, on the other hand, it is the negotiation of intimacy that is often problematic, the expressions of love, sadness, hurt, and gentleness that are the prime psychological challenge.

If we then project this pair of psychological portraits onto the practice of the rabbinate, the results are most striking. After all, if there is an emerging consensus among liberal Jews of our generation about the conduct of synagogue life, it is the recognition that the distance between the laity and the leadership, between the pews and the pulpit, has been excessively great in past years. Many of our congregants have begun to see the limits of the large congregation, which is characterized by lack of intimacy and lack of participation. Many rabbis, too, have begun to realize that the professionalization of Judaism, the lack of participatory democracy in the conduct of synagogue life, and the absence of real interdependence among the members of the community all run at cross-purposes with that which we all want to achieve.

What is most exciting now is the realization that, just as we as a community have identified this particular set of problems in synagogue life, we are welcoming into the ranks of the rabbinate a group of people who, by their very life experience as women, are distinctly qualified to contribute to this work. Surely, women rabbis who take pride in their female, relational orientation can be most helpful in breaking down the antiquated, male-associated stereotype of the distant, austere, authoritarian rabbi who performs Judaism for his congregation. Women, so often inclined to make issues of relationship primary, so often oriented toward helping others to grow, can have an important role to play in encouraging congregants to take responsibility for their own religious lives. With a leader who is primarily a facilitator, congregants would be forced to move away from the concept of Judaism as a spectator sport, forced to take a more active role in defining their spiritual questions and in shaping their own encounter with Judaism.

Of course, many male rabbis have already made great strides in this direction, so that I by no means wish to suggest that women have a monopoly on this sort of work. Yet, it is no accident that this new realization about the nature of congregational life arose in precisely that era that saw the emergence of women as partners in the lives of their communities. It is now clear that there is a striking link between women's psychological orientation and the particular kind of work that is called for in religious life today. This does not mean that only women can productively contribute to this work, but it does mean that the genuinely cooperative effort of women and men in this area is most important.

*W*omen in the Community—a New Encounter

Thus far, I have focused on women rabbis as the key to the feminization of Judaism. Yet, I see the ordination of women as a pivotal experience not merely for those relatively small numbers of women who will personally aspire to the rabbinate. Rather, I view the decision to ordain women as most significant in symbolic terms, as a declaration, finally, on the part of all of the non-Orthodox movements, that the equality of women is a priority for our communities. The leadership of the three liberal movements has, in effect, issued an invitation to all women throughout the country to step forward and enter into a new encounter with Judaism, to claim their new-found equality and develop it, with responsibility, with commitment, and with creativity. Only as a large number of women begin to take this invitation seriously will the decision to ordain women truly bear fruit. Only then will we see the ways in which Judaism will be reinterpreted, reappropriated, and transformed as, for the first time, it becomes a tradition that fully incorporates the particular insights and life experiences of women. In order for this to happen, all Jewish women must take upon themselves the responsibility to open the ancient books of Judaism and to study them afresh. This study must be careful and painstaking, allowing for the emergence of both love and anger, feelings of both connection and alienation. It must treat the classical texts with utmost seriousness, allowing them to speak in their own terms. But this activity must also be a spur to new creative work, new ideas about the ways in which the tradition can be made meaningful for modern women and men.

In short, women must engage in the most ancient and most modern Jewish act, the process of exegesis, of midrash. This process has always been the way in which our ancient tradition has maintained its continuing vitality throughout the centuries, as successive generations have opened and reopened the texts, rereading, reinterpreting, and appropriating old material for a new Jewish world. It is precisely this process that now promises to be a vehicle for the incorporation of women's wisdom into Judaism.

We have surely come a long way since Sally Priesand's ordination in 1972, and Sandy Sasso's in 1974, and mine in 1985. Then, the equality of women was just being articulated. We have lived to see the fulfillment of that dream and the articulation of a new set of goals. We are just now beginning to understand the tremendous potential for growth that the equality of women represents. We are beginning to grasp the nature of the grand opportunity that stands before us at this stage of Jewish history. For the first time, our community has the chance to draw on the leadership, the insight and life experience of all Jews.

Today, we can hear a much fuller chorus of Jewish wisdom, embracing the Torah, the midrash, the life experience of Jewish women in books such as this one. Jewish life is fuller for it; the Torah itself is fuller for it. May our efforts result in the enrichment of Torah today and always.

(This foreword was updated and adapted from its full version, which appeared in Ra'ayonot *5, no. 3–4 [summer–autumn 1985].)*

Acknowledgments

SO MANY OF MY FEMALE COLLEAGUES are great preachers, great teachers, and great writers. We are always in demand as speakers. When we get together at conventions and study text together, I am always impressed and sometimes astonished at the depth of insight and the collective creativity present. How was it possible that there had not yet been a compendium of female rabbis' commentary on the Torah? When I discovered that indeed no one had yet put together an anthology of female rabbinic interpretations of the weekly Torah portions, I knew immediately that this would be my chosen task. It has been a complete and utter joy, and a "labor of love" only in the most positive sense of labor, that which brings forth birth. From my first call for submissions until the last editing, I have continued to be inspired by the rabbis I have encountered through their writings.

Thus first I thank the 116 women rabbis who submitted essays for this book, and I regret that only the physical realities of time, space, and length prevented me from printing them all.

Stuart Matlins, at Jewish Lights, shared my conviction from the beginning that these impressive women need to be published, and that Jews of every denomination—as well as anyone interested in the Bible at all—ought to be learning from them. I continue to appreciate his wisdom. Elisheva Urbas, the editor's editor, has an amazingly keen eye and sharp focus. She has tactfully and thoughtfully shaped this book and all its contributions with her knowledge, and with her dedication to both scholarship and feminist critique. We all feel deeply indebted to her. Thank you also to Barbara Berson, who first guided this book in Canada.

And through this book, I wish to salute the first three women ordained—Sally Priesand (Reform), Sandy Eisenberg Sasso (Reconstructionist), and Amy Eilberg (Conservative)—and gratefully acknowledge, on behalf of all of us, that it was their hard work of breaking the path that made it possible at all for us to walk that path now.

My husband, Baruch Browns-Sienna, spent many long hours on the computer doing all those mysterious things that need doing in order to put together an anthology such as this. I deeply appreciate his continual support and belief not only in me but in the "cause" of Jewish feminism. To my sons, Noam, Carmi, and Micah, thank you for your patience, pride, and love. I live with the conviction that, one day, my boys will have a Judaism filled with the insights of women as part of the "normative" experience of just being Jewish. And to my mother, Terry, who should have been a rabbi herself, thanks for rubbing off on me.

Most importantly, thank you to those of every religion who continue to open their hearts and minds to the sage voices of women and to the unique gifts of female leadership.

I bless the Holy One, who has kept me alive, sustained me,
and brought me strength to see each new day.

Sh'vat 5760/January 2000
Toronto, Canada

Introduction

ON JUNE 3, 1972, the Reform movement ordained as a rabbi a young woman from Ohio named Sally Priesand. In that one moment, the face of the Jewish community was forever changed. It was, to paraphrase another great event, "one small step for a woman, one giant step for womankind."

Rabbi Priesand's ordination did not occur in a vacuum. She entered Hebrew Union College (HUC), the Reform seminary, during the women's-lib era of the 1960s. She often notes that her motive was never to "rock the boat," but simply to become a rabbi. Yet no doubt at that particular moment in history HUC had decided it was time to keep up with the new demands of women and the new advancements for women in the secular world.

Since the early nineteenth century, the denomination of Reform Judaism had, on paper, ensured the religious equality of women. The introduction of the ceremony of confirmation for both girls and boys in 1846 by Max Lilienthal in New York City attested to the growing religious emancipation of women; it was offered as an "antidote" to the all-boys experience of bar mitzvah, and there seemed no reason to exclude girls from the new rite. As early as 1851, Isaac Mayer Wise had removed separate seating from his synagogue, Anshe Emeth, in Albany, New York. In the 1850s reforming rabbis were arguing for the ceremonial religious equality of women, the abolition of *chalitzah* (a ceremony freeing a woman from marrying her dead husband's brother) and the status of *agunah* (a woman unable to ever remarry because her husband would not or could not grant her a Jewish bill of divorce). All these reforming discussions, however, were based on the assumption that men would continue to govern decision-making bodies in the Jewish world. Since men made the rules, men could bend them, or even break them, to "allow" women's entrance into male bastions such as bar mitzvah or *aliyot* to the Torah. This entrance was limited to what the male leadership felt was still "proper" for "ladies" of that era. It was not until the 1920s that the question was debated as to whether such opportunities for equal religious expression might also lead women to enter the echelons of rabbinic leadership.

In 1919 a woman named Martha Neumark began to study at the Reform rabbinical seminary. In 1921 she was allowed to lead a High Holiday congregation, thus marking her entrance into the professional rabbinic world. It was that move that prompted Kaufmann Kohler, president of the seminary at that time, to form a faculty committee to study the feasibility of ordaining women. When the debate around women's ordination did emerge officially in 1922, at a conference of the faculty of Hebrew Union College, it revolved around three themes. The first was halachic, and the rabbis studied whether Jewish law might permit such ordination. The second was sociological, and the rabbis wondered whether women could retain their devotion to home and family within the difficult and laborious tasks of the rabbinate. The third was communal, and the rabbis worried whether ordaining women would create an irreparable schism within the larger community. Yet despite these concerns, the faculty of the seminary voted in favor of women's ordination. But a few months later, the lay Board of Governors, upon whom the final decision rested, rejected the vote, and restricted ordination from the Hebrew Union College to men only. Though women attended the seminary as students from as early as 1900, they were not to be ordained. Writing on the history of women in the Reform seminary, Hebrew Union College–Jewish Institute of Religion, and looking at its roots in the late 1800s, Rabbi Gary Zola says, "Despite the fact that the presence of women in the halls of HUC goes back to the school's very first days, no one believed seriously that a woman would actually enter the rabbinate. Even though Isaac Mayer Wise, the school's founder and president, had declared publicly that he was ready and eager to educate and ordain women rabbis, no evidence exists to suggest that he ever actively sought or encouraged a woman to pursue ordination."[1]

It was in Nazi Germany that the first woman actually held a rabbinic title. In 1935 Regina Jonas, a student at the liberal seminary in Berlin, was empowered with a special diploma to "hold rabbinic office." She ministered to her people in the Terezin concentration camp, and died in Auschwitz in 1944. Twenty-eight years after her death and fifty years since the seminary faculty had formally agreed to ordain women, Sally Priesand became the first woman to be granted *smichah*, official ordination, from the faculty and lay body of a major rabbinic seminary. It took the merging of the counterculture 1960s, women's-lib of the early 1970s, and the personalities of both Priesand and the HUC faculty of the time to fully move from the idea of religious leadership for women to the practice of it.

Dr. Alfred Gottschalk, the president of the seminary who ordained Priesand, speaks on having been present in person at the historic change. He writes, "I will never forget that day. . . . After I finished reciting the words of priestly benediction, Sally descended from the *bimah* in order to return to her seat. At that moment, all of her classmates spontaneously rose from their seats and offered their sustained applause. All present felt the significance of that remarkable moment."[2]

The Reform movement knew there would be implications of Priesand's ordination. Indeed, the Reconstructionist movement soon followed suit, with the ordination of Sandy Eisenberg Sasso, in 1974; and the Conservative movement ordained Amy Eilberg in 1985. While the Orthodox movement does not ordain women, it has begun to deal with the demands of its own female leadership. A yearly Orthodox feminist conference in New York attracts thousands of participants. Most notably, in 1998 Lincoln Square synagogue, a modern Orthodox synagogue in New York, hired Julie Joseph as "congregational intern" in a pararabbinic position to offer counseling, classes, and other professional services, just short of preaching or leading worship.

The ordination of women has completely changed the face of organized Jewish life, in all the synagogue denominations, and in many facets of the Jewish community unrelated to the synagogue. Female rabbis often bring their feminist concerns into their work, along with a sense of collective responsibility as women. What were once considered solely women's issues, belonging to the Sisterhood or women's auxiliaries, are now discussed from the *bimah* and at conferences of major mainstream Jewish organizations. In sermons and study groups, the female characters of the Bible are studied, examined, and dissected as never before. The issues of sexual harassment and power hierarchies in organized Jewish life have come to the forefront. Gender stereotyping in textbooks is being analyzed and corrected. All this might have come about anyway, with the advances of feminism into Judaism. But there is no doubt that the presence of women in positions of religious and communal authority, influence, and decision-making has pushed what have been previously identified as "marginal" issues into the consciousness of the mainstream.

*W*omen as Rabbis: Some Personal Notes

When you close your eyes and picture "a rabbi," can you picture a young woman, a mother of three, a beardless, short figure who does not bellow or have a deeply resonant voice? We practice our authority differently than most of the rabbis we grew up with. We cry easily on the *bimah*. We hold our babies during Adon Olam. We nurse in our offices. I myself do not know anymore how to define rabbi. Gloria Steinem once remarked that when people would say to her, "Gee, you don't look forty," she would respond, "Well, this is what forty looks like!" "You don't look like a rabbi," I think to myself, as I picture my childhood rabbis, but this is what a rabbi looks like now.

The very notion of a woman rabbi challenges us to recognize that for centuries we thought male rabbis were the norm. We never before in our history referred to our rabbis as "male rabbis." Now that we have "Women in Judaism" courses, we see that we have been studying "Men in Judaism" all along, mistakenly believing that we had been learning "just Judaism." We have assumed that what we received was a neutral form of Judaism. By hearing the same stories retold now by women, by being at the same events now led by women, by simply sitting in the pews and looking up to see women in front of us, we have grown to understand that the "just Judaism" we inherited was not at all neutral, but filtered through men and the male experience.

When women were first ordained, the early pioneers spent energy trying not to be different, trying to fit in and be just "one of the guys." But as more and more women were ordained, and as women from different denominations with differing religious perspectives joined the Reform ordainees, the focus shifted to a sense of pride in a woman's way of doing things, and especially a woman's way of seeing text. Study groups and classes emerged in synagogues and living rooms as female rabbis were called upon more and more to examine the women of the Torah, or lecture on the issues of women and halachah, or guide women through learning to don traditional garb once reserved only for men, like the tallit or tefillin. Men and women both began to recognize the one-sidedness of the Jewish religious experience. What we considered to be "normative" Jewish thought, Jewish teaching, and Jewish commentary were almost exclusively male. To put it simply, seeing and hearing women from the pulpit has changed the way Jews see and hear sacred text, holiday celebrations, lifecycle events, and almost anything Jewish.

To be sure, there are some women in the rabbinate who do not identify as feminists. There are times when those of us who do identify as feminists just do a wedding or a funeral, or teach a Talmud class, or plan an event, and we don't wear our feminism on our sleeves. Our being female, however, is always apparent.

People are often disappointed when a female rabbi says no to a request because such a request might jar a Jewish sensibility. "But you're a woman," they protest. "We thought you would be different." We do not say yes to every request, even from feminists, and we do not change everything that is based on a patriarchal history.

Sometimes we vote for tradition, even with our commitment to feminism.

Women rabbis, like women in general, are not a monolith. This book reflects the flowering of diversity within that body of women in the rabbinate, which may surprise those readers who expected to hear "the voice of women rabbis" rather than "the many different voices of many different women rabbis." One author may suggest the exact opposite of what a second author suggests, which does not signal a failure of consistency. Rather, it projects in clear view the variety of ways that women in the rabbinate read the Torah, which actually imitates the way traditional commentators disagreed on the meaning of any given passage, which in turn mirrors the vast spectrum of ways that Jews have seen any given text through the ages.

Of course, the assumption that men and women see text—or anything, for that matter—differently is still a matter of debate. Feminist social theorists such as Carol Gilligan have posited that men tend to relate to the world in a hierarchical, authoritative and exhortative way, and women in a relational, inclusive way. Whether this is nature or nurture remains unproven.

Whether or not we are actually different from our male counterparts, I believe that most of the women in the rabbinate today would agree that we are *perceived* differently. Put simply, people experience female rabbis differently than they experience male ones. And they experience Judaism, the gender issues of the prayerbook, and the whole question of the male imagery of God differently with a woman rabbi. As Rabbi Ellen Lewis writes, "Women rabbis make things look different without even trying. When I first assumed my present pulpit, I tried to do everything just like my predecessor did. . . . What I found out was that, even if I did the same things he did, when I did them they looked and sounded different. . . . We still have the idea that, for all that we share with our male colleagues, our experience of the rabbinate is different."[3]

If our experience of the rabbinate is indeed distinct, then our experience of the central role of being a rabbi—teaching Torah—will also be distinct. If we hear the text differently than men, we will interpret it differently than men. How might a Torah commentary by women rabbis be different? I wanted to find out.

The Methodology of This Anthology

Rachel Adler, writing on feminist methodologies, suggests, "One crucial contribution will be the methodologies feminists have developed for understanding and using narrative. . . . As a method of vision, feminist narratives draw upon fantasies and desires, prophecies and prayers to imagine possible worlds in which both women and men could flourish. As a tool of critique, narrative can expose within abstract theories assumptions about the nature and experience of being human, what people know, how they love, what they want, and what they fear."[4] Other feminist methodologies include a critique of the text from within its social context as that context applies to women both in the biblical period and now; a critique of the traditional ways of "unpacking" the text that rarely "unpacked" it for women; and an analysis of the assumptions we bring to the text, based on a history of our own personal biases we have inherited from a patriarchal Judaism. All these "ways of seeing" are contained in the essays of this volume.

Therefore, a commentary written by women will contain messages of change within a traditional reverence for an unchanging text. Because this volume includes only the voices of women who have sought ordination, it necessarily privileges the thinking of reform (broadly defined) rather than tradition. This is not to suggest either that fewer women than men care about traditional halachah or that Orthodox/traditional women do not struggle with the implications of Jewish feminism. It is only to point out what is perhaps the most significant tension that these essays represent: the paradox of being agents of change who still maintain tradition.

At the same time, this commentary is a correction of the so-called neutral commentaries that came before, which assumed that women were included somehow, albeit in the margins or when a particular female character or legislation regarding women is introduced. The very existence of a commentary of women rabbis on all fifty-four weekly readings, not only the portions pertaining directly to women, challenges the notion that only those portions about women or containing female characters are relevant to an examination of the Torah and women. A complete feminist commentary on the whole Torah calls into question the marginality of feminist discussion and offers us the opportunity to go back and examine the "neutrality" of what we have learned before.

Will a book of Torah commentary exclusively by women rabbis be all the things that women rabbis are perceived to be? Will it be uniquely female, uncompromisingly feminist, enlightening from a woman's point of view, inclusive and approachable? Each reader will have to answer that question for herself or himself. This book will give you the unmatched opportunity to learn the whole Torah from women rabbis, and then decide. I cannot imagine you, dear reader, being in a place where you could hear every *parashah*, every Torah portion of the year, explicated by a different woman, so I have put you in a room with fifty-four female rabbis. I think you will agree that, indeed, these commentaries are enlivening, exhilarating, and uniquely different. They are different not only from the traditional commentaries you may have read before, but each one is different from the others. You will find that while we share a feminist vision and a feminist "spin" on our assigned portions, we each bring our unique self to the task.

Each contributor to this anthology has presented a *dvar Torah,* a homiletic explanation of the weekly Torah portion, from a feminist viewpoint. Each has given you her personal interpretation on the portion. Some have chosen one aspect of it while others looked at it as a whole. They are trying to teach you something new that comes from within their experience of being female.

The fifty-four rabbis writing in this volume were ordained from the Reform, Conservative, and Reconstructionist seminaries. It is my great sorrow that there are no Orthodox women rabbis represented, because there are, as yet, no Orthodox women rabbis at all. That is not to say that there are not great Orthodox female scholars and teachers. There certainly are, and you can find many of their writings listed in the bibliography at the end. They have much to teach us. But for my specific purposes, I present only ordained women who have been working as rabbis in the Jewish community.

They function as congregational rabbis, Hillel directors, professional academics, chaplains, and in a variety of other interesting rabbinic positions. They serve in the United States, Canada, Israel, and South America. Their biographies are at the end of the book. You will note that in the biographies, each has included a short statement of when and why she decided to become a rabbi—a question still asked very often of women in this field.

I am particularly honored that the first woman ordained in each seminary has agreed to be a part of this volume. Those three pathbreakers made it possible for the rest of us to earn the title rabbi, which we cherish so dearly. Other pathbreakers are included: the first woman president of the Reconstructionist Rabbinical Association, the first female rabbi to serve in Israel, the first Orthodox-trained female rabbi. The first generation of daughters of male rabbis is represented. (We are still waiting for the first daughter of a female rabbi!) Sometimes we joke that we will become truly normalized when we won't be the first woman rabbi to do *anything.* I include these "firsts" not only out of pride, but also out of a sense of duty, so that our children may have the role models that we did not have.

I hope, dear reader, that you will use this book. Bring it to synagogue or church with you as you hear the Bible read and explained. Write your own *divrei Torah* quoting the women within, their scholarship and their personal insights. Use it for your bat mitzvah or bar mitzvah as you try to tackle the portions you read on your special day. See this as a treasury of the Torah you have inherited—the traditional Torah—together with a new Torah, or teaching. Then together we can sow seeds of a truly egalitarian Judaism where, as Abraham Geiger said in 1837, "our whole religious life will profit from the beneficial influence which feminine hearts will bestow upon it."[5]

What You Need to Know
to Use This Book

TRADITIONAL TORAH STUDY must certainly seem daunting. Where, and how, does one begin to understand the many layers of a story? Even seemingly simple stories open up a host of questions when the reader begins to uncover how much material is missing, or repeated, or inverted, or detailed. Wordplays are common in the Bible, and a person who doesn't read Hebrew may well miss them altogether. One text may remind the reader of another text in a completely different place, have echoes of another story, or include references to an earlier or later event. Readers in a Diaspora context most certainly bring with them Christian connotations, inculcated by the general milieu, into the Jewish Bible. And all readers bring with them their own prejudices about the text, childhood memories, and "received wisdom" from a lifetime of sources.

A feminist will bring yet another whole set of questions. Where are women in the story? Are they visible, and if not, why not? Does this story teach us anything about the "character" of women? Or does it perhaps teach us about the biases of the male lens through which the story is viewed?

On the one hand, feminists can choose to reject the Bible outright as hopelessly sexist, unsalvageable for the modern woman. As

Naomi Goldenberg has written, "Although I admire the efforts of the reformers, I see them engaged in a hopeless effort. . . . Many feminists recommend ignoring parts of the Torah, but still claim the book as a whole is God-given. It is hard to deny that an eventual consequence of criticizing the correctness of any sacred text or tradition is to question why that text or tradition should be considered a divine authority at all. . . . In order to develop a theology of women's liberation, feminists have to leave . . . the Bible behind them." [1]

On the other hand, we can become skilled apologists with the claim that if we just understood the Torah better, we would see how our original concerns about women are simply unfounded. There may be some instances where women "seem" to be aggrieved or "seem" to be depicted in a negative light, but these few instances can be easily "fixed" by traditional commentators. Apologists usually claim that the problem lies not in the text but in the reader.

This book, however, takes the middle road. We neither reject nor apologize. Although the inclination of many of us is to say, "If only the text were different . . . ," we accept that the text as we have received it can be reread and understood in a new light. We uncover, recover, and discover. We explore, suggest, and speculate. Most importantly, we reappropriate the rabbinic use of parable, story, and metaphor, creating explications and interpretations called midrash in Hebrew. Midrash—coming from the Hebrew root *lidrosh*, "examine" or "interpret"—is the creative process of filling in the biblical gaps. Midrashim were written as early as before the first century C.E., and continue to be written today. They have been compiled into different collections at different times, from the third century to the sixteenth century C.E. Today's twentieth-century works are often labeled "modern midrash" to differentiate them from classical midrash, but both fit Barry Holtz's description: "Where the Bible is mysterious and silent, Midrash comes to unravel the mystery. Moreover, there are sections of the Bible that are simply confusing or unclear. Midrash attempts to elucidate confusions and to harmonize seeming contradictions. . . . [T]he Rabbis when examining the ancient texts of the Bible found it necessary at times to reread texts in the light of their own contemporary values and beliefs."[2] As modern midrashists, the authors of these essays look deeply into the biblical texts, and, failing to find women's voices or women's experience, may invent them. Like the classical midrashists, we may wander far from the original to get back to it. We fill in the details of women's lives, their thoughts, hopes, and dreams.

The contributors to this volume believe that with all its problems, the Torah is still, at its core, our spiritual guide. Thus we reject women's marginality as the central assumption, and rather, attempt either to write ourselves in, reinterpret ourselves in, or critique our absence. And when we are not absent at all, we find the strength of our inclusion and ponder its meaning for all Jews today. As Mary Ann Tolbert has written, this is a "conscious effort to retrieve texts overlooked or distorted by patriarchal hermeneutics. . . . [It] focuses its attention on texts involving women characters and explores their functions without the patriarchal presumption of marginality."[3]

We recognize patriarchy in the Torah, but invite you to read the Torah with nonpatriarchal eyes. Sometimes we have to turn a text over to uncover what might have already been there but has been censored out, ignored, or misconstrued by patriarchal bias. Other times we discover what is already there. And sometimes we ourselves cover over a layer of text with a completely new layer of meaning.

But all of these methodologies are quite traditional. Any Bible reader needs tools to "unpack" the text. Midrash is one such tool. Commentary is another. Since it is nigh impossible to ever know the original "intention" of a biblical text, the rabbis began to build a pyramid of interpretations, assumptions, and meanings based on their understanding of the Torah text. Starting with the Talmud in the second century, and continuing most strongly with the medieval rabbis, Torah was explicated from various points of view: the literal, the homiletic, the mystical, the legal. The rabbis who systematically wrote such interpretations are called the commentators, and their works, the commentaries.

To save the reader from having to learn who the commentators are or what the midrashic compilations are each and every time they appear, on pages 41–44 is a list of those quoted in the essays. This list is by no means exhaustive, but merely represents the commentators and collections quoted by the authors of the essays.

In order to bring the Hebrew text to an English-speaking audience, the contributors could have chosen from a large number of translations now available. But since all translations are, in a sense, interpretations, the vast majority of contributors decided to translate the text themselves. Unless otherwise noted, translations in each essay are the products of the contributors.

Finally, we, the essayists, offer our own brand of homiletic, our own feminist sensibility and sensitivity, and our own list of questions. Like the rabbis of old, we innovate while trying to stay true to the text. And like the rabbis of old, we are faced with the tension of creating a new interpretation while safeguarding the sacredness of the text. But that is, perhaps, the greatest beauty of the Jewish way of reading the Bible. Never was a Jew commanded to read the Bible only as an academic, intellectual exercise or as a proof of blind, unquestioned, unchallenged faith in the literal word. The words "why," "how," and "what if" were never forbidden in the academies of Torah study. And never was reading the text allowed only to the scholar. Learning Torah has always been an act of devotion, a spiritual practice, a holy act. Studying the Bible in a Jewish context has always been a democratic affair. Now, that democracy finally, blessedly, includes all its citizens.

Rabbinic Commentators and Midrashic Collections Noted in This Book

Isaac Abravanel: 1437–1508, a highly placed officer in Portugal, his commentaries include political observations and defenses of Judaism against the Inquisition.

Bereshit Rabbah: Known in English as *Genesis Rabbah*, a compilation of homilies on the stories of Genesis, from about the sixth century C.E.

Martin Buber: 1878–1965, philosopher and theologian. Though best known for his work *I and Thou*, in 1925 he also translated the Bible into German with Franz Rosenzweig and published several works of Bible interpretation.

Isserles, Moses ben Israel: 1530–1572, sometimes referred to as the Rema, from Cracow. He is best known for his halachic works.

Keli Yakar: The commentary of Solomon Ephraim ben Chaim Lunchitz, 1550–1619, from Lemburg, Poland. He relies heavily on midrash and psychological interpretations.

Lekah: Known as Lekah Tov, an eleventh-century C.E. collection of midrashim on the Torah and Five Megillot by Tobias ben Eliezer.

Maimonides: Rabbi Moses ben Maimon, 1135–1204, a Spanish physician and philosopher, known as a commentator, philosopher, and halachist. He is famous for his legal code *Mishneh Torah*, his philosophical work *Guide for the Perplexed*, and many other works. His acronym is **Rambam.**

Mekhilta: A halachic midrash on Exodus.

Midrash Tennaim: A halachic midrash on Deuteronomy.

Midrash Vayosha: Compilation of midrashim from 1100.

Moses Mendelsohn: 1729–1786, a philosopher, literary critic who is recognized as one of the leaders of the *Haskalah*, or Enlightenment. He wrote the *Biur* (Explanation) between 1780 and 1783.

Nachmanides: Rabbi Moses ben Nachman, 1194–1270, born in Spain. He spent his last years writing his commentary in the Land of Israel. His acronym is **Ramban.**

Nehama Leibowitz: 1905–1996, an Israeli scholar who compares and contrasts the insights of traditional commentators to glean new insights.

Philo of Alexandria: 20 B.C.E.–50 C.E., a nobleman and philosopher who wrote in Greek and who favored allegorical interpretations.

Pinchas Peli: 1930–1989, Jerusalem rabbi, was Professor of Thought and Literature at Ben Gurion University in Israel.

Pirke de Rabbi Eliezar: A very early midrashic collection traditionally attributed to Rabbi Eliezar ben Hyrcanus, who lived in the first century C.E.

W. Gunther Plaut: 1912–, German-born rabbi living in Toronto, whose *Torah: A Modern Commentary*, published in 1985, is considered one of the greatest liberal Torah commentaries of our time, encompassing not only traditional commentary in translation but modern historical, sociological, psychological, and literary insights into the text.

Rashbam: Acronym for Rabbi Shmuel ben Meir, Rashi's grandson, known for his piety and his strict insistence on retaining the most literal sense of the text.

Rashi: Acronym for Rabbi Shlomo Yitzchaki, 1040–1105, from France. Rashi is the best-known of the medieval commentators, famous for explaining the *peshat*, or plain meaning of the text, sprinkled liberally with stories, parables, and some fanciful suggestions of his own based on classical midrash. In traditional circles, Rashi is studied most often as the central vision of what the text really means.

Sefer Hahinuch: Believed to have been written by Aharon Halevi of Barcelona, 1230–1300, contains a commentary on the 613 mitzvot divided according to weekly *parshiyot.*

Shmot Rabbah: Known in English as *Exodus Rabbah,* a compilation of homilies on the stories of Exodus. From about the sixth century C.E.

Tanhuma: A fourth-century C.E. collection of midrashim ascribed to Rabbi Tanhuma of Palestine.

Tanhuma Yelammdanu: A group of midrashim that begin with halachic formulas and end with homiletic formulas.

Targum: Translation. During the period of the Second Temple, many different translations appeared in Greek and Aramaic. Such translations also serve as interpretations.

Targum Onkelos: Third-century C.E. Aramaic translation best known for its interpretive quality.

Targum Yerushalmi: A first-century Aramaic translation.

Targum Yonatan: A fragmented Aramaic translation drawing heavily on *Targum Onkelos.*

Tosafot: Collections of comments on the Talmud arranged according to the order of the talmudic tractates, relying heavily on

Rashi's talmudic commentary. Rashi's pupils and descendants began to expand and elaborate on their teacher's talmudic commentary in the twelfth to fourteenth centuries C.E.

Tz'enah Ur'enah: A Yiddish Torah interpretation, first published in 1618, generally thought to have been written for women by Jacob ben Isaac Ashkenazi of Yanof.

Bereshit / Genesis

RABBI LORI FORMAN

בראשית

Bereshit

The Untold Story of Eve

When the woman saw that the tree was good for eating and a delight to the eyes, and that the tree was desirable as a source of wisdom, she took of its fruit and ate.

(GENESIS 3:6, ASCHKENASY TRANSLATION)

THE TORAH BEGINS ANEW each time we read the biblical story of humanity's origin in *Parashat Bereshit*. There we read about the creation of the world, the relationship between the first man and woman, called Adam and Eve, and their eventual exile from the Garden of Eden. These stories of beginnings are part of the fundamental consciousness of Western civilization. Images, allusions, and assumptions abound when we read about this primeval couple, Adam and Eve.

Many of our common images of Eve are negative ones. Was Eve created from Adam's rib? Was Eve an empty-headed woman easily lured by the snake into biting into the forbidden fruit? Most often, Eve is portrayed as a temptress and seductress. Most of us have learned that Eve seduced Adam into eating the forbidden fruit from the Tree of Knowledge. These ugly views of Eve have paved the way for all Western religious traditions to denigrate women.

Christianity, perhaps, is most explicit in using these narratives to characterize women as evil and sinful. In the Christian Bible we are told, "Let a woman learn in silence with all submissiveness. I permit no woman to teach or to have authority over men; she is to keep silent . . . for woman was deceived and became a transgressor" (I Tim. 2:11–14).

Moreover, the church bases its extensive theology of original sin on these first narratives. Judaism, too, voiced its own condemnation of Eve. In an attempt to explain the three mitzvot incumbent on women—*mikveh, challah,* and Shabbat[1]—we read that these mitzvot were in fact punishment for Eve's transgression:

> Why was the precept of menstruation given to her? Because she shed the blood of Adam. And why was the precept of challah given to her? Because she corrupted Adam, who was the dough of the world. And why was the precept of the Sabbath lights given to her? Because she extinguished the soul of Adam.[2]

Given the far-reaching and scathing nature of these traditional interpretations, it is imperative for us as Jewish feminists to reexamine these stories found in Gen. 2 and 3. Let us look first at the creation of woman. Just how was woman created? Was she created from Adam's actual rib? There is another way to understand the verses of Gen. 2:20–24. We read there that Adam did not have a partner, so God cast a deep sleep on Adam, and while he slept, God removed one of his ribs *(tzelah),* thus forming woman. But in Gen. 1:27—in the first story of creation—we read, "And God created Adam in God's image: male and female God created them." This discrepancy has caused commentators to ponder: were man and woman created simultaneously, as related in chapter 1, or was woman an afterthought, as suggested by chapter 2?

The talmudic rabbis were also bothered by an overly literal interpretation of the verses in chapter 2. Carefully reading verses 20 and 21, they suggest that the word *tzelah,* most commonly translated as "rib," derives from the Hebrew word meaning "side." Thus, they declare that Eve was not created from Adam's rib. Rather, Adam was a bisexual, double-faced being—neither male nor female. During the deep sleep that fell upon this first human, its male and female sides were separated, creating man and woman as we know them today.[3] Thus, man and woman came into being not one after another, but simultaneously; in fact, joined together as one. This first story (chapter 1) relates the creation of this androgynous being, while the second story (chapter 2) relates the creation of gendered beings—man and woman. The mystics take this talmudic interpretation one step further, suggesting that when men and women fall in love, their yearning is none other than the primeval desire to reunite into the one being that was bifurcated in the Garden of Eden so long ago.[4] This view takes us a short trip away from the plain meaning of the verse in Gen. 2, but its midrashic assistance makes sense of the juxtaposition of the two stories, which the more belittling view of Eve leaves unresolved.

The second narrative that needs further discussion involves Eve eating the forbidden fruit. It is commonly held that Eve was seduced by the snake:

> Now the serpent was the shrewdest of all the wild beasts that the Lord God had made. He said to the woman, "Did God really say: You shall not eat of any tree of the garden?" The woman replied to the serpent, "It is only about the fruit in the middle of the garden that God said: 'You shall not eat of it or touch it, lest you die.'" And the serpent said to the woman,

> "You are not going to die, but God knows that as soon
> as you eat of it your eyes will be opened and you will
> be like divine beings who know good and bad." When
> the woman saw that the tree was good for eating and
> a delight to the eyes, and that the tree was desirable as
> a source of wisdom, she took of its fruit and ate, and
> she also gave some to her husband, who was with her,
> and he ate (Gen. 3:1–6).

Yet, the snake's seduction also involves undermining God's original warning: Not only will eating fruit from this particular tree not cause death, but rather, benefits will result from doing so. Upon hearing the snake's contradictory words, Eve looks at the fruit and comes to some very startling conclusions of her own. The fruit, she sees, is good for eating; it is edible and could satisfy hunger. It is pleasant to her visual sensibilities, satisfying her need for beautiful things. And Eve discerns that the fruit could make her wise, and increase her intellectual abilities. The Torah, surprisingly, explains Eve's inner motives, quite out of character for the Torah, which rarely divulges such personal reflection. Only after such contemplation does Eve actively reach for the fruit. It is not an impulsive act. This is not a passive scene. Eve, full of curiosity, reaches out for the gifts of life: food, beauty, and wisdom.[5]

Many of us may harbor images in our heads of Eve running to find Adam to share with him this delicious fruit. Actually, the Torah explicitly tells us that Adam was there next to her during this entire scene. The text clearly states that "she gave some to her husband with her" (Gen. 3:6). Adam is not off in some distant corner of the garden. He is present for this entire interchange between the snake and Eve and not once does he speak up! He does not intervene when Eve reaches out to eat the fruit, nor does he refuse to partake of it when she offers it to him. Then why don't the traditional commentators implicate Adam to the same extent as Eve in this violation of the Divine commandment? Perhaps their male bias clouded their ability to condemn Adam and Eve equally. A few verses later, when Adam hides from God, he himself is also held accountable, though he blames Eve, who in turn blames the snake. The biblical commentators use this verse to elaborate on human responsibility, and to explain why both Adam and Eve are banished from the garden. Yet, the rabbis do not condemn or belittle all men, as they do all women, based on this transgression. Their interpretive abilities were far from objective.

Moreover, nowhere in chapter 3 does Eve uses any means of seduction to tempt Adam into eating. There are no pleas, no tantrums, none of the feminine wiles that the verbs "seduce" and "tempt" suggest. In fact, the Torah does not mention Adam and Eve having a sexual relationship until chapter 4, after both Adam and Eve have eaten of the fruit and they have left the garden. Eve cannot be accused of employing any sexual advances; it was beyond her knowledge at this point. Sexuality as we understand it is mentioned only at the start of chapter 4, where we read, "And Adam knew Eve, his wife." This takes places after they have left the garden, not when they realize they were naked.

Eve is neither a seductress nor a temptress. These are male fears projected onto this story. Rather, Eve acts out of her own sense of adventure and curiosity. Though tradition has frequently seen her act as one of disobedience, without Eve's boldness, human history as we know it would never have come to pass. Adam and Eve might well have grown old in the Garden of Eden, but birth, life, and death would never have entered the world. Yes, Adam and Eve leave the garden. Hard work and the pain of life follow. Eve's name in

Hebrew is Chavah, which the Bible tells us is derived from the word *chayim*, "life." She is called "the mother of all the living." Eve knows that for life to continue, she must listen to her own conscience, expand her limitations, and reach out for what she knew intuitively would bring moral consciousness and human generativeness into the world—in other words, the fullness of life.

It is a challenge to refashion our images and attitudes toward a story that has become embedded in our culture's consciousness as the touchstone of woman's nature. Artistic renditions, literature, and poetry expand on the notion that men must take heed and protect themselves from woman's seductiveness. Such warnings derive from these misinterpretations of Eve. While the task is mighty, it is worth the effort. We can reclaim Eve and her spirit for ourselves, and thus finally recast Eve's legacy to speak of a woman who began human history by reaching for what was good, pleasant, and intellectually empowering.

נח

Noach

Mrs. Noah

*A*nd you shall enter the ark, with your sons,
your wife, and your sons' wives. (GENESIS 6:18)

SOMETIMES, WHEN STUDYING A TORAH TEXT, it is just as important to look for what is *not* mentioned, as to notice what is. This is particularly true when it comes to the role of women. In *Parashat Noach,* the word *ishto,* "his wife," is mentioned five times. Though her name is never mentioned, her relationship to Noah certainly is. Though she figures less prominently than he does in this drama (at least according to the plainest reading of the text), she is nevertheless critical to the story. And although the identity of our "Mrs. Noah" is not elucidated in the Torah portion itself, the ancient rabbis fill in some of those gaps.

According to rabbinic legend, Naamah is the name of Noah's wife. Interestingly, the original location for Naamah as the name of Noah's wife is not in *Parashat Noach,* but in the previous portion, *Bereshit.* At the end of a list of the descendants of Cain, Naamah is mentioned as the sister of Tubal-cain (Gen. 4:22).

Two midrashim from *Bereshit Rabbah* tell us something about her. Both midrashim employ wordplays on the letters of her name:

nun, ayin, mem. One suggests that her name comes from the Hebrew word *man'emet,* which means to sing or accompany, because it was her practice to sing to a drum on her way to worship idols. This musical talent was also noted in *Targum Yonatan* in Gen. 4:23: "I am (also) of the opinion that Naamah comes from the expression (singer of) sweet songs, as it is (found) in *(Bereshit) Rabbah."* The second notes that the letters of her name are also shared by the word "pleasing," and from this it can be inferred that her name refers to her pleasing deeds (*Bereshit Rabbah* 23:3).

Why, then, would some of the commentators want to teach that Naamah was involved in idolatry, a very grievous offense, when others linked her name to the doing of good deeds? Perhaps she was a bold and feisty woman who challenged the men in her family. Perhaps her musicality was seen as a disruption or a distraction as they went about their lives. Yet, on the ark, that music might have actually helped to soothe the hunger pangs of the various beasts of the field and sky as she and her husband made the rounds. No doubt, her good deeds accrued to her during this time.

But something about her character bothered the writers of the midrashim. Sweet singers of music touch chords deep within the soul. They cause the body to stir in ways that are not always controllable. Perhaps Naamah, and women like her, were threatening to the orderly and controlled world of the rabbis. Thus, female singers became suspect and derided. Rather than admit to being touched, even spiritually stirred by their voices, the rabbis sought to blame the singers for the feelings that they as listeners were experiencing. This logic persists today in the form of a halachic prohibition called in Hebrew *kol ishah,* which forbids men from hearing women's voices singing in most situations.

Other clues about her identity and her actions while on the ark all point to a woman of strong character. From another midrash in *Bereshit Rabbah*, we are taught that Noah and his wife did not have sexual relations while they were aboard their floating menagerie. They were forbidden by God from such intimacy. The midrash appears twice in the same compilation (*Bereshit Rabbah* 31:12 and 34:7), as if to say, "You might think this far-fetched, but it is true!" It was only upon their disembarkation that they were allowed to resume. Why would the rabbis include such a lesson? The simple answer might be that with all of their duties in the care and feeding of the animals, there was no time for intimacy. How sad. Surely, touching could not have been forbidden. It is a natural part of human behavior. Was there not such behavior on the part of the animal pairs in their care? Remember, this prohibition lasted longer than forty days. In the same midrashic compilation the rabbis teach that Noah and his wife were on the ark for a year (*Bereshit Rabbah* 33:7).

Naamah was a woman of beauty, a woman of musical talent, a doer of good deeds, and, for the rabbis, a threat to the male order. Their answer to the passions elicited by a woman like Naamah was to limit and restrict. Rather than trust that Noah could fulfill his obligations to the animals in his care, and also care for the sexual needs of his spouse, they imagined that he is prohibited from being intimate with his wife. Rather than condone the euphonious music that would burst forth spontaneously from the mouths of women, they singled out Naamah as an example of an idolater. Her music leads to the worship of false gods, and must therefore be condemned. Her beauty is a distraction, and so her husband must be controlled lest his passions get in the way of his duty. In turn, she is denied the physical intimacy of his company for the entire time spent on the ark.

I imagine that Naamah's voice was the reason that there was such peace among the animals during the deluge. It served to comfort them, and to keep them from looking with fear or desire upon one another. The notes of her song carried the prayers of her family through the dark storm clouds to the heavens above, and they were spared the worst of the roiling waves. She inspired her children, Shem, Ham, and Japheth, to work together with their wives, lightening their burdens and making the time pass more quickly. She soothed her husband when he was overwhelmed by the enormity of his responsibility to those in his care, and indeed, his responsibilities to the future.

I imagine that Noah would have been strong enough to control his passions, and the prohibition against intimacy would have been a prescription instead. I imagine that, like the animals who nuzzled and snuggled with their mates, Noah and Naamah nuzzled and snuggled with each other as the rain battered the wooden deck above them. The contentment and love they felt infused the air of every nook and cranny on the crowded ship. It was not an easy place to live, but their discomfort was eased by knowing that at the end of a long day, they had one another to hold. Together they sang songs of gratitude and love to Adonai, and to one another. And together, as the waters receded, they watched the rainbow as it stretched from horizon to horizon.

RABBI MICHAL SHEKEL

לֶךְ לְךָ

Lech Lecha

What's in a Name?

*A*donai's messenger found her by a spring of water in the wilderness, the spring on the way to Shur. He said: "Hagar, Sarai's servant, where have you come from and where are you going?" She said: "I have fled from my mistress Sarai." Adonai's messenger said to her: "Return to your mistress and let yourself be afflicted under her hand." Adonai's messenger said to her: "I will greatly increase your offspring and they will be too many to count." Adonai's messenger said to her: "For you are pregnant and will bear a son whom you shall call Ishmael, for Adonai has heard your affliction. . . ." She called the name of Adonai who had spoken to her "You Are the God Whom I See," for she said: "Do I truly see after being seen?"
(GENESIS 16:7–11, 13)

Parashat Lech Lecha contains within it two journeys, each of which encompasses both a spiritual and physical aspect. The first is the well-known story of Abram leaving his native land to follow God (Gen. 12). The second is subtler, but still powerful. It is the journey undertaken by Sarai's maidservant, Hagar.

In Gen. 16, Sarai, following ancient Near Eastern custom, gives Hagar to Abram in order that he may father a child, with Hagar acting as a surrogate for Sarai. Hagar becomes pregnant, and difficulties develop between Sarai and her maidservant, causing Hagar to flee. While she is in the wilderness, Hagar has an encounter with the Divine, in which she is told to return to Sarai. She is also presented with a name for her child, Ishmael, and is told his fate.

This encounter between Hagar and the Divine is a cause of discomfort in traditional Jewish interpretation. In Gen. 16:7, it is Adonai's messenger who finds Hagar. In the next four verses (16:8–11), Adonai's messenger speaks to Hagar.[1] In verse 13, Hagar names Adonai. This last verse causes much unease. Would God speak directly to a woman, and would she dare reply? According to one midrash, Hagar misinterpreted what she saw. It was a Divine messenger she encountered. God would never "condescend" to speak with a woman.[2]

Yet, Gen. 16:13 reveals the nature of the Divine revelation experienced by Hagar. Every time that God is mentioned in this narrative, God's Divine Hebrew name, YHVH, which is read as Adonai, is used. There is no doubt that it was Adonai's angel, or messenger, who first spoke to her, but at the very end of the chapter she encounters God directly. This pattern is similar to that of Abraham's Divine encounter in chapter 18, when the birth of Isaac is announced. There, three Divine messengers approach Abraham as he sits outside his tent (Gen. 18:1–2). But by the end of the chapter, the messengers have departed and Abraham is standing in God's presence (18:22).

What actually happens to Hagar during this encounter with the Divine? One can discover three occurrences in this *parashah* that mirror Abram's experiences. First, Hagar leaves her home, her personal *lechi lach,* "go forth" (fem.). Although it is not specified as such in the text, this parallels Abram's *lech lecha,* "go forth" (masc.). Thus, her leaving is similar to his departure from his home. Second, God makes a *brit,* a covenant, with her, in which she is promised that she will have numerous offspring, just as Abraham receives this same assurance in a more elaborate covenant that appears later in this Torah portion (Gen. 17:19). Third, she is told her son's name, just as Abraham will later be told his other son's name before his birth.

But here the parallel ends; for, most significantly, Hagar gives God a name. Abram has never done this, nor has anyone else. Throughout the early chapters of the Torah, Abram needs signs to substantiate his covenant with God.[3] Hagar is somehow more accepting, more comfortable with God. Hagar accepts her encounter for what it is. She takes the initiative and she names God.

What courage! In these early chapters of the Torah, the act of naming is highly significant. It is both empowering and embracing. The first human being names all the creatures and, in so doing, discovers that there is no fitting mate for it. Adam names his wife, Eve, placing himself in relationship to her. Eve names her children Cain and Seth.[4] God names the children of Sarah and Hagar. God will also rename adult individuals, beginning with Abram and Sarai. From the very beginning, humans name animals and humans name each other. Yet here, for the first and only time in a Divine encounter, a human, a woman, names God.

Hagar names God *el ro'i,* "God Who sees me." This is in response to God's naming her child Yishma'el, which means "God hears." In naming God, Hagar affirms that God sees as well as hears. Here, too, there is a parallel with Abraham. After the *akedah,* the binding of Isaac, Abraham calls the mountain where he offered his son "Adonai sees," personalizing his relationship with God through the familiar name Adonai. Hagar gives her relationship with the Divine a more formal aspect by using the title *el*, God. They have in common that both affirm God as seeing. Hagar is a woman who has had a spiritual encounter and is strengthened by it to such an extent that she is the first person in the Torah who has the *chutzpah* to endow the Divine with a name.

Consciously or not, Hagar has a sense of the Divine that is evident from the moment she flees Sarai. In her act of running away, Hagar stops by a spring of water and, not surprisingly, this is where she encounters God. Water often acts as a symbol of spiritual belief and strength in the Torah. The matriarchs Rebecca and Rachel are first introduced to us at wells. The children of Israel are strengthened by crossing the Sea of Reeds, and are spiritually weakened whenever there is a lack of water, complaining that they want to return to Egypt. In the later books of the Torah, water is used for spiritual purification. When the prophetess Miriam (whose name contains the word *yam*, "sea") dies, we are told that the people were without water. As the people lose faith and quarrel, Moses, spiritually frustrated, strikes the rock and brings forth water. In Genesis, just six chapters after Hagar's encounter with God, she and Ishmael will be sent out into the wilderness. When her water runs out, she will lose faith and sit down to watch her son die. But her "God of Seeing" will open her eyes and Hagar will find a well.

Hagar has arrived at a place of spiritual focus and renewal. Her encounter with God happens at a well that is henceforth called *Be'er-lehai-ro'i* (Gen. 16:14), commonly translated as the "Well of the Living One Who Sees Me." She has discovered a place of healing. It is at this same location that Isaac will seek comfort after the *akedah* and his mother's death.[5] Furthermore, this well is out of Kadesh. Not far away, between Kadesh and Shur, will be Abraham's home after the destruction of Sodom and Gomorrah. Abraham will also find solace here, as do Hagar and Isaac in their respective times of distress. It is at Kadesh that Miriam dies, and here that the children of Israel need to regain their spiritual strength before they can continue their journey (Num. 20).

Hagar is a woman of innate spirituality encompassing a sense of the Divine. Ironically, this can be seen by the omission of Hagar from the most significant part of the Torah portion *Lech Lecha*, the renaming of individuals performed by God. Abram's name is changed to Abraham (taken to mean "father of a multitude") and Sarai's name is changed to Sarah (meaning "princess").[6] Yet, Hagar is left out. Why?

The significance of the name changes is the addition of the Hebrew letter *hey* to both Abram and Sarai's name. This letter is significant because it is part of God's name. Before the name change, Sarai had a *yod* in her name, another Divine letter, with the Hebrew numerical value of ten. The letter *hey* is the Hebrew numerical equivalent of five. In changing Abram and Sarai's names, traditional explanations hold, God has distributed a symbol of the Divine name equally between the two of them. Yet, forgotten in all this is that Hagar also has the Divine letter *hey* in her name. There was no reason to change her name, because she already had a measure of the Divine presence.

Why is this ignored in traditional interpretations of the text? One can read the tradition as saying that Hagar is an outsider, the other, alien to God, by interpreting her name as *Hey ger*, "Adonai is foreign." Yet, all her actions in chapter 16 prove that this is not so. Hagar sets off on a journey and finds a holy place that others will find only later. She is met by Divine messengers, is told she will have a child, and that her offspring will be "too many to count." The

Divine messenger names her child; Hagar reciprocates by naming the Divine. Hagar is no stranger to God; she is comfortable with God's presence in a way that is less formal than God's relationship with Abraham or Sarah. Hers is a more personal relationship with God. This is symbolized by the Divine letter *hey*, which is a part of her name from the moment we first meet her. For surely, Hagar fulfills the destiny of her name, *hey gar*, "Adonai dwells" with her.

וירא

Vayera

Positive Pillars

*L*ot's wife looked back and thereupon turned into a pillar of salt. (GENESIS 19:26)

AS RICH AS THE TORAH PORTION OF *Vayera* is in family dynamics and parent-child relationships, there is one drama that we rarely discuss, its characters not even known by name. They are known to us only as appendages to Abraham's nephew, Lot.

Other than the one verse about Lot's wife turning into salt, we know nothing about her. This unnamed woman comes on the scene in Gen. 19 as quickly as she disappears. We do not know her thoughts or what she may have said either prior to or during the family flight out of Sodom. All we know is that she turned around, and this was not permitted.

Why is she even in the narrative? We are not emotionally attached to her, and therefore will not keenly feel a sense of loss at her punishment. The destruction of the city did not hinge upon her looking back, for God had planned this destruction anyway. Is the message supposed to be that we should not look back? What is so bad about looking back?

There was a directive earlier in our chapter (Gen. 19:14–17) instructing Lot not to look back. This command is second person masculine singular, addressed grammatically only to Lot and not to his wife or daughters. Only he is known to have been on the scene when the directive was given. And we can make sense of this mandate that Lot should not look back, for he has given us every indication of his hesitancy. His uncertainty is emphasized by the fact that the trope, the singing mark used on the word "lingered" in Gen. 19:16, is a *shalshelet*, a rare trope, found only four times in the Torah, which is characterized by a long, wavering embellishment. And remember how much Lot pleaded to live in the small city of Zoar. We can easily justify why such a directive was made to him, but presumably, Lot's wife is exempt from this prohibition. She should be innocent. She must be teaching us something.

Targum Yerushalmi on this verse states, "And because the wife of Lot was from the sons of sons of Sodom, she looked back to see what would be the end of her father's house." It concludes, "And behold, she stands as a pillar of salt until the time the dead are brought to life." This source now offers answers and new questions.

Targum Yerushalmi answers why she looked back. It was her home (which we may have presumed all along, but now we definitely know) and the home of many other family members as well. A parallel source within *Bereshit Rabbah* informs us that she even had two other married daughters who were left behind. It makes sense to us that any person would look back, but all the more so for Lot's wife, who had emotional and familial ties to Sodom. And it is understandable that her cries must have been, "What is to become of my home? My family, friends, and community?"

Looking back at our past is something we all do, or certainly should do. Where we are coming from is just as important as where we are going. Many of us try to bury our pasts, but the past is a part of who we are. To erase it is to deny a part of ourselves. It does not mean that we have to pretend to be proud of something in our past that we regret, or revert back to such behaviors. Still, our past, our looking back, is a part of the general composition of who we are, and it influences our lives and our choices in life. When done wisely, our looking back can even help influence others and their choices.

Thus, given that it is natural for all of us to look back, and given that the episode of Lot's wife is highlighted for some reason, what if she looked back for some greater purpose?

A *baraita* in the Babylonian Talmud states (in abbreviated form), "The Rabbis taught that one who sees . . . Lot's wife [as a pillar of salt] should give thanks and praise before God" (*Berachot* 54a). While it is true that the discussion in the Gemara goes on to challenge this idea—suggesting that we should instead say a traditional recitation upon hearing bad news—the question is nevertheless raised: Why should *hoda-ah va-shevach*, "thanksgiving and praise," ever be appropriate when seeing Lot's wife?

The *baraita* refers to her being seen as the pillar. The word for pillar, *n'tziv*, is used as a noun only this one time in the Torah, yet all through the Bible there are pillars, called *amudim*, made as covenant reminders or memorials. Pillars can also be warning signs or blockades. By their very nature and just by their presence, they cause us to stop in our tracks and at the very least acknowledge them. Hopefully, we also seek answers to explain the significance of their existence.

Some pillars can be direction markers, offering us guidance or causing us to stop and think about why we are going in a particular direction. We tend to interpret verse 26 to mean that God had turned Lot's wife into a pillar of salt as a punishment, but what if she herself radically chose to become such a pillar, both of memorial and of direction? Memorial of what and direction to whom? Lot's wife was a pillar to her daughters.

Perhaps the most powerful message she could send to them,

given her circumstances, was in her turning around, stopping, and setting herself up as such a unique memorial. As we fill in the silences, her message to them could have been, "This is where I come from, the only world I know. Remember that this too is a part of your heritage and will always be a part of who you are. Use the lessons it has taught you and build from them."

No doubt, the daughters had their silent soliloquies as well, although *Parashat Vayera* as a whole is as lacking in emotion and dialogue as it is filled with family conflicts. They must have wondered where they were going and why they were being forcibly led out. They too must have turned to look back. They may even have contemplated staying behind before the hail of destruction.

This now being the case, their mother's stance becomes stronger. In addition to being a memorial to the past, she now takes on the role of direction marker, pointing ahead to the future. As much as she does not want them to forget their heritage, she also knows that it would be self-destructive for them to choose to go back. As a pillar that causes them to stop and contemplate, she confronts them with a challenge, and her message now questions, "Wait! Do you know in which direction you are going? Why are you going this way?"

Remember that Lot's wife has no name—a significant fact mirrored in the idea that she is a pillar with a cryptic message. She is not telling her daughters to go one way or the other. The nature of many pillars is that they have no direct answers for us. They are purposely ambiguous, for they have many different lessons to teach us.

From observation and experience, we know that many parents, teachers, and role models send these types of messages all the time. As pillars of experience, they do not grab us by the hand and guide our every step. Instead, they give us signs, and give themselves as

signs. They try to steer us in the right direction, giving us the freedom to make our choices, even our own mistakes. Instead of
becoming dictators to us, they become directional pillars for us.

Thus, Lot's wife made herself a figurative pillar to her daughters. Instilling a sense of history, as we do all the time in Judaism,
Lot's wife gave the gift of memory and direction to them, and merited the blessing that her message was heard. She, above all others,
may be unknown by name, but not by deed. In response, God then
made her into the pillar of salt, but neither as punishment nor for
eternity. Recalling that salt is a valuable preservative associated
with Temple offerings, she can now be understood as a cause for
thanksgiving and praise, the *hoda-ah va-shevach* of *Berachot* 54a. And
as we recall *Targum Yerushalmi's* teaching that Lot's wife "stands as a
pillar of salt until the time the dead are brought to life," we are
further convinced of her positive stance meriting this resurrection,
particularly from what we learn in *Sanhedrin* 108a: "The people of
Sodom do not have a portion in the world to come." Yet Lot's wife,
from Sodom, is the one exception, who does merit a portion in
the world to come!

Lot's wife set herself up as this figurative pillar to her daughters,
offering to redeem them. If redemption means to have a new direction on life, and if life is not truly life unless we have options—
choices and free will—then Lot's wife does give choice, life, and
redemption to her daughters, during that history's bleakest moment.

And remarkably, what next follows is that this mother is in
turn ultimately redeemed through her daughters. They have experienced the destruction of their generation, and are fearful that now
may be the end of all life. Believing their father to be the only man
alive and hence the only source from which to generate life, the
daughters commit incest with the same man who proposed to offer

them to the people of Sodom as a gesture of "hospitality" to protect his guests (Gen. 19:8).

This part of the narrative has almost always been viewed negatively—a polemic against the ancestry of the Moabites and Ammonites, the traditional enemies of the Israelites. Nevertheless, there are three different interpretations from *Bereshit Rabbah* 51, which neutralize the offensive act.

The first interpretation examines why the daughters make their father drink wine. The midrash suggests that they knew their action would be a violation of their father, so they first strive to dull his faculties. The interpretation hints that God left the wine in the cave, and therefore their actions receive a Divine endorsement.

Second, many of the rabbis quoted in *Bereshit Rabbah* believed that females do not get pregnant the first time they have intercourse. Rabbi Tanhuma says that Lot's daughters removed their own virginity first, so that they would become pregnant this first and only time with their father. Regardless of how this can be understood, the daughters spare their father from a second violation and are rewarded the Divine gift of children.

Similarly, the midrash picks up on the language used in Gen. 19:34 when the eldest of the daughters urges her sister to participate in the incest. She says, "so that we may maintain life through our father," and the rabbis suggest that her chosen language presents a message of looking toward a universal future for all humanity, not just to her own offspring.

As abhorrent as their action toward Lot may be, and as much as we try to avoid this incest narrative in our Sunday school classes, the daughters' intent was honorable. These teachings help mitigate the offense and show us a positive side, but even more so, we can learn a great deal from the daughters of Lot. To the daughters, a life with choice and direction is crucial, and this is a lesson they learned from their mother. Not only are they survivors, but they can, in essence, laugh back at God (an important theme in this *parashah*) and bring life out of death. Simply having babies in a time of destruction and despair is a redemptive act. In turn, they too have learned to be pillars.

Because of their faith in the importance of humanity, Lot's daughters merited children who are remembered less as the ancestral enemies of the Israelites, and more as the ancestors of the Messiah. From the youngest of the daughters came Ben-Ammi, ancestor of Naamah, the wife of Solomon. From the eldest came Moav, and from Moav we have Ruth, the great-grandmother of King David. From these origins of Davidic messianism, Judaism teaches us that one of the many events occurring at the time of the Messiah will be the resurrection of the dead.

Thus we have come full circle: The mother teaches her daughters that they could be redeemed, and that they themselves could be a source of redemption. And not only do her daughters hear her message, but their message back to their mother is that she too, in the time of the Messiah, will be redeemed.

And what is the message for us in all of this? We should all learn to be memorials and messengers. Lot's wife as a pillar is a reminder of our potential to influence others around us. Each of our actions, just like those of Lot's daughters, can usher in the time of the Messiah. But until that time, whether as parents or friends, role models or leaders, we need to make ourselves into pillars. We need to give direction and support; to be stepping stones and not stumbling blocks, to bring redemption to the world, and as in *Berachot* 54a, to bring *hoda-ah va-shevach lifney ha-Makom*, "thanksgiving and praise before God."

RABBI RONA SHAPIRO

חיי שרה

Chaye Sarah

Woman's Life, Woman's Truth

N ow Sarah's life was one hundred years and twenty years and seven years, the years of Sarah's life. Sarah died. . . . (GENESIS 23:1–2)

THE NAMES OF *parshiyot* are significant. Although the name of a given *parashah* is derived from the first few words of that *parashah*, it usually captures the theme of the *parashah* as well. This *parashah*, then, begins with a strange irony. It is called *Chaye Sarah*, meaning "the life of Sarah," but the first event of the *parashah* is Sarah's death! Is the most significant event in Sarah's life her death? Does Sarah contribute nothing more important to this story then an occasion for Abraham to buy his first piece of land in Israel? From a patriarchal perspective, Abraham's actions after her death are what is crucial. Yet, if Sarah's life is, in fact, significant, what does this *parashah's* recording of her death tell us about her life? In order to answer that question, we need to look back at both the occasion for Sarah's death, and at her life as we have known it.

One answer is found in a midrash on the cause of Sarah's death. Although Sarah dies at the age of 127, presumably of natural causes, the midrash is interested in the fact that her death immediately follows *akedat Yitzchak*, the near-sacrifice of Isaac. There is, according to the Midrash, a connection between these two events: Sarah dies of grief when she learns of what Abraham nearly did to Isaac, her only son, the child of her old age.

> At that time, Satan went to Sarah and appeared to her
> in the guise of Isaac. When she saw him, she said to
> him: My son, what has your father done to you? He
> answers her: My father took me up hill and down dale,
> up to the top of a certain mountain, he built an altar,
> arranged the wood, bound me on top of it, he took
> the knife to slaughter me, and if God had not said,
> "Don't stretch out your hand," I would already have
> been slaughtered. He did not finish telling the story
> before she died. (*Tanhuma Vayera* 23)

Sarah is overcome with grief at the *akedah*, while Abraham seems to carry out God's orders unflinchingly. Traditionally, Abraham is seen as the ultimate servant of God in this story, willing to sacrifice his only son in obedience to the divine command. His allegiance to God supersedes all human ties, even to his beloved son. Kierkegaard has characterized Abraham's heroism as his transcendence of the ethical. What is great about Abraham, for Kierkegaard, is his ability to suspend ethical law in response to the Divine imperative, to realize that there is a Divine Commander who transcends even the Divine Commander's own ethic.[1]

From Kierkegaard's perspective, it would seem that Sarah cannot rise to the heroism of which Abraham is capable. She is "bound to the ethical," while Abraham transcends these narrow human categories.

There is yet another way to look at this story, a way implied in the words of the rabbis. Sarah dies because she knows that the sacrifice of their son is wrong, that God could not, would not, command such an act, and that any God who issued such a command must be rejected. Sarah knows that there is no category that transcends the ethical, that there is no God greater than human relations, that there is no commandment holier than the responsibility not to inflict pain on others. Sarah knows that relationships are the ultimate testing ground of morality, of faith, of God. Thus, Sarah is the greater hero in our story. Sarah's sense of the primacy of relationships is well characterized by psychologist Carol Gilligan's descriptions of the difference between men and women:

> [W]omen not only define themselves in a context of human relationship but also judge themselves in terms of their ability to care. Women's place in man's life cycle has been that of nurturer, caretaker and helpmate, the weaver of those networks of relationships on which she in turn relies. But while women have thus taken care of men, men have...tended to...devalue that care.[2]

Abraham is looking for truth on the mountaintop. Unsatisfied with the domesticity of normal, everyday life, he often seeks a higher truth with some transcendent meaning. Indeed, throughout the entire Abraham narratives, we see an Abraham frustrated with domestic life, seeking to live his life on some higher plane. Abraham is at his best when he is gazing at the stars, walking the length and breadth of the land, arguing with God over the justice of Sodom and Gomorrah. He is a failure, however, when it comes to meting out justice in his own home. For example, unable to deal with the conflict between Sarah and Hagar, he tells Sarah to "do what is right in her eyes" (Gen. 16:6). His abdication of responsibility shows his insensitivity to Sarah and Hagar's pain; his attitude is,

"Let the women work out their petty problems." Even after Isaac is born, he fails to see that this is the son promised to him, and that Ishmael and Isaac cannot both remain in the same house and carry on his lineage. In fact, it seems that it takes Abraham's nearly killing Isaac for him to realize the significance of this son to him.

Sarah's death says that this trip to the mountaintop, this near-sacrifice of a son, is unnecessary. There is no truth on the mountaintop, there is no *kedushah*, no special holiness up there. Truth is right here, at home, in cooking dinner, taking out the garbage, holding hands, raising a child. As Moses says in Deuteronomy,

> *Lo b'shamayim hi'*—It [Torah, truth] is not in the heavens, that you should say, "Who among us can go up to the heavens and get it for us, that we may observe it?" Neither is it beyond the sea, that you should say, "Who among us can cross to the other side of the sea and get it for us and impart it to us, that we may observe it?" No, the thing is very close to you, in your mouth and in your heart. (Deut. 30:11–14)

Sarah dies knowing that truth, a truth Abraham never learns. We return now to the original question: Why is this *parashah* called *Chaye Sarah?* What does it have to do with Sarah's life? One answer is found in the events of this *parashah.* Following Sarah's death, Abraham buys a plot of land from the Canaanites in which to bury her. Worried about his bachelor son, he engages his servant Eliezer to find a wife for Isaac. He himself marries again and fathers more children, and finally he writes a will and dies at the ripe old age of 175.

Without doubt, this is a very different Abraham than the Abraham we have known. There are no mountaintops, no wars with kings, no dramatic rescues. In fact, following the *akedah*, Abraham does not speak to God again; and, although throughout this *parashah* Divine blessings are invoked, God, too, is silent. What has become of Abraham, this mighty partner of God willing to sacrifice even his own son in obedience to the Divine imperative? Has Abraham merely grown old and tired of drama, or is this an Abraham who, himself traumatized by the *akedah*, has finally learned Sarah's truth? Has he finally internalized that truth is right here at home, that, as Dorothy says in the *Wizard of Oz*, "If I ever go looking for my heart's desire again, I won't look any farther than my own backyard, because if it isn't there, I never really lost it to begin with."

Perhaps, then, this *parashah* is called *Chaye Sarah*, "the life of Sarah," because with Sarah's death, Abraham finally learns to live her life; he comes down from the mountain and becomes a man of the heart, a man who cares for his family members and lives out his life on a human plane. He learns to find truth and meaning within the context of his family, in marrying off his son, in raising children, in the small acts of daily kindness that make life holy. Abraham learns that God is not enthroned in heaven, but that God sits wherever human beings let God into their lives.

With Sarah's death, Abraham is given a new and more humble, but ultimately more real, more human, vision of life. With her death, Abraham finally comes to understand and live *Chaye Sarah*— the lives of Sarah.

RABBI BETH J. SINGER

תולדות
Toldot

Rebecca's Birth Stories

*B*ut the children struggled in her womb, and
she said, "If so, why do I exist?"
She went to seek God. (GENESIS 25:22)

JUDAISM TEACHES THAT HUMANS WERE CREATED to act as God's partners here on earth. Rebecca epitomizes this essential value. Each
time Rebecca appears in the Torah she figures prominently in God's
plans. Rebecca first appears at the well; Abraham's servant catches
sight of her just after he prays to God for guidance in finding the
right partner for Abraham's son Isaac. Later in the narrative it is
Rebecca who sets up her son Jacob to receive his brother Esau's
blessing from their blind, dying father, Isaac.

This *parashah* opens with these words: *Eleh toldot Yitzchak,* "These
are the genealogical stories of Isaac." With the text's immediate
shift in focus to Rebecca, *Parashat Toldot* might well have opened with
Eleh toldot Rivka, "These are the genealogical stories of Rebecca." But
rather than interpret *toldot* as "stories," "generations," "line," or
"lineage," as is the plain meaning, we can play with its root, *y-l-d*
(birth), and imagine, "These are Rebecca's birth stories." Like all
women who have given birth, Rebecca has stories. She can tell you

stories of the difficulty of conception, for it took Isaac and Rebecca twenty years to conceive! The text claims that Rebecca was barren, but since Isaac and Rebecca were a monogamous couple, it is unclear which one was infertile. The Torah merely assumes it was Rebecca. *Parashat Toldot* records stories of a difficult pregnancy and an exceptional birth story. *Eleh toldot Rivka.* "These are Rebecca's birth stories."

Rebecca's stories are so consequential that they merit a prominent place in our Torah. With a paucity of detail concerning women's lives in the Torah, why else do we encounter a section filled with the intimate details of a matriarch's pregnancy and birth? It is because her stories are rich with meaning. She teaches us values—the values of prayer, of looking for significance in life's struggles, and of understanding our capacity to be God's partners.

The Power of Prayer

One remarkable element of this story is that, in the course of Rebecca's terribly difficult pregnancy, she goes directly to God: *Vatelech lidrosh et-Adonai*, "She went to inquire of Adonai." God responds to her inquiry with the world's first (Divine!) ultrasound. God tells Rebecca, "You've got twins!" Traditional commentators generally skip over this section, which is odd, since it is rare and powerful that God and any individual enjoy such intimate communication. With the words *telech lidrosh* we learn that it is Rebecca who initiated this human-Divine interaction. While the verb *lidrosh* means "seek" or "inquire," it also has the connotation of seeking God in prayer and worship. The verb is used for this meaning in many other places throughout the Torah.

It makes sense that a religious woman experiencing gut-wrenching pain would pray to God, but for what? In this case, she prays to better understand her pain. After all, pain may be better endured if the one in pain knows that something momentous will be the result of that pain. The spare detail imparted by these few words suggests that Rebecca is already in possession of a strong spiritual life when she goes to inquire of Adonai. When Rebecca prays, God answers her immediately.

The text does not address the nature of her relationship with Isaac. We can only surmise that it was intimate and loving, that throughout their years of infertility they supported and loved one another. But there is no doubt of the strength of Rebecca's relationship to God. This aspect of Rebecca's birth story suggests to us the possibility of attaining higher levels of self-awareness and understanding by seeking God in prayer, when faced with our own existential challenges.

*F*inding Meaning in Life's Struggles

Rebecca's words to God are heartfelt, yet puzzling. Feeling wretched from the struggle going on inside her womb, Rebecca cries out to God, *Im ken, lama zeh anochi?* Though the idiomatic meaning of Rebecca's words is, "If this is so, why do I exist?" we can break up the phrases as if they were pieces to a jigsaw puzzle. Imagine them as fragments of a prayer that Rebecca is unable to vocalize in one smooth utterance. Yet, God understands perfectly, because God can hear the longings of her heart, longings that connect the puzzle pieces. *Im ken.* "If so." Rebecca accepts the facts of her situation. *Lama zeh?* "Why is this?" She looks to God in order to find meaning in her suffering. Amidst her agony, that Rebecca spits out *anochi,* "I," suggests that her question is of an existential nature. God hears her *anochi* as: "But who am I? What is the meaning of my life in contradistinction to these beings growing inside of me?" When assembled, the puzzle pieces of Rebecca's heartfelt prayer teach us that asking existential questions is part of the spiritual process of discovering meaning in our lives. Life's greatest struggles can teach us who we are—if we are not afraid to ask the questions.

Being God's Partner

Rebecca's prayers are answered with God's assurance that she has a crucial role to play in the eternal process of the unfolding of God's holy creation. When Rebecca prays her prayer, *Im ken, lama zeh anochi?* we can make a midrashic interpretation: "What do you want from me, God?" God answers her in such a way that she comes to understand her role in nurturing the future of the Jewish people. In contrast to her husband Isaac's blindness, Rebecca is blessed with total clarity about her life's purpose and its implications for future generations. Realizing herself as God's partner, she makes decisions and carries out plans without hesitation.

Rebecca stands out among our male and female biblical heroes as a truly inspiring role model. She is clear-sighted, smart, humble, courageous, loyal, loving, and, above all else, spiritually connected and clear regarding her life's purpose. Her stories are essential to the story of the birth of the Jewish people. When we tell our birth story, we must necessarily tell the stories of Rebecca. She invites each of us to open our eyes to God's presence, to pray for awareness that our lives have meaning, and to direct our own actions in such a way that we, too, may be God's partners in the continual work of creation.

RABBI SANDY EISENBERG SASSO

ויצא

Vayetze

Wrestling on the Other Side of the River

With God-wrestlings have I wrestled with my sister and prevailed. (GENESIS 30:8)

WE ARE RESPONSIBLE FOR THE STORIES WE TELL and for those we choose not to tell. Our silences speak volumes about whom and what we value. The Torah text uses both speech and silence to open a window into the spiritual quests of our ancestors. Most of their pilgrimages lead us up a mountain or to some secluded place. We have climbed with Abraham up Mount Moriah, and with Jacob we have found ourselves alone by the river Jabbok. It seems that the true God-struggle takes place in solitary moments; the obligations of life's daily routine are a distraction. You close your eyes, take deep breaths, and you tune out the world. The spirit requires solitude and silence. Was that not why Abraham left his servants at the foot of Moriah, and why Moses made certain that no one approached Sinai? Why else would Jacob send his two wives, eleven children, servants, and cattle across the Jabbok before his divine struggle, which ultimately led him to reconcile with his brother, Esau? These are the stories we have chosen to tell.

79

But what of the stories we have chosen not to tell? What of those struggles that take place at the foot of the mountain, by the well, on the side of the river with Rachel and Leah? I always imagined myself with Jacob, soul-struggling, trying to wrest a blessing from a God whom I could not always understand. Then I came across a sermon that helped me reside awhile with Rachel and Leah on the other side of the Jabbok.[1] There I found amidst the clamor of daily routine a life of the spirit that had for too long been silent. There I discovered a spiritual life that involved not retreat but engagement.

The story of Rachel and Leah is told as a classic narrative of sibling rivalry between the unloved fertile wife and the loved and beautiful barren one. It is a story told from Jacob's perspective. We barely get a glimpse of what Rachel and Leah thought or felt. What if they were to speak to us and to each other? What would they teach?

Rachel and Leah's rivalry is not unlike that of Jacob and Esau. The brothers struggle for their father's blessing, the sisters for Jacob's love. The brothers vie for the rights of the firstborn, the sisters for the status of the fertile wife. But Jacob's long journey away from his brother's enmity leads him back. After Jacob's struggling with the angel, the two brothers meet. Esau embraces Jacob and they weep. Later they bury their father Isaac together. But there is no narrative that tells of a similar struggle and reconciliation between the sisters. With each new birth Rachel and Leah appear to grow farther apart from each other; they never find one another's embrace. They die and are buried apart. Rachel is buried alone in Bethlehem, on the way to Ephrat, and Leah with Jacob in Machpelah. The text leaves Rachel and Leah separated by jealousy, and Jacob and Esau in each other's arms. If we read the story through a woman's eyes, if we allowed Rachel and Leah to speak for themselves, would they find reconciliation?

In Gen. 30:8, in the context of Rachel's jealousy over her sister's ability to bear children, we read, "With God-wrestlings have I wrestled with my sister and prevailed." The Hebrew is *naftulei elohim*, which means "great wrestlings," or more literally, "God wrestlings." Later, in describing Jacob's encounter, Gen. 32:25 reads, "Then Jacob was left alone; and a man wrestled *(va-ye'avek)* with him until sunrise." While the Hebrew word for "wrestle" in this verse is not the one used for Rachel's struggle, the two contests are very similar. Yet Jacob's struggle is with the Ultimate, an event marking not only a change of name but of character. Rachel's wrestling is dismissed as nothing more than a fight with her sister. It is customary to view men's conflicts as serious confrontations and women's as nothing more than cat fights. But what if we imagine God in Rachel's struggle? Jacob does not let his adversary go until he blesses him. Does Rachel also wrest a blessing from her adversary?

Jacob's struggle tells us that before we can meet the other, reconcile with our enemy, find peace and acceptance, we must separate, find that space apart from others to come to know ourselves better. Fearful of his brother's anger and jealousy, Jacob had to flee from Esau, build a life apart from him in Haran, while Rachel and Leah build their lives in the same tent, alongside each other. Rachel's struggle teaches us that reconciliation is not a process *apart* from other people, but *with* them, and that we come to better know ourselves through the eyes of another human being. Jacob tells us that the spiritual search demands solitude. Rachel and Leah tell us that it demands engagement. In between, in the encounters of one with the other, the soul is nourished.

What Rachel sees reflected in Leah's soul are the unloved parts of herself. We don't read of Rachel as the unloved one. Yet her father offers her older sister to her beloved Jacob, callous to the feelings of his youngest daughter. God has presumably blessed Rachel with beauty. She was "of beautiful form and fair to look upon" (Gen. 20:17). Yet God does not bless her with the children for whom she yearns. She can claim neither her father's love nor God's. Her anger, her jealousy of Leah, is self-hatred for the love she cannot find in herself. Rachel is fearful of recognizing that the unloved Leah is not only a sister but herself. And Leah is fearful of recognizing that the barren Rachel is not only her sister, but indeed herself. The fullness of her womb does not compensate for the emptiness in her life.

The rabbis imagine that Jacob's struggle with the angel is in fact a struggle with his brother, Esau. So we imagine that Rachel's wrestling with her sister Leah is also a Divine struggle. In the end, the angel blesses Jacob. In the end, Leah and God bless Rachel. After the sisters' encounter, Leah gives Rachel mandrakes (Gen. 30:15), which seem to be either aphrodisiacs or fertility plants, and not long after that, Rachel bears a son, Joseph.

A medieval midrash provides us with another striking statement of reconciliation among all the matriarchs:

> Now all the wives of Jacob, Leah, Rachel, Zilpah and Bilhah, united their prayers with the prayer of Jacob, and together they besought God to remove the curse of barrenness from Rachel. On New Year's Day, the day whereon God sits in judgment upon the inhabitants of the earth, God remembered Rachel and granted her a son.[2]

The women are not competitors, but sisters. The result of their solidarity is new life, God's blessing. Just as Jacob's struggle is transforming, allowing him to emerge as Israel, Rachel's wrestling allows her to become a mother in Israel, a matriarch of our people.

At the end of Jacob's struggle, it appears that Jacob and Esau have resolved their differences. Yet tradition records their descendants as eternal enemies.[3] Rachel reminds us that reconciliation is ongoing, a healing process that continues even after death, for generations.

Rachel bears a second son and names him Ben Oni, "son of my sorrow," and she dies and is buried in Bethlehem, "on the way" to Ephrat (Gen. 35:19). Could her sorrow be regret over the rivalry with her sister? Could her burial "on the way" mean "on the way to reconciliation"? Jacob and Esau's children are enemies; Rachel and Leah's are not. Despite internal bickering and jealousies, they are still family. In fact, it is Rachel who greets Leah's children as they return from exile, and according to the midrash, prays to God for their return. Her prayer is extraordinary:

> If I, a creature of flesh and blood, formed of dust and ashes, was not envious of my rival and did not expose her to shame and contempt, why should you, Ruler who lives eternally and are merciful, be jealous of idolatry and exile my children? Forthwith the mercy of the Holy One, the Blessed One, was stirred, and God said, "For your sake, Rachel, I will restore Israel to their place."[4]

It is because of Rachel's prayer that God and the children of Israel are reconciled with each other.

Reconciliation is not a one-time accomplishment, but a process that continues. Our children carry with them our enmities, and our loves.

The story of Rachel and Leah ends with Rachel's tears. Jacob and Esau's story also ends in tears. The two brothers weep out of relief. For the moment, the battle they anticipated does not ensue. Yet their descendants do battle, and the conflict between them continues for generations. But Rachel's tears are different. In Jer. 31:15 Rachel is pictured as weeping for her children, "who are not." We read this passage on Rosh Hashanah, a time of turning and repentance, and see Rachel as a model for reconciliation. Rachel's tears, unlike Jacob's and Esau's, are vessels of forgiveness and healing. They bring her children home. In an age where our primary battles are within the Jewish family, we have much to learn from the struggle between two sisters.

Rachel and Leah teach us that reconciliation involves struggle, not only with the external enemy but also with ourselves. It asks that we see what we hate in the other as part of us. Jacob teaches us about the need for solitude, for detachment from the encumbrance of relationships and responsibilities in order to nourish the soul. Rachel reminds us that we also embark on the spiritual journey with others, that our character is formed in the midst of the demands and trials of daily life. She teaches us to find within all encounters the presence of God, and to wrest from that presence a blessing. We need both sides of the river after all. How good it is to abide for a while with Rachel and Leah, across the river Jabbok.

וישלח

Vayishlach

No Means No

While Israel stayed in that land, Reuben went and lay with Bilhah, the concubine of his father: and Israel found out. (GENESIS 35:22)

TOWARD THE END OF THIS TORAH PORTION, Reuben, Jacob's older son, lies with Bilhah. In an actual Torah parchment, this verse—Gen. 35:22—is written in Hebrew in a way physically detached from the rest of the writing. In Hebrew this kind of verse is termed *piska be'emtza passuk,* meaning a paragraph that ends in the middle of a verse. It is a mysterious verse. A conflict between father and son. A woman caught in between. It is great material for a soap opera!

We have no indications of the feelings, the reasons and the motivations behind Reuben's action. The Torah is sparse about feelings in general, so there is a lot of room for imagination. Maybe Reuben was trying to establish his power by sleeping with his father's concubine. Since he was the firstborn, he would be the one to receive all the responsibility and benefits over his brothers. By lying with his father's concubine, he was ensuring his power and supremacy over them.

The Talmud, in *Shabbat* 55b, suggests that when Rachel died,

Jacob moved Bilhah's bed to his tent. Reuben was very angry and said, "Is it not enough that my mother was so disrespected while her sister was alive? [Reuben was Leah's son.] Now my mother is going to be diminished by a concubine?" For that reason he went and lay with Bilhah. According to this midrash, Reuben wanted to avenge his mother. He committed adultery and incest, and also dishonored his father, to honor his mother. This does not seem in our day a fitting monument to the memory of his mother, though in the patriarchal context of its own time, Reuben might well have sincerely believed that it was.

Bilhah's voice is not heard, and we do not know how much she was a willing partner to this relationship with Reuben. The son might have had unresolved issues with his father, so Bilhah was put in the middle. Interestingly, when Jacob blesses his sons, he says that because of this transgression, Reuben's rights as firstborn are taken away.

None of the commentators deal directly with Bilhah. Their main focus is to condemn Reuben for sleeping with his father's concubine; in other words, for utilizing his father's property. Because Reuben was not written off from Jacob's will, the commentators explain that he actually repented of what he did, and was the first one to do *teshuvah*.[1] For that reason, the rabbis teach that he merited to have the prophet Hosea come from his tribe, because Hosea was the first to call the Israelites to repentance.

Still, not a word about this woman. How did she feel? Was she a willing partner? The clue to her feelings comes from the preposition *et*, in verse 22, which is used to mean "with" in the phrase "he lay with her." The word *et* is not translatable into English, but its grammatical function in Hebrew is to show that the word that follows it is an object—the object of the verb that preceded it. The verb form "he lay," *vayishkav*, used of a man with a woman implies a sexual encounter. It is usually followed by the word *im*, meaning "with." For example, when this verb form is used to describe the kind of encounter David had with Bathshebah (2 Sam. 11:4 and 12:24), or Jacob had with Leah (Gen. 30:16)—both times seen as either consensual or initiated by the woman—the preposition used after *vayishkav* is *im.* Yet when it comes to Bilhah, the preposition *et* is used, and seems to connote that Bilhah is an object of this act—as in vulgar English slang we might say that "he laid Bilhah." The use of the preposition *et* in our text implies that in this case of sex, force was a factor. There are only two other instances in the Hebrew Bible where the expression *vayishkav et* is found. Both are sex initiated by a man, done to a woman. First we see *et* in the rape of Dinah in Gen. 34:2, and then we see *et* in the rape of Tamar in 2 Sam. 13:14. This incident with Bilhah is the third. What do these three women—Dinah, Tamar, and Bilhah—have in common? In her story, Tamar is not a willing partner to Amnon. In her story, Dinah does not seem to be a willing partner to Shechem. Through a kind of inference that the tradition calls in Hebrew *gezerah shavah*, "the same claim,"[2] I would suggest that in Bilhah's case, too, she did not consent. It was rape.

Of course, we would not wish that Bilhah was raped. What would we gain from the Bible by having yet another story of humiliation and pain? But by using the preposition *et* in these three incidents, the Torah does have an important lesson: No means no. In these three instances, it is clear that the motivation for rape is not desire. The issue is power, as we have learned in our modern times. Rape is a violent act, an act of establishing authority and power through fear. In the case of Tamar, raping her would establish Amnon's power over his half-siblings, specifically over Absalom, who was next in line to succeed David. By raping his half-sister Tamar, Amnon tries desperately to establish his dominion over his brother's family. In the case of Dinah, she was a pawn in the fight between the possessors of the Land (Shechem and his father, Hamor) and the newcomers (Jacob and his sons). In taking her by force, Shechem tried to establish his power over the Land and his right to do whatever he deemed right in that Land. And in the case of Bilhah, we have Reuben trying to establish his power over his father's estate. His father was old, and the inheritance would be his, sooner or later. He begins to exert that power immediately to make sure that the message to the other brothers is clear.

This, then, is the spark that makes this *parashah* shine for us. This is a message as relevant today as it was centuries ago, as men continue to use and abuse women as pawns in the power game. These three examples show that making women suffer is not the road to attain power. Amnon is killed by his half-brother, Absalom, in revenge for his sister. Shimon and Levi kill Shechem and his people in revenge for their sister. And Reuben lost all of his privileges, including the rights of the firstborn. Rape is about power, but it will never secure the power that the rapist seeks. And every time a woman affirms, "No means no," we will all know that the Torah supports her.

וישב

Vayeshev

Power, Sex, and Deception

*T*hen Tamar put off her widow's garments . . .
and he thought her to be a harlot.
(GENESIS 38:14–15)

THE THEMES OF POWER, DECEPTION AND SEXUALITY are found in *Parashat Vayeshev*, highlighted especially in the story of Tamar and Judah. This story is a multilevel biblical narrative rich with intrigue, action, and significance for the Jewish people. Included are teachings concerning the lineage of the descendants of Judah, the applications of the levirate marriage, rabbinic sources for modesty, a pivotal text about public humiliation, a clue to Canaanite cultic prostitution, and the tradition of the red thread.

After the death of Judah's first two sons, he was reluctant to betroth his youngest son, Shelah, to Tamar, and made an excuse to her that he must wait awhile to marry. Tamar, now a widow, is sent back to her father's house to wait until Shelah grows up. Tamar suspects that Judah will never surrender his youngest son to her, yet she knows that she is entitled to a family by Judah's lineage, according to the rules of levirate marriage. It is at this point that she becomes an agent of her own destiny, securing her legacy with the Jewish people.

Tamar dresses as a prostitute, and tricks Judah into sleeping with her. Tamar exchanges her widow's clothes for the dress of a "sacred" prostitute. The Hebrew word used for this prostitute is *kedeshah*, from the same root letters as *kadosh* (*k-d-sh*), implying something holy, or in this case, a temple priestess involved in cultic worship through sex. She intercepts Judah on his way to the annual sheep-shearing festival, perhaps involving fertility rites.[1]

Judah's wife has died, and he is lonely, so when he spies a veiled prostitute on his way, he cannot resist the temptation, and approaches her. Tamar, who has been silent until this point in the story, speaks very cleverly, asking for payment before she agrees to the sexual encounter. She asks, as a pledge against that future payment, his staff and signet ring. The exchange is made, Judah seals the bargain, and he has intercourse with Tamar. Tamar gets pregnant from this encounter and goes back home to her family to wait. Later, Judah tries to find the *kedeshah*, the temple prostitute to whom he owes a payment, but is unsuccessful.

When Judah hears of Tamar's pregnancy and suspected infidelity, he demands that she be "brought out and burnt," for she is still under his patronage. Tamar again speaks, this time to state, "By the man whose things these are, I am with child." Judah, in recognizing his own signet ring and staff, acknowledges that she is more righteous than he (Gen. 38:26). As he is forced to acknowledge that it was his seed that impregnated her, she is vindicated.

The story concludes with Tamar giving birth to twins and having the midwife bind a scarlet cord around the first hand that shows forth out of the birth canal. The cord was the sign of who was actually the firstborn and therefore who would inherit the birthright blessing.

We first ask, Why was this story about Judah and Tamar inserted in the midst of the Joseph stories? Some scholars suggest that it comes to tell the story of Judah as an independent unit, and has no connection to the stories before or after. This chapter comes at a point in the Joseph stories allowing time for events to unfold.

Other commentators, by contrast, have noticed linguistic connections to the Joseph stories. The eleven brothers, sons of Jacob, have just sold Joseph into slavery and shown their father his bloodied multicolored coat. Although Jacob recognizes Joseph's coat, Joseph later is not recognized by the very brothers who betrayed him. Both times, the same Hebrew verb, *haker*, "recognize," is used. The word *haker* powerfully links the chapters, because these stories are built around the suspense of being recognized or not. The root *haker* is used when Jacob "recognizes his son's tunic" (Gen. 37:33), when Judah "recognizes his staff" that Tamar returns to him (Gen. 38:26), and when Joseph "recognizes" his brothers (Gen. 42:7).

There are several other words used in this story that link it to the chapters before and after. The words *ered, va-yered,* and *hurad* are all from the same root, meaning "go down." They are used when Jacob says, "I will go down mourning" (Gen. 37:35), when Judah "goes down" in the opening sentence to chapter 38 (Gen. 38:1), and when Joseph was "taken down" in the opening sentence of the next chapter (Gen. 39:1). *Nacham,* "comfort," also serves to connect the chapters. Jacob couldn't "be comforted" after losing Joseph (Gen. 37:35), yet Judah "was comforted" after the death of his wife (Gen. 38:12).

There are also thematic links that interweave the Judah narrative with the Joseph stories. One of the main issues is the matter of deception. Judah is a main player in the preceding chapter, when he sells his brother Joseph into slavery and helps convince his father that Joseph is dead. The brothers dip Joseph's clothes in a kid's blood. Judah is then deceived by Tamar, who, having changed her clothes, demands his staff and seal when he offers to pay her with a kid. In other words, Judah is given his due by the very means that he used against others—known in Hebrew as *midah k'neged midah*, "measure for measure." The biblical narratives use this pattern often. The Torah seems to see the matter of deceit as expedient and acceptable as long as the end result is the way things should be. For example, Tamar is not condemned for her part in the deception, and in fact she is rewarded with not one boy, but twin boys, and the lineage of King David.

This is the story of Judah's lineage, and most scholars agree that it contains elements that tie him to David, making Judah important enough to devote a chapter to him. The proper names in this story reveal some of the connections of Judah to King David. Tamar is a heroine of this story, and one of David's daughters was named Tamar. Judah's wife is named Bat-Shua, and David's wife was named Bat-Sheva. The towns mentioned in chapter 38—Adullam, Chezib, Timnah, and Enan—are all located within the southern kingdom of Judah that would be ruled by David at a later period of history. Finally, at the end of the narrative, Tamar's twins are named Peretz and Zerach. Although Zerach was officially the elder, because he stuck out his hand first, Peretz superseded him, and burst forth from the womb asserting his place in the world. As we know, this is a familiar theme in the biblical narratives. The youngest often surpasses the favored birthright position of the eldest. And King David is descended from the Perezites (Ruth 4:18–22, I Chron. 2:5, 9–15).

Tamar's Character

Tamar is a Canaanite woman who has lost two husbands and is childless, yet it is Judah who is comforted after his wife dies. As she is "banished" back to her father's house by Judah, she maintains her presence of mind to devise a scheme that will enable her to bear an heir to her husband's line. Her scheme to sleep with her father-in-law, although courageous, is motivated by the desperation of a woman trapped by the patriarchal mores of biblical society. A woman's status would have been determined by her ability to provide an heir. A childless widow would be only an object of pity.

Tamar is a very calculating and cunning woman, and does what is necessary to secure her progeny. Her very name, Tamar, a pun on the word "date," implies also that she is sweet, able to withstand a harsh climate, and nourishing to those around her. She is not afraid, and there is no sign of hesitation in her actions in Gen. 38:14. The verbs imply action. In the midst of her grief and abandonment, she proves that she is a woman who knows what she is doing and why. Tamar takes matters into her own hands, ignoring societal norms. She seems unconcerned about her family's reactions, and prepares herself sufficiently with Judah's items to protect herself from his anticipated punishment.

Judah's Character

As the patriarch, Judah has the final word, and Tamar is subject to his whim. In this story, Judah's position of authority is challenged and his foibles exposed. First, Judah marries a Canaanite woman, in contrast to Abraham's specific request that Isaac not marry any of the Canaanite women. Judah then withholds his third son, Shelah, from marrying Tamar, violating the terms of the levirate laws that hold a brother-in-law, or the family of the deceased man, responsible for the continuity of his lineage and property.

After Judah sleeps with Tamar, and she extracts a pledge, he sends an intermediary to find her. He is reluctant to go himself, and in fact is worried that he will be held in contempt for his actions. Finally, Judah's most damaging behavior is his overreaction to finding out that Tamar is pregnant. He seems to be furious, for he says, "Take her out and burn her." Adultery was usually punished by stoning (Deut. 22:21) and reserved for the daughters of Israel who were in a city, within shouting distance, and thus assumed to have been capable of calling out for help and receiving it. Judah doesn't take the time to find out the circumstances of Tamar's condition, but condemns her immediately. Perhaps this was his way of getting rid of the problem of marrying her off, as she was still his responsibility, even though she was living with her parents. As the story takes place in the border regions of the future kingdom of Israel, Judah also seems "borderline" in his behavior. This inappropriateness in him makes an especially strong contrast with Tamar's own behavior, so much more discreet and wise than his that even Judah himself learns from it before the story is over. And in light of his admission, *hi tzadkah mimeni*, "she is more righteous than I," it leaves us wondering why David's kingdom isn't named after Tamar instead of Judah.

Modesty

One of the issues our sages have had with this story is how to explain Tamar's behavior in a respectable light. After all, Tamar commits a rather bold act, sleeping with her father-in-law. In fact, different midrashim go to some lengths to protect her "reputation" by saying that the reason Judah didn't recognize his own daughter-in-law was that she had been properly veiled for reasons of modesty the whole time she had lived in his house.[2] This is the reason that she merits to be an ancestor of the Messiah, through her descendant David.

We also learn from Tamar that it is better to die than to publicly humiliate someone. She does not report directly that Judah is the father; rather, she sets it up so that he confesses. She seems willing to die rather than name him directly.

Sacred Prostitution

Another intriguing element of the story is the suggestion that Tamar seems very comfortable in the role of prostitute. It leaves us to speculate that perhaps she may have not only masqueraded as prostitute, but could have actually been a hierodule, a temple priestess in service to the gods. Hierodules were young women who served in a temple, taking part in ritualistic sex to insure the fertility of the land. To some, they were priestesses, to others, "sacred" prostitutes, or even temple slaves.

The text uses two words, *zonah* and *kedeshah*, to describe Tamar. In Gen. 38:15, Judah thought Tamar to be a *zonah*, a common harlot. In Gen. 38:21, his friend the Adullamite asks for a *kedeshah*, implying a temple prostitute, and the men of the place reply that there was no *kedeshah* there. What, then, is the difference between *zonah* and *kedeshah?* Tamar seems to be mistaken for both. What might these terms mean for our story and the explanation of Tamar's behavior? Do they shed light on Tamar's action and seeming familiarity with the role of seductress?

Some biblical scholars suggest that sacred prostitution did not exist, and explain the different usage of the terms by suggesting that, because the Canaanites used the term *kedeshah*, it may reflect their own terminology.[3] It could also be a distinction between language used for polite public speech, as contrasted to slang or private thought. Yet others argue that the exchange of the words *kedeshah* and *zonah* in Gen. 38, leaves no doubt "that there were cult prostitutes akin to Greek hierodules."[4] Evidence from the laws of Lipi-Istar of Isin and other Middle Assyrian law codes states that a *harimtu* (temple prostitute) was sexually active, could marry, but was forbidden to have children. Tamar was to be punished, then, for as a priestess, she would have been forbidden to have children.

There are other parallels with the Gen. 38 story that might suggest Tamar's role as an ancient priestess. Onan pours his seed on the ground, perhaps to keep Tamar, a hierodule, from getting pregnant. Execution by burning was specifically applied to female temple personnel condemned for transgressions. Fire was used because the executed were holy. This is similar to the injunction about the priest's daughter who must be burnt because her sin desecrates her father's priestly holiness (Lev. 21:9). This may explain why Judah uses the penalty of burning instead of stoning, which was the usual punishment for sexual crimes.

But other scholars conclude that Tamar could not be a temple prostitute. Judah was a prominent figure, too important a figure in the Genesis narratives to commit a cultic act with a prostitute. And if Judah were found participating in Canaanite ritual, this would deny his faith in the one God.[5]

Phyllis Bird argues that *kedaishot* are not prostitutes, but share common characteristics with prostitutes, including intercourse with strangers. If Tamar were a common prostitute, then there was nothing wrong with Judah visiting her. But if she were a temple prostitute, he would have been condemned. When Tamar was found to be pregnant, she was to be punished because of her alleged adultery— she was considered a part of Judah's household and promised to Shelah—not because she was a prostitute or *kedeshah*.

Returning to our text, this leaves us with some interesting possibilities. Perhaps Tamar becomes a hierodule temporarily, for the story, and to insure that her destiny is fulfilled. We are not comfortable with the notion that our ancestor of King David may have been a temple priestess, or even perhaps had friends in cultic circles who prompted her on how to behave. The fact is that the transaction between Judah and Tamar happens during the sheep-shearing festival. This was a major feast in the tribe of Judah, and "feasts were accompanied by ritual fornication with the magic intention of securing rich crops and herds."[6] Therefore, Judah's visit with a sacred prostitute would have been no surprise. Tamar seized this one prime moment for action, securing her, our, destiny. In any case, whether she was a common prostitute *(zonah)*, or a sacred priestess *(kedeshah)*, or temporarily pretending, her daring dance with illicit sex is surprisingly seen by our tradition as just, moral, and ethical. She is a woman who resorts to desperate measures, and in doing so, she shows Judah's lack of commitment, at least to levirate marriage.

The Red Thread

Finally, we learn here of the tradition of the red thread. The red thread that Tamar used, according to one story, is the same red thread that Rahav (Josh. 2:21) uses as a sign to let the spies know which house to protect. According to Ginzberg's *Legends of the Jews*,[7]

Tamar's twin sons, Peretz and Zerah, were sent out as spies by Joshua. This red rope that Rahav bound in her house was from Zerah. It was the same scarlet thread that the midwife had bound upon his hand to mark him as the child who, when Tamar gave birth, appeared first but then withdrew and was born second.

Although it is centuries later, we are still binding the sign of a scarlet cord. Red thread is still used ritually by women today at Rachel's tomb in Israel, where the red thread is wound around the tomb seven times. It is used to encircle the belly of a pregnant woman to protect a pregnancy. It is also used for good luck and other magical purposes.

The red thread winds its way through history from story to story, connecting us to tradition and to this *parashah*. We will know, as Tamar did, when we need to take action. This is the symbol of women's knowing/recognition of right and justice, of our power in situations that may seem beyond our control, and of God's continuous "weaving of the threads" of our lives.

RABBI DEBRA JUDITH ROBBINS

מקץ

Miketz

In Search of Dreamers

*P*haraoh . . . gave Joseph Asnat, daughter of
Potipherah, priest of On, for a wife.
(GENESIS 41:45)

DREAMING. With a pillow under her head and the moon high above, she dreams. Sitting at her desk, eyes wide open, with the sun shining through the window, she dreams. Dreams are visions, fantasy and exploration, glimpses of the past and the future. Some dreams need interpretation while others offer clear insight into our hopes and aspirations. Dreaming is a wonderful blessing. But not everyone has the luxury of paying attention to dreams.

Studies have shown that women, and especially teenage girls, are not always able to dream and fulfill their dreams. Thirty-five percent of teenage girls believe that they are not smart enough or good enough to achieve their dreams. Women, and especially young women, often feel devalued by our culture; they feel that they don't have the right to their dreams, or if they achieve them, they feel undeserving.[1] Jews believe in dreaming. Our tradition embraces dreaming by celebrating and studying the story of Joseph, the most famous dreamer in the Torah. Today's teenage girls need a variety of dreamers to emulate if they are to defy the statistics and embrace dreaming in their lives.

If only Asnat, Joseph's wife, who is mentioned only in *Parashat Miketz*, were able to speak to us. We might find that she, like many of her counterparts today, was a frustrated dreamer. The Torah tells us, "Pharaoh . . . gave Joseph Asnat, daughter of Potipherah, priest of On, for a wife" (Gen. 41:45). Asnat, Joseph's wife, mother of Ephraim and Menasseh (Gen. 41:50; 46:20), is a woman whose name appears only three times in the entire text of our Torah. We know very little about her. She is the daughter of a man named Potipherah (who may or may not have been the same Potiphar mentioned earlier in the Joseph story).[2] She is the daughter of a priest, and not just any priest—the high priest of On was known as the "Greatest of Seers."[3] Her name actually means "promised to Nut," the Egyptian goddess of death and rebirth,[4] one of the most prominent deities of ancient Egypt. She is hardly a woman we would expect to be among the matriarchs of Jewish tradition.

The rabbis of the midrash work hard to fill in the details of Asnat's life. They want to make her belong to the Israelite people, to explain why Joseph married a pagan woman. In a discussion of Joseph's new Egyptian name (Gen. 41:45), Rav Ahah suggests, "The name connotes: the one that was hidden here, you have come to reveal her."[5] This appears to refer to another midrash, one that suggests that when Dinah was raped by Shechem (Gen. 34:2), Jacob sent her away. But before doing so, he tied a disc around her neck to indicate that she was a member of his family. The legend indicates that the daughter whom Dinah gave birth to was Asnat.[6] Asnat was then abandoned by Dinah and adopted by the house of Potiphar, where she witnessed and later testified (as an infant!)

that it was Potiphar's wife who seduced Joseph and not Joseph who made the sexual advances.[7] We can give the early rabbis credit for trying to give Asnat a personality, but they do not give her what all young women need: ambitions, hope, faith, and, most importantly, dreams. The woman who spends her life in sacred relationship with Joseph, the one who is his *ezer k'negdo,* his helpmate in life, must also be a dreamer. She must be a woman capable of dreaming, and also gifted in remembering her dreams, interpreting them, and then, most importantly, acting on them.

Asnat of the Torah is like many teenage girls today. She is like many women of all ages. Women who have dreams but aren't encouraged to be like Joseph, to share those dreams and act on them. Imagine that Asnat was Joseph's wife because she was his true soul mate, his *bashert.* Imagine that she was able to dream and remember the dreams, interpret them for herself and for others, and act on them to bring about blessing, reconciliation, and transformation. Perhaps they were truly partners in the work described in the many chapters of the Joseph saga. Now imagine what it would be like if we could encourage women and men, of all ages, to shape themselves in the image of this Asnat—to be survivors, builders of relationships, protectors of Judaism, dreamers in the full sense of the word.

Phyllis Trible reminds us, "Women can receive divine revelation (like Hagar). . . . Women can be prophets—Deborah, Miriam and all the rest. Women are also sages. There are the wise women of Tekoah. . . . And women sing songs on various occasions . . . so women [in the Bible] do a variety of things. But I cannot think of an example of a woman interpreting dreams."[8] I'd like to believe Asnat is that woman. She is the woman who is able to see visions, interpret dreams, and turn them into reality. Asnat is the woman who can inspire teenage girls to move from the back row of the classroom where they are afraid to raise their hands, to the front of the room where they can confidently participate in the learning experience. Asnat is the woman who can motivate the underpaid and exploited office worker to demand better treatment in the corporate environment. Asnat is the woman who can encourage a battered wife to imagine a healthy, nonviolent, loving relationship and leave her abusive husband. Asnat is the woman who can inspire all women to dream.

Dreaming demands that a man or a woman have three basic areas of expertise. First, dreamers remember their dreams. Second, dreamers interpret the dreams and sometimes ask for help. Third, dreamers act on their dreams, often in partnership with other people and with God.

Dreamers remember their dreams. This doesn't mean doing what Pharaoh does, simply waking up with a start and being able to retell the dream (Gen. 41:8). This is not casual remembering. Rather, it is what happened to Joseph when years after his dreams of the sun, moon, and stars and the sheaves of wheat, his brothers stand before him in the Egyptian court, begging for food. "Joseph remembered the dreams he had dreamed about them" (Gen. 42:9). He remembered his youthful dreams, and perhaps he then shared them with Asnat. Perhaps they talked about them, together interpreted what they finally meant, and together devised the plan that would both test the brothers and bring about the reconciliation of the family. It is easy to get sidetracked, to lose sight of a dream or quickly abandon one dream for another. True dreamers, like Joseph and Asnat, are able to remember dreams and see them through to fulfillment.

Dreamers interpret their dreams. We all need help understanding our dreams; we need help to see what the real implications and meanings of our visions can be. The Talmud suggests the following course of action for getting help in interpreting a dream:

> But Rav Chisdah said: An uninterpreted dream is like an unread letter![9] Rather say: Have it made better in the presence of three people. Let the person gather three people and say, "I saw a great dream!" Let them respond by saying, "It is a great dream. May it turn out well. May the Merciful One make it turn out well. Seven times may it be decreed from Heaven that it should turn out well. It will most assuredly turn out well." Then, let them recite three Bad-Things-Turned-Good verses,[10] three Redemption verses,[11] and three Peace verses.[12] Then the person who has had the dream makes a donation to *tzedakah.* Then the three people recite, "Shalom to you, Shalom on us, Shalom for all Israel."[13]

Now this may seem like an ancient, semi-magical ritual to change the meaning of dreams from bad to good. But by sharing a dream with others, and using it as an opportunity to study Torah and do *tzedakah,* we remind ourselves that we are dreamers and that we have the capacity to turn those dreams to good ends.

The verses that are recited serve to remind us of three basic principles of Jewish life. First, we have the ability to do *teshuvah* (repentance). We can change ourselves and our world. Through our dreams we can turn ourselves and our lives from bad to good. Second, we are all in search of *geulah* (redemption). We are all enslaved in some ways, and our dreams can help us imagine freedom and move toward it. And third, we are all in need of *shalom* (peace). The quest for *shalom,* for true wholeness and peace, for ourselves, our families, our communities, and our world is that goal toward which all our dreams should be directed.

After we study the verses, after we are reminded of our core values, we give *tzedakah*. We share our resources, no matter how abundant or limited they may be. We give to others, lest we become like Joseph in his unadmirable youth, using our dreams only for our own personal advancement. We all need help grounding our dreams in values that are shared by our families, our schools, and our communities. Parents, teachers, rabbis, and friends can be among the three people of Rav Chisdah's plan, who help to shape and interpret the dreams so that they will indeed be great.

Being a dreamer means acting on one's dreams. It is not enough to comprehend and intellectualize dreams. We have to be willing to do something with them. Joseph did not act alone. All the people of Egypt invested in his plan and agreed to participate in both the collection of food and the rationing of food. Joseph was able to act on the dreams because he had faith in God. When Pharaoh asks Joseph to interpret the dreams about the cows and the grain, Joseph responds, "Not I, God will respond to Pharaoh's welfare" (Gen. 41:16).

No one can act on dreams alone. Everyone, and young women in particular, need to be embraced by families and communities that affirm dreaming. Dreamers have to have faith—in themselves, in other people, and in God. Dreamers know that God is in the depths of what sometimes seems like an empty pit, in the confining places that seem like prison cells, in the midst of power and glory and affluence. One midrash suggests that Asnat knew how important God was in the life of a dreamer. She urges Joseph to take their sons to be blessed by their grandfather because, she says, "I have heard that if one receives a blessing from a righteous person it is like receiving it from the *Shechinah*."[14] She wants her children, the dreamers of the future, to have a relationship with their God, to know that they are not alone in the world.

The following talmudic prayer, found in the traditional morning liturgy for the festivals, connects all the dreamers of our tradition and reminds us of the power of dreaming, in partnership with God, to bring *teshuvah, geulah,* and *shalom* to our lives and our world. Imagine it coming from the mouth of Asnat and Joseph. Imagine it coming from teenage girls at the start of each school year. Imagine it coming from the lips of women as they embark upon a new stage on life's journey. Imagine it in your own mouth.

> *Sovereign of the Universe, I am Yours and my dreams are Yours. I have dreamt a dream and do not know what it is. Whether I have dreamt a dream about myself, or my friends have dreamt about me, or I have dreamt about others, if they are good dreams, confirm them. Reinforce them, like the dreams of Joseph [and Asnat]. If they require a remedy, heal them, as the waters of Marah were healed by Moses, as Miriam was healed of leprosy, Hezekiah of his sickness, and the waters of Jericho by Elishah. As You turned the curse of the wicked Balaam into a blessing, so turn all my dreams into something good for me. . . . You Who are majestic on high, Who dwells in might, You are peace and Your name is peace. May it be Your will to bestow peace on us. . . . Amen."*[15]

Vayigash

Daddy's Girl

*T*hese are the sons of Leah, to whom she gave
birth with Jacob in Paddan-aram, together
with his daughter Dinah; in all, Jacob's sons and
his daughters numbered thirty-three.
(CF. GENESIS 46:15)

THERE ARE NO EXTRANEOUS WORDS IN TORAH, our tradition tells us.
No misplaced accent or adjective, no miswritten description. Each
sacred word has its place. It is fascinating, therefore, to play the ultimate Jewish word game: "How come?" How come, in the story
before us, Dinah is described as *bat Yaakov*, the daughter of Jacob,
when in the initial story about Dinah twelve chapters earlier she is
called *bat Leah* (Gen. 34:10)? Why the discrepancy, if not to alert us
to some important insight into our communal history, and by
extension, into our own lives?

As a child, I always wanted a large family—sisters and brothers
of every shape and size, loud dinners with lots of food and good
stories. There would always be someone to play with, to talk with,
and to love. When I became a parent, I realized that each of my
children needed all of my attention, so a brood like Jacob's, a baker's
dozen, was completely out of the question. Sometimes, as I stare

at the faces of my three sons, I wonder how it is possible to love another human being so much. At other times, I want to tear my hair out when they argue, hating the way our boys have assimilated our own faults so well that they mimic our own behavior.

Imagine being Jacob, the center of the universe for his household. Each wife had her tent and her responsibilities, her own children to feed and raise and mentor. Almost all were boys; only Leah would birth a girl, someone to be close to her in her waning years. Thus, it comes as no surprise that when Dinah, the only daughter, ventures away from the family compound, she is identified by her mother's line and not her father's, for all the children had a common father: "So Dinah, the daughter of Leah, went out to visit the daughters of the land" (Gen. 34:1).

The commentaries spend a good deal of time analyzing this point. Rashi claims that this verse shows us that Dinah was a "forward girl," just like her mother, who had gone out to meet Jacob and had told him to come to her tent. Dinah "went out" to find other girls to talk to, and that is when Shechem kidnapped her.[1] The Midrash goes further, and links this thought with a verse from Psalms: "Your wife shall be like a fruitful vine in the foundations of your home" (cf. Ps. 128:3). In other words, women should stay home, lest they get into trouble.

This "trouble" is the turning point, for what happens when Shechem rapes Dinah in the fields? Dinah, in that instant, becomes "the daughter of Jacob." Dinah is rejected, never again to be associated with Leah.

The rabbinic explanation is that Leah is responsible for the rape of her daughter: she bore her and raised her, and she should have taught her how to avoid the places too dangerous to frequent. Poor Leah: nearsighted, unloved, second to her sister Rachel despite her ability to produce strapping sons for Jacob, she has to suffer the indignity of mothering the only girl among all four of Jacob's women. Her shame is doubled when her daughter's only value is literally snatched away, and Leah cannot seem to cope with this reality.

Mothers always seem to get short shrift in the biblical text. They are painted as paranoid like Sarah, manipulative like Rebecca, jealous like Leah, and envious like Rachel. They are barren, they fight among themselves, they renege on promises, as Hagar discovered. So why are we surprised when Leah suddenly rejects her daughter?

Perhaps Leah envisioned something better for her little girl. Maybe she had her own fantasy for her, one that would showcase her beautiful child so that Dinah might become more than Leah could ever hope to be. And when she saw what Shechem had wrought, when her dream of something better was destroyed, a part of Leah died as well. The carnage of her sons, who decimate the town in revenge for their sister's humiliation, does not faze Leah, but the tearing of a small membrane shatters her completely.

Dinah is an oddity from the beginning. At her birth, unlike her brothers, her name was given no explanation. Every other name given a child linked him to his past, his future, or his mother's most intimate wish: Asher made Leah happy; Yosef was a plea from Rachel to God that she might bear yet another son. But Dinah is simply Dinah; her name, a feminine form of the word for "judgment" stands alone, and we are left to wonder why. Does Dinah become the "One-Who-Is-Judged" or the adjudicator? And whom would she judge?

I imagine that Dinah would judge everyone. She would judge her mother, who failed her during crisis; her aunt and stepmothers, whose support she had always had as she was growing up; her brothers, who destroyed her only remaining hope for marriage. Every relationship dissolved at the moment Dinah needed connection the most.

Real relationships need to be tested and stretched and not found wanting, if they are to last. From the start, Dinah stands alone. She is not part of the women's world that her mother and stepmothers have created. How do we know this? Because she left them. She went out to find something—or someone—who was missing in her life. Dinah, the daughter of Leah, having no peers in camp, went to find company. With a tent full of women—mother, aunt and stepmothers—Dinah ventured away to spend time with other girls. Could she have already felt marginalized, perhaps because she was not the boy her mother had hoped for? Could she have known that her only chance at finding unconditional attention was outside of the tent in which she had been raised? Would Dinah ever be, if not perfect, "good enough"?

"Good enough" is the true meaning of unconditional love. But good enough is not enough for Leah, because it does not bring Jacob's affection back to her. Good enough is not enough for Leah, because once again, she cannot surpass her sister's unique place in Jacob's heart. Good enough is not enough, because, despite her seven children, her arms feel empty. And Dinah, the only daughter to be born to Jacob, would forever be judged as damaged goods.

Dinah, the One-Who-Judges, might try to make sense of this by asking, "What can we learn from all these losses? Loss is a major part of living, and because of that, we need to understand how it changes our life and what we can do to stem its flow. If all of life is loss, and the only way to counteract the loss is to solidify what we have in relationship with others, then we must figure out a way to strengthen the connections we have.

In *I and Thou*, Martin Buber articulated an understanding of the world through relationship: he claimed that "we live in the currents of universal reciprocity."[2] We never function on our own, but always in relation to the world around us—to God, to nature, and to each other. Everything exists within a twofold dimension. Dinah always had the possibility of close relationship with her mother, her brothers, and the rest of her extended family. But these relationships were peripheral. Her brothers were furious about her rape because such an act sullied their family, not because they felt her pain: "The sons of Jacob came in from the field when they found out what had happened, and the men were livid and furious, because Shechem had made a mockery of Israel by raping Jacob's daughter, for such a thing was outrageous" (Gen. 34:7). Her trauma became their trauma, but instead of bringing them closer, it tore them apart. Had they really felt for her, the text might have highlighted their compassion for her after her trauma.

So how does Dinah then become *bat Yaakov*, the daughter of Jacob? Certainly, mothers and daughters, sometimes close enough to be sisters, can compete for the same man. And when the daughter eventually wins the father's heart, she risks losing her mother's love. Jacob, in time father to twelve sons, must have had a special place in his heart for Dinah. He chastises his sons for murdering the town and ruining his reputation, but he never rebukes his little girl. Dinah enters the protective embrace of her father from that moment on. As *bat Yaakov*, she survives the rape, the killing, and the isolation from her family, because she has one real relationship that had been tested and found true.

As Buber teaches, we cannot live in a world of "I-Its." He writes, "When we live our lives peripherally, existing without connection, we live in a world of I-Its . . . , people who feel disenfranchised on every level: they feel no bond to their spouses, their children, their work."[3] We need to live in relationship with people, loving and being loved for who we are, not for what we represent. Dinah, *bat Leah,* loses her mother, who has seen her as an instrument—a thing, an "It"—to capture Jacob's favor; she is judged for her potential, and dismissed when she loses it. And so she becomes *bat Yaakov* to regain her humanity. She cannot survive as One-Who-Judges or as one who is judged, and neither can we. We humans crave the closeness that we find in family and friends who love us unconditionally, and with the assurance of those special relationships to bolster our courage, we face the world anew each day.

RABBI BARBARA ROSMAN PENZNER

וַיְחִי

Vayechi

Serach Bat Asher—the Woman Who Enabled the Exodus

God will surely take notice of you and bring you up from this land. (GENESIS 50:24)

THE BOOK OF GENESIS, the first book of the Torah, ends on a cliff-hanger, like a good novel. Joseph swears on his Egyptian deathbed that his children, or his children's children would return to the promised land, which God swore to give to the children of Israel. The book closes with Joseph's death, leaving open the possibility for the sequel: *The Return of the Israelites.*

The Book of Exodus, the second book of the Torah, opens many generations later, so long after Joseph's death that the new Pharaoh in charge in Egypt has not even heard of Joseph and his phenomenal managerial talent. From Genesis to Exodus, we leap over what the Book of Exodus tells us was a period of 430 years (Exod. 12:40). In that period, the children of Israel grow from a tribe of seventy into a large people. But they also seem to have lost all knowledge of their past, their religious traditions, and their promise to return to the land of Abraham, Isaac, and Jacob.

Yet, they somehow maintained a connection that eventually led to their willing exodus from Egypt. Somehow, the Israelites kept alive Joseph's promise in this portion: "God will surely remember you" (Gen. 50:24). It was not Moses alone who enlivened the hearts and kindled the hopes of the slaves. Moses ignited a spark where the kindling had already been gathered, but who was it that prepared that fire for Moses' leadership? How could a people enslaved, humiliated, and cut off from their past, accept Moses' leadership and join together to return to their ancestral homeland?

One answer lies in a rabbinic tale, a midrash about a little-known woman who not only carried the "institutional memory" of the Jewish people, but was the only one to experience both the entry into Egypt with Jacob and the subsequent exodus with Moses. She is Serach, the daughter of Asher, and she is an unknown heroine of the exodus, one who provides a bridge between the last chapter of Genesis and the beginning of Exodus.[1]

Serach appears two times in the Torah. The first is in Gen. 46:17, where she is counted in the list of the seventy who went down to Egypt with Jacob. There, she is the only daughter mentioned of all of the progeny of Jacob's twelve sons. The sages who crafted the midrash were impressed by her presence in this list of sons and grandsons. She must have had an extraordinary story to be listed by name here and counted among the men! But even more astonishing is that she is mentioned again (Num. 26:46) in the list of those who left Egypt.

Serach is mentioned, almost parenthetically, among the clans of Israelites who left Egypt, leaving open the possibility that she was not necessarily alive at that time. After all, no one could possibly live that long, even given the extraordinary ages in the earliest accounts of Genesis. By the time of Exodus, a life spans no more than 120 years. But again, the fact that she is the only woman mentioned at all struck a chord with the sages, who reckoned that Serach held a place of honor (if not mystery) in the biblical narrative. Or perhaps they even knew the ancient origins of her extraordinary tale, which have faded from our sacred texts

Midrash One: Serach Tells Jacob That Joseph Is Alive

Serach was a woman of unusual gifts. Her talents, according to the midrash, were first recognized by her uncles, Jacob's sons. After trapping their haughty brother, Joseph, and selling him into slavery, they tell their father that he has been killed. Their scheme is foiled when Joseph reappears in Egypt, and they must inform their still-grieving father that Joseph is indeed alive. Serach is introduced in the midrash found on Gen. 45:26. Worried that the news might kill Jacob, or perhaps fearful of his retaliation against them, the brothers ask Asher's daughter, Serach, to convey the information. She waits until he is enraptured in prayer and repeats in rhyme, "Joseph is in *Mitzrayim* [Egypt], and has fathered two sons, Menashe and Ephraim." Because of Serach, the children of Israel may descend into Egypt with their father's approval. For this gentle and courageous act, according to the midrash, Serach's grandfather blesses her, saying, "My child, may death never rule over you, for you brought my spirit back to life," thus explaining the secret of her longevity.[2]

Midrash Two: Serach Confirms That Moses Is the Redeemer

Serach's father, Asher, apparently considered her the heir of the family legacy, and saw her as the wise and faithful leader who would continue the chain of tradition. In the midrash on Exod. 3:16, we learn that Asher entrusted Serach with the secret code that Moses will later hear at the burning bush—*pakod pakad'ti*, "God will surely take notice of you"—indicating that the time of the redemption has come. This code, the midrash tells us, was passed down from Abraham, to Isaac, to Jacob, to Joseph, who shared it with his brothers in our Torah portion, *Vayechi*, at the end of his life (cf. Gen. 50:24).

The midrash continues with Moses' appearance before the elders of Israel (Exod. 4:29–31). Unsure of the meaning of his signs and words, the elders turn to Serach, more advanced in age than the "wise men" of the time, asking for her opinion of Moses' credibility. Dismissing the signs and wonders, Serach then confirms that Moses is the rightful leader upon hearing that Moses had said that God had spoken to him, saying, "I have taken notice of you." Recognizing the secret code, she announces that he has passed the test, by using the words that she heard from her father.[3] Had Serach not been so wise, so trusted by her father or respected by the people, Moses' leadership might not have the imprimatur that we take for granted today.

Midrash Three: Serach Helps Moses Find Joseph's Bones

Finally, Moses depends upon Serach's penetrating memory once more, at the crucial moment before crossing the Red Sea. On his deathbed, Joseph made his brothers swear that they would bury him back in his homeland, as they did for their father, Jacob (Gen. 50:25). But the Egyptians embalmed Joseph with all the pomp and ceremony due an Egyptian leader, and his bones remained in

Egypt. The exodus thus becomes inextricably intertwined with the return of Joseph's bones. In Exod. 13:19 we read that Moses took the bones of Joseph with him before leaving Egypt. But how would Moses know exactly where Joseph was buried? How was he able to find those bones? According to the midrash on this verse, the Egyptians had slyly hidden Joseph's coffin in order to prevent the slaves from revolting and returning home. Once again, Serach advises Moses, telling him that the Egyptians had put Joseph's corpse into a metal coffin, which they sank into the Nile. Knowledgeable and forthcoming, Serach solves the last riddle that might have forestalled the exodus.[4]

Another Story

Serach enters the midrash like a phantom, someone we catch in the corner of our eye but cannot see in full view. In the Torah, she nearly disappears, like her sisters and nieces. Who would think to look in a list of names for such a heroine? Yet her presence, while almost invisible, carries great weight in the historical tale. Serach is a different kind of woman from the others we encounter in the more familiar stories, and her benevolent wisdom earns her a pivotal place in the Jewish saga.

In the Talmud, the rabbis also claim to have relied on her wisdom and memory. According to another midrashic account, Rabbi Yochanan and his colleagues were once debating the form that the waters of the Red Sea took when they parted. At that moment, Serach bat Asher looked in and interjected, "I was there. The waters were not like you describe, but rather like lighted windows."[5] And who could argue with someone who was there?

And so, Serach, a mysterious and wise woman, enters the biblical account to teach us to look in the dark corners for the true heroes, and not to overlook anyone just because they are old, or quiet, or isolated. Rather, we should treasure the gifts of memory, authority, and awareness that our grandmothers bestow.

Shmot/Exodus

RABBI REBECCA T. ALPERT

שמות

Shmot

Rediscovering Tziporah

*T*he priest of Midian had seven daughters. They came to draw water, and filled the troughs to water their father's flock. Shepherds came to drive them off, but Moses rose to defend them, and he watered their flock. They returned to their father Reuel, and he said, "Why have you come back so soon today?" They answered, "An Egyptian rescued us from the shepherds and he even drew water for us and watered the flock." He said to his daughters, "Where is he? Why did you leave the man? Ask him in to eat." Moses consented to stay with the man, and he gave Moses his daughter Tziporah as wife. She bore a son whom he named Gershom, for he said, "I have been a stranger in a strange land." (EXODUS 2:16–22)

NO FEMINIST TALE THIS, the story of the meeting and betrothal of Moses and Tziporah, at least not in the biblical text itself. We can name the elements that reduce women to property and render them invisible: Reuel (who is identified both by traditional commentators and later biblical scholars as one and the same with Jethro, Moses' father-in-law in later episodes of the story) owns the flock. He criticizes his daughters for their lack of hospitality. He rewards Moses for his deed by "giving" his daughter to him in marriage. Moses is the hero, saving the helpless daughters from the shepherds. The son that Tziporah bears belongs to Moses, and he names this son in remembrance of his experience in Midian. Moses and Reuel act; Tziporah and her nameless sisters are acted upon. Tziporah's mother isn't mentioned in the Torah's story. It is left for later commentators to imagine her into existence.

Later midrashim, both ancient and contemporary, rework elements of this story, giving life to its female protagonist, Tziporah. Through these retellings the story comes alive from a feminist perspective and enables us to see Tziporah as a much more complicated character in the story, one who acts rather than one to whom things happen.

The story of Tziporah begins with her name, which translates into English as "bird." *Midrash Tanhuma* suggests that Tziporah's mother gave her that name because she had the insight that, like the purification offering of two clean, living birds, Tziporah would be responsible for purifying her house.[1]

The ancient texts make Tziporah's nameless mother the one who names her. I wonder what made her think of this name. Perhaps she knew that Tziporah would take flight with this strange man, Moses. Or perhaps she named her for the goddess who came to her in a vision at the moment of Tziporah's birth.

Although no goddess worship is known to have existed in Midian, many of the ancient traditions worshiped goddesses in the forms of animals, particularly birds.[2]

I'd like to imagine that Tziporah learned from her mother, and harbored her own unorthodox religious beliefs. Perhaps she and her sisters were troubled at the well by the shepherds because Tziporah was known to be a believer in the bird goddess, the one for whom her mother named her. As an outcast because of her beliefs, she would share much in common with Moses, who struggled with his belief in the invisible God who spoke to him from a bush.

Midrash tells the story of the well where Tziporah and her sisters watered the flock. According to later accounts, it came into being at the creation of the world. It was the same well where Rebekah and Rachel met their husbands.[3]

Ancient sources identify Tziporah as a descendant of Abraham through the line of Keturah because of this connection,[4] and we will discover that Tziporah was indeed like Abraham in more than one respect. Linking women to water is a powerful perspective that we cannot overlook in telling this story, for it connects Tziporah not only to her ancestors, but to her sister-in-law, Miriam the prophet, and to Moses, the one who was drawn out of the water. So Tziporah has a proud lineage and a powerful connection to symbolic elements in our history—to birds and to water.

While the biblical story suggests that Jethro/Reuel knew immediately that he liked Moses and wanted him as part of his family, in the midrash, Jethro/Reuel was actually frightened of Moses at first because he did not like Egyptians. Rather than inviting him to eat with them and to marry his daughter, he threw Moses into a pit to die. According to this account, it was Tziporah who felt an attraction to Moses, and kept him alive in the pit, secretly feeding him every day.[5]

But perhaps Tziporah sustained Moses with more than food. Perhaps they also shared their lives—he telling of his identity as a Hebrew and his reasons for fleeing to Midian, as well as his concern about justice for his people that led him to kill a man; and she sharing with him the secrets of her profession as a shepherd, how to care for a flock, guiding and leading it while caring for each individual animal and learning its secrets. Perhaps it was then that she also shared her vision of the bird goddess with him, as he explored his feelings for the God of Israel—both knowing the commanding voice, though they called their gods by different names.

According to *Sefer VaYosha*, Tziporah took her fate into her hands, keeping Moses alive secretly and then only some time later telling her father that he still lived. In this version, Reuel/Jethro was impressed with Moses' ability to stay alive. Convinced of Moses' worthiness, he gave permission for the marriage. So it was Tziporah's cleverness that defined her fate, not her father's wisdom.[6]

In this midrash, Reuel consented to the marriage on one condition: one half of the children were to be raised as Midianites, and the other half as Hebrews.[7]

According to this midrash, Moses agreed to the marriage that Tziporah had masterminded and to raise half of his children as Midianites. As the story is told in the midrash *Lekah*, Tziporah was pregnant immediately, but she remained small, so that no one knew that she was carrying a child. The concern for this detail in the ancient midrash brings out the traditional commentators' awareness of Tziporah's humanity and shows how much ancient sources saw her as a person in her own right, not merely a shadow of her father and husband. This first child was hers as much as it was Moses'— more so, because he was to be raised as a Midianite according to plan.[8]

When the child was born, Moses did name him Gershom (meaning "I was a stranger there"), not only because Moses was a stranger in Midian, but also because, as modern midrashist Hanna Siegel suggests, Gershom, who was to be raised as a Midianite, would be a stranger to Moses himself.[9]

Gershom was raised in the ways of Midian and, as I imagine it, initiated into the rites of his mother's goddess. He was not circumcised, nor was he taught about his heritage as a Hebrew.

As the biblical story goes, it was sometime later that the king of Egypt died and Moses was called back to save his people. In the meantime, Moses and Tziporah lived together, tending the flocks in Midian. What would their life have been like? I can imagine that Tziporah continued to function as a shepherd while she raised her first child, teaching him her religious beliefs, living peacefully in Midian.

Of course, the main focus of *Shmot* is Moses' call to save his people, and Tziporah recedes into the background upon his return to Egypt. But she does return to the text in this *parashah* one more time, in a very bizarre encounter:

> At a night encampment on the way, Adonai encountered him and sought to kill him. So Tziporah took a flint and cut off her son's foreskin, and touched his legs with it, saying, "You are truly a bridegroom of blood to me!" And when he let up, she added, "A bridegroom of blood on account of the circumcision." (Exod. 4:24–26)

The midrash, and what we already know about Tziporah as a powerful actor, helps us interpret this very strange passage. The text never names the son who becomes circumcised. It might have been another son, since the text tells us that Moses returns to Egypt with "his wife and his sons" (Exod. 4:20). But perhaps this strange encounter was Tziporah's effort to leave her Midianite roots behind by circumcising Gershom so that he would not be a stranger to the Hebrew people among whom they were going to live. According to Rashi, Tziporah had a vision that Moses was being swallowed up by a serpent, a messenger of God. The serpent had swallowed him whole, all but his penis. Perhaps she construed this as a message from Moses' God that to save her husband's life she must show her acceptance of this God by making her son a Hebrew through the covenant cut upon the penis. Thus, she took matters into her own hands, and taking up the flint, circumcised her son, cutting the flesh of her own firstborn. In breaking her commitment to her father, she made Moses her bridegroom of blood, made Gershom an Israelite through the sacrificial act,[10] and also sacrificed her chance to pass on her goddess traditions to her firstborn. It was then Tziporah who, leaving behind her connections to her past, became the stranger in a strange land.

In this *parashah*, as it is interpreted through ancient and contemporary midrash, Tziporah comes alive as a courageous, energetic, clever, and visionary woman. She is a model from whom we learn about exploring visions and acting on your own behalf to attain your dreams. Like our ancestor Abraham, she teaches us about surrendering old beliefs for new ones, and about what it feels like to be compelled to take a knife to a child in pursuit of those beliefs. And she reminds us about the ancient world of the goddesses that were left behind and are now being rediscovered and reclaimed by Jewish feminists in our generation as a part of our heritage.

וארא

Va-era

The Many Names of God

*G*od spoke to Moses saying, "I am YHVH. I appeared to Abraham, Isaac, and Jacob as El Shaddai, but I did not make Myself known to them as YHVH." (EXODUS 6:2–3)

THE NAMES OF GOD ARE MANIFOLD. Each name bears a different image, nuance, reality. The names contradict, mix metaphors and often confuse. In the opening verses of *Va-era*, God admits to a confusion by design: "I am called YHVH but I was called El Shaddai, but I didn't tell them that I am also YHVH, but you should know I am that same God." We are beckoned amid the confusion to know the many names of God; if we could only say It, then perhaps we could understand It.

For so many years I searched for the different expressions of God. Yet, one name remained dominant: the King. I tried to erase the man with the white beard from behind the lids of my eyes and find a reasonable substitute—one that defies a male authority pulling at my life as the "King of the Universe." I longed to utter God's name and see wind or waves of purple light. I found myself on a treasure hunt, searching for more buried images and concepts that were undeniably female.

Suddenly I saw the word *shaddai* sparkling like gold from the mezuzah on the doorpost of my house. *Shaddai,* used in a biblical name for God, translates as "breast," and evokes the images of mountains and breasts, much like the mountain range the Grand Tetons. Dare we say in English what our ancestors understood in their native Hebrew? El Shaddai—the God of Breasts.

In the verses that open *Va-era,* the name El Shaddai is juxtaposed with the name YHVH. YHVH is a curious word. It seems to come from the word "to be." It is never pronounced as it is written. In fact, the true pronunciation was uttered once a year on Yom Kippur, in the second century in the great Temple of Jerusalem, by the high priest in the seclusion of the Holy of Holies, where no one else could hear. When the Temple was destroyed, the high priest lost his moment and we lost the sound of YHVH. As a proper noun, grammatically it ends in the feminine form, but we read it as "Adonai," a masculine name that is translated as "Lord." Is the feminine rendition of God's name the reason we lost the pronunciation? We are dangerously close to the goddesses of the pagan world when we evoke female images to describe the Deity. Is there conceptual room in a monotheistic system for conflicting, even competing, images of God, sometimes male, other times female? In the name of monotheism and in defiance of paganism, we became blind to the rich variety of ways we describe God.

Consider the opening verses of Genesis: In the beginning God created heaven and earth—the earth being unformed and void, with darkness over the surface of the deep and the spirit of God sweeping over the water—and God said, "Let there be light," and there was light.

Look closely and we reveal a description of the womb. The deep, unformed darkness is the womb, ripe with potential. The water is the amniotic waters that protect the fragility of life. There is the spirit of God within, windlike and soul-like all at once. God is the Mother, the force that makes sense out of the chaos. And then there is light: God births the world into being.

It was quite common in the ancient polytheistic world to describe creation as the result of the consorting of male and female gods. The Mesopotamian myth *Enuma Elish* is particularly interesting to us for its similarities to Genesis. The goddess Tiamat is slain and cut in half by the god Marduk. He forms the world from her corpse: her upper half becomes the heavens and her lower half becomes the earth, which is similar to the biblical creation, where the waters above are separated from the waters below. It seems that the Hebrew word for waters, *yam*, may share the same Semitic root as the name Tiamat. Is the Genesis story a distant relative to the Mesopotamian myth? Do they share the Mother? If they do, the two stories differ in tone and content: The Mesopotamian story creates the world in violence and death, while the Genesis story births the world gently and with goodness.

It was when I found the Mother that I understood the King. We mistake the metaphor for the literal. The King of the Universe is singular in his name and one in his essence. But it's not that God *is* the king; rather, God is merely *called* king. What God *is* is beyond description. What we mean is that God is *like* the King of the Universe, that there is a ruling principle that guides our spiritual life just as there is a ruling principle that governs the physical world. Every time I say, "King," I think, "Ruling Principle."

Maimonides has noted that "the Torah is written in the language of human beings." What he is teaching us is that we use words to describe truth, not to ultimately define truth. God defies definition. So when we use King of the Universe, we are not describing God in any literal sense, but rather, metaphorically.

The truth is, when we speak of God with male terminology, we tolerate contradiction. Consider *Avinu Malkeinu,* "Our Father, Our King." The Father conjures the image of a loving parent, a caring, intimate, accessible figure. Juxtapose that to the King, a distant, ruling, powerful, inaccessible figure. When Father and King are said together in one breath, the metaphor is mixed, as if to remind us not to take these words literally but figuratively. God is not a father and not a king, but if I were to describe my experience of God, I could say that at times God seems like a little of both.

Freeing God from the literal frees us all from narrow and, often, dangerous concepts. On one level, the Mother of Genesis liberates the female of our world. God is not only in the experience of men; she is now within the experience of women. Yet she has always been there, hiding.

We say and we pray to *Av HaRachamim. Rachamim* is derived from the Hebrew root that means "womb." The word is often translated as "mercy" or "compassion." I prefer to render it as "compassion," meaning "with passion." God loves us and envelops us with the same passion as that of a mother protecting her creation in her womb. Contrast this to the English words "hysterical" or "hysterectomy," which originate from the Greek *hystera,* "womb." In the Jewish culture, which values women, the essence of the female, her passion and great love, is a word assigned to God. In the Greek world, that emotion comes to us as excessive and negative.

What I like most about the feminine imagery of God is the mixing of the metaphors. The etymology of *Av HaRachamim* evokes the image of the Father of the Womb. When you mix metaphors

—father and mother, for example—you realize the truth is that God is neither. The truth is that only in recent memory have we forgotten female imagery to describe God. The mystics and kabbalists used a variety of images: When we pray and say, ". . . the Great God," God clothes himself with greatness. When we say "the Mighty," God clothes himself in might. When we say, "the Fearsome," God clothes himself in fearsomeness. The attribute through which God clothes himself through our prayers is called "Mother."

In more recent times, Reform Judaism has recalled the feminine imagery of the kabbalists and took a courageous step in *Gates of Forgiveness*, published by the Central Conference of American Rabbis. In their prayerbook they juxtapose "Our Father, Our King" with a feminine image by introducing a prayer that evokes the Shechinah and translates it as "Mothering Presence."[1] Years later, the Israel Movement for Progressive Judaism took a similar step when they published the following prayer in their Hebrew *Machzor*, the High Holiday prayerbook:

Shechinah, the source of our life—hear our prayer and have compassion for us.

Shechinah, the source of our life—remember that we are Your sons and daughters.

Shechinah, the source of our life—teach us to recognize our limitations.

Shechinah, the source of our life—guide us in the ways of pleasantness.

Shechinah, the source of our life—teach us compassion and tzedakah.

Shechinah, the source of our life—be with us for the sake of those who struggle for peace and justice.

Shechinah, the source of our life—turn our mourning to joy and our sadness to happiness.

Shechinah, the source of our life—bless our land and the work of our hands.

*Shechinah, the source of our life—gather Your children from the four
corners of the earth.*

*Shechinah, the source of our life—complete the building of Jerusalem
Your holy city.*[2]

What is so compelling in the Hebrew is that since Shechinah
is a feminine noun, all of the verbs that follow are in the feminine
grammatical form. The impact is breathtaking. The Mother has
reentered our prayers during the most holy of days of the year,
Rosh Hashanah and Yom Kippur.

Va-era seems to tell us that once God was known to Abraham
by the concrete image El Shaddai, the Great Mother, but now will
be known to Moses as YHVH, the God who sustains all being.

Apparently, our ancestors understood that the vastness of God
can be understood only if we use words that include as much of the
human experience as possible. God is like a judge, like a birthing
woman, like a compassionate mother, like a warrior, like a ruler, like
a friend. When seen clearly, God is not seen at all, at least not as
we see our mother or father. Rather God is, as Moses was told, a
great beingness that sustains the universe with grace and goodness.
We are challenged to find the combination of words that will help
us sense and experience the reality of YHVH.

RABBI LUCY H.F. DINNER

בא

Bo

Power and Liberation

*G*od said to Moses . . . , "For I have hardened
[Pharaoh's] heart and the heart of his servants
so that I may display My signs among them."
(EXODUS 10:1)

LIBERATION—FREEDOM FROM ENSLAVEMENT—requires breaking free
from both physical and psychological bondage. In the classic liberation story that culminates in *Parashat Bo*, master and slave alike
struggle for identity and autonomy in a time of dramatic change.
Pharaoh, the ruler-god of Egypt, comes begging for forgiveness
before the God of Israel. The Israelites, long oppressed and suffering, embolden themselves to demand gold and silver from their
oppressors. These dramatic role reversals signal the psychological
power exchange that necessarily accompanies physical liberation.

The portion opens by alluding to the change in cosmological
understanding that the Egyptians are about to experience. "God
said to Moses . . . , "For I have hardened [Pharaoh's] heart and the
heart of his servants so that I may display My signs among them"
(Exod. 10:1). "Among them" expresses the operative message of the
verse. Egyptian and corresponding biblical cultures held that their

deities were linked directly to their rulers' power. But now, with these final plagues, the Egyptians will come to realize the overarching power of the One God. The Israelites' God transcends political boundaries, showing forth instead the Divine omnipotent will.

The eighth plague, locusts, serves as the catalyst for the Egyptians' realization of God's pervasive might. God's strength magnifies the destructive potential of swarming locusts beyond all imagining or historical memory. Pharaoh is forced to summon Aaron and Moses, and to beseech their forgiveness before their God. Overwhelmed by the depth of destruction, Pharaoh summons Moses and confesses, "I have sinned before your God and before you. And now, please forgive my transgression . . . and plead with your God to remove this death from me" (Exod. 10:16–17). Though in the past, Pharaoh has pleaded for Moses' intercession to lift the plagues, never before has he admitted to standing guilty before both God and Moses. This eighth plague of all-devouring locusts initiates a critical shift in the center of power, with Pharaoh beginning to recognize that his authority is meaningless before the might of God.

For our enslaved ancestors, the weakness Pharaoh displays in admitting his guilt before them launches the shift in psychological balance between the Israelites and the Egyptians. It was not for the Egyptians alone that God displays this awesome show of strength. Liberation from the centuries of slavery pressed into the Israelite psyche requires more than just the absence of shackles. The Israelites have to be empowered to claim their freedom psychologically as well as physically. Thus, the impact of the plagues extends God's signs among the Israelites as well as the Egyptians. *Parashat Bo* begins by proclaiming the import of these final plagues not only for the Egyptians, but also for "you [the Israelites] and your children and your children's children . . . so that you will know that

I am Adonai" (Exod. 10:22). The Israelites, under the grip of bondage for so long, need their faith in God's sovereignty reaffirmed in order to prepare spiritually and emotionally for liberation. These final plagues put the Israelites in a position to seize upon the weakness exposed with Pharaoh's admission of guilt.

Whereas the plague of locusts strips the power from the Egyptians, it is the ninth plague, of darkness, that fortifies Israelite faith. When the ninth plague blankets Egypt, the darkness is so dense that the Egyptians cannot move from their places. The enveloping darkness blinds and immobilizes them. Yet, the text relates, "And as for all the Israelites, they had light in their dwellings" (Exod. 10:23). Some commentators explain that the Israelites dwelled in Goshen, away from the Egyptians, and Goshen was not affected by the plague simply because of its geographical separation.[1] Others describe a spiritual enlightenment that filled the homes of faithful Israelites.[2]

Freezing the Egyptians in darkness for three days while the Israelites enjoyed light, this ninth plague imposes a hiatus in Egyptian mastery that gives the Israelites a taste of the liberation to come. This temporary reprieve from slavery strengthens the Israelites' confidence, and makes them eager for freedom.

The Israelites' renewed faith in God and in their own power to overcome bondage shines through the verses immediately following the plague of darkness. Upon God's command, the Israelites boldly request and receive gold and silver from the Egyptians. The Israelites now see themselves as worthy of riches. Even before the physical liberation takes place, these two plagues shift the balance of power from the Egyptians to the Israelites. Masters now show respect for slaves, and slaves direct masters.

The transformation that the Israelites went through in moving from slavery to freedom parallels the road to liberation common to all those who face oppression. Liberation involves envisioning one's self and one's power in a new light. Before the Israelites could cross the Sea of Reeds, they needed to reaffirm their own self-esteem and worthiness. It was essential that they free themselves emotionally from the idea that they were destined to be slaves. So, too, all those who seek liberation traverse both physical and emotional hurdles in their quest for freedom.

For generations women have sought liberation from societies in which their rights and powers have been limited. Women have struggled to prevail over both the emotional and physical road-blocks to liberation. From education to suffrage, from employment discrimination to abuse and harassment, time and again women have fought the battle for basic rights and dignity. Throughout the struggle, the battle has been inward as much as outward. Even with freedom well in reach, many do not feel that they can claim their just reward. And like the Israelites, the lack of self-esteem of many women keeps them psychologically, if not physically, in chains. Women, too, must free themselves from the notion that we are "destined," by either nature or society, to be servants.

It is not enough to simply open the door to equality, when those in power, like Pharaoh, are unwilling to relinquish control. Even when Pharaoh seeks forgiveness, he quickly turns back to wielding control over the Israelites. The backlash to feminism today often feels like Pharaoh's retreat from his inclination to seek forgiveness. As doors have been opened for women, too often those in power have been unwilling to share that power. Women acquire the intellectual tools and job openings to cross the threshold. Once inside, however, many find little access to advancement. Male-dominated workplaces may open the door, but their leaders often are reluctant to accept the ideas and leadership of their female counterparts. So too, women, having played subservient roles for generations, wonder if they are not encroaching on territory that is not rightfully theirs.

In seeking freedom, one cannot overlook the importance of the inner changes that must accompany liberation. Women working side by side with men often still feel responsible for the bulk of household and parenting responsibilities. Those who are abused, once separated from their abuser, may not be able to envision a healthy relationship in the absence of abuse. These physical changes in status unaccompanied by a bold inner readiness for change keep the oppressed still locked in oppression.

Freedom for the Israelites went beyond their release from Pharaoh's grip. The Israelites did not move from being in slavery into assuming the dominating power that enslaved them, but rather, they sought their own vision of freedom in line with their belief in one God. Women reaching new freedoms in the workplace, political arena, university, and home do not automatically assume the roles once held by men. Instead, we forge a new path reflective of our own wisdom and vision. Women are changing not only the roles we play in society, but also we are taking part in a redefinition of society. Complete freedom entails men and women both coming to understand freedom and power in a new light.

Parashat Bo teaches us that the quest for liberation has to extend beyond physical release from persecution. True freedom demands more than loosened shackles: To be truly free, individuals need faith in their identity as free people and in their own unquestioned autonomy. As much as liberation is about release from forced servitude, it is also about the psychological and spiritual strength required to act according to one's own will.

בשלח

Beshalach

Miriam's Song, Miriam's Silence

*T*hen Miriam the Prophet, the sister of Aaron,
took her timbrel in her hand, and all the
women followed her with timbrels and in dance.
And Miriam chanted to them. . . . (EXODUS 15:20–21)

THIS DRAMATIC *parashah* chronicles one of the central events in the
creation of the Jewish people: the exodus from Egypt and the crossing of the Red Sea. Once the people have made their way though
the sea and reach dry land, they confront the hunger, thirst, fatigue,
and boredom of a journey that seems without end. In their anger
and confusion, they challenge the leadership of Moses. The portion
ends with a surprise attack by the Amalekite tribe.

Miriam the prophet appears in this portion as an effective and
established leader of the people. But then, as quickly as she appears,
Miriam and her timbrel fall silent. Ancient and modern scholars
have puzzled over Miriam's song—and Miriam's silence. This portion, like those that precede it, tantalizes the reader by introducing
a powerful woman whose story is so briefly explored in the text that
every generation of commentators is left with more questions than
answers. And every generation of readers is invited to consider the

place and the power of women's songs in our lives and our celebrations.

Who was this woman? What was her role in the unfolding story of the exodus? What has tradition said about her? What are Miriam's legacies?

This portion begins with a detour, a change of direction. God leads the people out of Egypt the long way, away from a war zone, enabling the newly freed slaves to taste freedom unmolested and unchallenged. The diversion described in the text in Exod. 13:17–18 reflects a change of direction in the text itself, a compression of the narrative events that has historically eclipsed the role of half the participants in this central drama in our people's history. The opening of this *parashah* suggests that the direct presentation of the story is sacrificed because it could bring to light tensions that existed between those who followed Moses and those who rallied behind Miriam. The text suggests that a more circuitous telling is preferred, a narrative that does not even mention Miriam until the drama of the sea crossing is complete.[1]

The text is spare and powerful as it describes this singular, extraordinary event: a miraculous journey by foot across the floor of the Red Sea. An inclusive reading of *am*, specifically the whole people in battle formation in verse 18, may reflect the ancient Near Eastern tradition of women warriors.[2] Once they have crossed through the walls of water, the people join Moses in the Song of the Sea, an eighteen-line poem of thanks that we chant with a tune reserved for this song alone. The Song gives us the name of the Sabbath on which this portion is read: *Shabbat Shirah*, "Sabbath of [the] Song."

At the conclusion of the song, we are introduced to Miriam, called *ha-Niviah*, "the prophet." This is not the first time we have met Miriam, although the young sister of Moses who hides in the reeds by the side of the Nile is not named (Exod. 2:4). Now comes the woman Miriam, whose name is interpreted in many ways throughout the ages. If derived from Egyptian sources, as is Moses' name, Miriam may mean "beloved." A Hebrew interpretation might be "the one who sees water."

Miriam is the first individual in the Torah to be called prophet. The text, however, never specifies how or why Miriam earned this appellation. Later rabbinic commentators were eager to discuss Miriam's status. One tradition from *Exodus Rabbah* 1:13 explains that Miriam convinced her parents to stay together despite Pharaoh's threats of death to all newborn boys, and to not only risk, but rather, attempt conception, because she foresaw Moses' leadership.

Miriam is also introduced here as the sister of Aaron, perhaps following the custom of identifying siblings with the firstborn of a family.[3] She steps out of the text with "a timbrel in her hand," which is startling when we remember that Miriam and the thousands with her are escaping slavery, and are being pursued by an angry, mounted army. What kind of people bring musical instruments with them as they run for their lives? And yet, Miriam makes a simple gesture and "all the women followed her with timbrels and in dance." The midrash in *Mekhilta* 10:84 explained the source of these instruments: "The righteous ones were confident and knew that the One who is in every place would perform miracles and deeds of might as they came out of Egypt, and they were prepared with instruments and dances." Contemporary scholars suggest that women in ancient Mediterranean cultures had a rich tradition of musical performance. The women—or all the people—were waiting for their acknowledged leader to initiate celebratory rituals that marked their safe arrival at the far shores of the sea.[4]

"Miriam chanted for them." Moses has concluded his song, and now Miriam begins her own victory ballad. Miriam repeats the opening line that Moses has sung: "Sing to God, for God has triumphed, yes triumphed; horse and rider has God hurled into the sea." Is this the whole of Miriam's song? Or is this simply a fragment? Many suggest that the song attributed to Moses was indeed composed by Miriam's hand. Others posit that the preceding poem was repeated in its entirety, accompanied with dancing and musical accompaniment, or that a separate celebratory poem was performed by Miriam and a band of women musicians, drummers, and dancers.[5]

Miriam's song of triumph is complemented by Deborah's battle song from Judges, chapters 4 and 5, which is chanted as the *haftarah* on *Shabbat Shirah*. These singular and ancient celebratory poems proclaim that God, acting with human agents, has brought victory to the righteous. The two songs act as an antiphonal hymn of victory won at great cost, which takes us back to the earliest days of our people's written story.

The strains of celebration fade and the Israelites' tedious journey resumes. By the end of three days, the people are faint with thirst. Water is a central metaphor in the unfolding of the exodus narrative, and the characters in the story are perpetually at risk of perishing because of either too much or too little water. Moses renders the bitter waters potable, and the people continue their journey (Exod. 15:22–25). But tradition teaches that Miriam is the true source of the waters that nourish the people. Throughout their wilderness journey, the Israelites depended upon the waters of Miriam's well, which traveled with them, "rolling up mountains and descending into valleys with them. Wherever Israel encamped, the well rested close by on an elevated spot opposite the entrance to the Tent of Meeting."[6] Some believe that Miriam's wells provided the water to complement the manna (Exod. 16:14ff.), refreshing the people's hopes as well as replenishing their bodies, and mirroring the imperative of both human and Divine sources of strength for the continuing survival of the Israelite people.

The portion that began by avoiding conflict concludes with a battle and the introduction of Joshua, the warrior who will become Moses' successor. Moses stands on a hill overlooking the battlefield, and when he raises his hand, the Israelites prevail. When he becomes weary, he is flanked by two who add their strength to his (Exod. 17:11–12). The reader might expect those two to be Aaron and Miriam, but once again, Miriam has been eclipsed by the patriarchal narrative. The two are named as Aaron and Hur. Rashi, perhaps uncomfortable with Miriam's single, childless state, identifies Hur as the son of Miriam and Caleb.[7] The biblical text again reads like a detour, circling away from the locus of leadership established at the shores of the sea. The portion concludes with resignation that God will continue to do battle against Israel's foes. But it is many generations before the Israelites again celebrate a victory with a song as powerful as Miriam's.

Contemporary Jews have begun to reclaim Miriam as a model for biblical leadership. For some, Miriam's well welcomes seekers into monthly *Rosh Chodesh* celebrations. Others study Torah in Miriam's name, adding their insights and questions to the commentaries of the generations. Many now dedicate a cup of water or wine during the Passover Seder to this woman who led the Jewish people out of slavery with song and celebration, and encouraged and nourished them as they journeyed for long years through the desert.[8] As contemporary Jews break Miriam's silence, and restore her memory as prophet and teacher, all of our songs are enriched, and our people's story becomes more whole.

יתרו

Yitro

We All Stood at Sinai

*A*ll the people answered as one, saying, "All that Adonai has spoken we will do!" (EXODUS 19:8)

And [Moses] said to the people, "Be ready for the third day; do not go near a woman." (EXODUS 19:15)

Parashat Yitro includes the chapter on the giving of the Ten Commandments. As the Ten Commandments are revealed to the Jewish people on Mount Sinai, did God address women as well as men? The Torah is very explicit in describing the people's acceptance of God's revelation: "All the people answered as one, saying, 'All that Adonai has spoken we will do!'" Then why did Moses, serving as God's spokesman, add the phrase "do not go near a woman" when he gave the people instructions on how to prepare to receive revelation? Why did he exclude women from these crucial preparatory moments?

Parashat Yitro also raises many questions about the perception of women's leadership abilities during early biblical history. In the beginning of the *parashah*, Moses' father-in-law, Jethro, believes that Moses is accepting too much responsibility. He tells Moses, "The task is too heavy for you; you cannot do it alone. Seek out capable

men to help you judge" (Exod. 18:17–21). Why didn't Jethro consider women as capable leaders? Miriam, for example, is described
a few chapters before as a prophetess. Jethro's own daughter Tziporah had shown decisive action in the desert when she circumcised
their son (Exod. 4:25). Why did Moses accept Jethro's implicit
negation of women as leaders?

To begin to answer these questions, we look back to Exodus,
chapter 18. Jethro advised Moses to seek help from other men when
answering people's disputes: "You shall also seek out from among
all the people capable *men* who fear God, trustworthy *men* who
spurn ill-gotten gains. Set these over them as chiefs of thousands,
hundreds, fifties, and tens, and let them judge the people at all
times" (Exod. 18:21–22). Moses took his father-in-law's advice,
and chose only men to be the "elders of the people": "Moses came
and summoned the elders of the people and put before them all that
Adonai had commanded him" (Exod. 19:7). Neither Jethro nor
Moses chose women to judge the people, despite Miriam's example
in leading the women as a prophetess. Both they and those who
passed these stories on were limited by their society's understanding
that women's primary roles centered on the home and children.

Evidence for this traditional role for women is shown in the
teachings of the great medieval Bible commentator Nachmanides,
elucidating verse 21: "Some scholars explain *anshei chayil* as men of
physical strength and zeal, such as have the ability to stand in the
king's palace (Dan. 1:4). Similarly, *eishet chayil* (Prov. 31:10) is a
woman of strength and industry in the work of the home."[1] In
response to this generally accepted view limiting women's role to the
home, it is important to note that the Bible contains examples of
women operating beyond that role. Deborah, for example, is a judge
(Judg. 4–5). Her advice and military knowledge are sought by her

people. They were not even willing to go to war without her leadership and assistance. Thus, although the Bible does show women in leadership roles, in *Parashat Yitro*, Moses and Jethro are trapped by the patriarchal bias of their society, in which women's leadership abilities are overlooked. At Sinai, Moses' limited perspective, not God's directive, is clearly seen.

Through the use of plural nouns we can assert that women and men were both present at revelation. Several times in Exodus, chapter 19, God calls to the entire Israelite people, without distinguishing between men and women. God said, "Thus shall you say to the house of Jacob and declare to the children of Israel" (Exod. 19:3). Rashi taught that "the house of Jacob refers to the women and the children of Israel refers to the men."[2] God then continues with this charge: "You shall be to Me a kingdom of priests and a holy nation. These are the words that you shall speak to the children of Israel" (Exod. 19:6). In both verses, God includes not only men, but also women in the revelatory experience. Torah also relates, "Adonai said to Moses, 'I will come to you in a thick cloud, in order that the people may hear when I speak with you and so trust you ever after'" (Exod. 19:9). God includes all the people, both men and women, in hearing God's revelation.

God continues, giving Moses specific commands for the people to help them prepare for this approaching intense spiritual experience. Both men and women are included in God's commands: "Go to the people and warn them to stay pure today and tomorrow. Let them wash their clothes. Let them be ready for the third day; for on the third day Adonai will come down, in the sight of all the people, on Mount Sinai. You shall set bounds for the people round about it" (Exod. 19:10–12). All the verbs and nouns used are plural, indicating the participation of the entire people.

God concludes the preparatory instructions with these words spoken to the total people: "When the ram's horn sounds a long blast, they may go up on the mountain." (Exod. 19:13). The verse ends reminding the entire people how they must act, both men and women, when they go up on the mountain.

These proof texts show that when God revealed Torah and commanded Moses, both men and women were equally included. Yet, Moses distinguished between men's and women's involvement in leadership and revelation. He first summoned only the elders, who were all men, and told them what God had commanded him. Later, after Moses came down from the mountain, he added the words that set men apart from women, "do not go near a woman" (Exod. 19:15). Rashi gives an explanation for Moses' addition: "This was in order that the women might bathe on the third day and be in a state of purity to receive the Torah."[3] Rashi noticed that Moses added these words to God's original command, and justified their inclusion. These words were not part of God's original commands to the entire people of Israel. When Moses served as God's spokesman, he limited women's involvement both as participants in revelation and as elders. What a great loss for that generation.

We draw strength from Torah's teaching that the Israelites positively responded to God's call that they should be a "kingdom of priests and a holy nation" (Exod. 19:6). Scripture relates the people's overwhelming acceptance of revelation with these immortal words: "All the people answered as one, saying, 'All that Adonai has spoken we will do!'" (Exod. 19:8). Both men and women accepted God's command to observe God's covenant. All the people accepted God's covenant in one unified voice.

A feminist reading[4] of *Parashat Yitro* teaches us that both men and women were present at the giving and receiving of the Ten Commandments. We now understand that Moses was limited in understanding by the conventions of his day. He also believed that only men were elders whom one consulted for advice. Torah posits the spiritual message of *Parashat Yitro:* men and women were involved at this momentous occasion of revelation. We reclaim God's original command to our people, both male and female, striving together to be a holy nation fulfilling God's Torah.

משפטים

Mishpatim

What Must We Do?

*Y*ou should not wrong a stranger, nor should you oppress him; for you were strangers in the land of Egypt. (EXODUS 22:20)

You should not oppress a stranger; for you understand the heart of the stranger. (EXODUS 23:9)

OUR TORAH PORTION BEGINS with a bold declaration: "Now these are the *mishpatim* [judgments, laws, rules] that you, Moses, shall set before them." Immediately, we are all ears. For this is just the question we all want answered. For millennia, human beings have been asking, How *are* we to act in this world? What laws should we follow and, more important, *why?* Which really matter and which are secondary? What does it mean to be a good person? We stand in awe before the sheer variety of answers our species has developed. And today, in our postmodern age, our awe is tinged with anxiety. Is there any guidance for us in our search for the good life? In this portion we find one distinctive, influential, and surprisingly modern—indeed, feminist—answer.

In Hebrew, the book of the Bible in which our portion is found is called *Shmot,* "Names," to reflect the first significant word in the book. In English, however, we use the Greek name Exodus, "Departure." Thus, the central laws and judgments that are required of the Jewish people are not presented in a biblical book entitled "Laws," but rather, they appear as an integral part of a story about the departure from Egypt. Context, in this case, is everything. These laws are not abstract ideas of a God who is above the fray, or something a philosopher came up with on a cool afternoon in her study. Rather, they are concepts that are intimately tied to the experiences of the Jewish people, in particular the experience of escaping Egyptian slavery.

In case that point is lost upon us, the Torah makes it explicit. Not once, not twice, but, according to Rabbi Eliezer the Great, thirty-six times (Talmud, *Baba Metzia*, 59b), the Torah says something similar to the verses quoted above. What an idea! People often remark about the unusual quality of the Jewish story. It seems odd for a people to so emphasize and recall a humiliating past. Having been a slave is not something one would want to remember or remind others of. Yet, in the Torah, the opposite is the case. The Jewish people are reminded over and over that they come from less-than-noble origins, and it is precisely this experience of slavery that forms the core from which moral obligations to other people are derived.

It is the most natural thing in the world to protect one's own family and clan, and to be unconcerned with, or even frightened by, the strange and different. It is precisely for this reason that the Torah has to teach us so many times to act counterintuitively, against our own immediate interests and inclinations. And the reason it gives is startling: you think the stranger is different from you, but you are wrong. The stranger *is* you. By virtue of being a member of the Jewish people, you were not only at Sinai, but also in Egypt. You remember the lashes of the slave drivers' whips as you lugged the giant stones. You know what it feels like to be oppressed, and therefore you must not oppress the stranger, however powerful and secure you now are. Indeed, as Nehama Leibowitz points out, because you have been oppressed you may be *more* tempted to lord it over someone else when you finally have power.[1] This is precisely what is forbidden.

This simple commandment against harming a stranger has a variety of implications, from the political level to the interpersonal. It speaks to questions of immigration policy, inclusion of the handicapped, and the treatment of the non-Jew in our own communities. The command to welcome the stranger can be understood to include openness to people, ideas, or even experiences that seem "strange" and therefore threatening. When we cannot muster true hospitality toward the strangeness in our lives, at least we should try to manage with grace.

The connection between the rules and the experience from which they derive poses the important issue: how a story spawns obligations. Ultimately, this portion of the Torah commands us to live in a certain way because we are part of the Jewish story, and also to ask ourselves some probing questions about our own lives: What has *my* story been, and what are the obligations that derive from that story?

Why does it matter that these "rules for a good life" come from a story about our ancestors in Egypt? The rabbis distinguished between *mishpatim* and *hukim*, two kinds of laws. For them, *hukim* are rules that have no rational explanation. *Mishpatim* are rules with a reason. And the reason is not a principle but story. It is in this way that the portion is most feminist. Carol Gilligan, in a classic work of early feminist psychological explorations, reported how she spent many years listening to people talk about their moral life and how they went about making decisions. She was operating with a model that suggested that there were stages of development of moral reasoning, each more sophisticated than the one before, which could explain the differences in the way people approached moral choices. But to her it seemed that many of these differences could be traced to gender. Often, although by no means always, there were characteristic ways of thinking about moral dilemmas that were shared by men, and other ways that were shared by women.[2]

The differences themselves, while quite interesting for our topic—men operated out of abstract principle, while women were more concerned with context and relationship—are not as important for our purposes as Gilligan's analysis. She does not believe that these different ways of thinking are hard-wired into the brain by genetics—the Y chromosome or the X. The association with one gender or another is merely an observation made in a particular time and place. In other words, the difference most likely derives from women's experience of the world, just as the Jews' commitment to the stranger and all that entailed derived from their experience of slavery.

At the time in which the women in Gilligan's studies grew up, women's lives in American society had been defined primarily by relationships and caretaking, while men had been encouraged to define themselves by individuation and achievement—"becoming your own man." Gilligan noticed two different kinds of ethics emerging: "an ethics of rights," often found in men's reasoning, and an "ethic of care," often associated with women. These "moral ideologies" are not really ideologies at all so much as results of different life stories and different experiences.

The idea that we find in our portion today—the connection between our slavery and our calling in this world—has penetrated every corner of the globe through its adoption by Christianity and Islam, each in their own characteristic way. Similarly, the experiences that have typified and even defined women's lives in the past—being a daughter, a sister, a wife, a mother, an enabler, a caretaker, a nurturer—retain profound value. Even if Jews were to know no oppression anywhere on earth, they would and should be indelibly shaped by their story. Similarly, even if all women were to expand into the many roles available for a human being, it would still be of value to recall their special stories and experiences and to honor the "voice" or "command" that may derive from them.

For each reader, the task before you is to look at your own story and notice the ways in which you have already been obligated by what you have experienced. Perhaps you have known a great teacher who has shaped your life, and you now feel called to teach. Or perhaps, as a child you experienced a terrible illness, and that challenge has been transformed into a deep commitment to visit the sick, or to be a hospital chaplain, or a doctor or nurse. Many of the things that happen to us in life are not optional, but we do get to choose whether we want to remember them. Ask yourself what your own stories have been. Which have you chosen to remember? Which to forget? How do you live differently because of them?

When I was a young pulpit rabbi in Manhattan, a mentally ill, homeless Jewish woman named Anna discovered our Saturday morning services. She regularly wandered in, sat in the back row with her shopping bags, and muttered to herself. She smelled bad, was occasionally disruptive, and made me nervous. I expected we would find a way to get her to leave. She was the quintessential stranger. Yet, somehow, we knew that this was not merely a case of compassion, or imagining that one day we might be in her shoes. Rather, we had all been there. We knew the heart of the stranger. She was there to test us: to mock our pious pronouncements if we could not welcome her, and to force us to grow into the people we claimed we already were.

In this unprecedentedly open society in which we live, we actually get to choose the greater stories with which we want to identify. We do not have to see ourselves as former slaves, but by becoming active members of the Jewish people, we may so choose to do so. If we are women, we may *choose* to embrace some of the traditional dimensions of women's roles such as nurturing and connecting, and the vision and voice that derive from them. The stories we choose to make our own become the stuff of our "experience," along with the particulars of our lives. And, in this way, through fate and through our active will, we select our memories, define ourselves, and discover what we must do.

RABBI SHARON L. SOBEL

תרומה

Terumah

Community as Sacred Space

*L*et them make Me a sanctuary that I may dwell within them. (EXODUS 25:8, JPS TRANSLATION)

HAVE YOU EVER NOTICED that when people walk into a sanctuary in a synagogue, their behavior changes, based on the physical characteristics of that room? If the sanctuary is a large, cathedral-like room with a vaulted ceiling, stained-glass windows, and a tall and remote *bimah* (podium), the immediate reaction is one of wonderment. People speak in hushed and reverential tones, as if they might disturb God by conversing more loudly. For many people, this type of sanctuary is an awe-inspiring and majestic place, a symbol of God's presence in their synagogue. If the sanctuary is a simpler kind of space, with wraparound windows looking out on a beautiful scene of nature, and a small, low-to-the-floor *bimah*, the mood it engenders is quite different. People enter the room talking and laughing. They don't hesitate to approach the *bimah* to speak with whoever is standing there before the worship service begins. For these people, God's presence is felt in their sanctuary by their closeness to nature and to each other. If someone who is accustomed to worshiping in one type of sanctuary visits the other, they have a tendency to feel uncomfortable praying, or they explain that they feel they can't connect to God, in any kind of space other than what they are used to at "home."

Why do we place so much emphasis on the sanctuaries of our synagogues? Can a physical space be holy in and of itself?

Before the creation of the first *mishkan* (sanctuary) in the Torah, the Hebrews worshiped God on hilltops, beside streams, or wherever they felt moved to pray. Abraham and Isaac traveled to Mount Moriah. Rebecca confronted God in her own tent. Jacob encountered God in a lonely place in the desert and near the river Jabbok. Moses met God at an ordinary bush in the land of Midian and at the top of Mount Sinai in the wilderness. Miriam praised God at the banks of the Sea of Reeds.

It was only after the Israelites were liberated from slavery in Egypt, and after they accepted God's Torah at Mount Sinai, that they were commanded to build a sanctuary. The instructions for erecting this sanctuary are given in great detail in this *parashah* from Exodus, *Terumah*. This *parashah* provides explicit directions not only for the erection of the structure itself, but also for all of the objects and decorations inside. The sanctuary was to contain the Ark of the Covenant, with its sacred stones upon which the Ten Commandments were inscribed. It was to be placed in the Holy of Holies chamber, inside the inner tabernacle. The opening of the Holy of Holies was to be covered by a curtain. Outside that curtain, there was a special altar for the incense, a table for the shewbread, and a golden menorah (lampstand). In front of the inner tabernacle was another curtain, outside of which are the laver and an altar for burnt offerings. Clearly, the sanctuary was designed for performing sacred rituals, which included the offering of sacrifice, and prayer to God.

The Torah seeks to clarify the purpose of the sanctuary when God instructs Moses to tell the people, *V'asu li mikdash v'shachanti b'tocham*, "And let them make me a sanctuary that I may dwell within them" (Exod. 25:8). What do these words really mean? Was God telling the people that without a sanctuary, a building, a place for the Ark of the Covenant, or altars for sacrifice, they would not sense the Divine presence in their lives? Does God truly require a building in order to "dwell" among human beings? What does it mean for God to "dwell within" the people? What does this tell us about our relationship with God?

Commentators are intrigued by the notion that God will not dwell *in the sanctuary*, but rather, *within them*, within the people. It is the physical act itself of building the sanctuary that will cause God to dwell within the people. The sanctuary is not for God, it is for the people; it is to be a visible symbol of God's presence in their midst. God's promise to dwell among the people is a recognition of the limitations of human beings in trying to understand that God is everywhere. The tabernacle is a concession to humankind and provides a visible focus for the idea of God's indwelling.

Therefore, it is not the physical space itself that causes God's presence to come into our midst, and it is not the physical space itself that is holy. Rather, it is the involvement of the community, expending its labor on God's behalf. It is the act of the community joining together to make a sacred space. It is the rituals that take place within that space that bring God's presence into the midst of the people. The purpose of the involvement of all the people in building the tabernacle is, as Torah commentator Pinchas Peli explains, to "convert the people from passive participants in their relationship with God, as constant recipients of God's gifts, into active partners."[1]

The indwelling of God among the people cannot take place as long as the people are passive, doing nothing to help bring the sacred into the world. God is saying, "My dwelling among them is on condition that *they* make the sanctuary." *We* must do the building to glorify God. This is emphasized in the text by the Hebrew verb *la'asot* (to "make"). It occurs two hundred times in the story of the building of the sanctuary.

The indwelling of God among the people is not contingent only upon the people's active participation in the building of the *mishkan,* it is also contingent upon the participation of *all* members of the community—men and women both. It becomes clear that the instructions of *Parashat Terumah* are given to both men and women when we look at *Parashat Vayakhel* in Exod. 35. Exodus 35 is the parallel description of the actual construction of the *mishkan* that corresponds to the instructions given in *Parashat Terumah.* Exodus 35 explicitly states that the instructions given in *Terumah* are intended for both men and women. This description of the construction of the Tabernacle provides the only biblical example of active female participation in an activity related to the official cult. When God states, "Let them make me a sanctuary," the word "them" refers to both men and women. In Exod. 35:1, Moses explicitly brings together *all* the community of Israel, which included both men and women. We see this in at least three statements in Exod. 35: "men and women, all whose hearts moved them, all who would make an offering" (Exod. 35:22); "all the skilled women spun with their own hands and brought what they had spun . . . ; and all the women who excelled in that skill spun the goats' hair" (Exod. 35:25–26); "thus the Israelites, all the men and women whose hearts moved them to bring anything for the work that the Lord, through Moses, had commanded to be done, brought it as a freewill offering to the Lord" (Exod. 35:29).

Therefore, the Torah text itself tells us that it is necessary for the *entire community*, which includes men and women both, to be involved in trying to bring God's presence into their midst. If only half the population is involved, if it is only the men who are doing the work and participating, then God's presence will not be felt. The community is whole and the community is holy only when both men and women are involved in sacred tasks together.

The task of bringing holiness into the world, which is the main obligation of every Jew, has always been seen in the Bible as a partnership, a combined project of humans and God. The holy can be manifest in three dimensions: space, time, and the person. God desires to encounter human beings by meeting them halfway as partners: in time, for the Shabbat, which God sanctified (Gen. 2:3) and commanded us to sanctify (Exod. 20:8); in space, by the building of the sanctuary; and in each person, through the mitzvot (commandments) or the sacred rituals, which bring us into God's presence every time we perform them.

We must start out on the path towards God, both in time and in space, in order for God to meet us halfway as partners in the act of sanctification. From this understanding comes the focus on building the tabernacle for God in the wilderness, and the emphasis we place on our sanctuaries in our synagogues today.

But what does it mean that the building of the sanctuary will cause God to "dwell within the people"? What does it mean that this will start us on our path towards meeting God? Torah commentator Nehama Leibowitz points out, "Surely these words contain a message of Divine love, a promise of intimate contact with God."[2] The typical image of God as portrayed by much of the Torah is an image of a distant, transcendent, parental, authoritarian figure. This notion from our *parashah* that God can dwell within the people is a shift in focus from the earlier biblical model of God as distant or remote from the people. It shows us that different models of relationships with God are necessary in order for us to live out our lives as a holy people.

Some feminists have been troubled that the God of the Torah seems to be primarily a transcendent God, and that this is the model that our male commentators and rabbis have perpetuated. This description of God in our *parashah* as an "indwelling presence," however, shows another angle. God wants to live among us, and God wants us to feel that Divine love in an intimate way. Commentator Isaac Abravanel reinforces this when he says, "The Divine intention behind the construction of the Tabernacle was to combat the idea that God had forsaken the earth and that His throne was in heaven and remote from humankind. To disabuse them of this erroneous belief, God commanded them to make a Tabernacle, as if to say that God lived in their minds . . . in order to implant in their hearts His presence."[3] *Parashat Terumah* helps us to understand that the traditional notion of God as only transcendent is a limited notion. It shows us that for God to truly dwell among us, both men and women must embrace immanent images of God as well.

So as we sit in our sanctuaries, be they small or large, intimate or grandiose, we need to keep in mind that it is not a particular physical space that evokes God's presence in our midst. Rather, it is we who will bring God's presence into our midst by making sure we include everyone—men, women, and children—in the sacred acts in which we participate.

RABBI SARA PAASCHE-ORLOW

תצוה

Tetzaveh

Finding Our Home in the Temple and the Temple in Our Homes

You shall instruct the children of Israel to bring to you clear olive oil, pressed for lighting, for kindling lamps regularly. (EXODUS 27:20)

THE TORAH PORTION BEGINS with the image of lighting the oil lights of the menorah in the Tabernacle or the Tent of Meeting. "It shall be a rule for all time, throughout the generations of the Israelites" (Exod. 27:21). Of all the commandments related to the Tabernacle, this is the one ritual that remained intact throughout the exile, and was easily moved from the context of the Temple into Diaspora experience. By reading women and their ritual role more fully into the life and development of the tradition, we can understand the Temple lamps as a ritual precursor for the lighting of Shabbat candles. The worshipful context and centrality of the Temple inform today's modern act. Thus, for centuries women have been responsible for evoking the spiritual legacy of the *mishkan*, the Tabernacle, when they have made their homes into sacred and hallowed spaces. In this way, the Temple texts become a source for enriching women's connection to the tradition and not an exclusionary text.

Seemingly in contrast to the persistence of the ritual of lighting lamps, *Parashat Tetzaveh* also relates another set of rituals: the intricate and detailed instructions for the ordination of Aaron and his sons—the priests of the people—how they must dress, and be initiated to serve God. These details about the creation of the sacred garments and then the bloody sacrifices and rituals surrounding the ordination are no longer functionally alive. In this model for Jewish life, the priests are set apart from the people, carry the burden of ritual responsibility, and serve as the spiritual fulcrum of the cult.

In the years since 70 C.E., the date of the destruction of the Second Temple, history has served as a democratizing force in Judaism. Over the course of centuries, the Jewish people endeavored to realize the words of God in Exod. 19:6: "You shall be to me a kingdom of priests and a holy nation." Yet, the rabbis also tried in certain ways to maintain the hierarchy of the priests. The word "Pharisee" derives from the word for "separation"; the early rabbis, like the priests, would eat only apart from, and not with, the common people. The tradition of listing the genealogies of the rabbis is a hearkening back to priestly authority, based on genealogy rather than learning. The rabbis also draw a parallel between the headdress of the priests and tefillin.[1] This hierarchy was then reflected in the behavior of Jewish men, who were, with a few known exceptions, the only ones wearing tallit and tefillin until the twentieth century. Today, although we have largely rejected the priesthood, in many synagogues the rabbi still replays the ancient hierarchy by enacting the religion for the people and echoing the role of the priest in both prayer and ritual.

Whereas men can easily trace their religious roles back to the established priesthood, and even connect their use of tefillin to the priestly headdress, women must strive to break into the ritual world of synagogue worship and prayer. Our *parashah* helps by providing insights into beginning a tradition of worship. There is a description of how the best craftspeople were put to work with the task of creating the sacred garments: a breastpiece, a robe, a fringed garment, a headdress, breeches, and a sash. They used gold, blue, purple, and crimson yarns and fine linen, as well as an array of precious and semiprecious stones. The Jewish people were preparing to serve God for the first time. Jewish women, as a community, are in a similar position today. There is a process of determining how women will worship, what are the garments, the times, the roles in community. It is Jewish women who have fueled a new trend of beautiful *tallitot, kipot, kiddush* cups, and *challah* covers. Just as their clothing gave the priests a sacred context, Jewish women are donning ritual garb and directing our hearts toward God in a new way.

The priestly clothing, furthermore, in current practice, communicates a powerful message of equality between men and women. At the time of death, all people are made equal through references to the priestly rites. In the ritual of *taharah*—the cleansing, clothing, and preparing of the body of a deceased person for burial—the names for the different parts of the shrouds are the names of the priestly clothing: *kutonet,* the long shirt; *avnet,* the sash; and *mitznefet,* the headdress. The dead person is being prepared to approach God. In death, we are all, men and women alike, dressed as priests.

The movement of Temple ritual to the home also evokes a more egalitarian model. In the Second Temple period, when the rabbis began the transfer of the locus of holiness from the Temple to the synagogues, there was also a transfer of ritual to the home, particularly relating to food and eating.[2] Along with the change in place, there was also a change in the participants. Men and women were expected to follow practices derived from Temple ritual to guide how they ate in their homes.[3] Women were included, and often central, in how Temple worship was played out in the home. Historically, across the Jewish world, women became the center of domestic Judaism, where generations were bound together through love and relationship, traditional values were transmitted, and food preparation was a central domestic religious act.[4]

It was not only rituals related to food that made their way into home ritual. The lighting of the *ner tamid*, the continuous light, serves in the text as the transition from the preparation and building of the tabernacle to the action of serving in it. The wording tells us that the light is for the people and not for God, when it says, "bring to you" (Exod. 27:20).[5] We are in need of a sign of God's nearness, and in this way we invite the Shechinah, God's presence into our midst.[6] It is not a setting where only the priests are allowed to approach God, but rather, the whole community is present.

Rashi asks why the text says, *tamid*, "continuously?" He understands "continuously" to mean "at regular intervals," like the "continual burnt offering," which was sacrificed once a day. It has become the custom to hang a lantern by the ark, always lit, to symbolize God's presence. There is, however, another reflection of the *ner tamid* in Jewish life that is in the tradition of Rashi. When women and families light Shabbat candles, they are rekindling this light; their homes are the places of worship, and they are welcoming God's light "continuously."

The Shabbat meal echoes the Temple ritual with the candles burning, ritual washing, bread with salt, and wine. Jewish homes now serve as temples. The Shabbat dinner is something that for centuries has not been the domain of rabbis and men, but of women and families together. It is women who have traditionally lit candles and thus invoked God's presence. Thus, the Temple rites have come to serve as a model for inclusivity and nearness to God.

כי תשא

Ki Tissa

The Women Didn't Build the Golden Calf—or Did They?

The people saw that Moses delayed coming down from the mountain [where he was receiving the Ten Commandments from God]. The people gathered against Aaron and said to him, "Rise, make us a god who shall go before us; for that man Moses, who brought us up out of the land of Egypt, we do not know what has happened to him." Aaron said to them, "Take off the rings of gold that are on the ears of your wives, your sons, and your daughters, and bring them to me." And all the people took off the rings of gold that were in their ears and brought them to Aaron. He took it from their hands and cast it in a mold and made it into a molten calf. And they said, "This is your god, O Israel, who brought you up from the land of Egypt!" (EXODUS 32:1–4)

TO READ THE STORY OF THE GOLDEN CALF from a feminist point of view, one must begin with *Rosh Chodesh*, the holiday celebrating the new moon, the new month of the Jewish year. Why *Rosh Chodesh*? Jewish tradition says that *Rosh Chodesh* was a holiday given to women as a reward for their refusal to give their earrings to be used to make the golden calf. A midrash explains, "The Holy One . . . gave the women their reward in this world and in the world to come. What reward did God give them in this world? That they should observe the New Moons more stringently than the men."[1] "More stringently" means that women were to take a holiday from work on *Rosh Chodesh*, making even more sure than the men were that they weren't performing any kind of work-related tasks. Just as men traditionally thanked God for stricter obligations to fulfill mitzvot from which women's exemption came to be understood as exclusion, so here the stringency of the women's obligation is seen as a reward.

But where does this notion that women did not participate in the building of the calf come from? "Aaron said to them, 'Take off the rings of gold that are on the ears of your wives, your sons, and your daughters, and bring them to me.' And all the people took off the rings of gold that were in their ears and brought them to Aaron." It does not say that the women refused. For a woman, reading these few lines with a feminist awareness not present in the Torah, the truth hits hard. For when Aaron speaks to "the people," he is speaking to the men, telling them to "take off the rings of gold that are on the ears of your wives, your sons, and your daughters." And therefore, when "all the people took off the rings of gold that were in their ears," "all the people" can refer only to the men.

We know this is an exclusion, because we know that when the Torah means specifically to include women, it does. For example, when the people of Israel begin to bring materials to build the *mishkan*, the Tabernacle in the wilderness, the Torah very clearly specifies, "Men and women came, all whose hearts were moved, all who would make a wave-offering of gold to the Eternal, brought clips, earrings, rings, and pendants—all gold objects" (Exod.

35:22). This kind of inclusion makes exclusion even more obvious. Just as Moses separated the women from "the people" before the giving of the Torah at Sinai by saying to "the people," "Be ready for the third day [the day on which God would come down on Mount Sinai]; do not go near a woman" (Exod. 19:15), so to build the golden calf, Moses' brother, Aaron, excludes women from "the people" by saying, "Take off the rings of gold that are on the ears of your wives."

Rebellion against such decrees seems inevitable, and various midrashim come to describe it: the women refused to give up their earrings for such a creation! *Pirke de Rabbi Eliezer,* for instance, imagines that the women heard what Aaron had said, "but were unwilling to give their earrings to their husbands. . . . [They] said to them: You desire to make a graven image and a molten image without any power in it to deliver."[2] As the men rebel against God, the women rebel against the men, choosing to remain faithful to God while the men try to remove their jewelery. Some midrashim suggest that Aaron instructed the men as he did because he knew that the women would refuse. Some say he imagined they would refuse out of vanity, not wanting to give up their beautiful gold rings.[3] But others, such as *Tanhuma Yelamdenu,* see an expression of faith in the women's refusal: "Aaron told them to do this difficult thing because [he was aware that] the women would not agree to it. They had seen the miracles and the deeds that the Holy One had wrought for them in Egypt, and what had transpired at the Red Sea and at Sinai, and so they went to the men and said: God forbid that we should renounce the Holy One, who has performed all these miracles and mighty deeds in our behalf, in order to fashion an idol."[4]

Why are the women so faithful to God? Have they made a promise we do not know of, some pledge behind the scenes? We might almost imagine them as married, remaining steadfast in their wedded connection even when an attractive alternative comes along. This possibility is heightened when we look at the Aramaic translations for the word "rings" in Aaron's instruction, "Take off the rings of gold that are on the ears of your wives." In Hebrew, a ring is a *nezem*, plural *n'zamim*, and "rings of gold" are *nizmei ha-zahav.* In Aramaic, though, seen in both *Targum Onkelos* and *Targum Yonatan* for Exod. 32:2–3, "rings" are *kadashei*, whose root is *k-d-sh*, related to the Hebrew *kadosh, kiddush, kiddushin.* All are generally translated as something having to do with holiness, but the root originally meant "set apart," for that is the definition of holiness. When they wed, a couple sets one another apart from all others, and the central ritual of wedding is *kiddushin*—the setting apart. It is symbolized by a ring, often made of gold. When Abraham's servant Eliezer goes to meet Rebekah and her family and to convince her to come back with him to marry Isaac, he brings her jewelry as engagement gifts, including a "gold nose-ring whose weight was a half-shekel" (Gen. 24:22, 30, 47). Here, too, the Aramaic translation reads *kadasha*, and here the ring is clearly a sign of betrothal.

Suddenly, these rings that the women refuse to give to their husbands as an offering take on new meaning. They must be a symbol of setting apart, of wedding or engagement. Perhaps the rings in their ears are engagement or wedding rings, symbols of the bonds these women share with their husbands, and thus too precious to give up for the making of foolishness like this golden calf. Even if their husbands do not share their compunction, they will insist on preserving those bonds. And this idol made of gold will surely shatter those bonds: how can they remain married to these easily swayed men?

Or perhaps the rings in their ears symbolize their connection to God, their way of setting themselves apart as a people linked to the One who cannot be seen, but whose miracles are fresh in mind. Women, seeing in this special link an echo of their promised fidelity to their husbands, hold fast to it, and refuse to let their husbands take the rings to create an alternate "god." For them, there is only the God who brought them out of slavery in Egypt, and they refuse further slavery to human-made gods.

It seems like a lovely picture—the women, more faithful than their men, refusing to part with their special, holy, setting-apart rings, refusing to participate in the creation of a golden idol, even as their men do participate. There is a problem, however, with this idyllic scene: Jewish tradition, using the same language, the same terms, sees this same scene as one of complete infidelity, by the whole people of Israel, women and men. And when it is viewed in this way, most often the metaphor used for the entire unfaithful people of Israel is that of the adulterous wife.

When Jacob and his family leave Shechem following the rape of Dinah and their violent destruction of the place and its inhabitants, Jacob says to his household, "Turn away the alien gods in your midst," and his family "gave to Jacob all the alien gods in their possession, and the rings that were in their ears . . ." (Gen. 35:2, 4). Similarly, the Book of Judges tells us of Gideon's victory over the Midianites, after which a man of Israel asks Gideon to rule over the Israelites. Gideon replies, "I will not rule over you, and my son shall not rule over you; Adonai will rule over you." He then asks each of them to give him the "earring [he had received] as booty." When they all did so, "Gideon made an ephod of it [this gold] and set it up in his town. . . . All Israel went astray after it . . ." (Judg. 8:22–27). The Hebrew for "went astray" is *va-yiznu*, literally translated as "they went whoring." Suddenly, *kol Yisrael*—"all

Israel"—is likened to a whore, a woman who will go with any man for pay or other reward. How surprising, then, to find that the Aramaic translation of "earring" in the Judges passage is *kadasha.* Again, a symbol of being set apart, but how and by whom? The prophet Hosea provides an answer. Speaking God's words, he describes the people of Israel not as a whore, but as an unfaithful wife, abandoning her husband, God, whose anger blazes: "I will punish her / For the days of the Baalim, / On which she brought them offerings; / And put on earrings and jewels, / And went after her lovers, / And Me, she forgot / —declares the Eternal" (Hos. 2:15). Once again, "earrings" are translated in the Aramaic as *kadasha*—again, the people of Israel is viewed as a woman set apart, here understood as "apart from God," rather than "a part of" or "apart with."

Little wonder, then, that *Exodus Rabbah* describes the building of the golden calf as follows: "It can be compared to a king who sent a marriage-broker to betroth a wife unto him, but while the broker was on his way, the woman corrupted herself with another man."[5] The king is God, the broker is Moses, and the woman is the people of Israel going astray after "another man"—the calf.

In this context, one of Moses' more puzzling responses to the golden calf becomes clear: "He took the calf that they had made and burned it in fire; he ground it until it was powder and strewed it upon the water and made the Israelites drink it" (Exod. 32:20). What made Moses think of this, we wonder—until we remember the biblical ritual of the bitter waters, designed to "prove" whether a woman suspected of adultery was in fact adulterous:

> The priest shall bring her near and stand her before the Eternal. The priest shall take holy [again, the root *k-d-sh*] water in an earthen vessel and shall take some of the earth that is on the floor of the Tabernacle and put

> it into the water. . . . The priest shall administer an
> oath to the woman, saying to her, "'If no man has lain
> with you, if you have not gone astray in uncleanness
> while married to your husband, stay clean of this bit-
> ter, cursing water. But if you have gone astray while
> married to your husband and have become unclean
> . . . may the Eternal make you a curse and an impreca-
> tion among your people, just as the Eternal causes
> your thigh to sag and your belly to distend, may this
> cursing water enter your body, causing the belly to dis-
> tend and the thigh to sag. . . ." (Num. 5:16–22)

Is Moses testing the people, as a jealous husband would test a wife, by having them drink the powdered calf? Does he hope to see in them some sign of remorse, of return and reconciliation? Marital infidelity was the ancient Israelites' clearest model for infidelity to God, for they saw their relationship to God in marital terms. Only marriage's intimacy would do to describe the close bond of God and Israel, so only the deep pain of marital infideli-ty would do to describe the rupture of that bond.

Women as well as men can well understand the use of marital metaphors to describe the bond between God and people. But modern women, long accustomed to a more equitable understand-ing of marriage than were our biblical ancestors, cannot help but be frustrated by the repetition of the metaphor of the straying wife for Israel's frequent lack of fidelity to God. There must be other metaphors we might use today to describe the sometimes shaky bond that grew between Israel and our God. And there must be a way to describe women's involvement in the building of the golden calf, that powerful act of rebellion against a God barely yet known, that does not fall back on the "saint-whore" contrast by which our tradition, as described here, either sees women as the righteous refusers or applies the metaphor of whore or adulterous wife to rebellious Israel.

Perhaps the image of rebellious teenager would serve us better today: Israel is coming into its own, following the childhood of Genesis, and is on the verge of accepting adult responsibility, symbolized by the Ten Commandments. At just that moment, the teenager foments one last, great rebellion, one that will grab the parents' attention fully, and will forestall the inevitable acceptance of responsibility. This image is accessible to all readers who themselves have been that rebellious teenager, or who are, or have been parents of same. It removes permanent blame from the perpetrator of this rebellious act, which the rabbis referred to always as "That Deed," seeing it instead as a normal part of a person's and our people's growth and development. Best of all, it removes the onus of perfect piety or wanton promiscuity from the women, who may now be seen as fully part of the whole people of Israel.

RABBI NANCY H. WIENER

ויקהל
Vayakhel

Of Women and Mirrors

*E*veryone whose heart prompted them and
everyone who was spiritually moved came,
bringing a Divine offering. . . . Men and women,
all whose hearts prompted them. . . .

(EXODUS 35:21–22)

WHY IS THIS PORTION, *Vayakhel*, different from all other Torah portions? In this portion, and this portion alone, the women of the
children of Israel are identified as a significant group within the
larger whole. Other portions mention individual women as part of
the larger narrative, but no other so clearly demonstrates the significant place that women qua women have within the larger community. Elsewhere we learn of the deeds of individual women. But
details of women's daily lives and activities are markedly absent.
We know something about how men spent their time—how they
labored and what concerned them. But this is the only portion that
gives us a taste of the variety of ways that women contributed to
the vitality and maintenance of the people's material and spiritual
life. In this portion, women respond to God's command to build
the *mishkan*, the Tabernacle, a dwelling place for God's presence
among the people. Women contribute to the spiritual life of the

people. Women are explicitly mentioned both alongside the men and independently of them.

At first glance, though, the uniqueness of this portion is not apparent. It begins with the words "Moses then assembled [*Vayakhel*, root *k-h-l*] the whole community of the children of Israel and said to them: These are the things that Adonai has commanded you to do" (Exod. 35:1). Moses' speaking to the community on God's behalf is nothing new. And God's commanding the people to carry out specific tasks is also nothing new. In previous encounters, Moses' instructions to the people on God's behalf are carried out exclusively by the men. As the portion begins, it seems that once again God and Israel will retain their established patterns. With the whole Israelite community before him, Moses enumerates specific instructions (Exod. 35:4ff.).

What follows, however, is nothing short of extraordinary in the realm of biblical narrative. The women suddenly become an important collective entity within the community of Israel. Women, too, hear and heed God's call. Not once, but repeatedly, this Torah portion specifically mentions the women. "Men and women, all whose hearts prompted them, all who wanted to make a wave-offering of gold to Adonai, came bringing brooches, earrings, rings, and pendants—gold objects of all kinds" (Exod. 35:22). *Everyone* brought what he or she had as an offering. This single sentence establishes that the "all" includes both men and women. So, grammatically speaking, the explicit repetition of "the women" in subsequent verses is really unnecessary, even superfluous. Yet, the Torah insists on repeating "the women" multiple times, underscoring the importance of their participation in this most sacred communal endeavor.

The Torah text reminds us that there are ways in which the responses of the men and women in the community are similar, and that there are ways in which members of each sex offer unique talents and gifts. "And all the women whose hearts' wisdom was in their hands spun what they had spun in blue, purple, and crimson yarns, and in fine linen. And all the women whose hearts prompted in them great skill spun the goats' hair" (Exod. 35:25–26). These two consecutive verses specifically mention the significant contributions of the female members of the people of Israel. The narrative continues, "And so the Israelites, all the men and women whose hearts moved them to bring anything for all of the work that Adonai, through Moses, had commanded to be done, brought it as a freewill offering to Adonai" (Exod. 35:29).

In this short section, Exod. 35:20–29, we learn much about the ways that women were capable of participating in communal endeavors. Contrary to today's popular conceptions, Israelite women did have their own possessions. Everything was not the property of their husbands. And they were recognized as having wills of their own! They could freely take from their possessions to make an offering to God. Their own hearts moved them to have their own relationships with God. Women's special skills and talents enabled the entire community to reach its sacred goal. With their own hands, they spun multicolored yarns and varied fabrics into articles to be used in the service of Adonai. In the hands of the women who excelled in particular handicrafts, raw materials were transformed into holy objects. The women gave generously of their time, handiwork, and possessions. The outpouring was so abundant that Moses eventually turned to the people, at the request of the artisans, and proclaimed throughout the camp, "No man or woman shall do more work for the holy offering! And the people ceased bringing; the effort had sufficed for all the work to be done and more" (Exod. 36:6–7).

The Torah unequivocally highlights that women are participating in the single most important sacred endeavor of the community of Israel's collective existence: the building of the *mishkan*, the place in which God's presence will dwell among the people and travel with them as they journey toward the Promised Land.

And then the narrative takes a significant turn. The efforts of the entire community become the backdrop for the tasks taken on by the great (male) architects and craftsmen of the *mishkan*. The portion mentions the contributions of women only once more as it describes the labors of Betzalel, the chief architect of the *mishkan*. The Torah says, "He made the laver of copper and its stand of copper, with the mirrors of the women who served at the entrance of the Tent of Meeting" (Exod. 38:8). In Midrash we are told that Moses did not want to accept the women's mirrors. Moses could not see that these seemingly profane objects could be used for a holy purpose. He could focus only on the sexual ends for which the women had used them. God, however, instructs Moses that without the mirrors and without the sexual drive they had inspired, the people of Israel would not have become as numerous as they are. God, rebuking Moses, explains, "Truly more precious to Me than all other gifts are these mirrors, for it is these mirrors that yielded Me My hosts." God sees the value of each offering in the intention of the giver, not in the form of the offering.

Never again are the women discussed in relation to the *mishkan*, or the Tent of Meeting. Never again do the women, capable of offering so much to God and the community, take such an active role in communal Divine service. At great length, the Torah explains the times that men are to bring offerings to God and the specific types of offerings they are to make. The women, who played such a significant role in the preparation of the community's most holy space, are now denied access to it. They cannot approach God once God has a specific dwelling place. It is amazing that this sacred project of the entire community, once completed, becomes the exclusive property of a few of the community's elite.

The institution of the sacrificial cult, with the completion of the *mishkan*, introduced a rigid status system among the children of Israel. Priestly and nonpriestly members of the community were now given specific roles. Only the priests and Levites could participate in making the actual sacrificial offerings. The nonpriests were expected to provide the offerings from their flocks and their crops. Vestiges of this rigid system are still maintained in the more traditional synagogues, in which *aliyot*, honors during the Torah service, are given first to the *kohen*, the descendant of the priests; then to the *Levi*, the descendant of the Levite; and finally to a *Yisrael*, anyone else from the community.

Another set of restrictions was placed upon those seeking to make an offering to God. Neither the thing being offered nor the person providing it could be ritually unclean or blemished. Both needed to be pure and intact. By establishing these norms, many members of the community were excluded from sacred service: the hunchback, the blind, the deaf/mute, the eunuch, and the person from whom uncontrolled bodily substances flowed—oozing wounds, menstrual blood. Based on these categorical restrictions, women were removed from serving God as visible participants and contributors to public worship.[1] It has been only in the last decades of the twentieth century, in the Reform, Reconstructionist, and Conservative Jewish communities, that women have achieved equal status in the realm of public worship—functioning as service leaders, rabbis, cantors, readers and interpreters of Torah.

The explicit inclusion of women in this week's portion is like a blast on the shofar. It stands in stark contrast to the deafening silence that pervades most of the Torah. This portion makes us wonder about the many ways that women's experiences were written out of our people's collective memory and history. It encourages us to seek out hints of the ways that women contributed to and participated in the life of our people. And it reminds us of how communal leaders often value the actions and lives only of those most like themselves.

As women, we are highly sensitized to the absence of women or the exclusion of women from our people's narrative. But women did not and do not have an exclusive claim to invisibility. We are not the only victims of collective amnesia. Each generation has members whose stories are included in the community's narrative, and those whose stories are consciously or unconsciously excluded. By erasing these lives and contributions from the contemporary narrative, we are making it all the more difficult for these hidden members to be included in our future narrative as well.

We have much to learn from our ancestors who contributed to the *mishkan*. For centuries, the most common phrase utilized to describe a Jewish community has been *kehillah kedoshah*, "holy community" (*kehillah*, k-h-l, the same root as the name of this portion, *Vayakhel*). Through their actions, the generation that contributed to the *mishkan* taught that a *kehillah kedoshah* should include all of its members. Over time, however, their teaching was eclipsed by the belief that it is *exclusion* that safeguards holiness. Drawing upon the example of the generation that contributed to and built the *mishkan*, I believe that the holiness of our contemporary communities is safeguarded through our commitment to *inclusion*, through our ability to appreciate the many gifts of all the members of all our communities. How worthy are our communities of the designation *kehillah kedoshah?* How receptive are we to the offerings of the hearts of those in our midst? Are the unique gifts brought by each of us before God and our communities valued? Do we set up barriers to inclusion? Do we have our own ways of designating some as more acceptable to God than others, and others as blemished or unclean? When we come together as a community, do we cast as wide a net as possible, or do we exclude some as our needs change or as our perceptions change? As women become more visible and active in contemporary communities, as our roles expand, how will we tell our communities' stories, and how will future generations remember them and tell them? Will there be those whose participation is absent or limited? Will there be those whose place in our histories is consciously erased or diminished?

The choice is ours. We can let our communities be like those of so many others that preceded us and most that surround us today. Our communities can discard and discount individuals who are not like the majority, not like those in power, or do not embody some unattainable ideal, believing that holiness comes through exclusion and uniformity. Or we can strive to follow the stunning example of this portion, and set our communities apart from most by encouraging everyone who hears and heeds God's voice, and wishes to participate, to do so. It is only by choosing the latter that we make each of our communities a holy community, worthy of being known as a *kehillah kedoshah.*

פקודי

Pekudei

The Birthing of the
Mishkan (Tabernacle)

*T*hese are the accountings of the *mishkan.*
(EXODUS 38:21, EVERETT FOX TRANSLATION)

Pekudei is the last of five *parshiyot* that discuss in great detail the building of the *mishkan,* the Tabernacle. I see the construction of the *mishkan* not just as a building project, but as a birthing process. As a building project, it comes to an end. As a birthing process, it continues throughout the generations.

Understanding the building of the *mishkan* as a birthing process is an idea inherent in the biblical text itself, specifically in the use of the word *pakad,* to "take account" (Exod. 38:21). The root *p-k-d* is found in many other texts, but two in particular stand out, for they shed light on this concept of birth. In Gen. 21:1, we read: *VaAdonai pakad et Sarah* ("Now YHVH took account of Sarah"), and in I Sam. 1–2:21 we read: *Ki pakad Adonai et Hannah* ("For YHVH took account of Hannah"). After God took account *(pakad)* of Sarah and Hannah, each woman gave birth.

In *Parashat Pekudei* there is a similar turn of events. God commands, and then the birth occurs. *Parashat Pekudei* begins with the phrase *Eleh pekudei hamishkan*, "These are the accountings of the *mishkan*" (Exod. 38:21). Four portions earlier, God commanded the people of Israel to build the *mishkan*. In this portion of *Pekudei* (Accountings) the people of Israel finally complete their building project.

Reading *Pekudei* in light of these verses that speak of Sarah and Hannah giving birth, we understand that, in a sense, the *mishkan* too has been birthed.

What does this image of birthing add to our understanding of the building of the *mishkan*? By reinterpreting the building of the *mishkan* in light of the birthing process, our perception of the building of the *mishkan*, and of its place throughout Israel's history, is given a new meaning. Three themes involved in physical birthing are labor, identity, and continuity, and each can be applied to the building of the *mishkan*.

*L*abor

The biblical text remains silent on the details of Sarah's and Hannah's labor. That is not surprising, given that the biblical text is known for its sparse detail. Besides, it need not give us a full report. We know that in most cases, giving birth is a physical process that requires a great deal of labor, deep breathing, focusing, and pushing. To give birth generally means to go through labor.

Similarly, the building of the *mishkan* required labor. The people did not merely have to bring their gifts to those in charge to make this project a success. Each person, each individual actually, had to engage in physical labor. In Exod. 39:43 we read, "Now Moses saw all the work (*melachah*, or "physical labor"), and here they had made it as YHVH had commanded, thus had they made." Building the *mishkan*, birthing the *mishkan*, was a very physical and labor-intensive process connecting the people of Israel to their creation.

*I*dentity

By giving birth, both Sarah and Hannah transformed their identities. After giving birth, each one was not only a woman and a wife, as she had been before, but each one was now also a mother, connected and responsible to the being she just created.

In building the *mishkan*, the Israelites' identity changed as well. Through the act of building, they became connected to their God in a new way. Though their identity as God's people had already been firmly established at Sinai, witnessing God's presence on the mountaintop of Sinai was frightening and distant, too unreal to comprehend. The act of God handing them an identity from above did not work for them. They had to be part of the process. They had to create an identity for themselves by bringing God into their midst, by bringing God's presence from the heavens above to the earth below. And so they did. The text is straightforward. The text that speaks of Sinai and of the cloud and the fire on the mountain directly precedes God's command to build the *mishkan*. (See Exod. 24:12–25:9.)

By giving birth to the *mishkan*, the Israelites came to experience their identity as God's people in a more intimate and involved way. God understood that they needed to be active participants in this process, for after the *mishkan* was built, God covered it with a cloud by day and a fire by night. With the birth of the *mishkan*, the experience at Sinai became a daily revelation of God's presence. With the birth of the *mishkan*, the experience of Sinai in the heavens above moved to the earth below.

Continuity

Just as Sarah's and Hannah's sons linked their parents to the generations before and after them, so too the *mishkan* (God's portable dwelling place) served as a link in the chain connecting the generations. It became a symbol of God's physical presence in Israel, guiding the people on their travels throughout the wilderness, and even remaining with them once they had entered the land of Israel. The *Beit Hamikdash* (the Temple, God's more permanent dwelling place) was next to fill that role. However, since neither the *mishkan* nor the *Beit Hamikdash* would continue to serve as God's dwelling place throughout history, God's presence had to be secured in something not tied to a specific place.

The rabbis succeeded in doing this by creating a new name for God based on the word *mishkan*. The word they created, "Shechinah," is a feminine name, suggesting God's presence in a very physical and immanent way. The rabbis understood that the people of Israel still needed to have a dwelling place for God, but that no one physical place would do, so they created a dwelling place for God in the form of a name. Said the rabbis in *Megillah* 29a, "Every place to which they [Israel] were exiled, the Shechinah went with them." Through the name Shechinah, the rabbis enabled God's physical presence to exist in exile.

By rereading the building of the *mishkan* in light of the word *pakad*, the *mishkan*, like the child, becomes a link in the chain. As the child is a link between past and future generations, so too the *mishkan* is a link between Sinai and Shechinah, a link in the continuity of our identity as a people connected to God. Today, we have neither Sinai nor the *mishkan*. What remains today of the Sinai experience and of the *mishkan* is the Shechinah. Because it is both name and place, we can enable it to dwell anywhere and everywhere.

Vayikra / Leviticus

RABBI SHOSHANA GELFAND

ויקרא

Vayikra

The Book of Relationships

*A*nd God called to Moses. (LEVITICUS 1:1)

THE BOOK OF *Vayikra* contains the laws instructing the priests on how to perform the sacrifices. This technical information is important, but we should also ask the deeper question of the purpose of these sacrifices. We begin by asking why one would want to offer a sacrifice to God, and why would God want to receive it. The answer will reveal that although Genesis is usually thought of as the biblical book focusing on relationships, it is actually *Vayikra* that is the Bible's "how-to book" for creating and maintaining relationships between people and God.

The Hebrew name of this book is the first clue regarding the subject matter of relationships, for the word *vayikra* ("and [God] called") summarizes the contents perfectly. *Vayikra*, like all books of the Hebrew Bible, derives its name from the first relevant word of the text. In this case, the first word is the key to the essence of the book that begins, *Vayikra el Moshe va-y'daber Adonai ai-lav may-ohel mo'ed lay-mor . . .* , ("And [God] called to Moses and God spoke to him out of the tent of meeting, saying . . ."). God calls Moses before speaking to him. This is a clue that "calling" must mean something more than the content of the words themselves, for if God had used words exclusively during this interaction, the text could have simply stated, "God spoke." Since the verb "called" is also used, there must be a deeper meaning to that action.

Another clue that this "calling" is important lies in the way the word itself is written in the Torah scroll. The first four letters *(v-y-k-r)* are written normally, but the final letter (a silent aleph) shows a certain peculiarity. It is written in what we would today call a smaller font, clearly half the size of the letters surrounding it. Since our tradition teaches that nothing in the Torah is superfluous, then not only does each letter have meaning, but even the way each letter is written comes to teach us a lesson.

While there are many explanations for the anomaly of the tiny aleph, one interpretation is that God is modeling good communication skills. In order to truly communicate with another being, whether a person or God, it is necessary to engage in what the mystics called *tzimtzum* (a drawing in or contracting of oneself), in order to make room for the other partner in the conversation. Were God to simply *speak* to Moses, then God would be dictating and Moses would be receiving the dictation. By first *calling* to Moses, God creates a situation whereby God's Presence has withdrawn inward to create room for Moses in the conversation. Moses can now be a partner, rather than a passive recipient. Thus, it becomes clear from the very first word that the content of this book is about relationships. God structures the relationship with Moses so that it is a partnership, one that can have true intimacy.

There are many other indications that this book is, in essence, about relationships, and that law, sacrifices, and priests are merely the means by which we might achieve the desired intimacy of the relationship. The whole concept of sacrifice, in fact, points to the desire for relationship. The word for "sacrifice," *korban*, comes from the root *k-r-b*, which means "to draw near." A sacrifice, therefore, is the means by which we draw near to God, and God draws near and is drawn near to us. The root appears constantly in the book of *Vayikra*, both in the noun form *korban* ("sacrifice") and the verb form *yakriv* ("offer a sacrifice, draw near"). Both words emphasize that while the action involved is highly ritualized, the end goal is to be near to God. Nahmanides states that indeed, the very purpose of the sacrifices is to get closer to God.[1]

This closeness is further emphasized by the name that the Torah uses to refer to God in *Parashat Vayikra*. With only one exception, the word used for God is the four-letter name spelled YHVH and not Elohim, the more generic name for God. YHVH (usually pronounced Adonai) is God's personal name, God's "first name," so to speak, as opposed to the more universal, general name Elohim. Just as my personal friends call me Shoshana, those who are close with God use the name Adonai. This indicates an inherent intimacy not present when God is addressed by title (just as Shoshana reflects more intimacy than Rabbi Gelfand). Furthermore, tradition connects the personal name of God with the attribute of *rachamim*, usually translated as "mercy" but actually deriving from the Hebrew root *rechem*, meaning "womb." There is no closer human relationship than that of a fetus growing in its mother's womb. They are two separate souls sharing the same physical body. When we use the name of God that recalls the attribute of *rachamim*, we call up the intimate image of the mother-fetus relationship.

Parashat Vayikra not only discusses in general how to draw near to God through sacrifice, but also specifies different types of intimacy through the archetypes of various sacrifices. For example, the portion begins with a discussion of the *olah* ("burnt-offering"). With this type of sacrifice, the entire animal is placed on the altar to be burnt. The word *olah* literally means "to go up," and as the fire consumes the offering and the smoke ascends to heaven, the desire of the offerer to ascend to heaven and unite with God is thus expressed. Unlike many of the other sacrifices, here the text uses the word *adam* to refer to the offerer (with other sacrifices, the word *nefesh* is used). While *adam* is often colloquially translated as "man," it does not literally mean "man" at all. *Adam* comes from the word for "earth," *adamah*, from which the first human being was created (Gen. 2:7). Some midrashim describe how this primordial being was then divided, with one side becoming male and the other female. Thus, the word *adam* actually refers to the first human creation, which contains both male and female characteristics.

It is no wonder, then, that the word *adam* is used in connection with the *olah* sacrifice. This typology of closeness is identified with intimacy to such an extent that the two beings involved—God and the offerer—become as close as is cosmically possible. The *olah* represents the kind of flaming passion in which the individual is totally consumed by the relationship with the other. The mystics refer to this kind of union as *devekut*, a clinging of the two entities. The great Jewish philosopher Martin Buber referred to this type of relationship as "I–Thou," where the bond of knowing the other is so intimate that the two entities unify.[2] Thus, the *olah* is a model of the Divine embrace, becoming passionately lost in one's relationship with God, blurring the boundaries between the self and the other.

While the *olah* may be momentarily satisfying, this kind of intimacy cannot be sustained continually. Therefore, there are other types of sacrifices that represent other ways of maintaining closeness. The *zevach shelamim* (peace offering), for example, is a type of sacrifice that is only partially burnt on the altar. The root of the word *shelamim* is *sh-l-m*, the same root as for the word *shalom*. This root's meaning conveys a sense of completeness. It is no wonder, therefore, that the root has also come to refer to peace, for peace is indeed a sense of total completeness.

Compared with the *olah*, what is striking about the *shelamim* is that the description of it does not use the word *adam* (the primordial male/female) for the person offering it. On the contrary, the text goes out of its way to specify that the *shelamim* offering itself can be either a male or female animal. The goal with the *shelamim* is thus not to lose one's own sense of self, but rather to maintain distinctions (like male and female), while being able to coexist in peace with those who are different. The *shelamim* is therefore only partially sacrificed to God on the altar. Another portion is given to the priests, while the remainder is eaten by the offerer, along with relatives and guests, at a meal following the sacrifice. The *shelamim* thus represents the closeness expressed through sharing. Each individual maintains a sense of self. Each person contributes the uniqueness of his or her soul, so that collectively, a sense of completeness is achieved.

The *zevach shelamim*, therefore, is the type of sacrifice used to symbolize family unity. In the Book of Genesis, following Jacob's flight from his father-in-law, Laban, we witness a covenant declaring peace between them. Immediately following the establishment of the covenant, we read *va-yizbach Ya'akov zevach ba-har va-yikra l'ehav le-echol lachem va-yochlu lechem va-yalinu ba-har*: "And Jacob offered a sacrifice in the mountain, and *called* his brothers to eat bread; and they ate bread, and stayed all night in the mountain" (Gen. 31:54). Two of the key words of this verse tie directly into the Book of Leviticus: *zevach* (the type of sacrifice) and *vayikra* ("and [Jacob] called").

Just as God calls to Moses at the beginning of Leviticus, demonstrating the desire for a relationship, so too does Jacob call to his family. Jacob's desire for intimacy with his family is a call for peace between them, a yearning for completeness, which can only be achieved by each individual participating in the relationship through eating the *zevach* *[shelamim]* sacrifice. Jacob offers the perfect example of the completeness attained by someone offering the *zevach shelamim*.

Thus, a sacrifice cannot simply be viewed as the offering of an animal. The meaning runs far deeper. Whether we are discussing the *olah*, the all-consuming passion that allows two entities to draw together and ascend upward as one, or we are focusing on the *zevach shelamim*, the familial love expressed through sharing of the self to create a collective whole, the purpose of *Vayikra* is not to overwhelm us with rules of how to offer the sacrifices properly; rather, the intention is to emphasize the importance of relationships. The sacrifice itself is merely a means to an end. In this book, the personal "womblike" God teaches us about closeness and intimacy. Being close to God and other human beings is the true message of *Vayikra*.

צַו

Tzav

Message and Messenger

*T*his is the ritual of the burnt offering: The burnt offering itself shall remain where it is burned upon the altar all night until morning, while the fire on the altar is kept going on it. The priest shall dress in linen raiment, with linen britches next to his body, and he shall take up the ashes to which the fire has reduced the burnt offering on the altar and place them beside the altar. He shall then take off his vestments and put on other vestments and carry the ashes outside the camp to a clean place. The fire on the altar shall be kept burning, not to go out: every morning the priest shall feed wood to it, lay out the burnt offering on it, and turn into smoke the fat parts of the offerings of well being. A perpetual fire shall be kept burning on the altar, not to go out. (LEVITICUS 6:2–6, JPS TRANSLATION)[1]

WHY DO WE READ TORAH? To learn the ways of God, to learn who we are as Jews. Torah also keeps us in touch with who we were. For thirteen centuries we spoke to God in the medium of animal sacrifice, a religious practice most Jews of today (though not all) no longer hope to restore.

On the day you read this portion, grab the *eitzei chayim*, the "trees of life," the wooden staves on which the sacred scroll is mounted, the text inscribed upon the skin of a once-living creature. Such a creature was once asked to speak to God for us. Now it carries God's message to us.

Tzav is the second portion of the Book of Leviticus, the book of the laws of the priests, the *kohanim. Zot torat ha-olah*, it begins, "Here are instructions concerning the burnt offering." And the text goes on to describe in explicit and repetitive detail the slaughter of the *korbanot*, the sacrificial animals, along with the offerings of flour and incense. Various occasions, specific supplications—each demands its particular ritual atonement.

The tone of the text is that of a policy and procedure manual. Can you imagine reading the job description of the supervising engineer of your local utility company? Envision the bank of computers, the ranks of dials, the rows of toggles and switches to be regulated. What chaos would ensue should the wrong button be pressed, the wrong command entered! But few of us know or care how energy enters our home, as long as we have light and heat on demand.

Just so, not every Israelite had to understand the minutiae of the sacrificial rite. They had only to present their gift, the beast appropriate for their expression to God of guilt or thanksgiving, sin or error. All categories of meaning—life and death, good and evil, sacred and profane—were mediated by this system of sacrifice managed by the sons of Aaron. The priests were specialists in this special language of ritual, and this distinction from the other tribes of Israel was an aspect of their holiness.

The priests' holiness, their special status, was expressed by rules set forth elsewhere in the Torah: their clothing, their hygiene, their food, and their family life were something apart from the mass of the people. To this day the role of *kohen* is remembered by our people with reverence, and many of us continue to confer special honor on those who claim priestly descent. How exalted is the priesthood—to communicate directly with God Most High on behalf of the people, to be able to address God by name and ask for their release from sin!

Oddly enough, the first regulation of *Tzav* concerns the end of the process. Each morning the priest must perform the mitzvah of *terumat hadeshen*, "lifting [and removing] the ashes [of the daily whole burnt sacrificial offerings]"[2] that burned on the altar for the night. But this is not so surprising. This sacrifice is a command for all time, a perpetual ritual cycle endlessly renewed with the new day.

What is more surprising is that the priest has to clear away the ashes himself. This nasty chore is not relegated to the Tabernacle's servant class, the priests' cousins, the Levites. The priest must change out of the splendid vestments, put on work clothes, and dispose of the ashes personally.

Clearly, and classically, this is a lesson in humility. Lest the exalted priest get too big for his linen britches, he must do some sort of common, dirty labor. He should know something of the life of those for whom he ministers. He should be reminded that his function, even when robed in precious fabrics, is a dual servitude: serving God, serving Israel. And the people, who see him at his task, will also be reminded that the priest is like them, a laborer on God's earth, a person.[3] The lesson will be drawn by priest and Israelite that humility is a component of the service of God.

No one denies that a sense of one's proper place in the order of things is a Jewish value: "The adornment of wisdom is humility; the adornment of humility is awe."[4] Is this all that the passage says to us who read it today? What does it mean for modern Jews, for whom the priesthood has ceased to function? Read hard, and demand that the text speak.

Our *parashah* instructs, "The fire on the altar shall be kept burning, not to go out" (Lev. 6:5), and again, "A perpetual fire shall be kept burning on the altar, not to go out" (Lev. 6:6). *Sefer Ha-hinukh* explains that the ashes are removed from the altar just so that the daily fire will burn better.[5] So the work of our priest is not just to take away what has been used up, but to improve what has been left. Humbling himself, he causes a brighter flame upon the altar, reflecting the fervor of the people. So in our sanctuaries today, the *ner tamid* (perpetual light) burns as the visible expression of the heated devotion of a people to its God.[6] Our faith is a flame of passion in which the material, the restrictive, the negative is burned away and truth revealed in the light and joy of Torah.[7]

So the priest who on that day cleans the altar has perhaps received the greatest honor of all, the greatest glory in the profoundest humility. And what of us, modern Jews without the sacrificial cult? We have been awarded by the Rabbis with that most daunting gift: we are both priest and people, responsible for our own spiritual welfare. How empowering, and how humbling! Taking comfort in the fact that our response to life as Jews always begins constructively in engagement with our tradition through its texts, there are still questions of attitude, particularly for women.

How do we adorn ourselves and our projects? How do we maintain a balance between humility and haughtiness, elegance and extremism, commitment and tired repetition, commandment and contrivance? How do we keep in touch with that spark of inspiration that keeps us true and focused?

Whose responsibility is it to maintain devotion and kindle sparks of understanding? Three thousand years ago the generations of the house of Aaron tended the channel of our people's burning desire to be a community close to God: the eternal flame. Today we rely on ourselves and each other.

What messages and images keep the fire going after the destruction of the Temple and the sacrificial cult? We can certainly be inspired by an image of ancient devotion although it is a picture in which women do not figure. The creative genius of rabbinic Judaism replaced the message and messenger of the sacrificial cult with the formula of study, prayer, and loving acts. Throughout the ages women have participated in these, although their experience is largely unrecorded and presumed unremarkable.

Even today, as women enter all aspects of religious life, we wonder about the quality of our participation. Will our roles be substantial or token? Must we sacrifice what is essential to our womanhood to gain respect, position?

For modern Jewish women reading *Tzav*, the drudgery of the priesthood has some ironic resonance; the glorious aspects are more remote. We are familiar with the claim that maintaining a Jewish home is holy. And so it is. Raising children, making *Shabbos*, maintaining *kehilla*, our classic tasks that created value for the community, should be a source of pride, beauty, and fulfillment to the individual. But that's not to deny the hard, thankless, often dirty work that they entail. It's just to recognize the potential for holiness in the most mundane activity.

We prize those moments in life when the occasion, the place, the company, the ritual evoke the sublime, the heightened moment. But we had better not count on these fleeting moments for our spiritual sustenance. Not every day is Yom Kippur; not every occasion is Bat Mitzvah or Confirmation, wedding or ordination. More often, we find ourselves taking out the trash.

Well, sisters, that too is holy.

RABBI ILENE SCHNEIDER

שמיני

Shemini

Kashrut, Food, and Women

*T*hese are the animals which are on all the earth
that you are allowed to eat. (LEVITICUS 11:2)

Parashat Shemini is divided into three main sections: the assumption
by the *kohanim* of their priestly functions; the deaths of Aaron's
sons, Nadav and Avihu; and the laws of kashrut. As with many
parshiyot, the inclusion of these sections together may seem arbitrary,
but there is an underlying logic: the setting of the boundaries
between the holy and the unholy, and the Jewish people's obligation to accept the word of God as binding, even when that word is
difficult or unreasonable to the human mind. The *kohanim* are
expected to perform their tasks without deviation. Nadav and
Avihu, who were overly zealous in their conduct, were punished
instead of praised for their devotion because they did not follow the
prescribed procedure exactly. The laws of kashrut are to be followed because they are given by God, not because of any other
stated reasons, at least within this *parashah*.

For modern Jews, the section of this *parashah* that has the most
resonance for us is the one dealing with the laws of kashrut. With
no Temple and no sacrificial rites, those *kohanim* who are still mind-

ful of their status are limited to its symbolic functions. And while we may be cautioned not to imbibe strong drink, as Nadav and Avihu did, we do not have any outright ban on alcoholic beverages. But kashrut, even for those who do not observe the laws, is still an issue. Even the Reform movement, which had historically rejected the laws of kashrut as archaic, has returned more recently to a debate about whether some kashrut standards should be included in their new platform.

According to the *parashah,* we are permitted to eat the meat of animals, but are restricted as to which animals are acceptable. We are allowed to eat only those mammals that have completely split hooves and chew their cud. Species like the camel, hare, and pig are prohibited; even though they have split hooves, they don't chew their cud. As for fish, only those with both scales and fins are permitted, thus excluding shell fish. All birds of prey were declared prohibited, along with some insects and crawling animals. In this way, the distinction was made between animals that were and were not permitted, between the clean and the unclean—in other words, between the holy and unholy.

Why have these laws been set? They may have been culturally determined. Just as some Asian cultures consider animals such as dogs to be staples or even delicacies, we in the West find the idea to be abhorrent. It could be that the taboo against eating the flesh of pigs was similarly distasteful (so to speak) to peoples living in the Middle East. These laws may have been established for humanitarian purposes. Just as we may not eat carrion or cruel animals, so must we, too, be kind in our treatment of others, both human and animal. Perhaps the purpose of the laws was hygienic. For example, by not eating pork, we prevent the disease trichinosis.

But traditionally, Judaism teaches that none of these rationales are truly relevant, for in the end, we observe the laws of kashrut because God has commanded us. Some traditionally observant Jews claim that it is only the nonobservant Jew who looks for reasons, in order to eventually reject the laws. After all, if kashrut is humanitarian, we can avoid the issue of cruelty to animals by becoming vegetarians. (For many Jews, being a vegetarian is the ultimate expression of kashrut.) If the reasons are hygienic, then the current FDA regulations, as imperfect as they may be, are enough to insure our health.

There are three seemingly peripheral issues about this *parashah* that fascinate me both as a Jew who observes kashrut and as a feminist: the "explosion" of talmudic laws about kashrut, the proximity of the *parashah* to Pesach, and the preoccupation with food by both Jews and women.

The laws as set forth in this *parashah* are fairly forthright; they describe the animals whose flesh we can and cannot eat. There is nothing in the *parashah* about separate dishes, or dishtowels, or automatic dishwashers. There is nothing about whether rennet or gelatin can be used to prepare cheese. Even the separation of milk and meat is from a later *parashah* (and possibly a different era in biblical history). In fact, most of the minutiae of kashrut are missing from the Torah. The regulations we follow today were set in later— including contemporary—commentaries. The process of refining and redefining biblical law continues to this day.

It is interesting (but probably coincidental) that the *parashah* is read around the time of Pesach, which is the holiday with the most intensive regulations about food. Kashrut laws are even more stringent during Pesach, with the exclusion of leavened grain products. It is also the one time of year that even those Jews who completely reject or at least ignore the laws of kashrut during the rest of the year feel an obligation to refrain from bread. Here again, many of the laws that we follow for Pesach are an outgrowth of biblical narrative, rather than set in the biblical text. There is nothing in the Torah about changing dishes or cleaning our ovens with a blowtorch. The oral tradition has as much force—if not more—than the written.

And finally, there is the preoccupation that we as Jews and as women have with food. Many of our holy days and holidays have traditional foods associated with them: apples and honey for Rosh Hashanah, latkes and doughnuts for Chanukah, hamentaschen for Purim, dairy products for Shavuot, and, of course, all the forbidden foods for Pesach. (I have often felt that Pesach is the final proof that God is male: no woman would have prescribed a holiday with so many regulations about cooking, cleaning, and food preparation!) The kitchen has been the traditional center of power—as well as source of servitude—for women (despite the oft cited statistic that the majority of celebrated chefs are men).

In addition, Western women in our era—whether Jewish or not—have a problematic relationship to food. We worry about whether we are too fat or (more rarely) too thin. If we eat too much on a date, we worry that the man will think us to be unfeminine. If we eat too little, we fear we will be suspected of anorexia. We feel guilty when we eat a piece of candy, so much so that we may even need to vomit afterwards. We feel that we must conform to the "ideals" set by fashion models and actors or be found unworthy. According to the Anorexia/Bulimia Association, more than five million Americans suffer from eating disorders. Only 10 percent of them are men, while the organization estimates that one thousand American women die each year from anorexia nervosa.

Although there are no statistics on the number of Jewish women with eating disorders, anecdotal evidence indicates that the percentage is high. In general, Jewish women suffer from problems of self-image. Our noses are too big, our hair too frizzy, our bodies too short-waisted, and our weight too high. In a November 22, 1996, article from the *Jewish Bulletin of Northern California*, Teresa Strasser quotes Joan Barnes Strauss as saying, "There's a colloquialism going around: Food, weight and body image issues is Jewish alcoholism." Strauss, former president and CEO of Gymboree and a bulimic for thirty years, now works to help others suffering from eating disorders. In addition, Jewish women are as much prey as any others to the distorted cultural norms presented by the media. Super-thin models are depicted on the covers of magazines that contain articles detailing the weight gains and losses of celebrities. These same magazines feature recipes for high-calorie desserts alongside diet tips.

Adolescent girls are at particular risk for eating disorders. They need to contend with their changing bodies, with parental expectations, with peer pressure, and with a growing awareness of their sexuality. Many, who feel that they can never be good enough to meet all these challenges, develop eating disorders. If they stay thin enough, then their bodies won't change. If they are thin, then they will please their parents. If they join their friends in purging and bingeing, they'll be part of the crowd. If they become anorexic, their periods will stop and they won't need to deal with their hormonal urges. These issues are at least as prevalent for Jewish teens as for any others. Even in the Orthodox community, eating disorders have become a problem. One woman in Overeaters Anonymous, a twelve-step program, has noted that Orthodox, Hasidic, and Lubavitch women attend regularly. There is a growing concern that the pressures to make a good first impression on an arranged date has led to *"shidduch* pressure," with young Orthodox girls starving themselves so they'll be more "presentable."

Kashrut and eating disorders involve control issues, but in different ways. With eating disorders, the control is internal: if we control our eating, we are better people. With kashrut, the control is external: we are following ancient laws and traditions that define us as a people. Of course, the issue isn't that simple. With eating disorders, there is also the external pressure of societal expectations. With kashrut, for nontraditional Jews, there is the voluntary aspect of the decision to observe the laws. But they both bring up the question, Are we controlling food or is it controlling us?

Kashrut and eating disorders also both entail a fixation with what we can and cannot eat. In addition, kashrut deals with how food is to be prepared and served. In both cases, we need to consider whether it is healthful for us to be so obsessed by so many details. In the case of eating disorders, it is clearly not healthful. But the matter is much more complex when dealing with kashrut.

To many of us, the idea that we must observe biblical (or talmudic) laws because God told us to do so is anathema. We need a rationale, not to reject the laws, but so that we can observe them without compromising our other beliefs.

To "keep kosher" is to remind oneself at all times that one is Jewish. We can elevate the act of eating, make it holy, make it special, and, paradoxically, remove from it the stigma that constant media messages have placed on this simple biological necessity. As women, we can feel that we are controlling our kinship with food; it is not controlling us. And just as importantly, we as Jews are affirming our connections with the Jewish people, past and present, and our folkways and traditions in a concrete, observable, and constant way.

תזריע

Tazria

Our Children/God's Children

*T*ell the children of Israel that when a
woman conceives and bears a male child . . .
(LEVITICUS 12:2)

A MERE EIGHT VERSES OF *Parashat Tazria* comprise God's instructions
to Moses and the children of Israel on the rules of a woman's purification after childbirth. We see in those verses that fear, as much as
joy, characterized the ancient view of childbirth. Immediately following labor and delivery, the woman was forbidden to have intimate
contact with her husband, for she was likened to a *niddah* (menstruating woman). This restriction ended after a week or two (depending on the gender of the baby), and then the woman's status was
changed to the more general category of *temayah* (one who is impure)
for another month or two (again, depending on the gender of the
baby). As someone who was impure, she was ritually unfit to have
contact with sacred food or to enter the sanctuary; however, she
might resume normal relations with her husband. At the end of
this second period of separation she brought a burnt offering and a
sin offering to the door of the Tent of Meeting (i.e., to the Sanctuary), which the priest then offered on her behalf. This restored her to

the status of *tehorah* (ritually fit, or clean), and from then on she might resume participation in any and all communal functions.

Our ancestors' apprehension must have sprung, at least in part, from the fact that it was not uncommon for women to die during childbirth. The stories of our own matriarchs include the sad tale of Rachel's death as she gives life to Benjamin (Gen. 35:17–19). A woman's monthly menstrual period would have been no less mysterious, and it too may have shared some of the fear of the postpartum period. For several days a woman bled uncontrollably, often heavily. We do well to remember that there were no discreet or disposable hygiene products in the ancient world. In modern Western society a woman's menstrual cycle is a private matter. In ancient society the time of a woman's monthly bleeding would have been more public knowledge. It is easy to imagine that these two physical states were equally confounding to our biblical ancestors. Thus, the Torah categorizes a woman as a *niddah* whether her bleeding is postpartum or menstrual, and in both cases instructs that she be kept apart in order to prevent her from contaminating others.

Welcoming a new child into the world, be it through childbirth or adoption, is an awesome experience. There is the inherent joy and the miracle of witnessing a new life. There is also the overwhelming sense of responsibility and the privilege of becoming a parent. We want to sing, to shout, to cry, to laugh, to embrace humanity, and to run away, all at the same time. Strong emotions bind the two parents together at this moment. Mothers and fathers today share more of the experience of the arrival of a new child than ever before, since many fathers are now present at the baby's delivery. How hard it becomes, therefore, to understand that according to this *parashah*, a woman and her husband are forbidden to touch one another just as their hopes for a child are fulfilled (or, heaven forbid, disappointed). To those of us who do not observe these mitzvot, it may seem unfair, unnatural, or unduly painful to prohibit the parents from physically comforting each other at such a time. How shall we understand the purpose and nature of a woman's segregated status after giving birth? What is the meaning of this practice?

Classical biblical commentary to the laws of *niddah* (Lev. 15:19–24) and to the regulations concerning the new mother views the woman's state as one of physical impurity. The classical commentators considered *niddah* (and states likened to it) as a period of physical defilement owing to the issue of blood. As such, a woman was forbidden to come in contact with her husband, so as to prevent his becoming contaminated. Modern Torah commentator W. Gunther Plaut, however, notes that the laws of *niddah* also safeguarded a woman and promoted her overall good health. He writes, "The law protects women from the importunities of their husbands at a time when they are not physically and emotionally ready for coitus."[1] Thus, we find that *niddah* is more than a physical state of impurity; *niddah*, it seems, encompasses the woman's general well-being.

Commentators of earlier generations saw it that way too. For example, the Yiddish Torah commentary *Tz'enah Ur'enah* takes a broader view of the term *niddah*. In the commentary to Lev. 12:2, *Tz'enah Ur'enah* draws a parallel between the period of impurity following childbirth and the period of mourning following a death: "The Torah states that a woman is in a state of impurity for seven days after giving birth. Similarly, there is a seven-day period of mourning for the dead. All is counted by the number seven."[2] This comment correlates a woman's state following birth with that of a mourner. A mourner is not in a physically altered state during *shivah* (the seven-day period of mourning), but rather, in a spiritually altered or emotionally altered state. Thus, if there is a parallel between the two moments in life—the week immediately following a birth and the week immediately following a death—it must be that the two are linked by their spiritual and emotional quality. Indeed, we are in a more vulnerable and acute spiritual condition at these two times. Although the *Tz'enah Ur'enah* does not expand on this parallel, it is interesting to note that a woman's status following childbirth is characterized by an intense first week or two, and then a less intense, although fairly restrictive, period of isolation, lasting a month or two, which correspond to the mourner's status during the *shivah* (first seven days) and the *sheloshim* (first thirty days). Moreover, one of the purposes of the *shivah* following a funeral is to free the mourners from other personal and communal obligations so that they may grieve and adjust to their loss. We may presume that the seven- or fourteen-day period following a birth served a similar purpose for the mother: freeing her from other personal and communal obligations so that she might tend to her new baby and adjust to this addition to her family. From this comparison we see again that *niddah* and its attending isolation encompass more than a woman's physical condition.

Ritually prescribed periods of isolation often serve dual purposes: first, they protect the community from contact with someone in a "contagious" state (whether that contagion is physical or spiritual); second, and simultaneously, they protect someone in a vulnerable state from the intrusions of the community. There is no doubt that the use of the terms *niddah, temayah,* and *tehorah* indicates that the newly delivered mother was viewed as contaminated by the birth and the ensuing issue of blood. That does not negate the fact, however, that for the seven or fourteen days following the birth, the mother's special status protected her and legitimated her need to focus on the baby and herself. The succeeding thirty-three or sixty-six days, then, provided an additional cushion of time during which she resumed her full role within her family but remained exempt from certain other communal activities and potential responsibilities. The legislation found in Lev. 12 guaranteed women a certain amount of recovery time following the birth of a child, and this may well have had a positive effect on women's lives.

But what of the gender difference that attended this sequestered time—double the time for a girl baby as for a boy baby? When we read closely, we find that *two* ritual processes took place after a woman gave birth. One was a communal process that focused on the gender of the new child, and expressed society's need to differentiate between the roles of men and women. The other was a sacrificial process that focused on the mother, and expressed her unique connection to God. From a feminist outlook, the communal process is the more problematic of the two. Here the mother remains separate for twice as long after giving birth to a girl as after giving birth to a boy. There is also a special covenant ceremony, a *brit milah*, required on the eighth day after a boy's birth, while there is no parallel ceremony required at any point for a girl.

Gender greatly influences every person's role and status within society. This was as true for biblical society as it is for our own. Thus, in ancient society, celebrating the arrival of a new child included acknowledging the differences between boys and girls. Our custom today of dressing girl babies in pink and boy babies in blue addresses the same immediate need to identify a child's gender. The ceremony of *brit milah*, then, was as much about the maleness of the child, as it was about covenant. *Brit milah* was, and still is, a father-son ceremony. Consider that for the entire period of the pregnancy and for the first seven days of the child's life, the mother was solely responsible for its survival. Human physiology dictates that fathers are peripheral to pregnancy and breastfeeding. Thus, on the eighth day after a boy's birth, precisely at the conclusion of the first most protected time between the mother and the child, the community held a special ceremony to mark the unique identity shared by father and son. In Lev. 12:3 it indicates that "he shall circumcise the flesh of his foreskin." Presumably, "he" is the father. Throughout the centuries this verse has been understood as obligating the father to circumcise his son and to enter him into the covenant (following the model of Abraham with his two sons, Ishmael and Isaac). Surely, the penis is the most powerful singular anatomical expression of a boy's shared identity with his father, and his differing identity from his mother. Through the communal ceremony of *brit milah*, the father was affirmed as moving, symbolically, from a peripheral to a central place in the boy's life. There was no need for the community to provide a similar vehicle for the mother with her daughter, because she was already the central figure in that child's life. *Brit milah* made the penis and maleness the central link to covenant and continuity. Comparably, a woman's uterus (i.e., her ability to bear a child) could be seen as her biological link to covenant and continuity. Today, the discrepancy between the explicit male link *(brit milah)* to the covenant and the implicit female link (childbirth) to the covenant has led to the creation of a variety of new communal rites and liturgies for entering girls into the covenant. In Israel, there is a new Hebrew term for the celebratory meal held in honor of the birth of a daughter: *britah*. As feminism and egalitarianism continue to influence Jewish life everywhere, we can hope that more of these kinds of communal celebrations will take place and include specific covenant ceremonies for girls.

This view of *brit milah,* however, does not explain the need to increase the "lying in" period for the mother when the child was a girl rather than a boy. But here again, a communal response to biology may explain the differentiation. The female infant was the potential mother of the next generation. She already possessed the potential power to conceive a child and give birth to a new life. She already held within her the same "contagion" as her mother, and thus society doubled the time of separation after a girl's birth, because biblical society recognized that there were now two women—one mature and one immature—in its midst.

The final verses of this passage (Lev. 12:6–8) detail the required sacrifices that a woman was to bring to the priest at the completion of her period of separation. She was to bring a lamb for a burnt offering *(olah)* and a pigeon or a turtledove for a sin offering *(chatat).* Baruch Levine cautions the modern reader against misunderstanding the English translation of the biblical term *chatat:*

> Ancient man seldom distinguished between 'sin' and 'impurity.' In man's relation to God, all sinfulness produced impurity. All impurity, however contracted, could lead to sinfulness if not attended to, and failure to deal properly with impurity aroused God's anger. The point is that the requirement to present a sin offering does not necessarily presume any offense on the part of the person so obligated. The offering was often needed solely to remove impurity. Childbirth, for example was not sinful—it involved no violation of law—yet a sin offering was required.[3]

In other words, the sin offering served as a vehicle for returning someone in a contaminated state to a pure state; it was not an indictment of that person. The required offerings provided a means of transition from the exceptional experience of giving life back to the everyday experience of living. Our ability as human beings to create in general, and to create life in particular, links us closely to God. At no other moment do we act so powerfully like God as when we bring forth new life. The ritual sacrifices following childbirth thus highlighted a woman's unique relationship with God through the shared experience of creation.

All women, regardless of their financial circumstances, were entitled to offer the sacrifices following childbirth, as we read in verse eight: "If she does not find at hand a sheep, let her take two turtledoves or two pigeons, one for a burnt offering and the other for a sin offering." Furthermore, with regard to this sacrificial ritual for the mother after childbirth, the gender of the child was insignificant: "Upon fulfilling the days of her purification, for either a son or a daughter, let her bring a lamb" (Lev. 12:6). The sacrificial process was an egalitarian process, and also a democratic one. All mothers and all babies, regardless of circumstance in the case of the former, and regardless of gender in the case of the latter, had the identical obligation to bring sacrifices to the priest. Human gender was unimportant with respect to the sacrificial relationship with God. These offerings acknowledged the act of creation itself and the way this act of creation transformed human experience.

We, who live in a different time, one far removed from concrete sacrificial connections to God, do well to note the valuable function that these sacrifices played in biblical society. The need to identify a child's gender was met through communal rituals of separation (for the mothers) and covenant (*brit milah* for the boys). Simultaneously, the need to celebrate the miracle of a child's very existence was met through appropriate sacrificial offerings. Only the gender-specific process continues into our day. It is our challenge, therefore, to search for a new and appropriate ritual in place of the ancient sacrifices, one that celebrates the Divine-human connection in the gift of each new child's life, regardless of gender.[4]

RABBI LAURA GELLER

מצרע

Metzorah

Reclaiming the Torah of Our Lives

*T*his is the ritual . . . concerning her, who is in her menstrual infirmity. (LEVITICUS 15:32–33)

Metzorah begins, "This shall be the ritual for the *metzorah*, the individual who had suffered from *tzara-at* [skin disease] at the time that he is to be cleaned." It continues with one of the most elaborate description of rites of purification in the Torah. This is followed by a detailed description of bodily discharge from sexual organs, and of the impurity of menstruation.

Purity and impurity (*taharah* and *tumah*) as categories were central to the cult conducted by the priesthood in the Temple in Jerusalem. While a person with impurity was not necessarily guilty of an offense against God, the impurities themselves threatened the sanctity of the Temple as a sacred environment. It was up to the priests to diagnose and monitor the condition that led to the impurity, and eventually bring the individual back into the camp when the condition abated. It was important to know when a person was *tahor* (purified), in order to determine whether he or she could approach the Temple.

But purity and impurity as categories are hard for us to grasp.

Rachel Adler once argued that they reflect a life-death nexus, with death being the major source of *tumah*.[1] It follows, then, that sexual emissions not connected to creating life would also be sources of *tumah*, as would menstruation, which represents the death of potential life.

In the biblical legislation, individual Israelites might be subject to *tumah* at certain times in their lives. But every adult woman would be subject to *tumah* often: every month that she menstruated, and then again after childbirth. Each month, except when she was pregnant or nursing, a premenopausal woman would spend some time out of the camp. Carol Ochs argues that while banishment from the camp was an extraordinary experience for most Israelites, for women it was a routine experience. She speculates about the impact on the camp when those who have been outside, who have been in a different place and have gained a new perspective, come back into the camp. She suggests that women bring the wilderness experience with them back into the tradition. In some profound ways, women are outsiders, and they know themselves to be outsiders.[2]

Since the destruction of the Second Temple, it would seem that the categories of *taharah* and *tumah* would no longer be relevant. After all, there is no longer a Temple to approach. But certain notions of purity are still operative within traditional Judaism: those that relate to the priesthood, and those that relate to women.[3] Because contact with a corpse conveys *tumah*, men who believe themselves to have priestly lineage are forbidden to have contact with the dead except to attend to the burial of their closest family. They are not permitted to marry women who have been divorced or women who have converted to Judaism, women whom the tradition might suspect of sexual misconduct. Yet while these prohibitions relate only to certain men (those who claim priestly lineage), all women are, according to traditional Judaism, still subject to *tumah*. Because a woman menstruates, she cyclically becomes *tameyah* (impure). Intercourse during the period of *tumah* is forbidden; after the requisite number of days (seven according to the biblical law, seven more according to the rabbinic legislation) the woman is to bathe herself in *mayim chayim* (living waters), usually a *mikveh* (ritual bath), and then she becomes *tehorah* and available to her husband.

Life-death nexus? Maybe. But still, primarily for women. Generations after we left the wilderness, in some ways women are still there.

The very end of the *parashah* (Lev. 15:32–33) includes these words: "This is the ritual . . . concerning her, who is in her menstrual infirmity." Perhaps ritual can bring us back from the wilderness.

In my second year at Hebrew Union College, in 1972, I was the only woman in the beginning Talmud class. Our teacher, Rabbi Julius Kravitz (*z"l*), was introducing us to tractate *Berachot*, the talmudic text on blessings. He began by explaining the rabbinic tradition that a Jew was to say one hundred blessings a day. A hundred times a day we were to stop and acknowledge the divinity present in our experience. Before we eat, after we eat, when we see the ocean, when we see a friend we haven't seen for a long time, when we see trees blossoming or a rainbow glowing—all of these moments evoke a blessing. Our teacher continued, "Every important moment in the lifetime of a Jew has a blessing." And I remember thinking, "Yes, that's true. Divinity is present at every moment; we just need to notice it. Every important moment in the lifetime of a Jew has a blessing."

Then I realized it wasn't true. There had been important moments in my lifetime for which there were no blessings.

Suddenly I became again a thirteen-year-old girl who had just gotten her first period. I ran to tell my mother and her response stopped me: "When I got my period, my mother slapped me."

"This is the ritual . . . concerning her, who is in her menstrual infirmity," says the Torah.

"Why?" I asked.

My mother responded, "I don't really know—something about losing blood and being a little pale."

We didn't speak of it again.

I put that experience away in a tiny corner of my brain. I forgot about it completely, until that moment in Talmud class. Suddenly, I knew that what my teacher was saying must become true: there should be no important moment in the lifetime of a Jew for which there is no blessing.

What if my mother and I had prepared for the moment of menarche not only by reading the clinical description of what would be happening in my body, but also by reflecting on the spiritual import of that moment? What if she and I had said a blessing? Something as simple as the *shehechiyanu*, or *she'asani isha*—thank you, God, for making me a woman. What a difference that would have made in my sense of myself, my feelings about my body, and my connection to Jewish tradition. It would have brought me in from the wilderness, back into the camp. Or perhaps it would have transformed the camp, changing it so that women's experience was fully part of Jewish experience.

"This is the ritual . . . concerning her, who is in her menstrual infirmity."

It was that realization that propelled me to ask the question I've been wrestling with ever since: What are the other moments in our lives for which we need a blessing, moments that our tradition has overlooked or misunderstood? Moments of connection and moments of loss—childbirth, weaning, miscarriage, abortion, infertility. There are so many.

I continue to wrestle with these questions. What are the moments in my life where divinity is present, moments that will call out for blessing? I think of important moments that are just ahead: menopause, growing older, and the challenges and transitions that are yet to come. I think of major birthdays, retirement, healing from illness, the necessary losses that I know will come as I get older. What rituals or blessings could help me mark those transitions, teach me how to value these transformations in my life?

"This is the ritual . . . concerning her, who is in her menstrual infirmity." Even the language seems wrong. Menstrual infirmity? The Hebrew is *ha-davah b'nidotah*—weak or infirm through her impurity. No wonder some women of my generation grew up calling their periods "the curse"! Our tradition views us as weak and we get slapped for it!

As Rabbi Chaim Seidler-Feller has written about this Torah portion,

> It would be an understatement to say that these laws offend the sensibilities of most modern rational individuals who respect a woman's person and the powerful biological forces that pulsate within her body. Despite reams of apologetic explanations, one cannot escape the conclusion that the niddah regulations, as they are known in rabbinic literature, are demeaning and disparaging, casting a cloud of impurity over a woman's natural life-giving abilities and transforming blessing into functional curse.[4]

In a fascinating discussion, Seidler-Feller analyzes the different ways Maimonides, the philosopher, and Nachmanides, the mystic, think about *niddah,* those rabbinic rules governing menstruation and the menstruating woman. For Nachmanides, it is a mythic category: defiling, contaminating and a source of contagion. For Maimonides, on the other hand, it is purely a legal prohibition originally intended to curb the mythological fears that penetrated our folk tradition from the surrounding pagan cultures. Unfortunately, it was the view of Nachmanides that had the greater impact on Jewish practice: Consider the opinion of Rabbi Moses Isserles, in the late sixteenth century:

> Some have written that a menstruant during the days of her discharge may not enter a synagogue or pray or mention God's name or touch a Hebrew book, but others say she is permitted to do all these, and this view, that she is permitted, is correct. However, the practice in these countries accords with the first opinion.[5]

Although Isserles clearly favors the views of Maimonides, he is compelled by the practice of the folk to legitimate the superstitious customs that Maimonides rejected.

And so it has continued through the generations, right until my grandmother slapped my mother to scare off the evil eye, which, she believed, hovers around you at times of transition. And it even continued as my mother told me her story. And not only does the superstition still continue, but also the mistaken perception that tradition somehow validates these superstitions still leaves women outside the camp. I remember the woman at her first Simchat Torah celebration in twenty years, dancing with joy at being so close to Torah. I remember her anguish as she ran up to me afterward, tears in her eyes. "Rabbi," she cried, " I have 'trafed' up the Torah. For the first time in my life I felt close to Torah! I was so carried away that I forgot I had my period! I ruined it for everyone!" And I remember all the women who have whispered to me over the years, "But how can you be a rabbi? What about your period?"

"This is the ritual . . . concerning her, who is in her menstrual infirmity."

If we can reframe the ritual, change the language, we can transform the community.

"This is the ritual for her, who has her menstrual period." This new ritual we create will celebrate the holiness present in our lives at such an important moment of transition. This blessing we will teach our daughters to say will help transform the wilderness into a bigger camp, with enough room to include all of Jewish experience and all Jews. We can reinterpret *tahorah* and *tumah* into categories of *kodesh* and *chol,* of holy and ordinary. We can name those moments of holiness in our lives and celebrate them. We can honor the Torah of our lives even as we struggle with the Torah of tradition.

The priest in the *parashah* looks at the affliction and sees the need for healing. The word for "affliction," *negah,* has the same letters as the word *oneg,* "joy." Each of us can look into our tradition and be part of its healing, transforming what has been an affliction into the possibility of wholeness and joy.

RABBI DAYLE A. FRIEDMAN

אחרי מות
Acharei Mot

After a Death . . . Then What?

*A*fter the death of the two sons of Aaron,
who died when they came too close to the
presence of the Eternal, God spoke to Moses.
(LEVITICUS 16:1)

IF WE REFLECT ON THE EVENTS AND EMOTIONS following the death
of someone close to us, we may remember emotions reeling out of
control, a general feeling of disorientation, and the sense that nothing would ever be the same. *Parashat Acharei Mot's* stolid exposition
of the events following the shocking deaths of Aaron's sons reflects
a general impulse to either contain or deny the emotional response
to loss. One can posit that this approach reflects male styles of
reacting to and expressing emotional distress, and also models a
negative and unhealthy response to grief. Not only are women utterly invisible and inaudible in this account, but women's ways of
grieving and healing are missing as well.

   Acharei Mot relates the aftermath of an incomprehensible tragedy
that occurred on the very day of the investiture of Aaron and his
sons to the priesthood, when God's presence had appeared before
all of the people. Following this ecstatic moment, Nadav and Avihu

218

were consumed by fire when they offered "an alien fire that God had not commanded" (Lev. 10:1). The response of *Parashat Acharei Mot* to these bewildering deaths is to provide a detailed set of instructions for the Yom Kippur rituals. These rites were to be performed by Aaron and the priests, and would effect expiation on behalf of the people of Israel. Those rites focus on individual and collective guilt.

Guilt is an almost inevitable concomitant to grief. Especially in the face of these devastating losses, Aaron must have been mercilessly reviewing his deeds to try to understand what he had done to allow his sons to err as they did. Thus, we can imagine that God's command at that time to perform what would become the Yom Kippur rituals of atonement (Lev. 16:2–34) resonated with his own sense of being in the wrong. In this context, the requirement that Aaron first make a *hatat* offering on his own and his household's behalf is particularly poignant, particularly in light of Rashi's suggestion that this offering also included the confession of sins. Whereas for the generations to come, the Yom Kippur rituals have offered liberation from the burden of guilt, for the bereaved Aaron they might well have only increased his suffering.

In addition to the concern with expiating past and future transgressions, the Torah text in *Acharei Mot*, as well as in Leviticus, chapter 10 *(Parashat Shemini)*, reflects two other responses to these deaths: minimizing the expression of grief and silence. There is an astonishing variety of rabbinic perspectives on Nadav and Avihu's actions and deaths. Some sources view them as arrogant sinners punished appropriately for a host of infractions, while others suggest that they were holy beings whose only sin was getting carried away with the quest for God's presence.[1]

Regardless of this tension between vilification and valorization, the text in *Acharei Mot* sends a clear message to the mourners: these losses that you have experienced prove that you are guilty, and you need to clear your slate with God. Similarly, in *Shemini*, Moses attempted to explain or rationalize the deaths: "This is what the Eternal meant in saying: Through those close to Me I am sanctified, and I make Myself known before all the people" (Lev. 10:3). He was then instructed by God to institute new restrictions in order to prevent such occurrences in the future. God commanded Aaron to refrain from imbibing intoxicants before entering the Tent of Meeting, and Moses offered Aaron, Eliezer, and Ithamar instructions for the proper locations for consuming the various sacrifices. The thrust of Moses' and God's reactions was, "Leave this mess behind you, and make sure you don't do anything to warrant such a punishment again."

This stark approach to the grieving Aaron, his family, and his community actually began immediately after the deaths. In *Shemini* we saw the second reaction to the deaths, a pattern of minimization of the emotional responses to loss. Aaron and his sons were explicitly forbidden to engage in the customary rituals of tearing their garments and baring their heads, on pain of death (Lev. 10:6). Rashbam explains that they must continue with their work as priests, honoring God not by mourning their loss but by keeping up "the work of the Creator." The community was allowed to "bewail the burning that the Eternal has wrought" (Lev. 10:6), but no consolation was offered to Aaron, his wife, Elisheva, and their surviving sons, Eliezer and Ithamar, the immediate mourners.

So far, we have seen the effort of Moses and God to shut down the emotional response to the death of Aaron's sons and to link these events with the need for expiation. But where, in all of this, is the grieving family? How do they respond to this cataclysm?

Their reaction to the loss represents a third pattern: silence. Their grief is invisible and largely inaudible. Elisheva, the bereaved mother, is simply absent from the text. There is no mention of her or her reactions in the accounts following the death, reminding the reader of Sarah, who is not mentioned in connection with the near death of her beloved son, Isaac (Gen. 22).

And what of Aaron, the leader, the high priest, the official spokesman of the people? The text in *Shemini* says simply, "And Aaron was silent" (Lev. 10:3). The reticence of Aaron, who is usually so full of words, is both striking and puzzling. Is this silence an absence of response, an expression of anger or despair, or, as the rabbis claim, a mark of acceptance of God's justice? *Biur*, the commentary written in the eighteenth century by Moses Mendelssohn and his associates, argues that Aaron's silence is an indication of "patience and resignation." Rashbam says that Aaron was silent *despite* his grief, since he believed that his sons had been honored in their deaths. Rashi teaches that Aaron was rewarded for his silence when God addressed him directly with the prohibition on intoxication.

Whatever the meaning of Aaron's silence, there is a singular moment when he is moved to speak in the aftermath of the deaths. Moses has gotten angry at Eliezer and Ithamar for failing to consume the flesh of a goat of a sin offering. Aaron responds, "Such things having happened to me! Had I eaten of the sin offering today, would it have found favor in the eyes of the Eternal?" (Lev. 10:19). Rashi argues that Aaron is offering a correction to Moses' halachic ruling on the obligations of a mourner, but *Biur* offers a radically different reading, suggesting that Aaron accepts the prohibition on exhibiting his grief, but refuses to pretend to be absorbed in the joy required by this ritual duty:

> If I restrained myself and did not weep in order to
> show publicly my acceptance of the Divine judgment,
> would it be well-pleasing in the sight of the Eternal
> to partake of the sin-offering in joy, whilst my heart
> is full of grief and sorrow; especially when the meat of
> the sacrifice has to be eaten in joy and not in grief?
> (*Biur,* ad. loc.)

Interestingly, Moses accepts Aaron's reasoning humbly (Lev. 10:20).

As they have been passed down, both the Torah text and rabbinic expansions on the events following the deaths of Aaron's two sons reflect men's responses to loss. The text not only omits women's responses to bereavement, it also inevitably creates norms out of male patterns of grieving. These norms are destructive, not just for women, but for men, for they deprive men of the opportunity to feel, express, and heal from bereavement in a healthy way. Moreover, the text's association of loss with guilt and expiation of sin could be particularly harmful to perfectly innocent bereaved men and women struggling with what they could have, or should have, done differently.

The responses to loss in this ancient narrative mirror male norms of grieving in our own society. Men in contemporary Western culture tend to mask or deflect grief. They do not verbally communicate about their feelings about bereavement.

> The majority of men react to the death of a loved
> one by keeping their thoughts and emotional pain to
> themselves most, if not all of the time. They appear
> not to need to communicate about the effects of the
> death, particularly about their innermost feelings.[2]

In addition, men tend to channel their reactions to loss by

"plung[ing] into action," conforming to "the cultural expectation that a man will not lose control of himself or the situation, nor will he be passive, helpless or afraid."[3] This response is particularly common among men who have lost a child. Male mourners also tend to throw themselves into work to avoid having time to grieve, but in this way, "other important components [of the self] are neglected and stifled."[4]

In contrast to the taciturnity and avoidance that characterize male grieving, women in our culture are more given to both verbal and nonverbal expression of emotions.[5] A study of the association of gender role and sadness found that "consistent with sex stereotypes, the feminine gender role was associated with *dwelling* [emphasis mine] on sadness whereas the masculine gender role was associated with *distraction* [emphasis mine] when sadness was experienced."[6] In response to others' troubles, "women tend to engage in both emotional and instrumental forms of communication. Men engage in less emotional forms of communication, preferring instead to provide support in the form of trying to deny, minimize or solve others' problems."[7] Men's inexpressiveness has been called "a tragedy of our society."

The women connected to Aaron and his sons would have responded to their deaths in a radically different manner than did Aaron and Moses. Imagine if we were to witness Elisheva's reaction, to hear *her* voice. No doubt she would not be alone, but rather, surrounded by women friends and relatives, as well as by the guilds of female wailers who routinely helped the community to grieve.[8] Keening, weeping, shouting, Elisheva might have cried out to God, sharing her anguish, if not her protest. With the women around her, Elisheva would have approached the Tent of Meeting, demanding that her husband and remaining sons put aside their liturgical work and join her in the holy rituals of mourning.

Perhaps, in Elisheva's tearful embrace, Aaron could have found voice for his sorrow. Surely, Elisheva's visibly traumatized presence would have moved God and Moses to have *rachmones* (compassion), to act to assuage her self-blaming; they might well have avoided heightening the mourners' inevitable guilt. They would likely have chosen a different moment for the instructions regarding the Yom Kippur ritual. Maybe, just maybe, if women had told this story instead of men, God's voice would have come to lovingly console Aaron, rather than to offer rules and structure.

As we listen through the silence of this story for the mournful voices of women, we may transform our understanding of loss, of grieving, and of healing. While nothing could erase the unfathomable loss of Nadav and Avihu, the voices and the ways of women might have offered solace to their suffering loved ones and perhaps, by extension, to bereaved men and women throughout the ages.

RABBI RACHEL ESSERMAN

קדשים

Kedoshim

Who Shall Be Holy?

*A*nd the Lord spoke to Moses: "Speak to all
the congregation, the children of Israel and
say to them: 'You shall be holy because I the Lord
your God am holy.'" (LEVITICUS 19:1–2)

WHAT IS THE MEANING OF A "holy people"? The Torah is considered to be the holy book for all the Jewish people throughout time
and space. Yet when I read Leviticus, I find myself wondering what
the Torah means when it speaks of the Jewish people.

The Book of Leviticus is filled with extensive instruction about
ritual sacrifices for an exclusively male priesthood. Biblical religion
centered on purifying oneself in order to bring sacrifices to God.
One major component of this ritual purification consisted of sep-
arating oneself from women, especially menstruating women. For
example, in Exod. 19:15, when Moses commands the people to
purify themselves in order to receive the Torah, he cautions them
"not to approach a woman." And Lev. 15:19 says that a menstruating woman is unclean and that "all who touch her will be unclean
until evening." In both cases, women are a source of impurity.

When I read these portions of the Torah, I feel forced to define the Jewish people as Jewish men. In chapter nineteen of Leviticus, however, in the Torah portion called *Kedoshim*, something different occurs. God asks Moses to speak to all the congregation and tell them, "You shall be holy." *Kol adat b'nai Yisrael*, all the congregation, not just the priests, or the Levites, but all the congregation—men, women, and children—is to be considered holy.

According to the verses that follow, being holy means following a combination of ritual and moral laws. Holiness in Lev. 19 is not just a matter of purification and sacrifice, of sweet savors being offered to God, but of everyday earthly rules that all—men and women—are expected to obey. Leave food in your fields for the poor; do not steal or lie; do not oppress your neighbor or be a tale-bearer. Even correct behavior in business matters, such as paying someone's wages in a timely manner, is necessary to make the Jewish people holy. I love the idea that the Torah offers us a way to be holy in our everyday lives. You do not have to leave your family or resign from society to find holiness. The path is there before you. Possibilities for holiness surround you in your everyday, workday world.

Is it possible that the Torah believes that everyone can be holy? Are women really included in this commandment instead of being excluded, as they are from most sacred rituals that were done in the Tabernacle and later in the Temple?

As much as I love the words "You shall be holy," as much as I want to embrace this Torah portion as inclusive, it is not that simple. The first two verses seem all inclusive—*kol adat b'nai Yisrael*, all the congregation. This seems to imply that women are included. There is a change, however, in verse three that challenges this interpretation. The verse states, "A man shall fear his mother and his father and guard my sabbaths." The Hebrew word used is *ish*, the

singular form for "man." The Hebrew plural of a word can grammatically mean either men or men and women, but here the word
used is clearly masculine singular. We move from the inclusive *kol
adat b'nai Yisrael*—all the congregation—to the exclusive *ish*, "man."
Will all of this community be holy? Or just men?

The verse contains an even greater puzzle. The verb used for
"fear," *yirau*, is in the third-person plural form. In Hebrew, nouns
and verbs must agree; a singular noun like "man" should have a
singular verb, not a plural one. Either the sentence is grammatically incorrect or, as the rabbis of ancient times would say, the use of
the plural is to teach us something. How does "all the congregation" in verse two come to be defined by the word "man" in verse
three?

According to Rashi, the laws of Lev. 19 were spoken "in an
assembly," an assembly consisting of men, women, and children.
Following his reasoning, the laws would pertain to everyone in the
community, and therefore everyone could be holy. His interpretation of Lev. 19:2–3 is more troubling. Rashi believes that the words
"you shall be holy" refer to the laws of incest listed earlier in Lev.
18, which is found in the previous week's Torah portion. He says,
"Separate yourself from incest and from transgression, in every
place you find a fence around incest, you find holiness." Rashi
understands the commandment "to be holy" to be within the context of sexual behavior of Lev. 18 rather than in the broader context of Lev. 19. The laws of incest in the former are told from a
man's point of view, but most of the laws in the latter are told from
neither a male nor female perspective. Shouldn't these laws be the
ones to make all of, not just part of, the people holy?

When looking at Lev. 19:3 ("a man shall fear his mother and
his father"), Rashi also questions the use of the singular *ish* for

man with the plural form of the verb "fear." His answer to the problem reflects his own bias. He says "a man has it in his power to do, but a woman has the authority of others over her." In simple terms, a man is his own master, but a woman has to obey others (her parents, her husband), and therefore she is not expected to obey this law. I can understand the rabbis' reason for exempting women from time-bound ritual commandments (e.g., excusing women from attending prayer services three times a day), since it is hard to perform a ritual that conflicts with other work that women were required to do by their husbands or parents. That should not prevent women from obeying other commandments, such as not cursing the deaf or putting a stumbling block in front of the blind, which are not time bound. Does taking care of her husband or children prevent a woman from keeping the Sabbath? Can't she still love her neighbor as herself? All these laws are found in Lev. 19. The whole congregation is supposed to follow these laws, according to Rashi. Women are supposed to obey them too, except when Rashi thinks it will be impossible for them to observe them. When he explains why the verse places the word mother before father ("a man shall fear his mother and his father"), he claims that it is because a son naturally fears his father more than his mother. Having exempted women from this obligation, Rashi speaks only of what a son must do. Women, daughters, are not included in his interpretation.

The halachic tradition could have taken a different direction. Instead of exempting women, it could have said that since God commands all the congregation to be holy and follow these laws, women must follow them too. Women should be freed from other obligations when it comes to pursuing holiness. Men are obligated to pray even if it interferes with their work. They are required to keep the Sabbath and the holidays even if it affects their livelihood. Only physical danger frees them from obeying the commandments. Why isn't the same degree of holiness required of women?

There are other verses in Lev. 19 that may make one question what the Torah means by "all the congregation." Verse twenty deals with the punishment of a man who has sexual intercourse with an engaged bondswoman. As in the verses on incest in Lev. 18, the man is the central figure. The verse speaks to him. In the second half of verse twenty-seven, God commanded the Israelites not to cut the corners of their beards. Isn't it obvious that this verse refers only to men? Here again, does the congregation—*kol adat b'nai yisrael*—consist of only men?

In verse twenty-nine we read, "Do not profane your daughter to cause her to be a prostitute." To whom is this verse directed? There is no verse telling parents not to prostitute their sons. When Rashi interprets this verse, he speaks only of a father prostituting his daughter. On the one hand, it is good to see that the Torah limits the power that parents have over children. On the other hand, we note that only women's actions profane the land.

Even though a literal halachic reading of the Torah might limit who belongs to the "holy congregation," I believe that the Torah teaches that all of us are holy. These commandments expect me to make holy every part of my life. It does not matter if you are studying Torah, or working in a store, or changing a baby's diaper, or digging a ditch. You can, you should, strive to be holy.

Women can strive for holiness not only in prayer and Torah study but in their everyday lives. Family and friendships give women a unique opportunity to translate the mundane into the holy, whether they are feeding and nurturing children, caring for elderly parents, or comforting a grieving friend. Our connections to others bring holiness into the world. We are a holy people because we treat others as holy.

We need to celebrate the holiness in our everyday lives. Each person should determine if her or his business decisions bring holiness into the world. While most of us can no longer leave food for the poor in the corners of our fields, we can carefully consider which of our donations of time and money could make us holy. We should consider the holiness of our words and actions toward our families, friends, and neighbors. Perhaps we need to recite the words *kodeshim tihiyu ke kodesh ani Adoney Elohaham,* "You shall be holy for I the Lord your God am holy," every morning so that we will search for ways to fulfill God's commandment. We, the congregation of Israel—every woman, child, and man—are called upon in this *parashah* to be holy.

RABBI VALERIE LIEBER

אמר

Emor

Elitism in the Levitical Priesthood

*H*e may marry only a woman who is a virgin.
A widow, or a divorced woman, or one who
is degraded by harlotry—such he may not marry.
(LEVITICUS 21:13–14)

LEVITICUS, CHAPTER 21, delineates the rules of the priesthood, which was centered in Jerusalem, the capital of the southern Jewish kingdom of Judah. Many limitations imposed upon priests involve their relationship to their own family members, notably, their wives and daughters. In examining these relationships we learn about both the power and the powerlessness of women in the institution of the priesthood.

It is important to read the Torah as a product of the historical and political situation in which it arose. In Lev. 21, one motive of the laws concerning the priesthood was to distinguish these priests from all others, including priests of pagan religions, earlier Jewish priests, and rival Jewish priesthoods in the northern kingdom of Israel. The intent of these passages was to legitimize the Levitical priests—priests who descended from Aaron and who were members of the tribe of Levi—as the only acceptable priesthood for the

Jewish people. For this reason, the behavior of these Levitical priests must be clearly defined, rigidly distinguishing them from priests of pagan gods and goddesses.

Most pagan religions in the geographic region of Canaan, where the Jews lived, employed women in their temples as priestesses. Furthermore, according to historian Julius Wellhausen and his followers, Jewish priesthood was not initially limited to the tribe of Levi.[1] Priestly functions, such as officiating over animal sacrifice, were practiced by members of each of the tribes, men and women alike.

Because other religions included women in their temple cult, and because early Judaism did not restrict women's access to sacrifice, the Levites found a simple way to distinguish the Israelite priesthood from its neighbors and predecessors by strictly forbidding women from religious duty. Meanwhile, they also faced a rival priesthood within Judaism. Wellhausen states that a group of non-Levitical priests served altars in the northern kingdom of Israel in the towns of Dan and Shilo. Over time, the Levites consolidated their monopoly of the priesthood, but not without great tension. Understandably, the other priests resented being shut out of their duties. In order to quell some of this tension, the Levitical priesthood attempted to define itself in a way that would render its priests beyond reproach. For the people to accept only these men as priests, they had to be the ultimate symbols of perfection and stability.[2]

The priesthood came to be defined as a social class markedly different from the general populace. The clothing they wore and their hairstyles set them apart visibly. The rigid standards they followed in sexual practices distinguished them morally. The limitations put on priests did more than create a mystique and an elite status. They also compensated for the jealousy of those shut out of the priesthood; people may have been envious of the priests' higher status, but few envied the obligations that they had to fulfill.

Though women were not allowed to be priests, the priests were encouraged to marry and continue the hereditary line of Aaron. In order to maintain the aura of elitism and ensure numerous priestly offspring, priests were forbidden from marrying many types of women. Leviticus 21:7 commands, "They shall not marry a woman defiled by harlotry *[ishah zonah v'chalala]*, nor shall they marry one divorced from her husband" (my translation). Why were priests restricted so? Harlotry, or prostitution, was not illegal in ancient Israel. A marriage between a prostitute and an Israelite was perfectly acceptable. So was a marriage between a divorced woman and an Israelite man.

The Torah does not pass judgment on prostitution, nor is prostitution defined as "defiling" anywhere else in the Torah. Leviticus 21:7 is less about harlots than it is about priests, and the need for priests to maintain families that were rigidly restricted, stable, and "perfect." Prostitution, though legal, was hardly mainstream. Because paternity of children was so important to the institutions of ancient Israel, a woman who gave birth to children of an unidentifiable father subverted society's most revered conventions.

On a practical level, a prostitute may have had children by other men, and therefore, conflicting emotional and financial obligations and alliances would arise for her priest-husband. This would complicate the priest's family life. On the other hand, if a prostitute were childless, this could be taken as a sign that she was unable to bear children. A barren woman could not produce the much needed male heirs for a priest and was therefore an unsuitable wife.

Leviticus 21:13–14 discusses two additional limitations on marriage, this time for the high priest: "He may marry only a woman who is a virgin. A widow, a divorced woman, or one who is degraded by harlotry—such he may not marry." The high priest is forbidden to marry a woman if she had ever engaged in sex. He is prohibited from marrying either a widow or a woman who had been raped or engaged in sex for any other reason.

In a talmudic discussion of these prohibitions, the rabbis and sages diverge from the Torah's focus on priestly behavior and instead focus on women's sexual behavior, particularly which woman can be defined as a *zonah*, or harlot. The Talmud passage in *Yebamot* 61a–b begins with the proposition that a priest is forbidden to marry a woman who is known to be barren unless he already has a wife and children. Rabbi Judah then expands the restrictions, saying, "A priest cannot marry any barren woman, because she falls under the definition of *zonah* (harlot)." In response to the later question, "What is the definition of *zonah?*" Rabbi Eliezer asserts, "*Zonah* implies from the language that she is a faithless wife." Rabbi Akiba sticks with the obvious, direct meaning, saying, "The word means a prostitute." Rabbi Judah reiterates, "A *zonah* is one incapable of procreation." The sages propose, "A *zonah* is a convert, a freed slave, or a woman who had tawdry sexual encounters." Rabbi Eleazar then claims, "If an unmarried man has intercourse with an unmarried woman, with no intent to marry her, he renders her a *zonah.*"

This passage of commentary extends the concept of *zonah* from an ordinary prostitute to any woman whom the rabbis see as straying from the ideal or norm. It indicates the fear and discomfort that the rabbis associated with women's sexuality. The impulse to define and control female sexuality is evident in this passage. For the rabbis, female sexuality is not just about sex; it is about a woman's power. If the rabbis could define women and their sexuality, women's power and identity could be harnessed and handled. They believed that for a priest—and perhaps any man who wished to attain elite status—a woman with uncontrolled sexuality or identity was a grave threat to his position. A woman whose sexuality was not in the complete service of her husband was unacceptable.

The rabbis use this biblical passage about the wives of priests to extrapolate their own more general thoughts about the kinds of women who are acceptable as wives for all Jewish men. Sadly, in this area, even among liberal Jews today, not much has changed. Granted, a divorced woman, widow, or convert is not usually seen to be sexually threatening in and of herself; but sexually active single women are judged more harshly than unmarried men who are sexually active. Men still want to own and master a woman's sexuality, so that her identity is defined by him rather than by her.

The story found in Lev. 24:10–16 is an example of the way that the struggle for priestly control is embedded in the narrative of Leviticus. The text tells of an unnamed man, the son of a nameless Egyptian man and a Jewish woman named Shelomit. The son argues with an Israelite man and speaks God's name in blasphemy. He is brought before Moses for the crime, and Moses appeals to God for the punishment. God commands that all who heard his blasphemy stone him to death.

This man, labeled "the Blasphemer," pronounced God's name. The priests had sole jurisdiction over such actions, and had forbidden anyone else to engage in any sacred activity associated with the worship of God in the absence of a presiding priest. The Blasphemer's utterance challenges the priestly monopoly over religious activity, and challenges the priestly definition of acceptable Judaism. This is similar to the way a *zonah* challenges the institutional definition of what is acceptable female sexuality.

Although the Blasphemer remains unnamed, his mother's name is recorded. This is surprising, as usually men are named while their female relatives remain unnamed. His mother's name is Shelomit, daughter of Dibri, of the tribe of Dan. About her, the commentator Rashi says, "The scripture exposes her by name to indicate that she alone was a harlot (zonah)."[3] Rashi further denigrates her by expounding on her name, saying that she was called Shelomit— from the root "shalom" or "peace"—"because she would babble, 'peace be with you; peace be with you.' She would babble words inquiring into the welfare of everyone." It is possible, I believe, that she was actually a respected leader who helped people to feel at peace, and who would minister unto the people. Perhaps Rashi is only half right, and she was a pastoral presence among her tribe of Dan. The Blasphemer's mother, Shelomit, was considered to be as threatening as her blaspheming son to the authority of the priest-hood and its vision of Judaism.

Finally, the text specifies that Shelomit came from the tribe of Dan. The tribe of Dan maintained its own altars, independent of the Levitical priests, for many years. The priests of Dan served the tribes of the northern kingdom, and did not follow the same rules as the Levitical priests in Judah. The presence of a rival priesthood and an alternative Jewish practice was intolerable for the descendants of Aaron. Any way that they could undermine its success helped them to gain full control over the religious lives of all Israelites through the downfall of their rivals in Dan. This entire episode can be seen as a threat to destroy any rivals.

Alternative visions of Jewish practice were never fully squelched by the Levitical priests. There were always men and women who practiced folk religion in the taking of vows, talking to the dead, and in worshiping a goddess or god from a pagan religion. In the biblical period, women who struggled for communal or social power were driven to find it outside of mainstream Judaism; they found themselves marginalized by ritual practice, laws of inheritance, and conventions of family life. Despite the struggle of some women, like Shelomit, for independence and influence, the priests managed to consolidate their control, and this text functions to warn women and others who might seek religious power that they would be punished severely. Seen in this light, the text serves to further limit the independence of the marginalized members of Israelite society and to encourage them to enter the mainstream.

Today, Jewish tradition still encourages women to embrace conventional family life and religious practice, but women's roles in Jewish ritual life have expanded in all streams of Judaism. For example, in the traditional community a few women have been empowered as *yoatzot halachah* (halachic advisors), a role similar to male *poskim* (interpreters of Jewish law), for halachic issues particular to women; some modern Orthodox congregations encourage women to study and teach each other Torah; women in most liberal Jewish communities are among the leaders and shapers of Jewish practice and thought as lay leaders, cantors, rabbis, and academics. Women rabbis are the "new Levitical priests." But instead of building up a mystique of "perfection" and elitism, we teach, preach, and practice inclusion. In my rabbinate, women and men, gays and straights, and interfaith families are welcomed into the community and embraced, each for their own gifts. Women leaders are trying innovative new rituals and bringing these alternative practices into mainstream Jewish life: *brit bat* ceremonies for baby girls entering the covenant, aging ceremonies to honor wisdom, and a cup for Miriam the prophetess at our Seder tables. We are reclaiming dormant "folk customs" like *Rosh Chodesh* celebrations, and we are putting our own feminist stamp on areas that were male-only areas of activity, such as the study of halachah, musical composition, and liturgical invention. Women in Judaism are no longer powerless in the religious sphere. We now are powerful, for we also define Judaism.

RABBINICAL STUDENTS
SHARON BROUS AND JILL HAMMER

בהר

Behar

Proclaiming Liberty throughout the Land

You shall make the fiftieth year holy. You shall proclaim liberty throughout the land for all its inhabitants. (LEVITICUS 25:10)

In the seventh year all are equal—this can indeed generate peace. (R. EPHRAIM LUNCHITZ, *Keli Yakar* ON DEUTERONOMY 31:12)

THE TORAH PRESENTS LAND OWNERSHIP as a major component of personhood. In the Book of Numbers the census is taken, and only those to whom land would be allocated are counted among the nation. This establishes a social structure that necessarily favors men over women, since we learn that women inherit land only under the rare circumstance in which a man dies leaving daughters but no sons (Num. 27:8). In an agrarian society with an economy primarily based on the produce of the land, it is clear that restricted inheritance must result in women's financial and social dependence on men. *Parashat Behar*, however, establishes an ideal system that has the potential to rectify this inequality.

Parashat Behar describes two unusual kinds of sabbaths—not the day of rest observed every seventh day, but year-long sabbaths. One occurs every seven years and is called the *shmita*, the sabbatical year, or in this passage, simply the *shabbat*. During the *shmita*, the land must not be planted, but rather, people must live off the wild growth of the earth while the land rests, and all debts must be canceled. Furthermore, the *shmita* relieves ownership of the land (Lev. 25:6–7). Rashi explains Lev. 25:6 to mean that the prohibition during the *shmita* year is "not only that you should not deal with [the lands] as an owner, rather, all people should be equal with regard to it, you and your hired servant and your settler." The Torah instructs us that during the *shmita*, all people have unrestricted access to the land, and individual owners must abandon their claims. The other year-long sabbath occurs every fifty years and is called the *yovel*, the jubilee. This is a time when Jewish slaves, even those who have chosen to be slaves, must be freed,[1] and all purchased farmland must be returned to the family that originally owned it. The message of both *shmita* and *yovel* is that the disposition of the land, its riches, and its citizens belongs to God, and humans are only permitted to interfere with that disposition temporarily.

Why is the renunciation of land ownership so crucial a notion that it is built into the calendrical cycle? *Shmita* is called *shabbat shabbaton* (the sabbath of sabbaths). The connection between *shmita* and Shabbat elucidates the essence of the laws of *shmita*, and also of *yovel*, which is the sabbathlike culmination of seven *shmita* cycles. Shabbat is traditionally regarded as a time for healing, renewal, and restoration of the cosmic equilibrium. The rabbis frequently referred to Shabbat as a foretaste of life in *olam haba* (the world to come).[2] Similarly, during the *shmita* and *yovel* years, the world mirrors the state of creation, in which land is ownerless, and God is its only master. God's mastery over people and land precludes people's mastery over material goods, and over one another.

Shmita and *yovel* specifically come to redress the inequalities of wealth and gender. Leviticus 25:6–7 teaches, "But you may eat the produce of the land during its sabbath—you, your male and female slaves, your hired and permanent laborers who live with you, and your cattle and wild animals in your land may eat all its produce." The careful choice of words emphasizes that *shmita* brings equality for all people, male and female. During the *shmita* year the male owners of land lose their privilege over women, over servants and laborers, and even over animals. The system of *shmita* and *yovel* ideally creates complete equality, in which gender and class distinctions no longer serve as obstacles to opportunity, in which all people have equal access to God's bounty. *Shmita* and *yovel* rectify the disequilibrium that pervades the years of work and ownership. They paint an image of *olam haba* in which men share their gifts with women and value the gifts that women have to share with them. It is a world in which no one takes priority over another person on the basis of gender or class. The message is an uplifting one for those who believe in the equality of all people. Just as the seventh day frees us from the enslavement and mastery of the workweek, so too the seventh year enables us to escape a flawed reality and indulge in the idealism of complete equality.

The Case of the Maidservant

The discussion of debts, poverty, and slavery in this text is a reminder to women of the consequences of economic disempowerment. The only woman directly mentioned in *Parashat Behar* is the *amah* (the slave woman), and this is significant because it indicates *Behar*'s concern for the most vulnerable members of society. The *amah* is listed as one of the people who will eat the wild produce of the land during the *shmita* year rather than harvested food (Lev. 25:6). In that respect, she is equal to all other Israelites, although she may have sold herself, or been sold by her father, into slavery (cf. Exod. 21:7). The *amah* is also one of the slaves who must be freed at the *shmita*. In fact, according to the rabbinic tradition, an Israelite *amah* had to be freed either in the *shmita* year, or in the *yovel*, or when she reached puberty—whichever came first—if her owner did not marry her. This was one of her protections against abuse.[3] Our own concern for women's vulnerability and our attempts to repair that vulnerability are mirrored in *Parashat Behar*, which shows a legal and moral concern for the poorest of the Israelites—the destitute who must sell themselves into slavery in order to eat, the debtors who cannot afford to pay interest on a loan, the paupers who must sell their family homes—and turns society nearly upside down on their behalf.[4]

Interestingly, a midrash in *Leviticus Rabbah* 34:8 quotes the case of Ruth and her benefactor, Boaz, when discussing the kinds of charity mentioned in *Behar*: "Who was it that showed kindness to one who needed kindness? Boaz to Ruth, as it is proved by the text: 'And Boaz said to her at mealtime' (Ruth 2:14)." Ruth, the stranger who must glean from the fields, is the quintessential model of a woman who does not lose her dignity or her destiny because she is poor and a stranger. Ruth refers to herself as an *amah*, a maidservant, when speaking to Boaz (Ruth 3:9), the same word that we find in *Parashat Behar*, and she epitomizes both the vulnerability and the strength of such a woman. Ruth's poverty is brought on by the loss of her husband and father-in-law, a situation that demonstrates why poverty has always been a women's issue, especially in societies that demand that women be economically dependent upon men. Yet,

Ruth's position in Israelite society does not alter her fundamental strength of character. In fact, although she is a widow and a foreigner, she becomes the ancestress of a king—her societal position is literally reversed. Ruth, as viewed through the eyes of *Parashat Behar*, is the *yovel* model of a woman: a divinely ordained egalitarianism gives her freedom to change her status and choose her religious identity, her life companions, and her inheritance, rather than allowing these things to be determined for her by the people around her. Boaz is the model benefactor who shares with the stranger not only his food but his soul.

In reality, it is unlikely that the land release of the *shmita* and the *yovel* gained any lasting economic equality for women, since women who had brothers could not inherit land. Nevertheless, the Torah presents us with the idea that existing social norms are temporary, that we can change them in order to better our lives economically and spiritually. The maidservant who lives off the charity of the land can become the maidservant who founds a new dynasty. In this biblical truth lies a powerful justification for the feminist reclamation of Torah.

The Meaning of *Ge'ulah* for Feminists

The road to that new dynasty, like Ruth's road, must be peopled with friends and supporters. *Parashat Behar* gives good advice on how kinsfolk can help each other in time of need. This help is called *ge'ulah* (redemption). A near relative is expected to redeem an Israelite who has been sold as a slave to a non-Israelite by paying his sale price to the "owner" (Lev. 25:49). A relative is also expected to redeem ancestral land that a poor individual has had to sell (Lev. 25:25). Although the principle of redemption only pertains to tribal and ancestral relations, we can extend it to include the larger community, for the Torah says, "You shall love the stranger" (Deut. 10:19). The Torah teaches that other people's misfortunes are our own problem.

The message for modern feminists is clear: sisterhood is powerful. Taking the mitzvah of *ge'ulah* seriously in our day means lending a hand not only to our families, but to our adopted networks of kinsfolk. We can practice *ge'ulah* toward each other in various private and public ways, including but not limited to political and financial support, spiritual community, and the gifts of the heart we give by our care and concern for each other. Specifically, we can practice *ge'ulah* as feminists. There are *agunot*, women chained to their husbands by Jewish divorce law, who need redeeming from slavery. There are women who are enslaved by society's view of their roles and bodies. There are poor women struggling to survive around the world. There are women enslaved by drugs or alcohol. There are women whose economic deprivation forces them into prostitution, and there are women whose families actually sell them into slavery. This *parashah* reminds us how much our kinsfolk need us to further their redemption.

Not only do we need to redeem those who are oppressed by others, but we also need to recognize when we ourselves participate in or benefit from oppression. *Parashat Behar* teaches, "You shall not do evil to one another" (Lev. 25:14). It is not easy to make a transition to equality, to give up the privilege of ownership or of presumed superiority. In his "Letter from a Birmingham Jail," written in 1963, Martin Luther King Jr. wrote, "History is the long and tragic story of the fact that privileged groups seldom give up their privileges voluntarily."[5] Yet, through *ge'ulah*, we too are redeemed. *Shmita* and *yovel*, which demand the redemption of our neighbors, challenge us to liberate ourselves as well.

The God-Concept of *Parashat Behar*

God may free slaves and redeem the land, but God's ascribed motivation in the text is disturbing. God's image is that of a slaveowner. "It is to Me that the Israelites are servants [slaves]" (Lev. 25:55). Some feminist theologians have questioned this concept of God, because even though it rejects the notion of human masters, it still keeps the relationship of master to slave as the theological ideal.

We should be particularly sensitive to the implications of this image, because it has been connected with the authority of men over women. God as the loving but authoritarian patriarch has intimations of men in the same role; for example, the prophet Hosea compares God to an authoritarian husband (Hos. 2:3–22). This image traps women in a series of rigid hierarchical relationships when what might be preferable would be to rethink the entire relationship structure. In fact, this is what many feminists have done. Various Jewish communities have experimented with ways of referring to God without invoking traditional hierarchical names. While the notion of commandedness and the idea of God's sovereignty are still meaningful for many feminists, feminism has forced the Jewish community to imagine God in new ways.

Perhaps one of these new images of God could come from *Behar* itself. In Lev. 25:12, we read, "For it is a *yovel*, it shall be a holy thing to you," *Ki yovel hi, kodesh tihiye lachem.* This can also be translated, "She is a *yovel* to you, she shall be a holy entity to you." God is our *Yovel*, the ultimate sabbath on which we rest, the place where we do not need to produce anything, but are accepted as we are. The word *yovel* comes from a root meaning "ram's horn."[6] God is the ram's horn that sounds our liberation from all that oppresses us.

What Is Liberty?

The Torah teaches, *Ukratem dror ba'aretz,* "Proclaim liberty through-out the land" (Lev. 25:10). The same language, *dror,* is used by the prophet Jeremiah to describe the *shmita* year (Jer. 34:8, 15, 17). In the Midrash, the rabbis ask why the Torah uses the unusual term *dror,* "liberty," with regard to the *yovel* and the *shmita.* Why not use the much more common language of *cherut,* "freedom"? Rabbi Judah answers that the origin of *dror* is *dira* (dwelling), and that one who is truly free is one who dwells in a dwelling.[7] In his commentary on Lev. 25:10, Rashi explains Rabbi Judah's elusive response: "One [is truly liberated when he] dwells in any place in which he desires, and is not under the authority of any other person." One medieval rabbi writes, "All strife originates from the attitude of 'mine is mine' and people claiming their prerogatives. But in the seventh year all are equal—this can indeed generate peace."[8] The *shmita* and the *yovel* each bring true freedom to the people—freedom from imposed authority, freedom from materialism, freedom from oppression, freedom from inequality.

"Then you shall blast the shofar" (Lev. 25:9). Jewish women are holding their breaths for the great shofar blast that guarantees our freedom. The *shmita* and the *yovel* are times for radical redefinition of what exists, and redefinition is one of the major tasks of Jewish feminists as we reimagine ourselves, our relationships, Torah, tra-dition, and God. While the *shmita* is still observed every seven years in the Land of Israel, the date of the *yovel* has been lost. We need to imagine a new kind of *yovel* in which we *amahot* of the Jewish people gain our freedom and claim our inheritance. That is a jubilee we would be glad to celebrate.

RABBI ELIZABETH BOLTON

בחקתי

Bechukotai

Mir Zaynen Do—We Are Here

When I break for you your staff of bread, ten women shall bake your bread in one oven; they will restore your bread by weight, and though you eat, you will not be sated. (LEVITICUS 26:26)

AT A SHABBAT MORNING SERVICE ONE FEBRUARY, I stepped out just before the Torah reading to accompany my preschooler to her children's service. The skilled and inventive leader always involves us all in prayer and Torah through movement. That Shabbat, a young boy played a mountain, Mount Sinai, to be exact, for the puppet Moses, who climbed up on him to receive the Torah. The service leader, playing Moses, dramatically recited all the rules that the people had to observe at the base of the mountain—don't touch the mountain; don't approach it for three days; wash your clothes—while I waited to see how she would dramatize, in an age-appropriate manner, Moses' additional injunction to the people, "Don't go near a woman" (Exod. 19:10–15).

Of course, she left it out. It was, after all, Moses' own elaboration of God's message, in any case. But it is a coded message at a "codify-ing" moment, the giving of the Ten Commandments, and

246

the transformation of the Israelite ex-slaves into God's treasured, holy people. Exactly who was being addressed at the base of the mountain—all the Israelites, or just the men? The moment is so critical that theologian Judith Plaskow entitled her study of feminist Judaism *Standing Again at Sinai.*[1]

If we women weren't *there*, where *do* we stand?

Every time that we encounter a Torah text that either egregiously omits women, or identifies women by name or as a group, it is worth noting. Such a gender-specific naming occurs in *Parashat Bechukotai*. Coming at the end of the Book of Leviticus, replete with its challenging and difficult passages around holiness, "purity," and women's status, these verses seem to reinforce an overall gloss of Torah text in general, and Leviticus in particular, as indicative of a diminished status for women in ancient Israelite culture.

Yet, once we assert our claim that we were *there*, we are obligated to figure out how to be fully *here*.

The first half of *Bechukotai* (Lev. 26:3–46) looks like a parenting handbook. God has instructed co-parent Moses to tell the children how to behave. If they are good, they'll be rewarded, and if they misbehave, they'll be punished. Undertaking the challenge of parenting a newly birthed and potentially unruly nation, God follows the classic covenanting formula of the day, consisting of blessing and execration/curse. The same formula appears again in *Parashat Ki Tavo* (Deut. 28–30).[2]

The blessings are brief and somewhat triumphalist, the curses ugly and inventive. "If you follow [literally, "walk" in my laws *[bechukotai]*]," the passage begins, "then I [God] will give you . . ." The list begins with good growing and planting outcomes—a must for an agriculturally based community—and follows with assurances of peace and military victories. The curses are much longer, and build up from the reversal of fortunes in the face of the enemy to a feverish list of doomsday horrors.

It is here that women are first named. In the face of devastation and desolation, God adds, "When I break for you your staff of bread, ten women shall bake your bread in one oven; they will restore your bread by weight, and though you eat, you will not be sated" (Lev. 26:26).

Here is how one commentator took note of this passage. The Rashbam explains that "ten" women should be understood to mean "many," referring to another passage in the Bible where the phrase "ten times" should be understood to mean "many times."[3] Like others in his era, Rashbam was interested in clarifying the literal meaning of the text. So when he continues his commentary on the verse by suggesting that the phrase "in one oven" tells us that one woman alone was not able to fill the oven with bread, we are invited to picture an actual community of women, helping each other with their daily domestic tasks.

While this may lead us on a welcome break from the harsh images of the text, Rashbam does not allow us to get too caught up in this vision of a women's world. He continues his analysis by explaining that the phrase "they will restore your bread by weight" indicates that the women will then return the bread, in meager weights of scanty rations, to their husbands. He also draws our attention to Ezek. 4:16, which also uses the phrase "to break the staff of bread." A contemporary commentator notes that this is the origin of the aphorism "bread is the staff of life."[4]

Yet, before we abandon the vision, let us imagine where it could lead us. Consider this stream of connections: The women of the community share an oven, baking bread together. During their long hours together they spell each other, take care of each other's children, sharing lore, and learning about their many tasks and responsibilities. They learn from each other, acknowledge each other's skills, and come to pay particular attention to those among them who have particular leadership qualities. Young and old, girls and women, as well as their menfolk, grant these sages and leaders the respect that is their due.

They may be largely unnamed, but how could they not be present? The reader, suddenly challenged to focus on women in the overall picture, is thus able to turn Rashbam's comment into a window, making it an opportunity to "re-vision" the biblical world.

Returning to the larger context, that of blessings and curses, we know from other passages in Torah, and Prophets as well, that some biblical women accepted, and deeply felt, the Divine's power to "bless" them with progeny or "curse" them with empty wombs. Their varying responses, from Sarah's laugh at the messenger's prediction that she would have a child after she stopped menstruating (Gen. 18:9–15), to Rachel's weeping and bargaining with her husband, maidservant, and sister (Gen. 30:1–24), show our foremothers resisting any sense of complacency or resignation regarding their fate. They are seen proactively responding to their circumstances, even though they may have understood their lives as being filled with both blessings and curses.

Contemporary translator and commentator Everett Fox characterizes Lev. 26 as "the first great monotheistic response to catastrophe, built on the idea that humans beings have the capacity to influence their fate by obeying or disobeying God."[5] In response to the theological underpinning of this chapter, Ellen Frankel suggests that we can read the *parashah*'s images as "Foreshadowing the Destruction," her heading for the following passage:

> Our Daughters ask: Moses warns the people that ter-
> rible things will happen if they fail to uphold God's
> laws of holiness: They'll face ruin and destruction,
> and the nations of the world will crush them between
> the millstones of history. As it is written: "Ten women
> shall bake your bread in a single oven and dole it out
> by weight," yet even such measures will fail to satisfy
> the people's hunger? Where do these horrific images
> come from . . . ?
>
> Our Mothers add: Such images recall our recent near
> destruction, when even one hundred women could not
> fill a single oven with bread but instead entered the
> ovens themselves and fed the hungry flames.
>
> Lilith the Rebel cries: But it was not our failure that
> led to the Holocaust. It was God's! Where was God
> when we were suffering?
>
> Mother Rachel adds: And where was the rest of the
> world?[6]

By situating a women's response to issues of suffering in the
voices of Rachel (who suffered), Lilith (who was excluded),[7] and
ourselves ("our" daughters and mothers), Frankel expands the window frame, enabling us to see the larger picture of women in the
Bible as leading to, and including, our generation and those to
come. She is also one of an increasing number of Jewish and
women writers to include in their work questions and visions
regarding women's experiences of, as well as feminist perspectives
on, the Holocaust.[8]

The issues of suffering, Divine absence, and human responsibility have challenged an increasing number of contemporary Jewish theologians, but they were also a concern to traditional
commentators. There are many parables in the Midrash and Tal-

mud that explore the concept of free will and its link to Divine reward and punishment.[9] Some hew to the framework cast by our *parashah*. For example, an early collection of midrash on the Book of Leviticus has the sage Rabbi Eleazar explaining that "God presented the Jewish people with a package from heaven, containing the Torah and a sword. If you do not live according to Torah, then you will be destroyed by the sword."[10] An alternate traditional view, that God rewards or punishes our behavior not in this life but in the afterlife, can be just as challenging to our sensibilities.[11]

The Book of Leviticus and the Priestly Code, with its many instances of separation and exclusion for women, comes to a final close with the addition of a coda, chapter 27, detailing donations for the upkeep of the sanctuary. Gifts are valued on a scale that counts women at one-half to two-thirds the monetary equivalent of men.

To the last, *Parashat Bechukotai* challenges us. If the text excludes us when we are not named, then should we include ourselves in such passages as blessings and curses? Surely, contemporary Jewish praxis would look different if we read the covenanting passages as excluding or exempting a whole class of Jews. And yet, this has been the experience of many Jewish women, who have searched in vain for a reflection of themselves in Torah, particularly once they move from the family narratives of Genesis and the nation-founding narratives of Exodus into the more disturbing prescriptions of Leviticus.

Just as the midrashists and commentators creatively struggled with difficult messages and images, so shall we. And just as the various cataclysms of Jewish history forced the subsequent generation to recast the forms—and content—of Jewish life, so shall we continue the process of visioning ourselves. As the song *Zog Nit Keyn Mol*, the hymn of the United Partisan Organization proudly declares, *Mir zaynen do*, "We are here!"[12]

Can a feminist rereading of *Bechukotai* and other passages of Torah with difficult theological implications help reestablish or reconfigure a healthy relationship with *brit* (covenant) for girls, women, Jews by choice, lesbian and gay Jews, Jews with disabilities, and all who question the notion of a Divine figure who rewards and punishes?

It can, and it must, for the simple reason that we were all *there*.

We were at Sinai, we witnessed the Temple's destruction, we stood at the abyss of history, and *we are here*.

Bamidbar/Numbers

RABBI SHERYL NOSAN

במדבר

Bamidbar

Beyond *Pidyon Ha-ben:* Blessings for Giving Life

I sanctified every first-born male of Israel . . . to be Mine. (NUMBERS 3:13)

AT A LOCAL RABBINIC ASSOCIATION MEETING I heard a familiar conversation. A colleague who was attending her first meeting since her maternity leave was bombarded with questions. "How's the baby?" "How many pounds?" "When was the bris?" "Is he cute?" And then, finally, someone asked the new mother, "And by the way, how are you?"

In our contemporary society, such a conversation, focusing on the newborn rather than the parent, may be commonplace. We assume that lavishing attention on the newborn child is natural, while considering the new parent as secondary. I suggest that such an assumption should be challenged, because it eclipses the miracle of creating a new life and obscures a lifecycle event worthy of blessings and celebration.

Parashat Bamidbar offers insight into some of our ancestors' assumptions about children and women. According to Num. 3:11–13,

255

> Adonai spoke to Moses saying: Behold, I take the
> Levites from among the children of Israel in place of
> all the first-born male issue of the womb from the
> children of Israel; the Levites will be Mine. Every first-
> born male is Mine, because on the day I smote each
> first-born male in the land of Egypt, I sanctified each
> first-born male of Israel, man and beast, they will be
> Mine, [for] Me, Adonai.

This text highlights biblical assumptions that conflict with our current sensibilities about children in families. First, today we assume that our children are *ours.* Parents may feel a particularly strong sense of ownership of their first child. In this *parashah,* however, it is clear that the first-born male is God's. Second, according to our modern ideal, we value all children equally, without preference as to gender, birth order, or manner of birth. The passage, however, reminds us that in biblical narrative and law, the birth of males is celebrated and valued more than the birth of females.[1] Furthermore, the text teaches us that biblical law accords the first-born male with a special status.[2] The first-born male has unique privileges (such as his claim to a double portion of his father's inheritance in Deut. 21:17) as well as unique obligations. The most important obligation is to God, who asserts a uniquely sanctified relationship with the first-born male, and claims rights to the first-born themselves. This claim is in compensation for saving the Israelite's first-born males when the first-born Egyptians were killed before the exodus from Egypt (Exod. 13:2; Num. 3:13; 8:17).

God's possessive claim on the first-born males is modified, however, by two provisions. First, God substitutes the men of the tribe of Levi for the first-born males of all the rest of the Israelites (Num. 3:11–13). Second, while God states that "every first issue of the womb is Mine," God informs the Israelites that they "must redeem every firstborn among [their] sons" (Exod. 34:19–20). This redemption technically frees the firstborn from dedicating his physical self and his life service to God through the Temple. It also frees him of certain ritual constraints and obligations. Because the Levites are taken in place of the first-born, they cannot be redeemed from their special service, constraints, or obligations. Similarly, the *kohanim* (the priestly tribe associated with the tribe of Levi) cannot be redeemed. All other Israelites, however, can be redeemed according to the instructions offered in Num. 18:15–16:

> The first issue of the womb of every being, man or beast, that is offered to Adonai shall be yours; but you shall have the first-born of man redeemed. . . . Take as their redemption price, from the age of one month up, the money equivalent of five shekels. . . .

Thus, God commands the people to redeem every first-born son, and God takes the Levites for Temple service in place of the first male issue of the womb. This redemptive exchange is the basis for *pidyon ha-ben,* the ritual for "the redemption of the first-born son."

Pidyon ha-ben is a ritual that continues to be practiced. According to tradition, following the eligible child's thirtieth day, the father gives five silver coins in the presence of guests to a man who claims priestly descent.[3] Certain formulas and blessings are recited, and a festive meal follows. The mitzvah of *pidyon ha-ben* may be observed only if a series of conditions are met. The child must be male. He must be the *peter rechem,* the baby who "bursts the womb" and is delivered vaginally (according to tradition, this excludes children born by Caesarean section as well as those born following a previous miscarriage of a fetus more than forty days old).[4] The infant may not be of priestly descent. If the father is descended from the tribes of Kohen or Levi, or if the mother is a daughter of a Kohen or Levi, the child cannot be redeemed from his priestly status and *pidyon ha-ben* is not performed (*Yoreh De'ah* 305:18).

These specifications exclude the majority of children from the mitzvah of the redemption of the first-born male. Nonetheless, for numerous reasons, the mitzvah can be meaningful when observed. First, the ritual of *pidyon ha-ben*, like every ritual, provides an opportunity to increase the sanctity in our lives and enhance our connection to God and tradition. Second, through *pidyon ha-ben*, families continue to recall the exodus from Egypt. In doing so, they echo overarching themes of freedom and responsibility, for while the first-born is now freed from obligation to the priesthood, he is not freed from obligation to God, Judaism, and the larger world. Thus, the move from slavery in Egypt to responsibility at Sinai is dramatically reenacted.

Finally, *pidyon ha-ben* reminds us of God's claim not only on the first-born, but also on all of us. As a family celebrates the redemption of the first-born, family members and friends all acknowledge that our Jewish ideal is for all of us to be "a kingdom of priests and a holy people" (Exod. 19:6).

While *pidyon ha-ben* continues to be practiced in its traditional form, many liberal Jews have sought new, more inclusive rituals. Today, rituals exist that expand our tradition, echoing *pidyon ha-ben* while emphasizing the redemptive potential of each child, regardless of gender or manner of birth.[5] These ceremonies are important, yet leave a gap, for no ritual has yet been embraced which recognizes the absolute uniqueness that accompanies a *first* birth, for only a first child changes an adult into a parent, or a couple into a family.

The precursor to birth-related ceremonies is found in the Torah, which offered a ritual for a new mother whereby she would bring sin offerings and burnt offerings to the Temple following her defined postpartum ritual impurity (Lev. 12:6). Such offerings were a gateway from a woman's experience of birthing back into the activities of the Temple cult. According to *Niddah* 31b, the sin offering was required because of what the woman might have said regarding her husband during the pain of childbirth. In contemporary times, some women continue the practice of going to the *mikveh* for ritual purification after giving birth.

Prayers offering thanks for successful births, and for the health, strength, and the well-being of mother and child, can be found in collections of *techines* (Yiddish prayers written by and for Jewish women, which were unsanctioned but popular in eighteenth-century Europe) as well as in contemporary liturgy.[6] *Birkat Ha Gomel,* the traditional prayer giving thanks for surviving dangerous situations, continues to be recited by many men on behalf of their wives as well as by women themselves after childbirth.

While many rituals and prayers are associated with childbirth, none of them focus on the change from person to parent. Our rich and beautiful heritage, while replete with blessings for mitzvot associated with special occasions and blessings that acknowledge God's role at these moments, offers no specific blessings for people to say at times of personal inner change. There are traditional blessings such as *ha-tov v'ha'mativ* ("Who has done good things for me") and *shehechiyanu* ("Who has kept us alive"), which may be recited at any important moments, but neither one specifically relates to the particular occasion of bringing forth life for the first time. There is no distinct blessing for a man to say upon becoming a father, or for a woman to say upon becoming a mother. Therefore, many contemporary Jews who wish to adapt the traditional form of blessings for these personal moments have sought to invent new *brachot*.[7]

In giving birth, a woman becomes a producer of life. It is fitting that she blesses God and celebrates her unique change. When a man's partner gives birth, he becomes a biological father, without whom there would be no new life. It is fitting that he blesses God and celebrates his unique change as well. *Parashat Bamidbar* reminds us of the significance and awesome sanctity accompanying the emergence of the first-born of a woman's womb. By celebrating being partners with God in the miracle of creation, men and women can, and should, sanctify not only their children's lives, but also their own.

נשא

Naso

Inscribing Jealousy on the Bodies of Women

NUMBERS 5:11–31 SUGGESTS A DISTURBING ORDEAL for a husband who suspects his wife of adulterous behavior. The biblical text describing the ordeal is somewhat unclear and seems to contradict itself in several places. This offers later commentators fertile ground for explanations and emendations.

Let us begin with the text.

The circumstances:

> ¹¹YHVH spoke to Moses saying,
> ¹²Speak to the children of Israel and say to them: Any man, any man [*ish ish*] whose wife goes astray committing a trespass against him [*ma'alah vo ma'al*],
> ¹³in that a man performs sexual relations with her with an emission of seed, and it is hidden from the eyes of her husband, and she concealed herself, and she became *temayah* [corrupted, defiled, inaccessible], and there was no witness against her, and she was not apprehended—
> ¹⁴and a spirit of jealousy washes over him, and he was jealous of his wife and she had become *temayah*, or a spirit of jealousy washes over him, and he was jealous

of his wife, and she had not become *temayah*—"

(The term *ma'alah vo ma'al* refers to using objects that have been set aside, specifically reserved for God. With this terminology the text equates an object set aside for use solely by God with a woman's body, set aside for use solely by her husband.)

The proceeding, stage one:

> [15]that man shall bring his wife to the priest, and he shall bring an offering for her—one tenth of an ephah of barley flour. And he shall not pour upon it any oil, and he shall not put frankincense on it for it is an offering of jealousy, an offering of remembrance, a remembrance of wrongdoing.
>
> [16]And the priest shall bring her near and stand her before YHVH.
>
> [17]And the priest shall take holy water in a clay dish and from the dirt that is [will be] on the floor of the tabernacle the priest shall take and place into the water.
>
> [18]And the priest shall stand the woman before YHVH, and shall bare the head of the woman, and shall place on her hands the offering of remembrance—it is an offering of jealousy—and in the hands of the priest shall be the bitter waters-that-induce-the-spell.[1]
>
> [19]And the priest shall adjure the woman and shall say to the woman, "If a man did not perform sexual relations with you, and if you did not stray in the ways of *tumah* under your husband['s authority][2] [or, "in place of your husband"], be clean through these waters-that-induce-the-spell.
>
> [20]And you—if you strayed under your husband['s authority] [or, "in place of your husband"] and if you incurred *tumah* and if a man placed his emission inside of you, other than your husband—

[21]here the priest shall adjure the woman with the oath of curse and the priest shall say to the woman, "YHVH shall make you a curse and a cause-for-oath[3] among your people in that YHVH shall make your thigh fall and your belly distend. [22]May these waters-that-induce-the-spell enter your innards to distend your belly and to cause your thigh to fall." And the woman shall say, "Amen, amen."

The proceeding, stage two:

[23]And the priest shall write these curses in the document and shall rub them into the waters of bitterness. [24]And he shall make the woman drink the bitter waters-that-induce-the-spell and the waters-that-induce-the-spell shall enter her and cause bitterness. [25]And the priest shall take the offering of jealousy from the hand of the woman and wave the offering before YHVH and offer it on the altar. [26]And the priest shall scoop out of the offering a token reminder, and he shall burn it on the altar and afterwards he shall make the woman drink the water. [27]When he has made her drink the water it shall be—if she has incurred *tumah* and she has committed a trespass [*va'tim'ol ma'al*] against her man—that the waters-that-induce-the-spell shall enter her and cause bitterness, and her belly shall distend, and her thigh shall fall, and the woman shall become a curse in the midst of her people; [28]and if the woman has not incurred *tumah* and she is *tehorah*, that she shall be cleared, and she shall conceive seed. [29]This is the *torah* of jealousy with regard to a woman straying from under her husband['s authority] and incurring *tumah*.

> [30]Or a man over whom the spirit of jealousy passes, and who becomes jealous of his wife, and places his wife before YHVH, the priest shall do to her all of this *torah*.
> [31]The man shall be clean from iniquity, and that woman shall bear her iniquity.

On the surface, it would seem that some basic assumptions underlie this ritual: women are required to remain faithful to their husbands, whereas no such restrictions are placed upon men; women are responsible for men's feelings of jealousy; and most importantly, a man's jealousy may work itself out on a woman's body.

*H*er Problem or His?

It would seem from verses 12–13 that the subject matter of this section concerns an adulterous woman, that is, a woman who has gone astray by being sexual with a man other than her husband. But the text uses four different literary expressions to demonstrate that this act took place without the husband's, or anyone else's, awareness: "it is hidden from the eyes of her husband"; "she concealed herself"; "there was no witness"; "she was not apprehended." Thus, the text seems to suggest what a husband should do if a woman commits adultery and he doesn't know it. But if he doesn't know it, why should he want to do anything? Seemingly, he would be oblivious to the entire episode.

While the text begins as if it is concerned with the subject of adultery, it soon becomes clear that this is not its topic at all. Although the opening, in verse twelve, seems to discuss an adulterous woman, the subject is the husband ("any man whose wife has gone astray"), rather than the woman herself (which might read: "any woman who has gone astray"). The subject of this section of Torah is not her adultery (which may or may not have occurred, since there is no actual evidence), but rather, his jealousy.

This is further corroborated by the continuation of the passage. While the passage begins by discussing a woman who has gone astray, and while we expect the punishment or consequences to follow, the text diverges for a moment to tell us that this must be done *whether or not* the woman has actually gone astray (verse 14). The same ordeal takes place even if clearly the woman has done nothing wrong. Again, the issue is not her transgression, but the husband's possessiveness and insecurity.

Why, then, does the text begin by addressing her sin rather than his jealousy? In an interesting narrative performance, the text wanders from one perspective to the next, giving us at one moment the subjective perspective of the individual man, and at another moment the objective perspective of a narrator. On the one hand, the individual man looks at his wife (who may or may not have done any "wrong") and says, "My wife has committed a trespass against me." On the other hand, the objective narrator is able to see the situation for what it is, to look at the man and see that it is his jealousy that is speaking, and not the actions of the woman. It seems almost as if the text keeps catching itself in the act of slipping into the subjective male perspective and, as it catches itself, moving back to the objective perspective. Thus, the text continually strays from treating her action as the difficulty, to acknowledging that his jealousy is the real problem at hand.

A second textual difficulty is found in verse fifteen: "for it is an offering of jealousy, an offering of remembrance, a remembrance of wrongdoing." Again, the language of the text is ambiguous. Whose wrongdoing? If it is an offering of jealousy that is to be brought, would the wrongdoing not be the jealousy itself? Read in this way, the text itself addresses jealousy as the wrongdoing that requires atonement. The man, not the woman, brings the offering. The text states that he brings it "for her," usually understood as "in place of her." But would it not make better sense that he brings it "on account of her," that is, "for his jealousy of her"? The word "jealousy" repeats itself in the text a total of ten times. It is his jealousy that requires remedy and sacrifice.

Just One Man?—the Social Problem of Male Jealousy

The repetition of the word *ish* (man) in verse twelve is a biblical literary device used to convey generality: "each man." The rabbis, however, often use word repetition as an exegetical tool, asking, "What does the extra word come to teach us?" Of this particular text, Rashi offers this commentary: *Ish Ish*, to teach that she transgresses against two men—against the man of war who is above (i.e., God [cf. Exod. 15:3]), and against her husband who is below.

The implications of Rashi's commentary are twofold. First, the medieval commentator takes the perspective only of the subjective male and disregards the objective perspective altogether, claiming this as an issue of her sin rather than his jealousy. And second, the earthly male husband becomes conflated with the heavenly male God, creating an alliance of the two "men" against the sinning woman.

If we explicate the doubling of the word *ish* somewhat differently from Rashi, the focus returns to what we can claim is the intent of the original biblical passage, concentrating on the men and not the women. Were Rashi to have looked at this from a feminist perspective, he might have written this: *Ish Ish,* to teach that this is not a case that might happen only once, with one man, but rather, that this is a societal problem that happens often, with many men.

This is a text meant to deal with a societal problem, one that we are still confronting today.

The Solution—the Humiliation of Women as a Societal Mechanism

The text makes it clear that this societal problem of men's jealousy is marked onto the bodies of women. In our Torah text, the woman's hair is exposed—a sign of disgrace associated with mourning or with leprosy. In the legal text of the Mishnah, the ordeal is embellished to include public humiliation and further degradation. Her clothes are torn to bare her breast/heart before the high court of seventy-one men (*Sotah* I:4–5). The combination of the ritual humiliation, the fear that this ordeal would have caused (whether or not she was guilty of the crime), and the drinking of the water mixed with dirt and ink, is a testament to the physical acting out of male jealousy on the female body.

Rabbi Toba Spitzer points out that the text, with all its difficulties, must be seen as taking responsibility for male jealousy as a societal problem, and for introducing a societal mechanism for its resolution. Whereas today men kill women in jealous rages—all of which the media represent as normative—in the biblical period jealousy was not an individual problem to be solved by an individual man in whatever way he saw fit. The biblical text attempted to deal with an otherwise impossible problem that could have worked itself out in more dangerous and painful ways.

While this may be true, it seems to me that in the final reckoning, the biblical solution is not dissimilar to today's lack of solution. While in our culture the jealousy of men is acted out on the bodies of women through physical harm and even murder, in the days of the Bible, though there was a societal mechanism in place, that mechanism was one of fear and humiliation. This brings to mind the feminist position that the role of the rapist (or in our case, the modern-day jealous husband) and that of the protector (or of the biblical ordeal, meant to "protect" her from a vigilante husband) are similar in nature. In both of our cases, modern day and biblical, the woman becomes a victim, unable to protect herself. Both treat woman as the cause of the problem and both see her degradation or physical harm as the solution to that problem. Neither solution takes the focus off the object of jealousy (the woman) and places it on the deserving subject (the man). Thus, even while understanding the problem as societal rather individual, the Torah text leaves us still demanding a better solution to an ongoing problem.

The Text's Internal Condemnation of Itself

The text itself, however, does not clearly condone this ritual or support the husband's lack of control over his emotions. In truth, the Torah may be seen as exhibiting ambivalence toward the husband's jealousy and toward the entire ordeal, ambivalence that is exhibited through the process of the ritual itself.

The ordeal ends when the priest writes the curses that he has spoken (verses 19–22)—curses that contain the four-letter ineffable name of God—on a sheet of parchment (verse 23), and places them in the bitter waters. The writing on the parchment, complete with the name of God, is erased, dissolving into the water. In fact, then, by bringing the woman before God to perform this ritual, the husband causes the name of God to be erased. This ordeal, which utterly humiliates an often innocent woman, ultimately results in the erasure of the holy name of God.

The act of humiliation itself, according to Jewish tradition, is tantamount to erasure. The rabbis of the Talmud claim that "one who shames another, it is as though s/he has shed blood" (*Bava Metziah* 58b–59a). By causing her shame, the husband has, in effect, murdered her, causing her erasure. In performing this ritual, the four letters of God's name, YHVH—letters that in Hebrew signify the essence of Being itself—are wiped out of existence, just as she is. The Torah's decisive statement is that the shaming of women is, in fact, the erasure of God.

By what means might we hold our own society accountable for the jealousy that often claims the lives of women? By what means might we bring before God an "offering of jealousy" that truly reflects and appeases the feelings of the jealous partner without inscribing itself on the body of the victim? *Parashat Naso* teaches us that only at that time when we can bring women back to full human status, only when each of us can take responsibility for our own actions in the world and not act out our feelings on others, and only when we can see each other and treat each other as full human beings will the name of God cease to be erased from the parchment.

RABBI RUTH H. SOHN

בהעלתך
Beha'alotecha

The Silencing of Miriam

*M*iriam and Aaron spoke against Moses
because of the Cushite woman whom he had
married; for he had married a Cushite woman.
(NUMBERS 12:1)

PERHAPS THERE IS NO WOMAN FROM THE BIBLE who inspires women today more than Miriam. Even more than any of the matriarchs, Miriam has been embraced and celebrated by Jewish women in *Rosh Chodesh* rituals, Miriam's cups at Seder tables, and in modern midrash, poetry, and song. The Torah presents us with the figure of Miriam standing at the sea with timbrel in hand, leading the women in dance and song. This powerful image suggests that Miriam was a true leader among the Israelites, a point supported by the prophet Micah: "I brought you up from the land of Egypt, and redeemed you from the house of bondage; and I sent before you Moses, Aaron, and Miriam" (Mic. 6:4). Miriam's Well, which, according to traditional midrash, accompanied the Israelites through their desert wanderings, providing the Israelites with sorely needed water and, symbolically, spiritual sustenance, has continued to inspire Jews in both ritual and lore.[1] Yet, Miriam is spoken of only five times in the Torah, with two of those references consisting of only a single verse each.[2] The longest narrative involving Miriam as a key figure comes at the end of our *parashah*. This is not the best-known story about Miriam, largely because it is such a complex and troubling narrative. It is a narrative that leaves us with more questions than answers about who Miriam was and how her role among the Israelites— indeed, how the role of women as a group—should be understood.

The opening verse of our story raises many questions, among which the first is, Who is this Cushite woman? It could be Tziporah, the Midianite woman whom Moses had married years before, whose father is referred to earlier in our *parashah*. But perhaps this reference is to a second wife. Miriam and Aaron are upset, yet the text is not clear as to why. Was it because this was a foreign wife, or because she was a second wife? And finally, the verse begins with the verb *vatedaber*, which means "she spoke," and yet, it is both Miriam and Aaron who speak out against Moses. The text grammatically implicates Miriam but not her brother. Why?

The second verse, rather than providing answers, only raises more questions. Numbers 12:2 continues, "They said 'Has Adonai spoken only through Moses? Has God not spoken through us as well?'" Here, it seems that Miriam and Aaron are questioning Moses' position as the primary leader of the Israelites rather than his choice of a spouse. It is as prophets that they compare themselves to Moses. They ask, rhetorically, whether they aren't also prophets. What is behind this challenge to Moses' authority? What grievance on Miriam and Aaron's part leads to these words? And how is this complaint related to the previous verse about the Cushite woman?

As the narrative continues to unfold, God responds in anger to Miriam and Aaron for daring to question Moses' singular role as prophet of Israel. God tells Miriam and Aaron that Moses is indeed in a category by himself as one who speaks to God direct-ly, *peh el peh*, "mouth to mouth." But even God's response leads to more questions. Why is there no reference here or anywhere else in the chapter to the Cushite woman of verse one? God departs in anger, and Miriam is stricken with *tzara'at*, a scaly, white disease of the skin. Miriam is singled out for harsh punishment and ultimate-ly shut out from the camp for seven days, but Aaron is not punished at all. Again, we are forced to ask why.

Several modern scholars suggest that the apparent lack of con-nection between verses 1 and 2 may be explained by the fact that these opening verses are actually fragments of different traditions pieced together.[3] Some scholars also note that God's response in verses 6–8, which begins, "Now hear My words," is a distinct lit-erary unit, more poetic in form, that might also have originated in a different context:[4]

> Now hear My words: When a prophet of Adonai aris-es among you, I make Myself known to him in a vision, I speak with him in a dream. Not so with My servant Moses; throughout My household he is trust-ed. With him I speak mouth to mouth, and not in rid-dles, and I appear plainly, and he beholds the likeness of Adonai. How is it then, that you were not afraid to speak against My servant Moses! (Num. 12:6–8)

This response from God never mentions Miriam or Aaron by name and could well have been uttered originally to a whole group of people. If we accept this theory of different textual traditions woven together, the murmuring against Moses and subsequent defense in this narrative may be evidence of a whole body of tra-dition that, in different ways, challenges Moses' behavior and exer-cise of power. These narrative fragments all question how other leaders and potential leaders were able to function alongside Moses. Set against the backdrop of our *parashah*, which begins with the consecration of the Levites and a delineation of their duties, and with the rebellion of Korach reported a few chapters later, Num. 12 opens a window on the challenges threatening Moses' seemingly unchallenged, singular leadership.

How Moses exercised and shared leadership is in fact a subject treated more broadly in our *parashah*. At first reading, the Torah emphasizes Moses' humility and ability to share the stage with others. In Num. 11, it is Moses who turns to God and asks that the burden of solitary leadership be eased. When God suggests that Moses delegate power and responsibility among seventy elders, Moses very willingly agrees. These elders begin to prophesy after God transfers some of the *ruach* (spirit) from Moses to them, and afterwards, two men, Eldad and Medad, remain prophesying in the camp. When Joshua and another young man run and report this to Moses in alarm, Moses responds, "Are you wrought up on my account? Would that all Adonai's people were prophets, that Adonai would put the Divine spirit upon them!" When others view Eldad and Medad's behavior as a possible affront to their leader, Moses appears humble and ready to share leadership with as many others as would present themselves.

But Num. 12 presents a more complex picture. On the one hand, we have the narrator's words, "Moses was a very humble man, more so than any other man on earth," immediately following Miriam and Aaron's complaints against Moses. These words support the previous chapters' description of Moses. And in Num. 12 itself, it is not Moses who rebukes Miriam and Aaron, but God. Yet, on the other hand, in this same chapter, Miriam and Aaron question Moses' behavior and their own respective roles as prophets. When they do so, God soundly rebukes them, and Miriam is singled out for harsh punishment. Were Miriam and Aaron forgetting their place and overstepping reasonable limits on their authority, or were they voicing legitimate complaints about Moses' exercise of power? Their complaints could well represent a larger faction of discontent. Perhaps the question of leadership among the Israelites during the wilderness period is more complex than we thought.

The punishment of Miriam stands out in particular as a challenge to the notion suggested in the story of Eldad and Medad that anyone who was willing and worthy could lead. If it had been Aaron rather than Miriam who had spoken, would he have been punished in the same way? It is hard to escape the conclusion that it is as a woman challenging male authority that Miriam is so sharply rebuked and singled out for punishment. Miriam's punishment, in its severity, would have been a clear warning to her and to all other women to remember their place. God's sentence—the scaly, white skin affliction and the requirement that Miriam be shut out of the camp for seven days—demanded that Miriam symbolically act out her own death. Aaron's words to Moses, "let her not be as one dead," say no less. Miriam's words against Moses were, in a sense, her last. They are the last words we hear from her in the Torah. The next mention of Miriam is her death in Num. 20.

Miriam's treatment in Num. 12 seems symbolic of her treatment in the Torah as a whole. The prophet Micah tells us that Miriam was a principal leader of the Israelites along with Moses and Aaron. Where in the Torah are the narratives that detail her leadership? Miriam was a prophet, we learn in Exodus. Why, in the entire Torah, do we have not a single example of her prophecy? Miriam has been all but silenced and banished from the narrative. All we are left with is shards, fragments of a tale, hints of a reality that we are left to ponder and dream.

Why was Miriam silenced? Was there conflict over Miriam's leadership in her own day? Were there Israelites who claimed her as their leader while others contested her right to lead? Perhaps she served as a leader of the women. The fact that the people would not move on without Miriam while she was healing from her skin ailment suggests that she had quite a loyal following. Biblical scholar Ilana Pardes suggests, "[I]n Moses' day a woman with the gift of prophecy would have had to be silenced and then buried in the wilderness for daring to demand a central cultural position."[5] According to Pardes, Moses and Miriam's world was not ready for a woman with the gift of prophecy. Miriam was silenced by the Israelites of her own time, who were unwilling to have a woman in such a high position.

But there is another possible explanation for Miriam's silence in the Torah. Perhaps in her own day Miriam *was* a prophet and leader, and it was later generations who, in retelling the tales, silenced Miriam and all but banished her from the text. Perhaps it was the later generations who were not willing to have a woman with the gift of prophecy standing strong, inspiring the women of their own day to seek public roles and voice demands for themselves. This would better explain the shards, the fragments of the tale that we do have—the various references to Miriam as leader and prophet without the detailed narratives that would flesh out these claims. It would also explain our enigmatic section of Num. 12, which cryptically suggests Miriam's fate in the Torah as a whole: a woman who did rise to power who was posthumously denied that power and silenced.

Where modern scholarship asks us to take a step back and view the Torah narrative from afar, traditional Midrash invites us to jump into the text from a particular perspective. Both approaches seek to fill in the gaps in the Torah text—the questions that are raised by the text without apparent answers—through close attention to the details in the text and creative reconstruction. But modern scholarship examines the text from outside of it while Midrash examines it from within. We have explored some of the possibilities of looking at the text in new ways from the outside. Now let us reenter the text from the inside, with Midrash as our guide.

One midrashic tradition identifies the Cushite woman of Num. 12:I as Tziporah, and maintains that Miriam's complaint in verse I about Moses' marriage to a Cushite woman is actually a complaint on behalf of Tziporah, who had a serious grievance against her husband.[6] The starting point for this midrash is in Num. II, the narrative immediately preceding our own, where Eldad and Medad were discovered to be prophesying. When the young man ran and told Moses, Tziporah said, "Woe to the wives of those men!" Miriam heard this and realized from Tziporah's complaint that Moses was not fulfilling his conjugal responsibility to Tziporah. Miriam then spoke about the matter with Aaron.

Another midrash provides us with the details of the conversation that took place between Miriam and Aaron. "Miriam said, 'The Word was upon me but I did not keep away from my husband.' Aaron said: 'The Word was upon me but I did not keep away from my wife.'"[7] Miriam and Aaron question why Moses' role as a prophet exempts him from his conjugal duties as a husband. The midrashim further explain that it was because Miriam spoke *lashon hara*, gossip about Moses to Aaron, that she was punished, even though her intent was ultimately for the purpose of seeing him fulfill his duties to Tziporah. Miriam should have known better, the midrashim seem to be saying. She should have acted as Tziporah's advocate by taking the matter directly to Moses.

These midrashim artfully link the challenges raised in Num. 12:1 about the Cushite woman and Num. 12:2 about Moses' role as prophet in relation to Miriam's and Aaron's leadership, which on first reading seem disjointed and unrelated. They also raise several issues of interest to us as women and feminists.

First, these midrashim suggest that Miriam may have occasionally or regularly acted as an advocate for other women. It is not hard to imagine that Miriam's particular leadership role was as a leader of the Israelite women. Exodus 15, where Miriam leads the women in song and dance, suggests the same. As a leader of women, Miriam would have played a major role during the desert wanderings.

Second, with the suggestion that Moses, in fulfilling his responsibilities as a prophet, neglected his wife Tziporah, these midrashim raise the question of how an intense spiritual life can coexist with an intimate relationship with another human being. Do these two relationships enhance one another or are they in tension? What is the relationship between sexuality and spirituality? Many traditions, including our own, are ambivalent about bringing the two together. From the separation of men and women at Sinai to the traditional separation of men and women in Jewish prayer settings, a sense of the conflict between sexuality and spirituality has been expressed through the ages. Some other religious traditions require celibacy of their most devoted members, those who will be dedicating themselves most fully to a relationship with God. Is this how we can explain Moses' behavior and God's defense of him? Did Moses' role as prophet demand that he be "on call" for God and preclude any other intimate relationship, particularly a sexual one? Or did the intensity of his relationship with God lead Moses away from full engagement with people?

The Midrash itself takes a definite stand against Moses' behavior. It acknowledges that while Miriam was wrong for turning to

Aaron instead of confronting Moses directly, her claims against Moses were justified: even Moses' responsibilities as a prophet did not justify his neglect of Tziporah.[8] And if this level of spiritual asceticism was inappropriate for Moses, how much more so for us. We ought to be cultivating a spiritual life that leads us again and again back into life, back into deeper relationships with others.[9]

The two approaches of critical scholarship and traditional midrash, one looking at the text from without and the other from within, both yield rich insights. We need not choose between them. On the contrary, we can weave together the insights that we gain from each of them. We mourn for the Miriam who was silenced and banished in Num. 12 and from the Torah generally. Our anger and sense of loss is real. But so too is the inspiration we draw from this woman who had to struggle and still struggles to be heard. Miriam of the Torah and the Midrash invites us to be prophets ourselves, to speak from the heart of our own visions and dreams. She invites us to be our sisters' advocates and to be direct in our advocacy, not to get sidetracked in simply ventilating our grievances to other parties. Finally, the figure of Miriam urges us to be brave enough to raise those issues that are of vital concern to women and men today, but about which no one seems willing to speak.

Miriam's banishment and silence stand out in stark relief against a textual tradition that puts so much emphasis on words. Who was Miriam? What words did she speak to the women of her day, to the men of her day, and to God? What would her words from so long ago say to us today if they had been preserved? The figure of Miriam calls out to women today to bring forth her voice in poetry, midrash, dance, and song.

RABBI LISA A. EDWARDS

שלח לך

Shelach-Lecha

The Grasshoppers and the Giants

*I*n our own eyes we were like grasshoppers, and
so we must have seemed in their eyes too.
(NUMBERS 13:33)

THE TORAH PORTION *Shelach-Lecha* is a thrilling, frightening one in
which the Israelites once again doubt God and whine about it, while
God becomes angry in a most troubling—some would say
"unGodlike"—way. In the second year of the Israelites' journey in
the wilderness, Moses, at God's behest, sends twelve spies/scouts
into the Promised Land, into Canaan, to see, says Moses,

> . . . what the land is. And the people who live on it—are
> they strong or weak, few or many? And the land in
> which they live—is it good or bad? And the cities in
> which they live—are they camps or forts? And the land
> itself—fat or lean? Are there trees or not? Be strong and
> take some of the fruit of the land. (Num. 13:18–20)

Ten of the twelve spies panic at what they see, and return with
alarmist, doomsday reports about the land and the supposed
"giants" who dwell there: "The land that we crossed over to scout
out is one that eats its inhabitants. And all the people that we saw

279

in it are giants. . . . In our own eyes we were like grasshoppers, and so we must have seemed in their eyes too" (Num. 13:32–33). Their report disheartens the rest of the Israelites (or at least the men, as we will see), who rail against Moses and Aaron and propose among themselves to return to Egypt (Num. 14:1–4).

This sin of the ten spies and the failure of faith that ensues is seen by God and Jewish tradition as second only to the golden calf episode in its severity, and the punishment follows suit. But why? The Talmud (*Sotah* 35a) and, later, Rashi suggest one possibility based on the last word in Num. 13:31. Following upon Caleb's calming words in the previous verse, "Let us indeed go up, and we will possess it, for we can prevail over it" (Num. 13:30), the faint-hearted spies speak out again, saying: "We cannot go up against that people, for it is stronger than we [*mimenu*]" (Num. 13:31). But grammatically, *mimenu* could mean either "than we" or "than he"; thus, it is possible that the ten spies are suggesting that the people in that country are stronger than He, that is, God. Such a failure of trust in God equals the insult of the golden calf, and leads God to reject this first generation as inheritors of God's land.

In fact, initially God wants to punish them even more harshly. Upon hearing the Israelites' willingness to believe the ten over the two, God at first wants to strike them all with pestilence and disown them, giving Moses a new people to lead. While some assume that it is the clever argument from Moses that dissuades God (Num. 14:13–18), that may only be Moses asking God to forgive them: "Please forgive the iniquity of this people according to Your great kindness, as You have lifted up this people since Egypt until now" (Num. 14:19); for this verse is followed by a simple response from God: "I forgive, according to your words" (Num. 14:20). We do not know exactly why God forgave, but Jewish tradition learns from these verses God's willingness to forgive in general. And annually, immediately following the chanting of Kol Nidre as Yom Kippur begins, we ask God to remember this moment—when we were most vulnerable and God most forgiving—by reciting these simple verses of Moses asking forgiveness, and God's gentle response: "I forgive, according to your words."

Although God does forgive and decides not to destroy the whole people, God still chooses a harsh punishment: the ten spies die then, and God decrees that as for the rest of the Israelite men, only Caleb and Joshua, the optimistic spies, will live to see the promised land. It is at this point that God decrees it will take forty years (corresponding to the forty days they scouted the land) to reach the Promised Land, and that every man who is now twenty and over will die before they get there. According to Jewish tradition, the incident of the scouts' return and God's decree against them took place on the ninth of Av. Thus, God's decree becomes the first of a long line of sorrows that befell the Jewish people on *Tisha B'av*, the fast day of mourning for many Jewish traumas throughout history.[1]

Tradition does not agree on whether this punishment was pronounced only against the men or against the women too.[2] Thus, some traditional sources and contemporary feminist perspectives both see this episode as a story about men, as opposed to women. In her interesting chapter on *Shelach-Lecha*, contemporary commentator Judith Antonelli quotes an unusual midrash from the seventeenth-century Polish commentator *Kli Yakar* (R. Shlomo Efraim). The midrash itself is inspired by God's opening words to Moses, *shelach-lecha anashim*, "send for you men," and it tries to answer two questions. First, why did God say, *shelach-lecha*, "send for you," instead of just *shelach*, "send"? Second, does the term *anashim* mean "men" only, or is it a generic term for "people" here? In the midrash from *Keli Yakar,* God gives Moses the following advice:

> With My knowledge from seeing into the future, it would be better to send women who cherish the Land because they don't count its faults. But for you *[lecha],* with your knowledge, if you think that they [masc.] are fit and the Land is dear to them, then send men. Therefore, send for yourselves *[shelach-lecha],* according to your level of knowledge, men. But according to My level of knowledge, it would be better to send women, as I said.[3]

Suppose that God really had offered these remarks to Moses. What does it mean that Moses did not take God's advice? Antonelli suggests, "[I]t illustrates how preposterous such a plan must have seemed to [Moses] and how preposterous he felt it would have sounded to the men in the wilderness if he had explained it to them."[4] That such a midrash exists, suggesting God's appreciation for women over men in this situation, is amazing. Beyond that, the text of the midrash invites questions and speculation. The midrash suggests that women appreciate the land because they do not *count* its faults. This is not necessarily to say that they do not *see* its faults. Is the midrash suggesting that God sees in women this trait of not counting faults?[5] How might the situation have changed if Moses had sent women to check out the land and the people dwelling there?

We can imagine other questions as well. What would have happened if all the scouts (whoever they were) had come back with a positive report, as Joshua and Caleb did? What if the Israelites had not wandered for forty years? What if that first generation of ex-slaves had been allowed into the Promised Land?

Another tradition derived from the ten scouts is the Talmud's instruction that it takes ten Jewish men to form a *minyan*, the minimum number required for communal prayers.[6] Why choose a negative gathering of men (the ten pessimistic scouts) to come up with the number for a positive gathering (a *minyan*)? One would think that the Rabbis would choose ten from the Ten Commandments, or seven from the days of creation, or some other number conjuring up positive connotations and powerful historical associations. The Talmud gives no explanation of why the pessimistic scouts inspired the number for a prayer quorum. Some say that the scouts' descendants must forever atone for the scouts' sin of failure of faith, both in their own strength and in God's. We gather in communal prayer, then, in part to do ongoing *teshuvah* (repentance) for this sin of our ancestors. Antonelli suggests seeing the *minyan* "as a kind of *teshuvah* (repentance) for the negative consequences of male bonding."[7] We might also speculate on what Jewish prayer would look like, and what role women might have played in it, if this incident had not occurred, or if Moses had followed God's advice to send women.

But what may be the worst offense the spies committed was to see themselves as grasshoppers. Up against giants (the Nephilim and the Anakites), "In our own eyes we were like grasshoppers, and so we must have seemed in their eyes too" (Num. 13:33). We are, in fact, never told how those spies appeared to the inhabitants of the land. We know only what they themselves projected onto the inhabitants. One midrash suggests that God was upset with the spies not for their own self-perception but for projecting that self-perception onto others:

> "I shall forgive them this remark," said God. But when they said: "And so we were in their sight," God asked: "Did you know how I made you appear in their sight?

Who can say that you did not appear in their sight as angels? What have you brought upon yourselves?" (*Numbers Rabbah* 16:11)

What if, in fact, they had appeared as angels to the inhabitants of Canaan? What if the spies had had more faith in their own strength or God's? The midrash writers alert us to the spies' failure, and remind us not to project onto others our own insecurities, for the consequences are grim for such failure of imagination. "What have you brought upon yourselves?" God asks the spies in the midrash. And the answer is in the Torah story itself: by assuming themselves to be less than they are and others more than they are, the spies have brought about their own demise, for the spies will die now and their followers will wander forty years and die before they reach the Promised Land (Num. 14:26–38).

As women, or members of minority groups, how often we have taken on the grasshopper image in our own eyes, and assumed that others view us the same way? How often do we fixate on how we look to "them," and fail ourselves in the process? If women had more faith and confidence in their own strength, how different the world might look to us all. How different it might be for us all.

Another midrash notes that all Israelites over the age of twenty were condemned to die in the desert, and speculates that "even those who silently disagreed with the majority and favored Joshua and Caleb" were left to die in the wilderness. And why, the midrash asks, did those silent ones—who favored God's favorites—receive the same punishment as the dissenters? "Because they did not speak up" (*Numbers Rabbah* 16:23). In the 1980s, the early years of AIDS, the organization known as ACT UP, which specialized in public demonstrations demanding more government intervention in the fight against AIDS, had as its motto, "Silence = Death." Long before ACT UP, Judaism taught the need to speak out when one disagrees, and the dangers of silence in the face of the wrongdoing of others.

The source of the problem for the ten scouts is their own self-image, and how that self-image shapes their confidence and ability to act. "In our own eyes we were like grasshoppers, and so we must have seemed in their eyes too." As women, we can identify: we well know how self-negation can hold one back, how quickly we can lose confidence if we feel belittled. But our *parashah* gives women the opportunity to see themselves in another way, for the spiritual message of the *parashah* comes to us through Joshua and Caleb, the optimistic spies, the ones who, according to God, had a *ruach acheret*, "a different spirit."[8]

All of us are the inheritors of the insight of Caleb and Joshua, as well as of the anxieties of the rest of the Israelites. Caleb and Joshua teach us how attitude and faith can help us overcome fear and negative thinking. As long as we women are not grasshoppers in our own eyes, we can use our *parashah* to find within ourselves "a different spirit," the spirit that brings with it the faith to forge ahead despite the obstacles.

RABBI ELYSE D. FRISHMAN

קרח

Korach

Authority, Status, Power

*T*hey combined against Moses and Aaron and said to them, "You have gone too far! For all the community are holy, all of them, and Adonai is in their midst. Why, then, do you raise yourselves above Adonai's congregation?"
(NUMBERS 16:3)

IN THIS *parashah* and the previous one, four sections are linked to each other. First, near the end of *Shelach Lecha*, the Israelites find a man deliberately gathering wood on Shabbat. Not knowing the proper punishment, the people bring that man to Moses, and God instructs Moses that everyone must stone him to death. Second, this episode is followed by the mitzvah of wearing *tzitzit;* gazing upon them should remind one to "not follow one's heart and eyes in lustful urge." The *tzitzit* are a reminder to observe mitzvot, to be holy to God, to remember God (Num. 15:32ff.). The third section, at the beginning of our *parashah,* is the story of the rebellion of Korach. Fourth, at the end of *Parashat Korach,* God finalizes the distinctions of the Kohen (priest), Levite, and Israelite.

The punishment of stoning the wood gatherer is the first and only incident of capital punishment actually applied in the Torah.

The episode must have been devastating for the people. Clearly, it proved God's seriousness. The sages note that the ensuing mitzvah of *tzitzit* was a lesson about the need for ritual to discipline rebellious inclinations. They suggest that Korach's challenge is, in fact, a rebellion against that discipline and requirement of ritual mitzvot.

One would think that the people were cautioned sufficiently against rebelling after the stoning of the wood gatherer. How was Korach now able to incite several hundred people to rise up against Moses and Aaron? The rebels proclaim, "You have gone too far! For all the community is holy, all of them, and Adonai is in their midst. Why then do you raise yourselves above the Lord's congregation?" (Num. 16:3). Korach implies that Moses is hypocritical. He impugns the characters of both Moses and Aaron. And Moses responds, "Adonai will make known who is God's, and who is holy" (Num. 16:5). We do not judge each other; that is God's task, and we are not God. Moses continues, "Is it not enough for you that the God of Israel has set you apart from the community of Israel and given you access . . . to perform the duties of Adonai's Tabernacle, and to minister to the community and serve them?" (Num. 16:9). Why are you not satisfied with the tremendous responsibilities you have already acquired?

Is this merely a power struggle? Or is this also a struggle with personal worth, with understanding one's role and purpose in life?

Thus far, the stoning, the mitzvah of *tzitzit*, and the rebellion teach that even with the discipline and structure of tradition, ego can pervert anyone's intention. How easily Korach twists and challenges the reputations of Moses and Aaron, ascribing his own ambition to them. How easily the people listen and are fooled. How little Korach understands the true responsibility and burden of authority and power that rest on Moses and Aaron.

At the end of *Parashat Korach*, then, is the attempt to prevent this confusion from ever reoccurring. God finalizes the distinct roles of Kohen, Levite, and Israelite. Judaism has upheld these ancient positions to this day. On Shabbat morning, as seven *aliyot* are celebrated during the reading of Torah, the first *aliyah* is given to the Kohen in the congregation, the second to the Levite, and the third to the Israelite. Why is the Kohen chosen for the first *aliyah*? It seems to reflect a hierarchy of importance: the Kohen ranks higher as the first *aliyah*.

Yet, I would suggest that the third *aliyah* is as significant as the first. The Israelite matters as much as the Kohen in the modern reading of the Torah, though for different reasons. In *Mishnah Gittin* 5:8, the order of *aliyah* is described: "The following rules were laid down in the interests of peace. A priest is called first to read [Torah], after him a Levite, and then an Israelite." "In the interests of peace" means to prevent argument about who merits being called to read. Yet, why is the priest called first? Is this because the priest is most coveted? Indeed, *Gemara Gittin* 59b discusses giving the Kohen this responsibility because of the verse in Lev. 21:8, "And you shall sanctify him [Aaron]." "Sanctify" actually means "separate," from the root *k-d-sh;* the priest will be separated, distinguished from everyone else. Is the priest, then, more important than everyone else?

Consider the Gemara's conversation about the eligibility of persons called for the third *aliyah*. The first priority went to scholars who were appointed *parnasim* of the community; that is, general leaders of the town council who oversaw the distribution of *tzedakah*. The Gemara continues, "after them, scholars who are qualified to be appointed as *Parnasim* of the community, and after them, the sons of the scholars whose fathers had been appointed *Parnasim* of the community, and after them heads of synagogues and members of the general public."

Why was the leader responsible for *tzedakah* distribution selected? Perhaps because that person merited the trust of the community. Unlike the Kohen or Levite, whose positions were inherited rather than "earned," the *tzedakah* distributor required a high moral character.

Interestingly, tradition weighs the third and seventh *aliyot* as extremely important. Why? In the traditional world of mitzvot, obligation garnered greater honor than choice. Men were credited for fulfilling time-bound mitzvot, to which they were obligated by the Talmud; women were discouraged from participating on a voluntary basis, because of the serious nature of obligation. Yet, a different perspective emerges from these *aliyot*. The Kohen and Levite are obligated to come up, but the serious discussion about who merits the third *aliyah* highlights its importance. The honor goes to the most trusted individual in the community. The honor goes to the one who merits it by virtue of moral character, not role distinction. The order and appreciation of *aliyot* offers this possibility: being chosen to participate on the basis of moral character ranks that volunteer at least as high as the one obligated. Voluntary, ethical commitment is treasured.

The modern Kohen fulfills a duty to offer the *aliyah*, just as in ancient times the priest offered the *olah*. Note that both *olah* (burnt sacrifice) and *aliyah* (ascending the *bimah*) are offerings. Linguistically, the words share the same root, a-l-h. The *olah* is an offering of an object; the *aliyah* is an offering of oneself. For the Israelite alone, this *aliyah* is a voluntary offering of oneself—and the selection of that person is based on moral character. This is why it receives high honor.

Why not call the Israelite first and the Kohen third? One answer might be that, in practical terms, a Kohen and Levite must be present for the *aliyah,* and they are far fewer in number. The obligation for a Kohen or Levite to participate in the ritual may be a greater burden for the reluctant participant. So they are called upon first and second, to give them recognition for the responsibility they fulfill. In being called, it is not the individual who is recognized, but the role fulfilled. The Israelite? There are so many! Who will be selected to represent the community? The person called up for the third *aliyah* will have honored the community through the quality of demonstrated leadership.

Role does need to be acknowledged. The position of priest or Levite bears great responsibility; misusing one's authority or duties brings grave danger. Korach understood none of this. He saw only power in the leader's role. His challenge was a mirror of his own character; he sought to raise himself above everyone.

Authority and status are conferred in two ways: determined by title, such as police officer, or earned by merit, such as mentor. The former is hierarchical, the latter relational. Relational authority builds respectful communities with moral integrity. Hierarchical society is completely role differentiated; personal worth is determined by your title: husband, wife, physician, teacher, man, woman. Relational community values character: supportive husband, understanding wife, compassionate physician, empathetic teacher. And of course, the greatest challenge is to understand the worth of each person, and to value each contribution. This is not communism, which negates individualism. This is the highest expression of individualism, where each person contributes uniquely to the community.

Western society, a patriarchal one, faces a challenge to its hierarchical structure each time it is confronted with unethical leaders—abusive teachers, physicians, clergy, spouses, parents who misuse the authority conferred by their titles. Shock comes from betrayed expectations that the title conveys morality. Yet in a feminist, relational system, a person's status, privilege, or honor is born from ethical behavior and reputation. Heroes and heroines have courage, moral strength, and wisdom. In a relational society, they may be found in every walk of life.

M. Scott Peck, in *The Different Drum*, tells the story of a monastery now struggling to survive despite its previous centuries of spiritual richness. The monks were at a loss. The abbot decided to seek the advice of a rabbi in a nearby village; after all, the Jews had survived despite adversity. What was their spiritual secret? The abbot and rabbi met, but the rabbi could not answer the abbot's question. "I only know," said the rabbi, "that one of you is the Messiah." "What!" thought the abbot. "One of us is the Messiah?" He hurried home and shared this with his monks. They looked at one another, thinking, "Tom? He's so quiet? How could he be the Messiah? Ah, perhaps he teaches us to listen more carefully. Joseph? He's so stubborn! Oh, this teaches perseverance." And so on. Each monk suddenly began to regard the others differently, and the atmosphere of the monastery began to evolve. In time, the place again flourished spiritually.[1]

The Kohen is acknowledged for role, not character. The Israelite is acknowledged for character, not role. How easily we confuse these honors!

Certainly one's work and responsibilities may effect a personal, spiritual, ethical transformation. One's character can blossom according to the situation. Korach understood none of this.

Moses' authority and power were obvious; the people were terrified of his ability to commune with God and not die. Though they occasionally challenged Moses, they never threatened him. Aaron, on the other hand, gained his role as high priest for no apparent reason other than that he was the elder brother of Moses. And to Korach, this was a precious appointment, greatly coveted. While it was obvious that God had chosen Moses, who chose Aaron? This was something Korach could wrest for himself!

Moses recognized this as he cried out to Korach, "Who is Aaron that you should complain about him?" (Num. 16:11). Moses knew that Aaron was not hungry for power. Imagine Aaron as the quiet introvert, excellent in his ritual position. He was not the charismatic visionary that his younger brother was; Aaron was the thoughtful, careful person needed to fulfill the duties of high priest.

Did Aaron's character evolve into this leadership position? It did not need to, for there was no call for the high priest to do more than the duties described. But in Num. 17:8–15, Aaron went further. God wanted to strike everyone dead because of the rebellion. "Then Moses said to Aaron, 'Take the fire pan and put on it fire from the altar. Add incense and take it quickly to the community and make expiation for them. For wrath has gone forth from the Lord; the plague has begun!' Aaron . . . ran to the midst of the congregation, where the plague had begun among the people. He put on the incense and made expiation for the people; he stood between the dead and the living until the plague was checked." Aaron went beyond the instruction, and took it upon himself to make certain that the people were saved. What a terrifying moment, and what courage he displayed, staying with his people, protecting them from death. It is almost as though Aaron's presence, not the incense or the expiation, checked the plague. Was it Aaron the high priest or Aaron the compassionate one whose presence made the difference?

One thing is certain: Aaron ripens here into mature leadership.

Was Aaron ever power hungry? Did he demand glory for himself? No. His humility was outstanding. Nor did Moses, powerfully burdened, ever ask anything for himself. From the inception of our Exodus story, he asked God, "Why me?"

The Chasidim reflect that each person in a community has a particular role. Each person may be regarded as a vessel concentrating one of the aspects of the Divine. One individual's character emphasizes glory, another's judgment, another's strength, intuition, or wisdom. The *rebbe* is the *keter*, the crown of the community, from and to whom all flow. Each position, each person, is crucial to the spiritual health of the community. All contribute holiness to the whole.

So it is with each of us. We are blessed with gifts. One is a talented musician, another a composer. A third sculpts, while a fourth plants gardens. In the field of personality development, Isabel Myers distinguished sixteen different personality combinations.[2] Introverts, extroverts, artists, scientists, critics, empathics—all are necessary for society to function creatively, ethically, and successfully.

Judaism emphasizes the worth of each person, the fulfillment of each person's sacred potential, and the recognition of our contributions. Korach's grave sin is that, promoting his own power, he would destroy the ethical society. He thought that title, rather than the character of each person, wielded power and importance. His most ironic claim accuses Moses and Aaron of setting themselves above the people.

Structure matters; roles are important. But we learn that for the majority of us, true worth is determined by personal offering and ethical reputation. How we behave determines our status in an ethical society.

RABBI AUDREY S. POLLACK

חקת
Chukkat

Blood and Water, Death and Life

*T*his is the statute of the law that Adonai has
commanded, saying: Speak to the children of
Israel that they should bring to you a red heifer,
pure, which has no blemish, and which has never
had a yoke upon it. (NUMBERS 19:2)

Chukkat covers a thirty-eight-year period in biblical history. It begins
with the ritual concerning the ashes of the red heifer and ritual
purification to be performed by the priests in the event of contamination. It continues with a brief recounting of Miriam's death
and with the accounting of the leadership of Moses and his brother, Aaron, in the wilderness, as the people cry out yet again that they
have no water and that they regret having left Egypt. It is at this
juncture that Moses' patience breaks down and he strikes the rock
to get water for the people, although God had commanded him
only to speak to the rock. This is said to be Moses' fatal flaw, the
sin that seals his fate so that he will not be permitted to enter the
Promised Land. The portion continues with Aaron's death and
the mourning period for Aaron, and concludes with a series of con-
quests and journeys through various lands on the way to the
Promised Land. One of the most striking things about this *parashah*

is the recurrence within it of elements that speak to the spiritual and physical experiences of women—blood and water, impurity and purity, death and life.

The Red Heifer

The description of the red heifer and the rites concerning it (Num. 19:1–10) seem strange to us. Indeed, even our sages could not explain the meaning of the rite, only that, "The ritual is commanded by God. It is set out within the Torah law. That is what justifies its observance, not some rational interpretation."[1] That is why it falls under the category of *Chukkat,* one of the four laws of Torah for which there is no rational explanation.[2]

The ritual itself, however, and its associations with purity and impurity and life and death, is reminiscent of women's rituals of purification in the *mikveh.* The ashes of this red heifer, a female cow that is completely red, that has never been used for work or borne any young, are mixed with water to create waters of purification. That the animal is to be a young female, virginal and untamed, suggests a connection with the power of women's reproductive cycles. It evokes the power of the life force present in blood: the red coloring of the heifer and its virginity symbolize a power that has not yet been brought forth, and an as yet untamed animal reminds us that this life force is beyond our power to control. The words, *mei niddah,* used here to describe the sprinkling potion made of water mixed with the ashes of the red heifer (Num. 19:9), are the same words used to describe the waters of the *mikveh,* in which a woman immerses herself after her menstrual period and after childbirth to change her status from *temayah* (translated as "impure") to *tehorah* (translated as "pure"). Thus, we see a connection between the red color of the heifer and its association with blood and the subsequent waters of purification for women after the menstrual period.

Furthermore, the ashes and water potion of the red heifer is sprinkled on someone to render them pure again after they had come into contact with a corpse. This sprinkling of the water and ashes potion signifies a separation between death and life. Anything associated with death (a corpse, vessels, clothing) is specifically capable of transmitting contamination or impurity, which can then be purified only through the waters of purification. It is the sprinkling of the waters that marks the purification of the individual, and his or her movement from associating with death to that of life. Similarly, women's immersion denotes a separation between the menstrual period, during which no life has begun, and the possibility of life in the coming month. It is worth noting, however, that the ashes of the red heifer by themselves had the power to contaminate, or make impure, both those who prepared it and their clothing (Num. 19:7–10). The ashes are able to both purify and defile. Ashes, by themselves (which are, after all, from a dead animal), made the priest and his clothing impure. But when mixed with water, a living substance, they also have the opposite effect, to render purity from impurity. In fact, in the description of how this sprinkling potion is to be concocted, the text says that "they shall take for the unclean person some of the ashes from the fire of cleansing, and shall add to them fresh water in a vessel" (Num. 19:17). Ramban comments on this verse, "The meaning is not that he should first put the ashes [of the Red Heifer] into the vessel and then pour the water upon the ashes, for our Rabbis have taught that if one places the ashes in the vessel first and then the water it invalidates [the water, so that it may not be used as water of purification]."[3] The water is thus the significant part of the equation of this process of purifying. Water is also a significant element in the rest of the Torah portion.

Miriam's Death and Miriam's Well

"The whole community of Israel arrived at the wilderness of Zin in the first month, and the people stayed at Kadesh. Miriam died there and was buried there" (Num. 20:1). Rashi comments on the juxtaposition of the section narrating Miriam's death with the section regarding the red heifer. Although these two events are widely separated chronologically, they are placed close together in the text. Rashi states that this is "to suggest the following comparison: what is the purpose of the sacrifices? They effect atonement! So, too, does the death of the righteous effect atonement."[4] Thus, the effect of Miriam's death upon the people is to bring purification to them because of her righteousness, in the same way that the sprinkling of the red heifer potion is said to bring purification. What is interesting, however, is that despite Miriam's righteousness and her important status in the community, there is no explicit mention of the community's mourning for her. Later in the portion, when Aaron dies, his death and the community's subsequent mourning for him are distinctly described: "Moses stripped Aaron of his garments and clothed his son Elazar in them, and Aaron died there on the top of the mountain; then Moses and Elazar went down from the mountain. When the community saw that Aaron had died, the whole house of Israel wept for Aaron thirty days" (Num. 20:28–29). Instead of mourning, what follows the notation of Miriam's death is the people's cry against Moses and Aaron because there is no water:

> The community was without water and they united
> against Moses and Aaron. The people challenged
> Moses, saying, "If only we had perished when our
> brothers perished before God! Why have you brought
> the community of God into this wilderness to die
> there, we and our animals? Why did you bring us up
> out of Egypt only to bring us to this terrible place, a
> place with no grain or figs or vines or pomegranates;
> and not even water to drink!" (Num. 20:2–5)

Instead of mourning for Miriam, the people seem concerned only for their own needs. Most of the commentators do not note the lack of mourning. They are interested, however, in the cry for water immediately following Miriam's death. They suggest, "[W]e may learn from it that during the entire forty years in the wilderness they had the 'well' through Miriam's merit."[5] In other words, it was because of Miriam's merit and her righteousness that the people had water to drink throughout the forty years in the wilderness. With her death, however, the water supply ceased.

The well that our sages refer to was a mobile well given by God as a reward for the good deeds of Miriam. Miriam's well accompanied the Israelites throughout the forty-year journey in the desert, providing for them a plentiful supply of fresh water wherever they went. According to *Mishnah Avot* 5:9, Miriam's well was one of ten special things that God created on the eve of the first Shabbat.[6] This same well gave water to Ishmael in the wilderness of Beersheba; it is the same well where Isaac's servant Eliezer met Rebecca, where Jacob met Rachel, where Moses met Tziporah; and the same well had given water to the people earlier on, when Moses struck it at Horeb. The *Tz'enah Ur'enah* explains the association of the well with Miriam:

> Pious women are compared to a well. The more water
> one draws from a well, the more water it contains. The
> more good deeds and charity done by women with
> their money, the more money will the women have. . . .
> Women do not have many commandments, but they
> must give charity, and so they are likened to a well.[7]

When Miriam died, all of a sudden the water ceased flowing, causing the Israelites to cry out in thirst and fear. According to one tradition, the gift of the well was to be limited to the time of wandering in the desert, and thus Miriam had to die shortly before the entrance into the land of Israel.[8]

The *Tz'enah Ur'enah* makes a passing reference to mourning after Miriam's death: "As soon as the well ceased flowing, Israel gathered around Moses and Aaron, who were weeping for Miriam. God told them: 'Because you are mourning, shall all of Israel die of thirst? Stand up, take your staff, and give water to Israel.'"[9] According to this interpretation, there is no mourning described, because God commanded Moses and Aaron to get on with the business at hand. Though Miriam certainly deserves a more satisfying explanation, there is none. The commentator Alshich does make a direct link between the lack of mourning over Miriam's death and the lack of water. He states, "Indeed, because they did not shed tears over the loss of Miriam, the source of their water dried up, for it was as if her merit did not matter to them."[10] The comparison of lack of tears—the people's cheeks were dry—with the statement "the community was without water" gives a deeper meaning to the passage. When Miriam was around and they needed her, they were grateful. But once she was gone, and thus no longer useful, they turned their attention elsewhere.

Is this a metaphor of how we treat the women in our lives? We might understand the lack as not only a lack of drinking water but as a reference to the people's inability to shed tears. Perhaps they were so stunned by the loss of Miriam that they were unable to express their grief directly. Instead, they cried out against Moses and Aaron, projecting and transferring their grief onto Miriam's brothers. Or perhaps they did not react to Miriam's death in such a way that would give comfort to her brothers. They seemed to care only that there was no water, and acted as if Miriam's death were unimportant. We can imagine that Moses and Aaron were deeply shaken by the loss of their sister, and this may have been the reason that Moses reacted with such anger toward the people when he struck the rock, instead of speaking to it, as God has commanded. In grief mixed with rage—such a normal reaction—Moses lashed out at the rock to produce what Miriam could have produced with only her presence.

In our *parashah*, when the journey is almost complete and Miriam dies, there is a song about waters, the Song at the Well in Num. 21:17–18. On both ends of the journey, leaving Egypt and entering Israel, water represents life and transition. These waters of transformation are a part of women's physical and spiritual experience—the waters of birth, the cleansing waters of the *mikveh* that separate the past from the future possibility of life, the change of status from one stage of life to another. In essence, these waters are a transitional element from death into life as our people move from wandering in the wilderness toward living as God's eternal people in the land that we have been promised by the merit of our ancestors, women as well as men.

RABBI DIANE ARONSON COHEN

בלק
Balak

The End of Abuse

God opened the mouth of the donkey, and she said
to Bil'am, "What did I do to you to make you hit
me three times?" Bil'am replied to the donkey,
"Because of your impudence! If there had been a
sword in my hand I would have killed you!" The donkey said to Bil'am, "Aren't I the donkey that you have
ridden all your life until this day? Is this the kind of
behavior you are used to from me?" He said, "No."
(NUMBERS 22:28–30)

THE TALMUD QUOTES RABBI HANINA: "I have learned much from my
teachers, and from my colleagues I have learned more than from my
teachers, but from my students I have learned more than from all of
them."[1] The Mishnah asks, "Who is wise?" and responds, "One
who learns from all persons."[2] The implication is clear: there is
much to be learned from all those around us, whether we perceive
them to be learned or not.

What is less clear is that there is also much we can learn from
animals. *Parashat Balak* records the efforts of a king to commission
a soothsayer to curse Israel on its trek from Sinai to Canaan. Balak
sends Bil'am to pronounce curses over Israel, curses that are turned

to blessings when Bil'am sees the beauty of Israel's camps. In our daily prayerbook, we say the same words each morning that Bil'am said: *Mah tovu ohalecha Ya'akov . . .*, "How beautiful are your tents, O Jacob [and your dwelling places, O Israel]!" Balak sends messengers to Bil'am; Bil'am hesitates and even seeks advice from God on whether to proceed. Later, Bil'am has an encounter with an angel of God:

> Bil'am got up in the morning and saddled his donkey and went with the officers of Moab. God was furious because he was going, so an angel of the Lord was stationed on the road to impede him. [Bil'am] rode on his donkey, and his two young men were with him. The donkey saw the angel of God standing on the road, with his drawn sword in his hand, so the donkey turned away from the road and went into the field; then Bil'am struck the donkey to turn her back onto the road. The angel of God stood in the path of the vineyards, a fence on this side and a fence on that side. The donkey saw the angel of God and pressed against the wall, pressing Bi'lam's leg against the wall—and he continued to strike her. The angel of God moved further and stood in a narrow place, where there was no room to turn right or left. The donkey saw the angel of God and crouched behind Bil'am. Enraged, Bil'am struck the donkey with the staff. God opened the mouth of the donkey, and she said to Bil'am, "What did I do to you to make you hit me three times?" Bil'am replied to the donkey, "Because of your impudence! If there had been a sword in my hand I would have killed you!" The donkey said to Bil'am, "Aren't I the donkey that you have ridden all your life until this day? Is this the kind of behavior you are used to from me?" He said, "No." (Num. 22:21–30)

There is a good deal written about Bil'am's personality in the classical commentaries noting the miraculous idea of a speaking animal. The commentators suggest that a speaking animal can perceive that which a human cannot. The *Keli Yakar* tells us that God intended for the donkey to speak only "for the glory of Israel." That is, just as God can allow an animal to speak, God can control the speech of humans. Thus, the entire incident of the donkey is a point of honor for Israel, and a sign of God's concern for Israel's welfare. Nachmanides quotes *Bamidbar Rabbah* in reporting that once the donkey had spoken, she died, so that she should not become a focus of idol worship.

What I have always found astonishing is the absence of concern about Bil'am's treatment of his animal. This is not a young animal: she rhetorically asks Bil'am, "Aren't I the donkey that you have ridden all your life until this day?" This was an animal strong enough to bear a young man on his journeys and is still carrying the well-known sorcerer as he travels from place to place. In all the years of her service to Bil'am she has given him no trouble. And yet, the commentators do not react to Bil'am's violent treatment of his loyal retainer.

This neglect goes far beyond the treatment of animals. The commentators do not see the abuse, the venting of anger or frustration on an individual, human or animal, that has been part of one's life. The donkey sees something her master cannot, an angel of God blocking the way, sword in hand, and the donkey stops to protect her master—and is beaten for it.

How does she stop the abuse? She speaks up. She does not even bother to explain why she has stopped in her tracks and crushed her master's foot against a wall. Explanations are unimportant. Whether her behavior is appropriate or not, the abuse was not. And she says so: "What did I do to you? Is this the kind of behavior you are used to from me?" Essentially, "What are you doing? Have I ever behaved like this before? What have I done that warrants your abuse of me?" And astonishingly, Bil'am is without words. He does not attempt to explain or justify his behavior. His donkey's castigation has brought him up short, and he can say only, "No." No, nothing you have done warrants my abuse of you.

Bil'am's behavior and the donkey's response translate in our modern day to an issue of empowerment. In this ancient text, we have an example of an angry man, frustrated at his donkey's uncharacteristic behavior, and unable to do anything but hit her. And we have the donkey speaking out against her master and his behavior. While the classical commentators tell us that she speaks to diminish Bil'am in the eyes of those around him, a careful reading shows us that the donkey never does tell Bil'am about the angel. It takes God's "uncovering" Bil'am's eyes in order for him to see what had been troubling his animal. The dialogue between Bil'am and the donkey focuses only on his abuse and her refusal to accept it.

What a powerful lesson to learn from a donkey! And what an astonishing truth to find in Torah, a truth overlooked by generations of commentators. What we learn from the donkey is clear: if we are on the receiving end of any kind of abuse, we have an obligation to speak out against our abuser. Modern psychology tells us that whether or not saying "Stop!" has an effect on the abuser, it does reduce the sense of helplessness in the one abused. Speak up. Speak out. Talk back to someone hurting you. Let them know that what they are doing is simply wrong.

The most painful part of this episode is the lack of closure. The angel asks Bil'am why he struck the donkey, adding, "If she had not turned away from me, I would have killed you and let her live!" (Num. 22:33). In the next verse, Bil'am replies to the angel, "I have sinned, because I did not know that you were standing opposite me on the road." Even though only moments before he has been able to speak to his donkey, his words now are exclusively to the angel. We might excuse his failure to address the donkey as a reaction to fear in the presence of the angel. Or we might agree with the midrash that suggests that the donkey, having spoken her piece, dies.

Or we might wonder whether she is still standing by the road, watching the encounter between Bil'am and the angel, her back still smarting from the blows inflicted by her master. She is wondering when her pain will be acknowledged, when salve might be applied to the cuts in her flesh. Once the donkey has spoken, she is never again mentioned, her role in the narrative having been played out.

The donkey that carried Bil'am from the days of his youth behaved strangely. In frustration, Bil'am struck her. God opened her mouth—gave her the courage and strength to speak out—and with her words she stopped the abuse. The logical close to the episode, at least by modern standards, would have been for Bil'am to say more than just, "I have sinned," to speak words of regret for his violent behavior. This he does not do. What might the rabbis have learned, what might they have taught, based on an expression of regret on the part of this sorcerer?

How might they have explained words of humanity coming from the lips of someone commissioned to curse Israel? They might have explained these words as they explained *Mah tovu ohalecha Ya'akov.* Just as God would not allow Bil'am to curse Israel, neither would God allow him to walk away from a beaten animal without acknowledging his wrongdoing.

This text is missing from the commentaries, but it is not missing from the realities of our lives today. The story of Bil'am and his donkey provides an important model of an abuser, reacting by venting misdirected anger in verbal abuse or physical violence, and the recipient of his abuse, finally deciding that she has had enough.

RABBI PAMELA WAX

פינחס

Pinchas

Daughters and Inheritance Law

*T*he plea of Tzelophechad's daughters is just: you
should give them a hereditary holding among
their father's kinsmen; transfer their father's share to
them. Further, speak to the Israelite people as follows:
"If a man dies without leaving a son, you shall transfer his property to his daughter. If he has no daughter, you shall assign his property to his brothers. If he
has no brothers, you shall assign his property to his
father's brothers. If his father had no brothers, you
shall assign his property to his nearest relative in his
own clan, and he shall inherit it." This shall be the
law of procedure for the Israelites, in accordance with
the Lord's command to Moses. (NUMBERS 27:7–11, JPS
TRANSLATION)

FROM OUR EARLIEST ENCOUNTERS WITH TORAH, we become well aware
of the biblical concern with matters of inheritance and succession.
Who will receive the birthright? Who the coveted blessings? In Genesis, most notably, there is always a favorite, there is jealousy, and
there are the numerous permutations on the theme of brother vying
with brother (or sister with sister): Cain and Abel, Isaac and Ishmael,

Jacob and Esau, Leah and Rachel, Joseph and his brothers.

In Num. 27, we are presented with a radically different model of sibling relationships: five sisters who are, incredibly, unified with one another regarding their parental inheritance. Their common "enemy" is not one another, but rather the patriarchal system that denies them a share in their father's land. Having died without sons, their father's name will be lost for posterity when the tribal lands are subdivided among clans and families, unless his daughters themselves receive his stake.

Mahlah, Noah, Hoglah, Milcah, and Tirtzah—the daughters of Tzelophechad—petitioned Moses, Eleazar the priest, the chieftains, and the whole assembly to grant them a share in their father's estate: "Let not our father's name be lost to his clan just because he had no son! Give us a holding among our father's kinsmen!" (Num. 27:4).

This being a case not provided for in the original legislation, Moses brought their case before God. God deems the daughters' claim a just one. While this rendering of law is a victory for the five daughters of Tzelophechad, it is a Pyrrhic victory at best. Had Tzelophechad had sons, the biblical text clearly indicates that the five sisters would not have benefited from their father's share of land, for daughters would not inherit when there were sons in the family. This fact is especially interesting considering the fact that some other ancient Near Eastern cultures did bequeath equally to daughters and sons.[1]

Sons, apparently, were considered "safe" heirs, not only because they insured the perpetuation of the family name, but also because they insured the integrity of the family property. With daughters, there was always the expectation that they would marry outsiders who would then succeed to the family property. (This concern is made explicit in an addendum to the Tzelophechad story in Num. 36, in which further legislation limits the five sisters' choices of husbands to members of their own clan. I imagine them returning to Moses in a rage, demanding an explanation for this further injustice.) The five sisters were not claiming personal belongings of their father, but rather, his share in the division of the tribal land. The repercussions of this seemingly small detail are manifold. Would not this Torah text suggest, then, that this law was specific to the division of the tribal lands, and therefore not binding on postexilic generations? Or, if deemed specifically a law for the land of Israel, the later rabbis could have considered inheritance a matter of civil law for which the principle *dina d'malchuta dina* ("the law of the land is the law") would be invoked in the Diaspora, thus allowing that inheritance be a civil matter, informed by other cultural norms under which Jews lived. Furthermore, might it not be read merely as a statement on a daughter's rights to real estate (the "immovables"), but be silent in regard to the "movables," that is, any other personal belongings?[2]

Lastly, since the Torah passage says nothing about a mother's estate, shouldn't a daughter inherit from her mother, if not from her father?

We now look to the rabbinic texts to understand how the Rabbis interpreted this Torah text regarding daughters and inheritance. Did they, in fact, recognize this to be a law for a specific situation in Israelite history, the ancestral inheritance in the Holy Land? Did they invoke the principle of *dina d'malchuta dina?* Did they give daughters the right to inherit equally with sons, or at least to inherit any movables, since the original legislation concerns real estate? Would they allow for the daughter inheriting from her mother's estate, if not from her father's? Unfortunately, the answer to all these questions is no. Despite compelling reasons to allow daughters to inherit, and despite legal ways in which they might have liberalized the law in Numbers to attain this goal, the Rabbis did not do so. In *Mishnah Baba Batra* 8:5, their conservative reading of the Toraitic inheritance law is made clear:

> If one says, "My son so-and-so, that is the first-born, shall not take a double portion," or, "My son so-and-so shall not inherit with his brothers," he has said nothing, because he has made a condition contrary to what is written in the Law. . . . If one says, "So-and-so shall inherit from me," when there is a daughter, or, "My daughter shall inherit from me," when there is a son, he has said nothing, since he has made a provision contrary to what is written in the Law.

The Rabbis, in fact, created two laws that were harsher to daughters than those originally imposed by Torah. First, she could not inherit from her mother's estate any more than she could from her father's (*Baba Batra* 111a). Second, should her brother predecease her, his children would take precedence in succession to her father's estate. Torah law in Num. 27 outlined the order of succession as being the deceased's sons, followed by the deceased's daughters (where there were no sons), followed by the deceased's brothers. Rabbinic law, however, created a concept of "inheritance from the grave," whereby the deceased's grandson or granddaughter (issue of the deceased's son) would supersede the deceased's own daughter in the event that the son himself were no longer alive to inherit the father's estate directly. In this case of a family where the inheriting son predeceases the daughter, *Mishnah Baba Batra* 8:2, unfortunately, goes to great lengths to keep the inheritance out of the daughter's hands:

The order of inheritance is as follows: "If a man die and he have no son, then you shall cause his inheritance to pass to his daughter" (Num. 27:8). A son takes precedence over the daughter, and all the offspring of a son take precedence over the daughter; a daughter takes precedence over the brothers, and the offspring of a daughter take precedence over the brothers; brothers take precedence over the father's brothers, and the offspring of brothers take precedence over the father's brothers. This is the general principle: whoever has precedence in an inheritance, his offspring have also precedence, and the father has precedence before all his offspring.

This way of interpreting the Torah's order of succession made it possible for a granddaughter or grandson to benefit from their grandfather's estate, to the exclusion of his daughter, a direct descendant! Inequitable inheritance law was deemed justified on the basis that a son (and therefore his children) was "closer kin" than was a daughter (*Baba Batra* 110b).

Occasionally, courageous rabbinic voices surfaced, suggesting or supporting a position of equality regarding the inheritance rights of sons and daughters.[3] These arguments supporting a daughter's inheritance rights were, however, ignored or ridiculed. The Palestinian Talmud, for instance, rejected any such lenience by stating that it was "the sages of gentiles" who say that "the son and daughter are equal" when it comes to inheritance (*Baba Batra* 8:1). Imma Shalom, the only woman with a voice in all of the cited literature on daughters and inheritance, supported, unfortunately, the status quo, which disinherited daughters (*Shabbat* 16a–b). Where were the spiritual descendants of the daughters of Tzelophechad? Were there no daughters who made claim on their own account?

There is no doubt that there were fathers throughout the ages who wished to bequeath to their daughters as well as to their sons. Dowry is generally understood by Jewish law to have been the daughter's substitute for inheritance, though the Rabbis were exceedingly concerned that a daughter's right to dowry would make her a de facto "heiress." They therefore created not only explicit monetary limits to dowry that would not disenfranchise sons from their rightful inheritance, but they made it very clear to call daughters "creditors" rather than "heirs" in regard to their rights to a dowry. Even with the best intentions, however, dowry could not truly serve as an adequate substitute for inheritance, because of her husband's title to it.

So, how did fathers who loved their daughters circumvent the law in order to bequeath to daughters some of their worldly goods? The answer is through "gifts."

The preexisting system of inheritance was "passive," in that a parent didn't have to do anything, write anything, or say anything for there to be a normal course of action upon their deaths. It was clear that the first-born son would inherit a double portion, and that the other sons would divide the remainder. Daughters receive nothing, except perhaps maintenance and dowry. Where there were daughters only, they would share the estate equally. However, under the influence of Greek and Roman law, in which wills were commonplace, Jewish law integrated a form of "active" inheritance. Such dispositions, in contemplation of death, dramatically changed the nature of inheritance law, making way for a total overthrow of the preexisting system of intestate inheritance law.[4]

The Rabbis' initial resistance to wills went hand-in-hand with their conservatism regarding inheritance. Their disdain for any transgression of inheritance law was often specifically levied against those who willed or gifted property to those other than legal heirs.[5]

Part of the change in regard to gifting was created by the new value of *kavod ha-met*, "honor for the dead." That a dead man's request should be fulfilled as a religious duty was gaining in importance as a religious value, and was deemed one of the highest of Jewish values because one acts on behalf of another without expectation of reward in return (*Gittin* 14b–15a). The obligation to fulfill a dead man's request was expressed, for instance, in this passage: "A dying man once instructed those around him that a palm tree shall be given to his daughter, but the orphans proceeded to divide the estate and gave her no palm tree. . . . They must give her a palm tree and divide the estate all over again" (*Ketubot* 109b).

A much more significant change in favor of daughters came in medieval Jewish law with the testamentary provision of *sh'tar hatzi zakhar*, "deed of half the male share," in which a daughter was granted half of a son's portion.[6] The daughter's right to her father's estate under this deed "is like general inheritance rules," meaning that she would share both the rights and the disabilities that her brothers would encounter in taking their inheritance. And yet, a daughter was entitled to this inheritance only if she married.

All of these innovations and discussions regarding daughters and inheritance law derive from Num. 27 and the story of the daughters of Tzelophechad. Today, we recognize the emotional ramifications of inheritance and the division of estates. Inheritance is not just a legal matter, but also a deeply emotional matter, having deep spiritual and psychological meaning. Being "part of the loop" of succession paves the way, we know, for healthy grieving. It helps a person feel properly loved and provided for by his or her parents. For centuries, daughters had no such assurances. Inheritance, delivered after the death of a parent or loved one, has the potential to serve as a source of comfort for the mourners. Was only her brother's grief to be assuaged at that time of deepest grief?

I imagine that Mahlah, Noah, Hoglah, Milcah, and Tirtzah, the five sisters whose legal petition before Moses and the elders resulted in a legal victory for themselves, would be distraught to learn that the inheritance law created from their personal victory led to centuries of discrimination against women in inheritance law. Nonetheless, we applaud their courage and remain indebted to them for raising their voices in protest and drawing our attention to their cause.

RABBI STACY K. OFFNER

מטות

Matot

Women Speak Louder Than Words

*If a woman vows a vow to Adonai or binds a bond in
her father's house while she is a youth, and her
father hears her vow or the bond she has bound upon
her soul, and her father is silent, all her vows shall
stand and all the bonds that she has bound upon her
soul shall stand. But if her father restricts her on the
day he hears, all her vows and all the bonds that she
has bound upon her soul do not stand. (NUMBERS 30:4–6)*

WORDS ARE CHEAP. We see words strewn all over the place. We send
more words out into the universe all the time. Long gone are the
days when the writing of words actually took the painstaking time
of careful execution with fountain pen and ink. We quickly type out
words with our e-mail software, then press "click," and with a
swoosh, the words are gone out into the world, not to be retrieved
or taken back ever again.

Technology has changed the way we use words. Being able to
exercise the "delete" command allows us to be much less careful in
our approach to writing. Imagine how much more careful we would
be if the use of a feather quill might allow the reader to see our
initial intentions beneath any cross-outs. E-mail, voice mail, phone

conversations, tape recordings—all suggest faster talking, faster ways of getting our message across, more words pouring out into the vast universe of talk, talk, talk.

In the ancient Near East, significant documents were chiseled into stone. A word that is chiseled into existence is a carefully crafted word. Midrash teaches us that God gave us two ears and only one mouth in order that we might listen twice as much as we talk.[1] But in our time, talking is the method of the moment. Talk-radio, talk-shows, talk, talk, talk.

And that is why *Matot* offers us such a precious gift. *Matot* does not treat words as cheap or expendable, but as the incredibly powerful blocks upon which an entire society stands or falls. *Matot* focuses upon the most powerful kind of word that a person can utter: a *neder*, "vow." A *neder* is an extraordinarily powerful kind of word, because it is not just a word of description. It is a word of action. When a person makes a *neder*, it involves a promise or a commitment, and an obligation involving future behavior. If you were to say today, "I vow to smile whenever I see a stranger," your immediate words would lock you into future actions. So even if you didn't feel like smiling, even if you meant it when you said it but circumstances have changed, *Matot* reminds you that you can't simply "delete" the words you have uttered.

"If a man vows a vow to Adonai, or swears an oath to bind a bond upon his soul, he shall not violate his word, for all that has gone forth from his lips he shall do" (Num. 30:3).

Traditionally, Judaism has taken the making or uttering of vows very seriously. There is a whole talmudic literature of rules and regulations regarding good vows, bad vows, and the situations in which vows are valid or invalid. So crucial is keeping a vow, that even today, traditional Jews will not make the slightest promise—"I'll come to your party"—without adding the disclaimer, *b'li neder,* that is, "no vow intended." And no wonder. Do we always do according to that which goes forth from our mouths? What a different world it would be if each one of us took the words that we utter so seriously that we never violated a single one. We admire people who honor their word. As a rabbi, I am often visiting with families soon after the death of a loved one. It is a time when people tend to reflect upon the most important qualities of a person's character. How often I hear "His word was his bond" as one of the highest compliments someone can pay to another person. *Parashat Matot* inspires us to ensure that our word be our bond, that we not violate our word, that we do according to all that goes forth from our mouths.

But wait! Just when we were about to accept this awesome responsibility that is spelled out in Num. 30:3, just when we were about to embrace the spirit of this verse of Torah, we read on. The next verse continues,

> If a woman vows a vow to Adonai or binds a bond in her father's house while she is a youth, and her father hears her vow or the bond she has bound upon her soul, and her father is silent, all her vows shall stand and all the bonds that she has bound upon her soul shall stand. But if her father restricts her on the day he hears, all her vows and all the bonds that she has bound upon her soul do not stand. (Num. 30:4–6)

A woman's word is placed in contradistinction to a man's word. A man's word is inviolable, whereas a woman's word may be annulled by a man. Many feminists have long rebelled against this apparent prejudice against women. In 1895, Elizabeth Cady Stanton wrote, "We see from this chapter that Jewish women, as well as those of other nations, were held in a condition of perpetual tutelage or minority under the authority of the father until married and then under the husband, hence vows if in their presence if disallowed were as nothing."[2] But far from a condition of "perpetual tutelage," Rashi is careful to explain that the phrase "in her youth" refers only to a period of less than one year that falls between childhood and womanhood.[3] At least in Rashi the period of a woman's dependency is limited. Still, it is clear. Even though Rashi takes pains to explain that Jewish tradition limits the period of a woman's dependency, if a man vows a vow, it stands. If a woman vows a vow, it stands only with her father's permission. With the introduction of the verses regarding women's vows, *Matot* is no longer only about the importance of our words. Now it is about the difference between the words of men and women.

And in truth I must say that I do find a difference. As I consider the accolade "His word was his bond," I note that it is said most often by family members about the men in their lives. I do not hear that high praise being used to describe the women. Surely, it is not because the women are less trustworthy than the men; rather, it suggests that men and women use words in distinct ways.

When I think of women and words, I see images of women talking *together*. Women tend to say what they think with highest regard for the personal relationship rather than for the public record. The words are free-flowing. Indeed, Carol Gilligan, in her groundbreaking book on the different ways in which men and women see the world, suggests that "masculinity is defined through separation while femininity is defined through attachment."[4] Women use words to promote attachment. I see women talking with such a sense of trust in each other that they do not measure their words. In truth, it is as though one woman has the words, and the other woman holds the "delete" button, knowing, in love, which words to discard and which to save. Perhaps it is precisely that fluidity of language amongst women that causes the Torah to be so concerned with the power of women's words. In contrast to the Torah's usually cautious and limited use of words, the constant flow of words emanating from a daughter's mouth may have been viewed by the father as dangerous, in light of the extreme seriousness with which traditional Judaism takes the uttering of vows. A father's ability to absolve a woman of her words may therefore have been offered as a kindness. Traditional Jews today still recite *hatarat nedarim* every year, grateful to be freed from their vows. But that is different yet from someone else unilaterally absolving you without your request.

Surely, many women today do not rejoice in being absolved of responsibility for their words. They want the responsibility. They want to be obligated.

I remember going to a traditional synagogue many years ago where it was the custom for men to wear yarmulkes and *talleisim.* Only the rare few women wore them. It was my personal custom to wear a *tallis,* but not a yarmulke. An usher came over to my seat and handed me a yarmulke. He explained that if I was going to wear the *tallis,* I had to wear the yarmulke.

What a liberating experience that was. How odd—to feel a sense of liberation because I was being required to do something! Being required meant, for me, being taken seriously. Taking *Matot* seriously means that I must seek to be required to adhere to its message, even when the message was originally directed only to men.

Wouldn't it be interesting if, just as I seek to be required to adhere to the verses pertaining to men, men were required to adhere to the verses pertaining to women? Not only would women be obligated by their words, but men would learn the power of their words and be prepared to accept limitations upon them from others. Numbers 30:4ff., which limits a woman's vow specifically to when she lives with her father or husband, would be understood to symbolize all persons living in relationship with others. All young people, male and female, who live in their parental home—though they may not like it all the time—are not fully independent. They need to understand that their parents have a part in all that they say and do. *Matot* teaches us that their vows cannot stand without parental approval.

The same is true for married partners. Adults who are married have committed to a partnership. Therefore, adults must share their oaths and their vows with their spouses, and their spouses are entitled to input. *Matot* teaches us that the vows of married persons cannot stand without spousal approval.

One reading of our *parashah* might suggest that it is a sexist reminder of an age when men were free to utter vows and women were not. Another reading might suggest that the time has come to cast off the limitations that were placed upon women and allow men and women both to accept the responsibility for the vows that they utter. Still a third interpretation would encourage us to consider the different ways that men and women use words to communicate. I think we do best to see a fourth possibility: men learn from women and women learn from men, and together we accept readily the responsibility entailed in uttering vows, while also sharing those responsibilities with the people close to us, with whom we live in treasured relationship.

RABBI HARA E. PERSON

מסעי

Masa'ei

Boundaries and Limits

*T*he daughters of Tzelophechad did as God
had commanded Moses. (NUMBERS 36:10)

CREATING ORDER OUT OF CHAOS is one of the primary themes in the
Torah. God sets an example in the very first portion, and throughout the rest of the Torah, human beings strive to continue God's
work. Chaos is frightening, dangerous, and leaves too much to
chance, while order, through the establishment of boundaries, puts
everything in its rightful place. *Parashat Masa'ei* is a portion about
those boundaries. There are the physical boundaries of land, the
social boundaries of appropriate behavior, and the boundaries
defined by gender. In this portion, women represent a snag in an
otherwise tight narrative seam.

The itinerary of the Israelites' trip through the desert is
recounted, station by station, plotting a line across a landscape, as if
across a graph. That line leads to the steppes of Moab, at the Jordan near Jericho, where the focus turns to possession and borders—
what belongs to whom. Numbers 34 reads like a surveyor's map, as
it lays out the physical boundaries of land in topographical detail.
It is not enough that the exact borders of the land be specified,

but within the land itself, there are to be subboundaries that divide each clan from the others. Even the exceptions must be taken into account. The tribe of the Levites, who do not inherit a portion of land, are to be a communal responsibility, cared for by all the other tribes. The large groups are to be allocated greater portions than the smaller groups.

The institution of the cities of refuge (Num. 35:22–28) addresses the limits of acceptable behavior and allows for another exception to the rule. A solution is found for a situation that could potentially threaten the stability of the group. Those who have committed unintentional homicide have a place where they can belong and exist. Within those limits they are safe, while outside, they cannot be protected.

Limits are not to be pushed; risks are not to be taken. Safety is found in following rules, and staying within the parameters.

It is only the intentional murderer, a person who purposefully tears apart the fabric of civilization, who has no place at all within its borders. The text warns, *lo tachanifu et ha'aretz*, "do not pollute the land" (Num. 35:33). Blood does not belong spilled on the ground. But it is not blood itself that is a polluting agent; rather, it is the way in which blood is spilled that pollutes. Blood in its rightful place within the body is not pollution. Mary Douglas, an anthropologist who studies religious systems, writes about dirt as being a matter out of place. She writes, "Where there is dirt there is a system. Dirt is the by-product of a systematic ordering and classification of matter, in so far as ordering involves rejecting inappropriate elements."[1]

In the context of this *parashah*, Douglas's ideas are useful in understanding the importance of boundaries. The one who has intentionally murdered is that inappropriate element. No one has the right to take anyone else's blood. The system cannot tolerate such behavior, and there is no room for that person anywhere.

It is not coincidental that the next issue dealt with in this portion is women. Women are also potentially inappropriate elements who don't fit into the system, and thus have the capacity to be agents of pollution. Thus, the matter of the daughters of Tzelophechad is preceded by a cautionary text about the danger of overstepping the boundaries, for, just as murder undermines order, so do women who push against the limits of their social and familial roles. One way to effect order is the creation of laws that limit and define appropriate behavior. Phyllis Bird writes, "One of the chief aims of Israelite law is to assure the integrity, stability, and economic viability of the family as the basic unit of society. In this legislation, however, the interests of the family are commonly identified with those of its male head."[2]

In *Masa'ei*, women surface as destabilizing elements who challenge the order that the laws provide.

The heads of one of the clans approach Moses to discuss a problem concerning the daughters of Tzelophechad and their right to inherit. This is the second time these five daughters are mentioned in the text, having been previously discussed in *Parashat Pinchas*, chapter 27. Because their father died leaving only daughters, they asked to be given his portion. Moses brought their case before God, and their wish was granted. This event caused new laws of inheritance to be created, among which is a law that daughters can inherit from fathers if there is no son. The daughters of Tzelophechad set a significant precedent. They stepped outside the boundary and survived.

The overriding concern in the second part of their story appears, however, not to be the daughters themselves, their welfare, or their rights, but rather, the disposition of the sum of the tribe's holdings if they are allowed to inherit. The question raised here is not their question, but that of the men of their tribe. If the daughters marry, the land that they possess would become the property of the tribe into which they marry, and their family's possession would be diminished. So it is decided that they may marry anyone they wish, as long as it is someone from within the tribe.

This second part of their story must be read in light of the previous chapter. In Num. 27, it is the daughters who approach Moses and direct him toward their situation: *va-tikravnah b'not Tzelophechad*, "And the daughters of Tzelophechad came forward" (Num. 27:1). They are the active participants in this encounter. In contrast, in Num. 36, *yikravu roshei ha-avot*, "The family heads came forward" (Num. 36:1). In this second piece of the story, it is the male leaders who bring the problem to Moses. In Num. 27, each of the daughters is clearly named at the outset: "The names of his daughters were Mahlah, Noah, Hoglah, Milcah, and Tirtzah" (Num. 27:1). They are still "his daughters," but they are named, and thus are individuals. In Num. 36, however, eleven lines intervene between the time they are mentioned and the time they are called by their individual names. The whole time that their case is being discussed, they are simply the daughters of Tzelophechad. It is only in Num. 36:11, once the case has been decided, that their names appear in the text.

Throughout the discussion of the dilemma, the daughters are passive observers while the men, together with God, try to create a system of order that will enable them to retain control over the women and over the land. But once a resolution has been reached, the daughters act as they have been told to do. In contrast to Num. 27, their actions here are actually reactions: "The daughters of

Tzelophechad did as God had commanded Moses" (Num. 36:10). They became wives to the sons of their uncles; in other words, as Sforno points out in his comment on this verse, not only did they marry within their tribe, but they married their closest relatives. The language used in these lines reveals that even the actions they do take are passive. The expression *ken asu*, "so they did," is an expression often used to denote action taken in response to a command from God,[3] sometimes even against one's will or better judgment.[4]

An implied sense of resignation can be read into this phrase. The daughters did so, because they really had no other choice. As Jacob Milgrom points out, by marrying their first-cousins, in effect they do not really inherit, but simply pass the portion on to the family of their father's brother, who would have inherited if they had not been allowed to.[5]

In this conclusion to the story of the daughters of Tzelophechad, their power is diminished and their victory is dampened. Now that they are wives, they have been woven back into a familiar role, and their inheritance is safely back in male hands. These sisters had the potential to pollute—to be matter out of place. But they are put back into their place, and danger is averted. Order prevails; chaos has been controlled.

These five sisters are generally regarded in a positive light by the rabbinic tradition. In a discussion on Num. 27:4 about the order of their names, Rashi mentions the intelligence of the sisters. After all, as Rashi also points out, unlike most other laws in the Torah, Moses waited to give an answer on this issue until he was addressed by the sisters. Because these daughters had so much merit, the law was written through them. Today, their victory might not seem like a victory at all. Yes, they gain the right to inherit, but only temporarily, and they are restricted in their ability to choose marriage partners. Is Rashi right in attributing intelligence to these sisters? In the context of a world with extremely limited options for women, they truly did act with remarkable intelligence. It is not them but their kinsmen who bring the issue of their marriages to Moses, for that is not their main concern. They have achieved the right to inherit land and continue their father's name. But once a decision is reached about whom they can marry and the future of their land, they act quickly. Sforno wonders why they chose to marry their first-cousins, when they had some choice about whom they could marry. He suggests, again in his comment on Num. 36:10, that it was exactly because they were the closest: once they saw that God did not want their inheritance to be removed from the tribe, it made sense to keep the land in the family as much as possible. But perhaps there is another angle. Though the language about their marriages leaves them in the passive role, stating that "they became wives to the sons of their uncles" (Num. 36:11), the text presumes that the sisters chose their husbands, and not the other way around. They have been commanded directly by God to become wives to those who appealed to them (Num. 36:6). The choice, albeit limited, has been left in their hands.

So why, indeed, this particular choice?

Phyllis Bird writes, "One consequence of patrilineal organization is that women are to some extent either aliens or transients within their family of residence. Married women are outsiders in the household of their husband and sons, while daughters are prepared from birth to leave their father's household and transfer loyalty to a husband's house and lineage."[6]

The wisdom to which Rashi referred is a subtle intelligence. Though the daughters have taken the risk of pushing limits, they also know that limits are not infinitely elastic. They understand that there is a time for creating new paradigms, and a time for working within existing systems. They do not want to be like the example of the intentional murderer, who has pushed the limits so far that there is no longer any place for him. By choosing to marry within such a closed circle, they are most likely marrying people who know them, and who know their father. There is no need to prove themselves, and no need for the kind of transfer of loyalty that Bird speaks about. They will be neither aliens nor transients within the households of their first-cousins, and thus they have a greater chance for some level of authority. Within the circle of their extended family, they are not matter out of place, but at home. What is more, by all marrying cousins, there is a greater chance that they will stay close to one another. That they acted twice in union implies a sense of closeness between the sisters. This way, they will be able to maintain their relationships and call on each other for strength and support. As a group, they are clearly a force with which the Torah must contend. Sisterhood is indeed powerful.

Devarim/Deuteronomy

RABBI ANALIA BORTZ

דברים

Devarim

Essence and Transcendence

*T*hese are the words that Moses addressed to all Israel on the other side of the Jordan. Through the wilderness, in the Arabah, near the Suph, between Paran and Tophel, Laban, Hazerot, and Di-zahab, it is eleven days from Horeb to Kadesh-barnea by the Mount Seir route. It was in the fortieth year, on the first day of the eleventh month, that Moses addressed the Israelites in accordance with the instructions that the Lord had given him for them, after he had defeated Sihon, king of the Amorites, who dwelt in Heshbon, and Og, king of Bashan, who dwelt at Ashtarot [and] Edrei. On the other side of the Jordan, in the land of Moab, Moses undertook to expound this teaching. (DEUTERONOMY 1:1–5)

MOSES STANDS ON THE OTHER SIDE OF THE JORDAN. He can see the beautiful land that belongs to him, the land that God had given to his ancestors, the land of his dreams, of his yearning. Moses is going to teach all the precepts and the laws that God asked him to do. In this job, he, the teacher, has to transfer all the foundation of the people of Israel.

We stand in front of a double image of one leader. On the one hand, we see his sadness because he is on the other side of the Jordan. Yet, on the other hand, he begins to teach again. Moses has to give up, not because he wants to do that, but because this is a request from God and he has to obey.

Our identification with Moses' suffering is almost inevitable. His words move us. During forty long years Moses had devoted his strength, his best energies, to caring for his people, to the point that he sometimes tried to give up. But he continued, so that a slave people, plunged into a cruel exile, turns into a free and proud nation. This people settles in its own land, territory that besides sheltering them, represents the supreme bastion of freedom, and in it, the presence of God. In his long task of guiding people with a slave mentality, used to comfort more than challenge, Moses is about to crystallize his work.

How can he not see it fulfilled? The threshold of satisfaction in this task was simply the Jordan River. To step on the soil of the Promised Land would have been (for this 120-year-old man, the great leader of our people, who saw God face to face, but who always lived in the exile) the maximum obtainable satisfaction.

Go ahead, Moses, just a few steps to make your dreams come true! But Moses' request to cross the Jordan, limit of the illusion, is denied: "These are the words that Moses addressed on the other side of the Jordan" (Deut. 1:1). Moses begins to say goodbye. The Book of Deuteronomy is the five farewell letters of Moses.

It hurts us. In the image of the greatest prophet watching and missing the land he will never enter, we can see the reflection of one of the most frequent human feelings: disappointment. A destroyed illusion, deep frustration, a dream that will never come true. Both sink and drown in our own Jordan River, insurmountable limit between expectations and achievements.

This is the sense described by the poet Rachel in a poem titled *"Ish U'Nebo Lo"*: each one has his own Nebo. What does Nebo mean? Nebo is the name of the mountain from which Moses watched the Promised Land, that land on the other side. Moses will never stand on it. Nebo is the symbolic place of all our disappointments—grave of the desired goals not fulfilled. Nebo is the reality of what Moses wishes to do but is forbidden, although he wants to cross the threshold.

It was very difficult for our commentators to understand why God didn't agree to his request. Why doesn't a plea that moves us so much also persuade a great and benevolent God? Why does the leader's desire fall into despair?

The exegetes took the first words of the Divine answer to Moses, *rav lach*, as an expression of the incomprehensible: "Enough! Never speak to me of this matter again!" (Deut. 3:26). *Rav lach*—an expression of difficult translation that might mean "It's enough" or "It's enough for you." In that way, the dialogue between God and Moses, between a father and a son, will begin.

The book of *Devarim* is all the words repeated again and again so that God's message would be clear. Moses has to convey this message, the words of God that cut him off from the possibility of finishing all the work, that say to him that it is enough.

In *Midrash Sifrei*, it is suggested that the intention of Deut. 3:26 is "It's enough, don't entreat me more, so it wouldn't be said in the future, how strict the Master is (that is, God)." As the verdict is unfair, this interpretation depicts God asking not to be questioned. Another explanation of *Tosafot* looks for justification for the denial of the request in the words of Moses himself, when the rebellion of Korah took place years ago while crossing the desert. Korah had challenged Moses' authority, and he had answered *rav lachem* (Num. 16:3), that is, "Enough for you." Moses had sent away Korah's rebels with the same word that God uses to deny Moses' request.

Nevertheless, it is possible to interpret the expression *rav lach* in another way: "Much is yours, much you achieved. Now you have to give way for the personal fulfillment of others, of those who come after you; those who are your future, whom you have borne in this long pregnancy of forty years, this people who tries to grow up, this people that you, Moses, you yourself have conceived."

Why might the text describe Moses as pregnant with the Jewish people.

It is remarkable that in the first verses of our *parashah* the Hebrew root *a-v-r* is repeated twice. The location of Moses seems to be very important. Our scholars have interpreted this word in various ways. Even though it may include different meanings, the word is the same, and as no letter exists by chance in our biblical text, the meaning of this invites us to study it with particular care.

The text speaks of words that "Moses addressed to all Israel, on the other side of the Jordan," *asher diver Moshe el kol Israel be'ever ha'- Yarden* (Deut. 1:1). And again the text uses *be'ever ha'Yarden* in "On the other side of the Jordan, in the land of Moab, Moses undertook to expounded this teaching" (Deut. 1:5). Later, in speaking to Moses, God uses *atem ovrim*: "And charge the people as follows: You will be passing [*atem ovrim*] through the territory of your kinsmen" (Deut. 2:4). And Moses will say, *E'evra beartzecha baderech*, "Let me pass through your country" (Deut. 2:27).

After so many times of using the root *a-r-v* as a noun for the static location of Moses and as a verb for the dynamic steps of the people, the teacher, Moses, mentions his pupil, his continuity, and says, "I also charged Joshua at that time, saying: You have seen with your eyes all that the Lord your God has done to these two kings; so shall the Lord do to all the kingdoms into which you shall cross over [*asher ata over shama*]" (Deut. 3:21). At the last words of the *parashah*, the leader encourages his pupil. Moses himself is suffering, but he knows that is the moment to give Joshua the force to carry the people, and to cross the Jordan.

This root, *a-v-r*, with meanings such as "go over," "get wroth," "cross," and "go ahead," has another kind of meaning as well, one that leads to our image of Moses' pregnancy. Moses is crushed that, after his intensive work, he will not be allowed to even set foot in the land. Moses is *be'ever*—on the other side. In the *Midrash Tannaim*, Rabbi Yehoshua connects the usage here with the same Hebrew root meaning "pregnancy." Rabbi Yehoshua uses a graphic image of a woman who is unable to bend over because of her pregnancy. This image implies that Moses is being punished because of external factors, namely, the behavior of the people, over which he had no control. These people are "inside" him. He, Moses, carried these people, making them alive. Rabbeinu Bahya ben Asher, quoting an allegorical interpretation based on the *Zohar*, also compares the etymology of this verb *avar*, with the word *ivur*, which means "gestation."

On not passing to the Promised Land, Moses will die on the other side of the Jordan River. His soul and his spirituality will rest in the people of Israel, and so each generation will be able to have a small part of his greatness. All the members of Israel will be, therefore, spiritual heirs of Moses, children of his legacy. From Moses, a whole people has been born, who will transmit his message from generation to generation.

God addresses this "mother delivering her people" in the feminine: *rav lach*. The usual way of addressing a man in this case would have been *rav lecha*, and, although in the parchment text of the Torah the dots that indicate vowels do not appear, we come away from the text with the impression that God does see Moses as in some sense female, pregnant.

Moses modifies his attitude after this scene. He reconsiders his situation, realizes that being *me'ubar* (pregnant) means to be *me'ever* (beyond). To be finishing this gestation is "beyond." It is his own possibility of transcending, to give others the possibility of conquest. This multiple pregnancy will itself be the fulfillment of his task.

Moses now looks toward the future. He, who was born in the water, who was rescued from the water that saved his life, who opened the water of the sea that saved his own and his people's lives, who demanded water so that his people would not die, is now the carrier of a new amniotic liquid. This liquid contains a whole people who stand before the water of the Jordan for a new conquest, a new rebirth. Today, among those waters, he allows a people to develop and be born, so as to grow, to cross the fluid, to conquer the Land.

Moses' vision changes completely. He doesn't complain to God anymore. He teaches the people: "On the other side of the Jordan, in the land of Moab, Moses undertook to expound this teaching" (Deut. I:5).

Moses is completing his fortieth year in the desert. This number represents a completed situation, fullness. A pregnancy lasts forty weeks, until the fetus is completed. Each year represents a week, and Moses is about to reach his term.

It does not matter how many children Moses has; the dedication and devotion to each one in particular is like that of a mother with her children. Each one is unique and exclusive. Thus, Moses speaks to the people of Israel in general, and to each one in particular.

Moses teaches, then, the rules, precepts, and commandments to his children, to us, and registers them and us in the school of life. He accompanies them and us by the hand; he leads them and us, until they reach the moment of his farewell.

In this *parashah*, Moses starts his first farewell speech. It is hard for him to say goodbye. Moses is like a true *Yiddishe mama* saying, "I want to accompany you so that you can fulfill yourself and your goal, and . . . so that you don't leave me alone!"

And now, Moses has delivery pains. Each contraction is a step ahead toward Mount Nebo, the precise place that will enable him to look at the future.

This future will be endowed with balance between his death and the life of his people, his children. He does not want anesthesia. His dialogue with God is sincere and mature. Any epidural would not allow him to see his work fulfilled; it would not allow him to feel that unique capacity of conceiving, begetting, giving birth, that precise instant in which essence turns into transcendence. It would not allow him to be this people's mother, in the deepest sense of the word.

ואתחנן

Va'etchanan

"A Land Flowing with Milk and Honey": Sexualizing the Land

*A*nd this is the instruction—the laws and rules—that Adonai your God has commanded [me] to impart to you, to be observed in the land that you are about to cross into and occupy, so that you, your children, and your children's children may revere Adonai your God and follow, all the days of your life, all God's laws and commandments that I enjoin upon you, to the end that you may long endure. Obey, O Israel, willingly and faithfully, that it may go well with you and that you may increase greatly [in] a land flowing with milk and honey, as Adonai, the God of your ancestors, spoke to you. (DEUTERONOMY 6:1–3)

THIS SECTION OF *Parashat Va'etchanan*, which immediately follows a reiteration of the Ten Commandments (in Deut. 4:44–5:30), serves as reminder that if the Israelites obey the instruction imparted by Moses, great reward will ensue, and they will enter and occupy a land flowing with milk and honey. What exactly is this land of milk and honey that the Israelites are waiting to receive? And why is it that we do not in fact enter the land at the end of the Book of Deuteronomy? Moses dies before his people enter the land, and indeed, the Book of Deuteronomy ends before we ourselves have witnessed the *eretz zavat halav u-devash*, "a land that flows with milk and honey." The narrative ends before we have been satisfied, and we are left awaiting entry into the fertile territory that we are told will nourish and sustain us.

The image of a lush agricultural environment is enticing for a nation that has been wandering in a dry desert for forty years. The phrase "a land flowing with milk and honey" is found in five other places in the Book of Deuteronomy itself.[1] Generally, commentators see in the phrase the concept of abundance. This is indeed a sensible explanation, considering that owning a milk-producing herd of goats and having the ability to produce honey, whether through gathering it in the wild or rendering it from various fruit syrups, would have indicated agricultural success in biblical times. It is most likely that the usage of the words "milk" and "honey" may be seen as metaphors for fertility and wealth rather than as literal categories. Contemporary commentator Jeffrey Tigay summarizes this perspective:

> "A land oozing milk and honey" came to be a proverbial description of the fertility of the land of Israel, representing the products of animals and the earth, of herders and farmers. It is not merely a neutral descriptive phrase, but carries positive overtones. It is not always meant literally. The scouts who toured the Promised Land brought back grapes, pomegranates, and figs as a confirmation that it was indeed "a land oozing milk and honey" (Num. 13:23, 27). Since they did not bring back milk products, they must have

meant the phrase as a general reference to fertility
rather than specifically to milk and honey.[2]

Metaphors of milk and honey, while certainly correlated to
the notion of abundance, may also be viewed as allegorical tools
that sexualize the land, portraying it (her) as a female body. The virgin territory awaits the virile influence and consumption of the
Israelites. It is a ripe land, a land that gushes like a surrealistic milky
breast, and its honeyed orifices are anticipating the acts of occupa-
tion, even penetration, and then conceiving and multiplying for its
masters. As Moses prepares the Israelites to enter the land by
instructing them in God's laws and commandments, they are also
preparing to become newly masculated after being cared for by God
as if they were infants when they were wandering in the desert.

The Hebrew root z-w-v (Deut. 6:3), "flow, ooze, gush," supports this reading. Tigay states that "the Hebrew verb refers to bodily organs leaking fluids and, in poetry, to water gushing" (see Lev.
15 and Ps. 78:20).[3] This same word refers to the issue of blood
from a menstruant woman, a discharge of semen from a man, and
the gushing of the intestines when a person is pierced with a
sword.[4]

The root z-w-v refers not only to the flow of bodily fluids, but
also can refer to a liminal state of one form or another. Each time
the term appears, it is with reference to the threshold between life
and death. In the case of the person who has been pierced with a
sword, the threshold between living and dying is rather obvious. Perhaps the threshold is less perceptible in regard to semen and menstruation. The discharge of these two fluids does not represent a
situation of imminent life and death. They are, however, the fluids
that symbolize the human ability to create life, and each time that
they are visible represents a loss of that procreative possibility—

sperm or an egg that has failed to create new life is in essence a small death. Flowing water, too, not commonly found in the middle of the desert, is a conspicuous biblical reminder that water truly is a fluid that bestows and maintains life, and without which death is certain.

The flow of sexual fluids is not treated casually in biblical or rabbinic tradition. This is indicated not only in the biblical texts on semen and menstruation, but also in the laws of family purity and proper sexual conduct discussed in later rabbinic sources.[5] It is important to ask, therefore, why the word root *z-w-v*, while often associated with the flowing of the "forbidden" fluids of bodily discharge, would be juxtaposed with the enticing fertility of the Promised Land. Why is a word with a connotation of sexual distress, inappropriateness, or prohibition used to discuss the land that is meant to embody the loftiest object of the people of Israel's desire? Perhaps the use of the root *z-w-v*, in this particular context, is indicative of ambivalence toward desire itself.

It is not only this word root that may signify sexual overtones in Deut. 6:3. As previously mentioned, the usage of the words "milk" (*halav*) and "honey" (*devash*) also convey sexual content. It is without question that these words in Song of Songs 4:11 and 5:1, for example, are laden with sexual and sensual meaning: "Your lips, O my bride, drop as the honeycomb: honey and milk are under your tongue, and the scent of your garments is like the scent of Lebanon" (Song of Songs 4:11); "I am come into my garden, my sister, my bride: I have gathered my myrrh with my spice; I have eaten my honeycomb with my honey; I have drunk my wine with my milk. Eat, lovers, drink: be drunk with love" (Song of Songs 5:1). Clearly, the honeycomb, the honey, and the milk are the fluids of female sexual response.

Having ascertained that "a land flowing with milk and honey" connotes a feminized land, discussed in terms that evoke images of female bodily emissions, let us return to the issue of the amalgamation of desire and ambivalence, communicated through the language of our text. Anne McClintock, in her essay "The Lay of the Land: Genealogies of Imperialism," discusses a similar issue later on in the historical spectrum. Although the historical periods and social settings are entirely different, parallels may certainly be drawn between the two texts being explored. McClintock analyzes Columbus's comment during his exploration of 1492, that the earth was shaped like a woman's breast with a nipple. She states, "Columbus' breast fantasy draws on a long tradition of male travel [and territorial conquest] as an erotics of ravishment."[6] McClintock's thesis is that the feminizing of land and the usage of female images as boundary markers inherently coincide with male anxiety:

> What is the meaning of this persistent gendering of the imperial unknown? As European men crossed the dangerous thresholds of their known world, they ritualistically feminized borders and boundaries. Female figures were planted like fetishes at the ambiguous points of contact, at the borders and orifices of the contest Zone. Sailors bound wooden female figures to their ships' prows and baptized their ships—as exemplary threshold objects—with female names. Cartographers filled the blank seas of their maps with mermaids and sirens. Explorers called unknown lands "virgin" territory. Philosophers veiled "Truth" as female, then fantasized about drawing back the veil. In myriad ways, women served as mediating and threshold figures by means of which men oriented themselves in space, as agents of power and agents of knowledge.[7]

McClintock posits that the establishment of feminized boundaries and borders is a kind of compensatory gesture, countering a male loss of boundary by overemphasizing a ritualization of boundary, which is often paired with military violence. While we cannot entirely overlay McClintock's conclusions onto the biblical text, we are able to verify that cities are often personified as women in the Hebrew Bible in discussions of war. Nahum 3:1 and 3:5–6 are examples of the destruction of a city being described as a female victim. Pamela Gordon and Harold C. Washington, through looking at Nah. 3:5–6 and other prophetic texts, refer to rape as a biblical military metaphor that still has relevance in contemporary times.[8]

A biblical tradition that personifies land and borders as women who are to be sexually desired and/or occupied is a challenge for our feminist sensibilities. Deuteronomy 6:3 personifies the land as female, and creates a scenario wherein the masculinized Israelites desire, and consequently ready themselves to move in and occupy, the female body/land. The ambivalent attitude toward desire as expressed in the language of Deut. 6:3 hints at the duality of desire and repulsion inherent in the male construct of femininity. The fact that the land is feminized, and thus the female objectified, naturally results in an incomplete picture of woman. We see the female as passive, as something to be entered, crossed into, and occupied. This equation of women and land, and consequent objectification of women, creates a situation whereby we see women as able to be either desired or reviled. Either option is equally possible when we do not see her as a whole being, as *who* she is rather than *what* she is. The (female) land's boundaries are there to be desired or conquered. The linguistic association of "forbidden fluids" with the delicacies of milk and honey *(z-w-v)* in Deuteronomy points directly to this friction.

If the phrase "a land flowing with milk and honey" linguistically evokes an image of male arousal and of revulsion, an image of the need to occupy the female body, an image of violence and boundary crossing, then the notion that the Israelites never do enter the land at the end of the Book of Deuteronomy leaves us with a powerful message. On some level, we may claim that the Book of Deuteronomy is unwilling to have us enter the land under these circumstances. Until the body is seen in her wholeness, we are not considered ready to enter her. Our entry must be a partnership, a gentle and mutual ingathering. In the meantime, until we can see the land in this way, we are left standing outside, in the desert.

RABBI GILA COLMAN RUSKIN

עקב

Ekev

Circumcision, Womb, and Spiritual Intimacy

*A*nd now, Israel, what does the Lord your God require of you, but to fear the Lord your God, to walk in all God's ways, and to love God, and to serve the Lord your God with all your heart and with all your soul, to keep for your good the commandments of the Lord, and God's statutes, which I command you this day? Behold, unto the Lord your God belongs the heaven, and the heaven of heavens, the earth, with all that is therein. Only the Lord had a delight in your ancestors to love them, and God chose their descendants after them, even you, above all peoples, as it is this day. Circumcise therefore the foreskin of your heart, and be no more stiff-necked. (DEUTERONOMY 10:12–16)

AT THE AGE OF EIGHT DAYS, every Jewish baby boy dramatically enters the eternal covenant between his ancestors and God by undergoing ritual circumcision. Family, friends, and community witness the surgical procedure, which consists of cutting and removing the foreskin from the baby boy's penis. The power of the ritual derives its ancient roots from the Book of Genesis, when Abraham was commanded to circumcise himself and all males in his household. The ceremony, in its bloody physicality, visibly affects everyone in the room, reminding us of the fragility of life.

In *Parashat Ekev*, in Deut. 10:16, we are once again commanded to circumcise. But in this new context, it is not a genital circumcision; rather, it is a metaphoric reference: "circumcise the foreskin of your heart." How do we understand this leap from the literal/physical to the metaphoric/spiritual? And how can women, in particular, comprehend this metaphor involving male anatomy?

This ultimate male metaphor, circumcision, appears many times throughout the Bible. Rashi, in his comments on Exod. 6:12, cites examples from Jeremiah (uncircumcised ear and uncircumcised heart), Exodus (uncircumcised lips), Habakkuk (intoxication), and Leviticus (fruit of a tree). Rashi's comment on Exod. 6:12 identifies this reference to the foreskin as "that which obstructs." Thus, an ear that is "uncircumcised" blocks the ability to hear and to understand.

The text in Jeremiah refers to the prophet's frustration with the people of Israel, who will not hearken to his message: "To whom shall I speak and warn, that they will take heed? Behold their ear is blocked [*arela oznam*] and they are unable to listen!" (Jer. 6:10).

"How will Pharaoh listen to me when I have 'uncircumcised lips' [*arel s'fatayim*]," protests Moses when God commands him to go before Pharaoh and demand, "Let My people go." Moses means that his lips are somehow obstructed, and thus it is difficult for him to express himself orally.

Habakkuk uses the term "become uncircumcised" (*ha-arel*) to refer to the state of intoxication that "obstructs" glory and introduces shame: "You are sated more with shame than with glory; you too will drink and become confounded *[ha-arel]*" (Hab. 2:16).

A second text from Jeremiah sheds light on the meaning of the words from Deut. 10:16, "circumcise the foreskin of your heart": "Behold the days are coming," says God, "when I shall deal with everyone who is circumcised for uncircumcision: with Egypt, with Judah, with Edom, with the Children of Ammon, and with Moab, and with all those who dwell in the remotest corners of the wilderness; for all the nations are uncircumcised, and the house of Israel is of uncircumcised heart *[arlay lev]*" (Jer. 9:24–25). The physical act of circumcision of the foreskin is not enough, declares Jeremiah. If one's heart is "uncircumcised," then the physical circumcision is seemingly nullified, rendering the Jews equal to the uncircumcised nations, who do not follow the mitzvot and who are not part of the covenant.

Based on these examples, the metaphor of foreskin and circumcision is this: just as a blocked ear interferes with the full potential of hearing, and a speech impediment interferes with the full potential of speaking, a foreskin prevents the penis from its full potential of spiritual feeling.

So what does it mean to "circumcise the foreskin of your heart"? Alternate translations range from "you shall cut away the barrier of your heart" to "remove the thickening from around your heart." As we look at the context in Deuteronomy, we notice that this metaphoric command comes as part of an answer to a rhetorical question, "Now, O Israel, what does Adonai your God ask of you?" (Deut. 10:12). The answer: "Only to fear Adonai your God, to walk in all of God's ways, to love God, and to serve Adonai your God, with all your heart and with all your soul, to observe the commandments of God and the statutes that I command you this day for your benefit" (Deut. 10:12–13). The adjuration "circumcise the foreskin of your heart and no longer stiffen the neck"

(Deut. 10:16) seems to indicate the necessity of removing all obstacles and impediments to the expression of this love and fear of God and commitment to mitzvot. When the foreskin of the heart is removed, the spiritual sensation is also made more intense, as contact between the self and the Divine becomes unobstructed.

Throughout the Book of Deuteronomy, there are numerous references to *ahavat ha-Shem* (loving God) and *yirat ha-Shem* (fearing God), the most familiar being the first paragraph of the Shema, which is found in Deut. 6: *V'ahavta et adonai elohecha b'chol l'vavcha,* "You shall love the Lord your God with all your heart." In these many passages about *ahavah,* the formula is included: in order to love your God, you must walk in all of God's ways by following God's commandments.

In the talmudic tractate *Berakhot,* the nature of *yirat ha-Shem* is clarified: "Everything is in the hand of Heaven, except for the fear of Heaven." The scriptural source for this statement comes directly from our passage in *Ekev:* "And now, Israel, what does Adonai your God ask of you? Only to fear Adonai your God and walk in God's ways" (Deut. 10:12). Clearly, this action of loving and fearing God is the one decision that each of us must make ourselves; it is a courageous and monumental volitional act that demands an individual's strong commitment to a life of mitzvot.

But the passages from Hab. 2 and Jer. 9 indicate that the Jews could be fulfilling mitzvot and still be described as *arel* (uncircumcised). If one is engaging in drunken behavior (Habakkuk) or in any immoral or unethical acts (Jeremiah), then physical circumcision, which is the sign of the covenant, does not "count." Without the vulnerability and *kavannah* (intention and focus) implied by "circumcising the heart," the merely automatic act of fulfilling a mitzvah is hollow, not hallowed.

Thus those who are routinely circumcised (men) can still be, in a spiritual sense, uncircumcised. And those who do not undergo a ritual circumcision (women) potentially can be "circumcised." For truly, half the population of the Jewish people never undergoes a *brit milah*. Does this metaphor, which transmits a spiritual message about taking the risk of opening up the tender places to achieve a deeper intimacy, exclude women from the potential intense and gratifying relationship that a male Jew can achieve with God; or does it include them covenantally in a new way?

This *parashah* requires of women an extra leap of imagination to understand fully the meaning of the metaphor of circumcision. In its richness of imagery, however, *Parashat Ekev* also requires men to take that extra leap of imagination. In the opening verses of the *parashah*, we are told of the rewards that will be bestowed as a result of hearkening to God's commandments: "Adonai your God will safeguard for you the covenant and the kindness that God swore to your ancestors. God will love you, bless you and multiply you, and God will bless the fruit of your womb" (Deut. 7:12–13).

How can a male, who has no uterus, and no potential for carrying a child within him, comprehend that experience? How can he understand the awesome responsibility/privilege of nurturing life within our bodies, and the desperate desire for that child to be blessed with health, beauty, intelligence, and happiness? Only by taking that extra leap of imagination will he be able to apply this female yearning for the care of this baby within her to his relationship to God as well.

"Circumcise the foreskin of your heart" means, "Remove whatever barriers that interfere with the total intimacy of loving and fearing God, which will lead to the ultimate fulfillment of one's life in covenant." "And you shall be rewarded for observing God's mitzvot by God blessing the fruit of your womb" then means, "May all for which you have taken responsibility, all of your creations, flourish, and may they be endowed with the holiness that can be granted only by a true intimacy with God."

RABBI LAURA M. RAPPAPORT

ראה
Re'eh

A Time to Tear Down,
a Time to Build Up

You must completely destroy all the sites at which
the nations you are to dispossess worshiped their
gods—on the high mountains, on hills, and under
each leafy tree. Tear down their altars, smash their pillars, burn their sacred posts with fire, and cut down
the carvings of their gods, obliterating their name
from that site. (DEUTERONOMY 12:2–3)

FOR FEMINIST WOMEN AND MEN, ideologically reared on visions of
ethnic and religious inclusiveness and the nurturing embrace of
diverse peoples, reading *Parashat Re'eh* can be a disturbing experience.

One doesn't need a feminist background—only a basic knowledge of twentieth-century political history—to reel in horror at the
conjured images of wiping out sacred objects, and even all memory, of non-Israelite religious communities. The changing of names
in order to revise history reminds us of Russian Communists
attempting to reprogram their comrades through the renaming of
cities and the ongoing rewriting of history texts. The wanton

351

destruction of once cherished property brings to mind zealous young Maoists searching private homes for priceless Chinese art and antiquities to demolish. It recalls scenes of early supporters of Ayatollah Khomeini annihilating every vestige of Western culture and influence, and bonfires in any number of settings, burning books not deemed acceptable to current modes of thinking,

And through our memory of these events, we perceive a link between the destruction of material goods and the destruction of life. It seems that once one loses respect for highly regarded possessions, one loses respect for the possessor as well.

It does not take long for the text to make this leap:

> If your brother, your mother's son, or your son or daughter, or the wife of your bosom, or your closest friend entices you in secret, saying, "Come let us worship other gods," whom neither you nor your fathers have known . . . , do not assent or hearken to him. Show him no pity or compassion, and do not shield him; but take his life. Let your hand be the first against him to put him to death, and the hand of the rest of the people thereafter. Stone him to death, for he sought to draw you away from the Lord your God. . . . Thus all Israel will hear and be afraid, and such evil things will not be done again in your midst. (Deut. 13:7–12)

Who among us can fail to shudder at the thought of loved ones informing on one another's private words and acts?

We are certainly not the first to recognize the danger lurking in exhortations to annihilate another culture. Those before us had many vivid associations with revolts and atrocities even more horrifying than our own. We, like our Jewish ancestors, search to fit these harsh scriptural words into a scheme that promotes the true divine purpose of our written and oral tradition: to usher God and holiness into the world and into our lives.

According to Jewish tradition, Torah speaks to us in a multitude of voices. This divinely inspired literary gift contains layer upon layer of meaning. Among these voices is the one that communicates in the language of revolution.

This holy book calls for radical and unprecedented social change. The chasm between the worldview advocated by the God of the Israelites and the worldview of contemporaneous cultures is of inconceivable width and depth. This God—making His/Her debut on the worldwide deity-worshiping scene—demands from followers a shift in values, priorities, ethics, and daily behavior. This God promises the newly forming community that it will dwell in its own land, under its own system of leadership. This God requests no less than individual and communal revolution.

Inspiring human beings to make a complete break from the status quo has never been a simple task. Among the essential components of this challenging undertaking are a dynamic and charismatic leader and extreme rhetoric. There is no room for subtle nuance in the parlance of revolution. Everyone must be clear that big changes are on the horizon. Radical social reform requires incendiary words of passion to motivate new adherents to act. Overstatement is the trademark of incipient movements for change.

This radical prose may strike postbiblical ears as dangerously extreme, but no one can deny that social change requires some destruction of the existing order. Even young children recognize the bulldozer as the preeminent sign of a building project. Whether it be Judaism or modern feminism, establishing a new mindset necessitates some pillar razing and altar smashing. Included in the cultural jetsam that must be cast off to make room for a new way of life are familiar assumptions and stereotypes, language that both expresses and shapes our attitudes and cherished icons. The Torah text is unflinching in its presentation of this reality.

But this inflammatory voice of revolution is only one of those that speaks to us from Scripture. We also hear a more pragmatic voice, urging action of a less dramatic nature. This other voice adds a different dimension to the holy endeavor of building and sustaining a new people.

In *Re'eh*, God instructs the Israelites concerning the observance of the three pilgrimage festivals: Pesach, Shavuot, and Sukkot. How interesting that the commandment to obliterate alien religious customs is followed so closely by the commandment to observe festivals clearly rooted in pagan culture! The Pesach season, culminating in Shavuot, began as a Canaanite farming festival. And, according to the rabbis of the Mishnah, Sukkot observance in its early years actually included liturgical reference to idolatry. The following account describes the Sukkot celebration in Second Temple times: "When [the priests] reached the gate that leads out to the east, they turned their faces to the west and said, 'Our fathers . . . worshiped the sun toward the east, but as for us, our eyes are turned toward the Lord'" (*Sukkah* 5:4).

The text that sparked passion with its revolutionary rhetoric now speaks to us in the voice of the real and the practical. In actuality, developing and sustaining a new movement involves a balance between destroying and incorporating the old. As we read in the Book of Ecclesiastes, "There is a time to tear down and a time to build up" (Eccles. 3:3).

Only God can create *ex nihilo*—from nothing. Human beings improve, expand, and reform, but in ways that connect us with our past. While our ideals may lie in visions of a drastically different future, our nature drives us to blend the innovative with the familiar. Deeply ingrained patterns, whether genetically or culturally determined, will inevitably temper iconoclastic radicalism.

In the early years of the women's movement, revolutionary rhetoric flowed freely and liberally. Every association with the traditional female role was deemed oppressive and demeaning, from marriage and childrearing and stereotypical female careers, to bras and leg shaving and the color pink. Religion and government and other well-entrenched institutions shaped largely by men were likewise dismissed as tyrannical patriarchy.

The use of inflammatory overstatement was necessary in this nascent phase of feminism. How else can one arouse the oblivious masses? Nothing shakes people out of complacency like the provocative language of extremes.

Gender revolution stirred in the liberal Jewish realm too. Some advocated disregarding much, if not all, of Jewish tradition, so corrupted was it by patriarchal attitudes. Many disregarded extremism, but the ideological milieu made it difficult to ignore that Judaism had become heavily one-sided and distorted through its centuries-old exclusion of women from leadership and religious power. Minds opened to the realization that for Jewish tradition to be balanced and whole, women's voices needed to be heard. The Divine spirit resides within all humanity—women as well as men—and our liturgy and theology needed to acknowledge this, our highest truth. For this to happen, some aspects of the male-dominated tradition needed razing indeed.

We are now several decades past the ordination of the first woman to the Reform rabbinate, and the revolutionary dust has settled. In the secular and the liberal Jewish worlds alike, the rousing voice of revolution has been largely replaced with the voice of pragmatism. What was torn down is now being reexamined. Women tentatively try on each discarded item: how will it fit in this new feminist age? Should it be returned to the trash heap? Can it be cleaned off and reclaimed for use, albeit in a more "enlightened" way?

In society at large, women reconsider traditional roles. Can we reclaim homemaking? Motherhood? What about our daughters' desire for ballerina and princess costumes? Similarly, Jewish women contemplate their tradition. Is there a place for *mikveh* in the lives of nontraditional women? Should they embrace the traditional form of prayer? What about the teachings of men who barred women from all houses of study?

At each point in the process we ask, Have we surrendered our gains, or successfully incorporated our past? Have we torn down when we should have built up? Built up when we should have torn down? Achieving balance is a delicate procedure. We see the scale tip to one side and then to the other. Ours is eternal vigilance.

God enjoins us in *Parashat Re'eh* to live up to an ultimate vision of joyful inclusiveness: "You shall rejoice before the Lord your God with your son and daughter, your male and female slave, the Levite within your gates, and the stranger, the fatherless, and the widow in your midst, at the place where the Lord your God will choose to establish the Divine name" (Deut. 16:11).

Re'eh reflects the conceptual ideal of the entire Torah: humanity achieves holiness through the active process of balancing human needs, human desires, and lofty values. We Jews are to break from the ways of other peoples, but not entirely. We are to question common assumptions, yet adhere firmly to traditional holy principles. We are to be poised to build up or to tear down as the need arises.

Clearly, there is no single answer, no single path. Ecclesiastes teaches us that "to everything there is a season" (Eccles. 3:1). For Jews, as well as for feminists, finding the path of truth requires a lifelong search with hearts and minds open wide to life- and God-affirming possibilities.

שפטים

Shoftim

Principles for Feminist Approaches to Torah

*J*udges and guards set for yourself in all
your gates. (DEUTERONOMY 16:18)

THE OPENING VERSE OF *Parashat Shoftim*, the Torah portion beginning
with the Hebrew word for "judges," refers to appointing appropriate officials for courts of justice, who "will judge the people with
mishpat tzedek [righteous judgment]" (Deut. 16:18). It is a fit beginning for a Torah portion that appears to be exclusively concerned
with rules for an orderly and holy society.

Shoftim is a pastiche of laws and principles about justice, exclusive worship of the Holy One, witnesses for capital cases, treatment
of accused murderers, obedience to authorities, restrictions on leaders, standards for prophecy, refuge for those who commit
manslaughter unintentionally, conduct during wartime, and purging
the community of impurity when a dead person's killer cannot be
identified. It is part of Moses' lengthy final oration to the Israelite
nation. The entire fifth book of the Torah, Deuteronomy, is a loving, parting lecture from this teacher, this stutterer-cum-orator.
He must leave them soon—he will not be allowed to accompany

them into the Land of Israel—and he must pass on his wisdom before his death. There is no time for neat outlines; they must hear it all, in the order in which it comes out.

In virtually all of the prescriptive portions of the Torah, when the text addresses the individual, Hebrew grammar (which has no neuter) suggests a male listener by the use of the male pronoun or verb conjugation. In Deut. 17, in our portion, the passage concerning idolaters does specify several times both men and women as potential violators (this specification of the female actor is relatively rare in biblical law). Women also appear explicitly toward the end of this portion as captives during war. And surely, women are included in the whole Israelite nation that Moses is addressing.

The *parashah*'s themes speak more subtly, though, to contemporary women's concerns. A theme that runs through so many of our portion's commandments—regarding appropriate worship, the nature of witnessing and of prophecy, the nature of authority and its limits—is that of truth. To whom should we listen? Which teachings and practices? Which words? These questions are at the heart of contemporary Jewish women's journeys. Several principles from *Parashat Shoftim* have particular significance for our lives as Jewish women.

The Nature of Prophetic Truth

In Deut. 18:21, after having prepared the way for successor prophets, Moses acknowledges that the people may wonder, "How shall we know the word that God has not spoken?" How will they recognize that which is not holy? His answer in verse 22 is simple: "When a prophet speaks in God's name, if the thing does not follow or come to be, it is a thing that God has not spoken." The anxiety about knowing which apparent products of human imagination are consonant with God's will continues, rightly, to our own day. Whether our belief is in a God who indeed has a will, or an understanding of God as a less personal Source of blessing and life, feminists and critics of feminism both want to know, How do we determine what is holy?

Although Moses' answer appears to be simple—it might be explained as "if it turns out to be true, it was true"—his words shimmer with possibility and subtlety. Moses' instruction, itself words of prophecy, suggests that the Jewish people need not jump to label new things as either holy or unholy, appropriate or inappropriate, accepted or rejected. Time will tell what is right for a holy community. Experience will be our teacher.

Contemporary Jewish women are creating new rituals, weaving midrashim, challenging legal interpretations, and transforming scholarship. Those who fear change often need to make quick assessments. Instead, Moses' words implicitly encourage us to be open and patient, to realize that the perspective of the passage of time will instruct us about what works, what is good and holy and true for our holy community.

Trees That Yield Fruit

The rabbinic principle of *bal tashchit* (literally, "do not destroy") is derived from this *parashah*, from Deut. 20:19–20. The biblical text itself contains the specific prohibition against destroying fruit-bearing trees during war. *Bal tashchit* has subsequently come to connote an entire environmentally conscious category of behaviors, in order to avoid wasting—and treating without respect—precious God-given resources.

This posture suggests a strategy for feminist Jewish approaches to Torah, to Jewish texts and teachings. It is all too easy to see women's exclusion, to name sexist traditions and interpretations, and to experience the pain of struggling toward full participation in Jewish life. *Bal tashchit* reminds us that Torah, too, is an *etz chayim*—a fruit-bearing tree of life. We may be tempted at times to name certain texts as beyond the pale, as outside the acceptable limits of Jewish tradition for Jewish women—in other words, to tear down this tree. Reading beyond the plain, contextual meaning, *bal tashchit* cautions us: this tree bears fruit. You do not need to eat all its fruit, but neither should you tear it down. It has been growing for a long time. You may yet find shade under its branches, or find its fruit sweet in ways that you cannot predict.

Cleansing Our Communities

The very last law of *Parashat Shoftim*, in Deut. 21:1–9, is that of the *eglah arufah*, the "heifer whose neck is broken." After an entire portion that assumes the just and methodical administration of law and religious culture, this law responds to an occurrence that has no neat resolution: a person is found slain, lying in a field, and her/his killer is unknown. The elders of the nearest city must take a heifer that has not been used for any other work or purpose and has borne no offspring, and break its neck. In the tractate *Sotah* ("Suspected Adulterous Woman") of the Babylonian Talmud, one sage suggests that the ritual should take place with an animal that bears no fruit, on ground that does not bear fruit (that is, uncultivated ground), to make atonement on behalf of the community for the death of an individual who in turn will not produce more "fruit"—subsequent offspring, the performance of mitzvot.[1]

There is a great deal of wisdom in the notion that we need a way to cleanse our communities of wrongdoing, even when there is no one obvious to blame. As Jewish women, we see historic exclusion from significant roles and rituals; we encounter sexist rabbinic blind spots; we are troubled by painful narratives. We sense that the ancient rabbis were no worse on "women's issues" than other men of their time, and that in many cases they were ahead of their time—for example, in providing certain kinds of economic protection to women.[2]

But still, we feel hurt and anger when we encounter aspects of our beloved tradition that seem to undermine, limit, or even oppress women. We need to find ways to ritually acknowledge the pain we feel at these encounters. There is often no one individual or group to blame, and we are not interested in fruitless fingerpointing. At times, though, we want our Jewish communities to acknowledge that injury has been done; that some stories are damaging to us all; that some laws must change, and that until they do, individuals suffer. We need a way for our communities to help heal the damage that is done, even when blame cannot be neatly assigned and problems remain unsolved, or unresolved.

Torah: Turn It and Turn It

In Deut. 17:18–19, Moses tells the people that when they have a king, "while he is sitting on the throne of the kingdom, he shall write a copy of this Torah in a book . . . and it shall be with him, and he shall read it all the days of his life." In their immediate context, these words probably refer to the specific *torah*, or set of laws regarding limitation on the king's power, and the importance of his remembering that he is, in the end, one of the people, and thus obligated to be an agent of God's will. Yet, the visual imagery suggests, for leaders and for all of us, a combination of humility and grandeur in keeping Torah near to us, so that we may delve into holy texts to keep learning, every day of our lives.

We Jewish women have never been more involved in studying and teaching Torah and in religious leadership than we are today. We cling to the Tree of Life; we find shelter in its shade; we climb in (and occasionally prune) its many branches; we water its roots so that it may grow stronger and healthier. An early rabbinic sage, Ben Bag Bag, is quoted as saying this about Torah: "Turn it and turn it, for everything is in it."[3]

We have faith that nothing of our holy strivings is foreign to Torah, to the possibilities in our sacred tradition. As human links in an ancient chain, we recognize that what Rabbi Amy Eilberg has called "holy chutzpah" is essential to bringing Jewish tradition and community ever closer to its messianic ideal. We move forward with a sense of power, and of awesome responsibility.

RABBI JUDITH GARY BROWN

כי תצא

Ki Tetzey

The Accused Woman

*I*f a man marries a woman and cohabits with her but then he hates her and he invents charges against her and defames her, saying, "I married this woman; but when I was intimate with her, I did not find evidence that she was a virgin"—in such a case, the girl's father and mother shall bring the evidence of the girl's virginity before the elders of the town at the gate. And the girl's father shall say to the elders, "I gave my daughter to this man as a wife, but he hated her. So he has invented charges, saying, 'I did not find your daughter to be a virgin.' But here is the evidence of my daughter's virginity!" And they shall spread out the cloth before the elders of the town. The elders of that town shall then take the man and flog him, and they shall fine him a hundred shekels of silver and give them to the girl's father, because he has defamed a virgin in Israel. Also she shall remain his wife; he shall never be able to divorce her. But if this thing is true, and evidence of the girl's virginity was not found, then they shall bring the girl to the doorway of her father's house, and the men of her town shall stone her to death, because she did a deplorable thing in Israel, committing fornication in her father's house. Thus you will rid yourself of evil in your midst. (DEUTERONOMY 22:13–21)

Parashat Ki Tetzey continues the enumeration of laws for the social well-being of Israel. In general, this *parashah* deals with laws that are focused on the private, inner workings of the Israelite community—specifically, who can be a part of the community and how those within the community should interact with each other. But *Ki Tetzey* abounds with laws that truly challenge our women's sensibilities.

By Maimonides' count, this Torah portion contains a total of seventy-two laws. Among these, Deut. 22:13–29 functions as a unit of legislation, dealing with marital and sexual transgressions. This section begins with a case of alleged misrepresentation. At the time of their wedding, the woman was supposed to be a virgin. After consummating the marriage, however, her new husband now claims that she had not been a virgin. The case, with its two possible conclusions (innocent or guilty), is fleshed out. This is followed by four brief cases dealing with different types of sexual transgressions.

In Deut. 22:13–21 (our focus) we learn that the man may be motivated by hatred *(usene'ah)* toward his wife and that he is fabricating the charges. We then learn how the case is to be handled by the community: The husband makes a claim to the elders of the community, and then the parents supply evidence and argument to disprove his claim. The husband is either found guilty and then punished, or, if the husband's claims are judged to be true because proof of the wife's virginity could not be found, then she is punished by being stoned to death.

The process seems close to what we would experience in today's court system, but let us look at the specifics, for they provide much information that is troubling. The father and mother are made responsible for proving their daughter's virginity. What would comprise evidence of her virginity? Verse 17 elucidates: "'But here is the evidence of my daughter's virginity.' And they shall spread out the cloth [ufarsu hasimlah] before the elders of the town."

The parents are responsible for providing the "piece of evidence," which is the cloth/garment with evidence of bleeding, resulting from the first intercourse that causes the breaking of the hymen. Could this be the only evidence that keeps this girl/woman from being stoned to death (Deut. 22:20–21)?[1]

There arises another difficulty: the parents are required to provide this evidence only after the charges are made. The parents would most likely have a lot at stake regarding the outcome of this case. They probably love their daughter and would not want to see her put to death. Thus, one could imagine the relative ease with which they could manufacture the evidence to save their daughter's life. On the off-chance that they were very angry with their daughter—so angry that they would not care if she lived or died—the parents would still be motivated to provide the evidence, because it would be their reputation at stake if their daughter were to be found guilty. Also, the parents would lose out on the hundred shekels that they would collect from the husband if he were to be found guilty of defamation.[2] Thus, the parents would have to be insanely angry with their daughter in order for them not to be motivated to produce the evidence, for it would be very much in their interest to prove her innocence.

But the wife loses regardless of the outcome. She may be vindicated by the evidence, but she does not receive the monetary award. As Abravanel points out in his commentary on Deut. 22:19, the wife does not receive the award, since her property became her husband's—in essence, the slandering husband would be paying himself.

Even if she is found to be innocent of the charges, the wife may still have been damaged. Unfortunately, as we have witnessed in our own news headlines, once an accusation is made, some question is left regarding just how innocent the innocent are. Rashi, in wrestling with the question of why the parents are the ones responsible for proving the daughter's virginity (Deut. 22:15), cites *Sifre:* "Let those who have reared this depraved child [*gidulim;* literally, "evil plant"] be exposed to contempt because of her." In essence, an assumption of some guilt is made; otherwise, the husband would not have suspected unchastity.[3] Thus, Deut. 22:19 tells us that the wife's father receives the one hundred shekels from the husband because her reputation was besmirched. The reasoning is that the father would be the one truly disgraced because the community would assume that he did not raise a virtuous daughter, and so he receives back double the bride-price established for virgins in Exod. 22:16. The father may have other daughters for whom he must find husbands, and if the community were to have any doubts about the accused daughter's total chastity or appearance of chastity, the father might not be able to make good marriage deals for his unwed daughters with other families. Since he might suffer financially, the father receives a monetary award.

So the woman, accused and proven innocent, has her character forever somewhat besmirched. And for all her innocence, she is accorded one final blow: as part of the husband's punishment, in addition to flogging and fine, "she shall remain his wife; he shall never have the right to divorce her" (Deut. 22:19).

At this point, many of us would cry out, "Injustice!" If the husband detests her so much that he would slander her, how could giving her a "life sentence" with the man be doing justice by her? Here, we need to step back and take a broader look at the culture of the time. The text can speak fully to us only if we allow it some historical context.

Much of the Book of Deuteronomy is similar in style and content to ancient Near Eastern law texts. The environment of this time (seventh century B.C.E. or earlier) viewed women as being of significantly inferior status. The husband had full control of the woman—he could take her as a wife, and, if he did not like her, he could be rid of her by saying, "You are not my wife," and then giving her one-half minah of silver. By accusing her of not being a virgin, the husband would be able to divorce the wife without having to return the bride-price of fifty shekels, which is equivalent to one-half minah of silver.[4] Deuteronomy, however, reflects some of the innovation that was particularly of Israelite character of the time. Here, concern for the obviously disadvantaged—women—motivated the ruling that the husband could not be rid of her, and thus he must support her for the rest of her life.

Of course, it is unfortunate that the wife is not given the right to choose to leave him. But this would be expecting too much innovation for that time. We can look for some advances in the rights of the wife in the texts of the next developmental period of Jewish civilization, the rabbinic period.[5]

This *parashah* is replete with laws that raise challenging issues for us: laws concerning women taken captive in war, adultery, rape of an engaged virgin inside versus outside the city, levirate marriage, a woman accidentally injuring a man's genitals. What slaps at our modern sensibilities as we read this Torah portion is the unmistakable presence of subordination and control of women of the biblical period. More to the point, it is the subjugation of women's sexuality that is most notable here. Yet, there seems to be virtually no control placed on men's sexuality during the biblical period.

Why? Again, understanding the historical context may shed some light.

In the biblical period a husband might pay a bride-price to his wife's father and join the wife's family and work for them, as was the case with Jacob and Rachel and Leah. Or the wife joined the husband's family, and the addition of their offspring economically benefited the husband's family, as was the case with Ruth and Boaz. In either case, the woman was mostly viewed as the "conduit" by which the family increased their productive work force and by which heirs would be provided—and those heirs were, for the most part, male offspring.

We see, then, that the value of women in this society was closely linked to their power of reproduction. In order to control the family and its financial security and success, women were treated as a commodity, with rights of exclusive "ownership" passing from the father to the husband. In this patriarchal society, strict control of women's sexuality ensured the continuation of the family-based social order.[6] It was the family's—primarily the father's—responsibility to control and protect the sexual purity, and thus the procreative fitness, of the daughters. This translated into monetary value, in the form of the bride-price, not just for the individual daughter in question, but also for all daughters of subsequent marrying age, and into family name value, in the form of reputation and standing in the community. As we learned, in the event that the daughter is found guilty, "then they shall bring the girl to the doorway of her father's house, and the men of her town shall stone her to death, because she did a deplorable thing in Israel, committing fornication in her father's house" (Deut. 22:21).

How can we live with knowledge that the Torah seems to objectify the role of women to such an extent? After all, it seems that women were merely a means to an end in the perpetuation of a patriarchal society. From our foray into the historical background and context that the Torah shares, I believe it fair to say that the Torah did not create this worldview; rather, it inherited the world-views of the surrounding cultures, although it did incorporate some innovation.

The rabbis of the talmudic period did progress to a somewhat more complex understanding of the role of women in society. Women were viewed less as objects and more as subjects in society. For example, in the case of rape, although the Bible provided only for the father receiving the bride-price of fifty shekels of silver (Deut. 22:28–29), the rabbis demanded that the rapist must also compensate the woman for her physical and psychological damage (*Ketubot* 43a–b). And although, according to our biblical text, the rapist was compelled to marry the woman, under talmudic law, the girl could refuse to marry the rapist (*Ketubot* 39b).

If we look to our texts as representative—evidence, if you will—of the development of our current social mores, we would see a progression toward our more balanced understanding of women's and men's roles in society. It is in this way that we can most powerfully experience the dynamic nature of our heritage. Our task, then, is to listen to the voice of history as we seek to uncover what the text is trying to tell us, and to honestly acknowledge our reactions to that text. We may not find the answers we want, but we will develop a better understanding of where we have been and of how far we have traveled. And perhaps we will discover those who traveled this same path before us.

RABBI NANCY WECHSLER-AZEN

כי תבוא

Ki Tavo

The Basket Ceremony of Gratitude and Hope

When you come to the land that Adonai your God gives to you as a heritage, and you occupy it and settle in it, you shall take some of every first fruit of the soil, which you harvest from the land that Adonai your God is giving you, put it in a basket and go to the place where Adonai your God will choose to establish God's name there. You shall go to the Kohen who is there at that time and say to him, "I declare this day before Adonai your God that I have come to the land that Adonai your God swore to our ancestors to give to us." The Kohen shall take the basket from your hand and set it down in front of the altar of Adonai your God. (DEUTERONOMY 26:1–4)

WITH ITS CEREMONIAL ENACTMENT of the themes of gratitude and hope, *Parashat Ki Tavo* endures as one of the most compelling pieces of Torah. Called by Philo of Alexandria the "basket ceremony," Deut. 26:1–15 offers a liturgical declaration and personalized prayer for a farmer to recite when he brings the first fruits to the

Temple. In no uncertain terms, the text declares that God, not humanity, is the source of the land's fertility. The recitation unfolds as a brief précis of Israel's history that will eventually find its way into the Passover Seder. More than anything else, these verses teach about reciprocity. God brought us to this desired place by way of an admittedly arduous journey, and we bring back to God symbols of the fulfillment of our heart's longing.

> You shall then recite as follows before Adonai your God: "My father was a fugitive Aramean. He went down to Egypt with meager numbers and sojourned there; but there he became a great and very populous nation. The Egyptians dealt harshly with us and oppressed us; they imposed heavy labor upon us. We cried to Adonai, the God our fathers, and Adonai heard our plea and saw our plight, our misery and our oppression. Adonai freed us from Egypt by a mighty hand, by an outstretched arm and awesome power, and by signs and portents. God brought us to this place and gave us this land, a land flowing with milk and honey. Wherefore I now bring the first fruits of the soil that You, Adonai, have given me." (Deut. 26:5–10)

Images of majestic oxen crowned with olive leaves come to mind. Their horns overlaid with gold, we imagine them swaying to the music of rhythmic flute. Bringing first fruits to Jerusalem is a dizzying, slow, undulating promenade filled with the ardent perfume of ripened figs and grapes. The baskets are held on the farmer's shoulder while he recites the passage from Deut. 26:3–5. When he utters the words, "My father was a fugitive Aramean" (Deut. 26:5), he removes the basket from his shoulder and holds it by the rim. The kohen then places his hand beneath the basket and waves it. Once the formulaic words have been said, the basket is placed by the side of the altar, and the farmer prostrates himself upon the ground.

Entering the land in this way serves as a powerful ritualized bridge connecting the past with the present. The farmers are reminded of both their personal and historical suffering, as well as their ability to overcome difficulties by placing God at the center. Once articulated, they no longer need to carry symbols of enslavement on their persons, but rather, the potential of new life: first fruits.

Thus, a three-step formula for how to enter a new place or a new chapter of our life is set before us in this Torah portion. First, elevate your personal dreams: "You will take some of every first fruit of the soil . . . and put it in a basket and go to the place where Adonai your God will choose" (Deut. 26:2). Second, acknowledge pain and survival of that pain: "The Egyptians dealt harshly with us and oppressed us; they imposed heavy labor upon us. We cried to Adonai . . . and Adonai heard our plea. Adonai freed us from Egypt" (Deut. 26:6–8). And third, let generosity extend from your happiness: "You shall enjoy, together with the Levite and the stranger in your midst, all the bounty that Adonai your God has bestowed upon you and your household" (Deut. 26:11). The future, the past, and the present are woven together, making the basket the perfect symbol for the moment.

How do women read this *parashah?* The most obvious challenge is the seemingly endless battle of female marginality. The Hebrew text is defiantly male. Women are missing. The "fugitive father" (Deut. 26:5) is recalled, not the mother. "He" (the farmer) brings the basket to the male priest, the kohen. The kohen, a man, takes it from him.

Within the realm of imagination, however, we can visualize a kohennet as a gracious elder, a wise woman who receives with dignity and kindness what we offer as first fruits in our basket. Also, *Parashat Ki Tavo* can be reframed as a dignified ritual for women when we "come to the land" (Deut. 26:1) through reaching milestones in our lives, that is, when we enter a previously uncharted era. For surely, aging women have received no gifts from our youth-obsessed culture. We have no rituals or basket ceremonies as we enter our older years. At one time, showing one's age was a gift given to humanity. Meant to provide honor, it was given by God on request:

> And it came to pass that when Isaac was old, Rabbi Judah ben Simon said: "Abraham requested the appearance of old age, pleading before God: Sovereign of the Universe! When a man and his son enter a town, none know whom to honor. But if You will crown the father with the appearance of old age, one will know whom to honor." Said the Holy One to him: "As you live, you have asked well, and it will commence with you." Thus from the beginning of the Book until here, old age is not mentioned, but when Abraham arose the appearance of old age was granted to him. And Abraham was old, well stricken with age.[1]

This midrash teaches us that the natural signs of old age are meant to show a life well lived. Contrary to the pervasive view of the media, Judaism reminds us that beauty includes a certain veneration, rewarded only after having lived many years.

Ki Tavo calls us to reexamine what we hold sacred in our life's basket. How do we elevate our dreams? How can we honor what we have learned through survival? How can we celebrate our lives with greater joy and generosity?

When I turned forty, I was fortunate to spend some time on

retreat. I reflected on my life—peering into my future as well as looking into my past. Using *Parashat Ki Tavo* as a friend, I welcomed her three-point formula as a guide into middle age. With pen and journal in hand, I quietly and reverently began the process of bringing my own basket of first fruits before the kohennet, a gracious elder, a wise woman. "Elevate personal dreams"—I thought about who I was in that moment and what ways I could imagine developing in the next chapter of my life. "Acknowledge pain and survival of that pain"—I recalled experiences that wounded me and felt deeply affirmed to see how those dark places once dominated me, but are now just a part of my life's weave. "Let generosity extend from my happiness"—because to reach my fortieth birthday is a *simchah*, I celebrated with gratitude several times with loved ones. From a place of thankfulness for the many blessings in my life, I made a commitment to give *tzedakah* as an extension of my heart's fulfillment.

> Now if you obey Adonai your God, to observe faithfully all God's commandments that I enjoin upon you this day, Adonai your God will set you high above all the nations of the earth. All these blessings shall come upon you and take effect, if you will but heed the word of Adonai your God. (Deut. 28:1–2)

What if "obeying Adonai your God" meant not submitting to an external authority, but rather, honoring the God within us? What if "observe faithfully" meant treating ourselves with more compassion, as souls created in the image of God? That would give us permission to celebrate our years, and the signs of those years, with less shame. It would encourage us to acknowledge the past and clarify our enthusiasm for the future. As a response to its own plea to honor God, the text offers everyday blessings to those who follow their innermost, highest selves. Some of the blessings are unequivocally framed in feminine imagery of fertility and nurture. The *parashah* reveals at last enduring contributions of women. Through the blessings, Torah offers essential tidings of birthing, carrying and preparing food.

> Blessed shall you be in the city and blessed shall you be in the country. Blessed shall be the issue of your womb, the produce of your soil and the offspring of your cattle, the calving of your herd and the lambing of your flock. Blessed shall be your basket and your kneading bowl. Blessed shall you be in your comings and blessed shall you be in your goings. (Deut. 28:3–6)

What is the blessing for our basket and kneading bowl? Baskets and bowls are the stuff of women, of home and hearth, of comfort and nourishment. They are the gifts of stability that women bring to the new nation. Though absent from the text, women are not wholly absent from the ceremony. The basket and bowl are our offerings for the future. Inside are our elevated dreams, our acknowledged pain, and our gratitude and joy.

RABBI MIRIAM CAREY BERKOWITZ

נצבים

Nitzavim

Women and the Covenant

Y ou are standing this day, all of you, before the
Lord your God: your heads, your tribes, your
elders and your officers, all the men of Israel,
your little ones, your wives [or, "women folk"],
and the stranger who is in the midst of your
camp. (DEUTERONOMY 29:9–10)

AFTER FORTY YEARS OF LEADING THE JEWISH PEOPLE through the
desert, Moses prepares them to enter the land of Israel, where, he
hopes, they will become a proud people in their own land. It is not
enough to be independent, though. Moses wants the people to be
faithful to God, living according to the guidelines of the Torah. He
wants them to affirm the covenant that God presented to them at
Sinai, the covenant that they accepted with the words "All that the
Lord has spoken, we will do" (Exod. 19:8).

What exactly is a "covenant"? What does it ask, and what does
it promise in return? How do Jewish women in particular fit into the
covenant set forth in *Parashat Nitzavim?* According to Anita Diamant,

> *Brit,* the Hebrew word for covenant, is the way Jews
> describe and define their relationship to God. A
> covenant is a contract—an agreement between respon-

sible parties, a two-way street. According to tradition, the document that spells out the rights and responsibilities for both sides in this agreement between God and the Jewish people is the Torah—the first five books of the Bible.[1]

Diamant enumerates four types of covenant found in the Torah: the rainbow, Shabbat, *milah* (circumcision), and the Torah itself. Are they separate covenants, or all part of the same encompassing pledge? And what are the repercussions for Jewish women today?

The covenant of Noah extends to all peoples, indeed to all living things. In the story of Noah, God promises never again to destroy the earth by flood. The rainbow is given as a sign of this pledge. God establishes this covenant "with you [Noah] and your offspring to come . . . and with every living thing on earth" (Gen. 9:9–10).

The covenant of circumcision, also called "the covenant of Abraham," is, of course, limited to male Jews—boys, who are circumcised, and their fathers, whose obligation it is to see that the mitzvah is done. Not only are girls spared any physical sign of entry into this covenant, mothers are not even commanded to have their sons circumcised. If for some reason a father is not available, the duty for making sure that the baby boy is circumcised passes to the *bet din*, the rabbinic court. Thus, women are not implicated in the covenant of Abraham in any way.[2]

The Sabbath, a covenant of cosmic significance, does address all Jews: "The people of Israel shall keep Shabbat, observing Shabbat throughout the generations as a covenant for all time. It shall be a sign forever between Me and the people of Israel, for in six days God made heaven and earth, and on the seventh day God rested and was refreshed" (Exod. 31:16–17). It seems clear from the context that, unlike circumcision, Shabbat is intended as a gift and responsibility for all Jews. Furthermore, the rabbis specify in the Talmud that women are obligated in all aspects of the Shabbat (see Babylonian Talmud, *Shavuot* 20b).

What of the covenant of Torah, the pact that demands the most of its parties, while promising God's protection and love in return? The covenant of Torah, which begins with the dramatic Sinai experience and is cemented in *Parashat Nitzavim*, once more affirms, despite mild ambiguity, God's commitment to the entire Jewish people and urges them all to accept the demands of the Torah, our side of the agreement.

At Sinai, the content of the covenant is inclusive, according to both Torah context and later rabbinic interpretation. God calls to Moses, saying,

> Thus shall you say to the house of Jacob and declare to the people of Israel: "You have seen what I did to the Egyptians, how I bore you on eagles' wings and brought you to me. Now then, if you will obey Me faithfully and keep my covenant, you shall be my treasured possession among all peoples. Indeed, all the earth is mine, but you shall be to me a kingdom of priests and a holy nation." (Exod. 19:3–6)

The rabbis interpret "the house of Jacob" as referring to the women, who not only receive the Torah but also learn it *before* the men, "the people of Israel" (Rashi on Exod. 19:3). Thus, in the rabbinic interpretation, not only are the women mentioned, they are mentioned first, because the women typically would be the ones to pass on Torah to the children, ensuring continuity of the heritage and the laws. We do not need commentary, however, to tell us that a pact made to safeguard the values, laws, calendar, and daily practices of a people necessitates involvement of all its members. Thus, the covenantal act, the promises and demands God makes to and of the people, encompasses the entire nation.

In *Parashat Nitzavim*, women's status is not quite so clear-cut, but the case still stands for women's inclusion in the covenant of Torah. Moses does speak specifically to the men: "You are standing this day all of you before the Lord your God: your heads, your tribes, your elders and your officers, all the men of Israel, your little ones, your wives [or, "women folk"], and the stranger who is in the midst of your camp" (Deut 29:9–10). The women are portrayed as relational to the men, and, if anything is to be made of the order of listing, second to the bottom in the hierarchy. Women come after the children, above only the strangers. But women are clearly enumerated among those "standing this day." While referred to as adjuncts of their husbands (or fathers)—the common view of women in any patriarchal society—the women are definitely present and accounted for. The content of the message is unequivocal:

> [Y]ou should enter into the covenant of the Lord, and into the oath, which the Lord your God makes with you today, that God may establish you today as a people, and that the Lord may be to you as a God, as sworn to you and to your fathers, to Abraham, to Isaac, and to Jacob. I make this covenant, with its sanctions, not with you alone, but both with those who are standing here this day before the Lord our God and with those who are not with us here this day. (Deut. 29:11–14)

The covenant extends throughout time to men, women, and children in every generation; to those born Jewish and to those who will become Jewish; to those who stood at Sinai and to those for whom Sinai is but a distant collective memory. It is a demanding idea, but an embracing one.

What are the implications of being included in the covenant with God, of being bound by our ancestors' decision that fateful day four thousand years ago to say, "Yes, we will be your people"? Covenant enjoins with it responsibilities as well as rights. "I command you this day to love the Lord your God, to walk in God's ways, to keep God's commandments, statutes, and ordinances" (Deut. 30:16). Being covenanted means reaching out to grasp the Torah and incorporating it into your life.

Today, many women are embracing the "women's mitzvot," such as making Shabbat in the home, raising and educating children, and immersing in the natural waters of the *mikveh*. Other women are drawn to the more public roles that were once reserved for men: praying in a *minyan*, taking on the obligation of tallit and tefillin, becoming rabbis, cantors, and community leaders. Still others focus on the "mainstream mitzvot": keeping kosher, observing Shabbat and festivals, avoiding gossip *(lashon hara)*, giving *tzedakah* (financial contributions).

In our time, more and more women are taking their places in the covenantal community by studying Torah, in the hope that learning will lead to action, but also for its own sake *(lishmah)*. Whether it be in small groups of women teaching women in private homes, in mixed *yeshivot* or university classrooms, on rural retreats, in Israel or in their local synagogues or community centers, studying Torah and passing on this pillar of Judaism ensures that our participation in the covenantal relationship with God will be not only de jure, by right, but de facto, in fact—proved and sustained by our actions.

Now that many women have opportunities to study Torah, those opportunities must be seized and cherished. *Parashat Nitzavim* brings home this point forcefully. Moses summarizes his message to the people:

> For this commandment that I command you this day,
> it is not too hard for you, neither is it far off. It is not
> in heaven, that you should say, "Who shall go up for
> us to heaven and bring it to us, and make us hear it,
> that we may do it?" Neither is it beyond the sea, that
> you should say, "Who shall go over the sea for us and
> bring it to us and make us hear it, that we may do it?"
> But the word is very near to you, in your mouth and
> in your heart, that you may do it. (Deut. 30:11–14)[3]

Moses encourages even as he challenges. Only when a Jew takes the initiative to participate in the commandments and to learn does he or she become an active, deserving member of the covenant. The choice is up to her or him to make.

Our *parashah* opens with, "You are standing this day, *nitzavim* [inclusive plural, "all of you"], before the Lord your God" (Deut. 29:9). What clues does the word *nitzavim* give us about the essence of the people's attitude as they stood in preparation to hear Moses' parting words? An intratextual answer (from elsewhere within the Torah) proves fascinating.

When Miriam stood by the river to see what would become of her baby brother, Moses, the Torah says, *"vatetatzav* Miriam" (Exod. 2:4). J. H. Hertz comments that this means Miriam not just "stood by" but "took her stand."[4] *Vatetatzav* and *nitzavim* share the root *y-tz-v,* meaning "firmly planted, unshakeable, committed." This commitment of striving to forge a relationship with God, revere the world that God created, and learn about, internalize, and pass on Jewish ways of life is especially important to people who do not have a physical sign in their skin to remind them every day of their covenant. But by seeing ourselves as *nitzavot* (feminine plural), standing and firmly planted, eager, brave and proud before God, Jewish women can bring to life the spiritual covenant that, introduced at Sinai and reaffirmed in *Parashat Nitzavim*, has been engraved not physically, but metaphorically, on our hearts.

RABBI ROSETTE BARRON HAIM

וילך

Vayelech

Guardians of the Tradition

*B*e strong and bold.
(DEUTERONOMY 31:23)

THE TORAH PORTION *Vayelech* begins with Moses announcing his retirement as the leader of the people, and his charging the people to "be strong and bold," thus reassuring them that God will remain with them. Moses then appoints Joshua as his successor, and offers him similar words of encouragement. The portion continues with Moses committing this law—the Book of Deuteronomy—to writing, and giving it over to the priests for safekeeping. Moses instructs the leaders to read the law to all the people during the feast of Tabernacles at the conclusion of every sabbatical (seventh) year. Afterward, when God tells Moses that his death is imminent, Moses publicly presents Joshua as the new leader of the people. God next reveals to Moses what fate shall befall the people, and commands Moses and all the people to write a poem to remind the people of God's deeds and continued loyalty to the people. Finally, Moses commands the Levites to put the book of the law in the Ark as a witness for the people, and Moses prepares to recite his poem.

Two themes in the portion are particularly striking. The first is the manner of selecting and presenting a successor to a great leader. The second is the way in which a sacred document is entrusted into the hands of leaders, even as it is meant to be accessible to all the people.

Establishing a successor can be very difficult, even in the simplest of situations. But this is no simple situation. Moses has had a unique relationship with the Divine, and has led the people through difficult times. During those years, even though his own authority over the people was well established, Moses did not always find the people to be completely cooperative. Moses' method of establishing a successor in this portion is, therefore, very instructive.

First, Moses announced his impending retirement. In essence, he prepared the people to think about the possibility of a new leader. Then he called to Joshua, who had been his support for some time, and who through some difficult events had earned the people's trust. Moses presented him as the next leader in a public ceremony "in the presence of all Israel" (Deut. 31:7), for just as Moses had led all the people, so too would Joshua lead all the people. Sometime soon thereafter, when Moses was about to die, he and Joshua went into the Tent of Meeting, where, the Torah records, God charged Joshua with the same words Moses had earlier used: "Be strong and bold" (Deut. 31:23). In essence, that moment represented the Divine calling to Joshua.

The way the leadership was transferred and the person to whom it was transferred reveal several key elements for our own time. A great leader needs to prepare the people to be ready to accept a subsequent leader. This preparation includes making it clear to the people that the former leader will not live forever, finding someone well qualified and respected to continue the job, and publicly investing the leader's trust in the successor. The importance of a leader demonstrating trust in the next generation of leadership must not be underestimated. The successor, too, must undergo some emotional transition from—to borrow language from the legal profession—being "second chair" to becoming "first chair." In that experience there is something Divine, perhaps even a "Divine calling." Leaders, whether women or men, must look for successive leaders who meet these high standards established by Joshua's appointment long ago.

Since Moses and Joshua, there have been subsequent transfers of the leadership of our people along a chain of authority. The Talmud, in *Pirkei Avot,* begins with a description of how the chain of tradition has been passed down: "Moses received the Torah at Sinai and handed it down to Joshua; Joshua to the elders; the elders to the prophets; and the prophets handed it down to the Men of the Great Assembly."[1]

These guardians of the tradition also reflect one leader investing the next with sufficient authority to rule, and the newly invested leaders showing themselves meritorious and worthy of the support of the community. Commenting on the importance of each leader in the chain of tradition, one author wrote, "If all that was involved in the chain of transmission was the mechanical transfer of a written scroll, then it becomes difficult to understand the importance attached to the individual persons or groups comprising the chain of tradition. If, on the other hand, what was involved in 'receiving and turning over' was the mastery of the comprehensive interpretation of Written Law, its proper applications and possible extensions, then the crucial role played by each link in the chain becomes clear."[2]

The crucial role played by each link in the chain is vitally important, and reflects her or his individuality. Two significant post-Mosaic persons whose names do not appear as links in that chain, but who play a crucial role in preserving and transmitting the tradition, come to mind. One was the prophetess Chuldah. The only prophetess mentioned during the period of the monarchy, Chuldah was the one to whom King Josiah brought the Book of Deuteronomy when it was found in the Temple. Although Jeremiah lived during her time, King Josiah wanted Chuldah to validate that this was indeed the book of the covenant that Moses had earlier entrusted to the Levites.[3] In considering the chain of tradition, one must recognize the importance of this woman. Not only was she a prophetess, she also conducted an academy in Jerusalem;[4] and it is only by her say that we are assured of the authenticity of the Book of Deuteronomy, in which the earliest links of the chain are described, and in which our portion is found.

Another important woman to consider in this chain is Beruriah. Famous in her own right as one of the only women in the Talmud to be taken seriously, she was also the daughter of Rabbi Chananiah ben Teradyon and the wife of Rabbi Meir. Her opinions are recorded by name, and her contributions evaluated by subsequent commentators. In fact, an aggadic passage records the tender way in which she told her husband of the death of their two sons by describing their presence on earth as a loan from heaven now returned to their Maker.[5] Her wisdom is recalled when tragedy strikes and bereaved parents must pronounce the words of Job: *Adonai natan, v'Adonai lakach, yihi shem Adonai mevorach,* "God gave, God took away, blessed be the name of God."[6] Her teachings represent her own thoughts and most assuredly influenced the thinking of the rabbis who were her contemporaries.

387

Though never officially passed a "mantle of leadership," these two women were recognized by the public as worthy leaders in the chain of tradition. Their crucial contributions have created and enriched the Judaism we now practice. And they are not alone. The important contributions of scores of other women throughout Jewish history have been overlooked as well.

Looking at the way in which the chain of tradition has been passed down, beginning even in the early books of Torah, a well-known, modern-day proverb comes to mind: "Behind every successful man, there is a successful woman." We need to draw out the other successful women, without whom there may not have been great teachings or continuity. Imagine if our matriarch Rebecca had not intervened in the course of Jewish history. It is she who controls the story whereby the Jewish tradition is preserved by linking the patriarchy of Isaac to Jacob instead of to Esau (Gen. 27). Imagine if Tamar had not held her father-in-law, Judah, accountable for raising up a line in his deceased son Er's behalf (Gen. 38). Tamar is the crucial figure for the evolution of the rest of Jewish history, for it is from the union of Judah and Tamar that Peretz, the ancestor of Boaz, is born. And from Boaz, the great-grandfather of David, the messianic line will be established. We need to be sure that we are not satisfied to keep our great women behind our great men anymore.

Our matriarchs and other strong female characters play a central role in the stories of our early history. Later, their involvement is made to seem limited and even marginal. Their contributions become associated with the private domain and the home. Constance Buchanan, a political sociologist, makes the point that limiting women's leadership to the privacy of their home was a mechanism of control, sometimes control for the sake of eliminating the strong woman's voice that challenged the less effective man's.[7] So too, in Jewish life, women's voices have been overidentified with the private sphere and undervalued in the public domain.

As their character and contributions are again appreciated in the public realm, where leadership must be reestablished, women are not seen as "mechanical" transmitters of the traditions but as enrichers of the heritage that has come down to us from Moses and Joshua and Chuldah and Beruriah. For indeed, the Torah was entrusted into the hands of *all the people,* as it is written in this portion: "Gather the people, the men and the women and the little one, and the stranger who is within your gates, so that they will hear and so that they will learn, and revere the Eternal your God and take care to do all the words of this teaching" (Deut. 31:12).

We, too, like an ancient people in the face of new leadership, and like Joshua upon taking over the leadership, are charged to "be strong and bold." Our new leadership will surely include women, as it does now. It may take strength and boldness to reimagine our tradition with the face of a female Joshua. We hear the charge, and we will be strong, for we all have a crucial role as good guardians of the chain of tradition.

RABBI NINA BETH CARDIN

האזינו

Ha'azinu

Understanding the Anger

*A*nd [God] said: "I will hide my countenance from them and see how they fare in the end. . . . I will incense them with a no-folk, vex them with a nation of fools. . . . I will heap misfortunes upon them and use up my arrows on them."
(DEUTERONOMY 32:20, 21, 23)

HA'AZINU IS THE NEXT-TO-LAST *parashah* of the Torah, and the very last one in the annual cycle of weekly Torah readings. We approach *Ha'azinu* with the melodies of the High Holidays fresh in our minds, our souls lifted by an ancient liturgy that promises us the possibility of redemption and renewal.

It is this attitude of hopefulness that makes this text so difficult to read. *Ha'azinu* is a *parashah* full of prophecies of betrayal and hurt, anger and pain. Neither the reader in the synagogue today nor the Israelites gathered on the banks of the Jordan long ago are prepared for such sharp words. The Jews in the Torah are expectant, ready to cross the Jordan and begin a new life in the Land of Israel. They are born of the desert into a life of freedom, distanced from the stunted generation that built the golden calf. Unlike their parents, they did not rebel repeatedly against God. They are young and

390

eager, and willing to take risks. They know that they are at the end of their wayfaring and wanderings.

Yet, their eagerness to enter the Promised Land is tempered by their fear that Moses is about to die. Torn by two great emotions of arrival (finally!) and loss (too soon!), they turn expectantly to their lifelong leader, teacher, and guide for words of comfort and vision that will sustain them through this difficult time of transition.

But what an odd speech Moses offers. The Israelites long to hear words of love and devotion. Moses foretells tales of betrayal, vengeance, and punishment. They desire words of encouragement and valor. Moses proclaims their vulnerability and weakness. "Jeshurun [Israel] grew fat and gross and coarse," he says, prophesying about how the Jews will behave once they enter the Promised Land, "and forsook the God who made him. They sacrificed to demons, no-gods, gods they had never known. . . . And God said: 'I will hide my countenance from them and see how they fare in the end. . . . I will incense them with a no-folk, vex them with a nation of fools. . . . I will heap misfortunes upon them and use up my arrows on them'" (Deut. 32:20, 21, 23).

How terrifying this must have been for the Jews of old. The Torah does not record how they responded. But what of us? How do we, loyal readers of the Torah, make sense of this harsh, problematic text?

One way is to look at it historically, examining the context and purpose of its writing. To what was it responding? What was its aim? How was it designed to serve the needs of the Jewish people? Scholars conjecture that this poem—for that is what most of the *parashah* is—does not belong here, that it was not crafted as part of Moses' farewell address on the east bank of the Jordan at all. Rather, it was created later, most likely sometime after the conquest of the Land of Israel. it was then imported to this *parashah* because of its grand language and powerful and, in retrospect, accurate prophecy. Its original purpose, therefore, was not to speak at such a liminal and vulnerable moment about Israel's future infidelity and suffering. (Note that the verbs of Israel's wrongdoing are all in the past tense.) Rather, it was designed to speak to a generation who recently suffered defeat at the hands of the enemy, and who were in need of comfort and encouragement (Deut. 32:36). How did it comfort such a generation? To believe that there is reason and purpose and order to the suffering we experience is often comforting. It means that the world is not ruled by randomness and chaos, but moves in accordance with God's will. To be told that our suffering is a justified response to our wrongdoing means both that we can control our destiny by how we act and that God is just. This poem leaves the people believing that although God punishes them, God still loves them unconditionally and that after they are punished, they will be forgiven. God will come to their aid, and they will be victorious once again (Deut. 32:43). Belief in this relationship of infidelity, punishment, and redemption carried the Jews through many a dark time.

Such a reading may be historically satisfying. But if we take the integrity of the text seriously, we cannot stop here, for the Torah itself presents the poem as Moses' closing charge. So we are again forced to ask, in the context of the story, How could these words have meaningfully aided the Jews gathered on the banks of the Jordan?

Perhaps we can imagine this poem as a medical prognosis. When we are faced with a serious illness, we turn to our doctors for a truthful picture of our future. We want to know what therapies are available, how difficult they will be, and what we will experience.

We want to be able to plot the course of the illness, how long it will take us to recover, and what we will be like once (and if) we do. In such a case, knowing the details of the future is not cruel or harsh; but on the contrary, often reassuring. It enables us to prepare ourselves and to see beyond the moment of pain, to imagine ourselves in control of our knowledge, if not our destiny. Perhaps that is the point of this song—to let the Israelites gain strength to carry them through their dark days by giving them a vision of a more peaceful and faithful time to come. The poem speaks words of God's tough love, but ends with God's eternal covenant.

Or perhaps it is something else entirely. As moderns familiar with the psychodynamics of loss, we can suggest another reading. This song can be seen as an expression of Moses' feelings about having to die without entering the land. Instead of addressing his anger to God, against whom it is properly directed, Moses weaves it into his final farewell to the Jewish people. That is why it is here. Moses' long farewell speech to the people occupies the entire Book of Deuteronomy. The man who protested when he was first chosen by God that he was not a man of words (Exod. 4:10), filled a book whose name is *Devarim,* "Words." And now that his words are spent, now that the moment of leave taking is upon him, Moses is overwhelmed by his pain. He lashes out at his family, his people, because he can't or won't present his raw anger to God. The poem can be read as an expression of this frustration, this sense of being cheated, the jealousy, helplessness, and burden of loss. Moses chooses to hurt his loved ones because he is overwhelmed with hurt. This part of *Ha'azinu,* according to such a reading, would have little to do with the Israelites and everything to do with Moses.

These three readings reflect three values of Jewish feminist exegesis, especially when faced with a problematic text.

Honesty. This excursus answers the very first question that each reader of a difficult passage must ask: How can I, the reader, be honest to the text? As a class of Jews whose voices were ignored or recast in the male key, feminists know the pain and loss of being silenced. We, of all readers, must resist silencing others. No matter what the text says, or how it says it, we must begin our exploration of it by allowing it to speak to us on its own terms.

Redemption. We can then move to the next question: Given what we now believe the text says about and for itself, how can we redeem it in its own right? What could have been its goals and motivations? How can we understand its sacred values in terms of the assumptions of its day? This does not mean that we must excuse it, forgive it, or accept it. Indeed, we can still find it seriously problematic. But it does mean that we should seek to understand it in a way that it would choose to be known.

Reinterpretation. How can we read ourselves into the text, meaningfully, aesthetically, psychologically, politically? How can we authentically and creatively reread the text so that our (re-)visions can be represented, or so that we are no longer present only in the silences, or in the margins, or as objects in someone else's world?

There is another, very common, aspect of feminist reading that can be demonstrated in regard to *Ha'azinu. Compensation,* as it is often called, involves surfacing, highlighting, and exploring the places where women, or women's images, appear. When reading carefully, we can find several places in this *parashah* where women's images peek out and can be highlighted.

For one, this is the only place in the Torah, and one of only two places in the Bible, where the daughters of Israel are named and made visible in their own right and not simply folded into the phrase "children/sons of Israel" (Deut. 32:19). As elsewhere in the world of literature, so too in the Bible, poetry seems to open the boundaries of language and vision.

For another, hidden in the angry and vengeful words of this poem is a gentle interweaving of images of God as both mother and father, the most powerful presentation of this kind in the Torah. "Is God not the father who created you? The One who fashioned you and constantly sustains you?" the poem asks (Deut. 32:6). "God found him in a desert region, in an empty howling waste. He swaddled him and watched over him and guarded him. . . . He spread His wings over him and bore him along on His wings" (Deut. 32:10–11). "God fed him honey from the crag, with oil from the flinty rock" (Deut. 32:13). "You [Israel] neglected the Rock that begot you, forgot the God who brought you forth" (Deut. 32:18).

The images of father and mother tumble together, showing through the usually opaque masculine scrim of the text, forming a dual image of God as father and mother. There are words of birthing, nurturing, and caring, of unconditional compassion, protection, and love. There are even two versions of parenthood, one as biological, the other as adoptive. We can read these two not as contradictory, but as emphatic, doubling the intensity of parental compassion, much like the dual image of mother and father doubles the intensity of parental love. But, the poem says, despite all this, Israel still rebelled and turned away from God—thus the need for punishment.

We are not surprised at the punitive response, given our familiarity with God's anger and jealousy. And yet, we are left to wonder if the softer images of mother were not overwhelmed by the male images throughout the poem, indeed throughout the Torah. If the image of woman stood on its own and was not simply grafted onto a male view of God, what might Moses have said instead?

Can we imagine how the female-imaged God would have responded to her rebellious children (even mothers have rebellious children); how a mother might speak of vengeance and war (even mothers have to contend with war); how a mother might speak of a wayward child? What would a mother say of children whose first forays into freedom and prosperity led them to excess and unhealthy indulgence, children who would suffer at their own and others' hands as a result, children who would need the strong hand of a parent to help them climb out of their mess and give them the courage and confidence to set out on their own again?

If God had been allowed to speak in a woman's voice, or be heard speaking in a woman's voice, perhaps the poem of *Ha'azinu* would have begun like this:

> *Give ear, O heavens, let me speak.*
> *Let the earth bear witness to the words I utter.*
> *For the heavens braced my back when I brought forth this people*
> *And the earth heralded the first strong cries of my child.*

The challenge to complement our sacred text with more gender-inclusive midrashim belongs to all of us who dare speak the voice of Judaism in a higher key. How might feminist midrashim reimagine this poem? It is still a bit early for us to know, but authentic, enriching responses will emerge with the generations. The era of sacred texts composed in a woman's key has begun, anchored by the sacred presence and eternal authority of the Torah.

RABBI SANDRA J. COHEN

וזאת הברכה

V'zot Habrachah

The Loss of Moses

So Moses, servant of the Lord, died there.
(DEUTERONOMY 34:5)

IN THE END, MOSES DIES. The leader of the Israelites, who shep-
herded them from slavery to Sinai and then to the edge of the
Promised Land, is mortal. The verses of the Torah portray the
story of Moses' last days in expansive terms: he was the most humble of men; he saw God face to face; he was the greatest prophet.
In this last tribute, however, something is missing. The words do
not tell us about Moses the son, husband, father, and friend. The
public hero is mourned in the Torah text, but it is only generations
later, in the Midrash, that Moses the person emerges. The spaces
between the words hint of Moses' striving for—and loss of—his
life's goal, and the Rabbis bring this human struggle to life, allowing us to mourn him.

V'zot Habrachah, the last *parashah* of the Torah, is divided into
two distinct portions, despite its brevity (forty-one verses).
Deuteronomy 33 contains Moses' last utterance to his people, and
they are words of blessing. Moses speaks to (almost) each tribe,
reminding them of their virtues and faults, and blessing them for

the future. Omitted is the tribe of Simeon, which remains unblessed and unacknowledged. In Moses' summing up of the corporate future of the Israelite nation, there is room for only the mythical twelve tribes—not the thirteen that exist in reality. Such a scarcity model—as if there is a set, limited amount of blessing in the world—underlines the political and communal nature of the blessing; in loving relationships, there would be enough for everyone. But here, in his last utterance, Moses the political leader hands down his legacy to his followers, with his cautions and directions for the future.[1]

These final blessings recall the blessings of Jacob to his sons and their progeny at the end of his life (Gen. 49), with one crucial difference. There, Jacob speaks personally to the strengths and weaknesses of each man, recalling his past actions and admonishing him for the future. It is an intimate act, the father passing down wisdom to his boys. Jacob's blessing is deeply personal, born of lives lived together. Jacob's acquired name, Israel, will become the name of his descendants for all time: the children of Israel, the house of Jacob. Because of this personal connection, Jacob's deeds and his person will live on through his children.

In stark contrast, Moses speaks to no one personally. He addresses the body politic, not the individuals, and his words obscure rather than enhance any human connection between him and his audience. When he blesses his own tribe of Levi, for example, he speaks of their righteousness at the instance of the golden calf and at the waters of Meribah (Deut. 33:8–9). But he does not even mention his own brother, Aaron, whose actions were crucial in these trials. Moses makes no reference to his nephews, who will serve as high priests in the Promised Land, nor to his sons, also Levites, who will not. The blessing is generic, for the whole and not the part. It is as though Moses had no personal relationships with or no blessing for those closest to his heart.

This image of Moses' last days as leader and not as man continues in the second part of the *parashah*. The last chapter of the Torah chronicles Moses' death in twelve simple verses. He ascends Mount Nebo, views the Promised Land, then dies. "The children of Israel mourned Moses in the plains of Moab for thirty days; then the days of mourning for Moses ended" (Deut. 34:8). The sages note that when Aaron died, the "entire house of Israel" mourned him (Num. 20:29), whereas Moses is mourned only by *b'nai yisrael*, the children or sons of Israel, implying only the men. Rashi explains that Moses was the teacher of Torah, but Aaron was involved personally with the whole community, making peace between men and women and among families.[2] The public misses Moses' role, the Torah implies, but the community does not miss the person. Quickly, the community moves on, under the leadership of Joshua. The Book of Deuteronomy concludes with a tribute to Moses: "Never again has there arisen in Israel a prophet like Moses" (Deut. 34:10). Gone is the leader of the Israelites.

But what of his family? And what of Moses' own fear and longing for life in the face of death? Is he really such a calm, stoic figure, accepting the Divine decree and willingly handing the people over to Joshua and his soul to God? The Torah's tale is the story of a great man of history, painted in broad, bold strokes. But the Midrash, anticipating perhaps the feminist search for the person behind the role, returns to this tale with a finer brush, to fill in the details that made Moses a unique, human soul, not simply a spokesperson for God.

In the careful hands of the Rabbis, Moses confronts his death as any person would, going through the classic stages of mourning, beginning with denial and bargaining and ending finally in acceptance of God's will. The sages did not use our modern terminology for the process of facing death, but they knew what it was to be human. No longer a proud, independent leader, Moses becomes like any one of us. As the Rabbis flesh out the story of Moses' fight for life, we get a glimpse of a different, fuller Moses. At first, Moses did not believe that he would really die before entering the land of Canaan; after all, in response to Moses' intervention, God had forgiven Israel for the golden calf and many other rebellions. Surely, Moses thought, God would forgive him also, and repent of such a harsh decree. But the Midrash teaches that God became angry that Moses did not take the threat seriously, and so sealed his punishment with God's own name, making it irrevocable.

With the poignant desperation of a person whose life's dream is about to be denied, Moses cried out, "Lord of the world . . . You already tested me at the time when the golden calf was made and I destroyed it. Why should I die?" He even, in a supreme act of chutzpah, compared himself to God, who killed "all the firstborn of Egypt, and shall I die on account of one single Egyptian that I slew?" God rebuked Moses, reminding him that God gives life, takes it away, and returns it, whereas Moses does not. Thus, God forced Moses to remember the difference between human and Divine. Moses is the leader of the Israelites, but he is mortal. He is not their god. Joshua can—and must—take his place. And although all of creation pled his case, Moses' death was still decreed.

At this point, the Rabbis teach, Moses began to bargain in earnest. He offered options in partial acceptance of the decree, hoping that relinquishing leadership or even his life would be enough for God, and Moses would nevertheless realize his dream of inheriting the land. He asked to live two years in the land of Canaan; God replied, "I have resolved that you shall not go there." Moses begged, "If I may not enter it in my lifetime, let me reach it after my death." This, too, God refused.[3] It is time for Joshua to lead, God told Moses. And Moses must neither live on as leader nor become an idol after death.

The Rabbis understand the human impulse to deny the inevitable: Moses, perhaps deliberately, misunderstood the decree. As one midrash tells it, Moses offered to become Joshua's disciple, living in his service, just as Joshua once served Moses. He stood in Joshua's presence as the new leader taught Torah, and followed Joshua into the Tent of Meeting, where God spoke only to Joshua. "What did the Word say to you?" Moses demanded to know. Joshua replied, "When the Word used to reveal itself to you, did I know what it said to you?"

Moses could not bear this anguish of living diminished, without his intimate relationship with God. "Rather a hundred deaths than a single pang of envy," he cried out. "Master of the Universe, until now I sought life. But now my soul is surrendered to You."[4] And finally Moses understood that he too must die. It is human to die with unfinished business and unfulfilled dreams.

Beyond this, the Rabbis' stories hint that Moses—and they—understood the need for personal reconciliation before death. Not only did he teach his final bits of Torah and bestow his blessing on the community, but in the Midrash, Moses also concerned himself with saying goodbye to Israel, with the care of his family, and with his own burial.

> Acknowledging their years of struggle together, Moses turned to the children of Israel as one friend would to another. "Because of the Torah and its percepts, I

troubled you greatly. Now please forgive me." They replied, "Our master, our lord, you are forgiven." In their turn they said to him, "Moses our teacher, we troubled you even more, we made your burden so heavy. Please forgive us." And he did.[5]

This is no corporate blessing, as in the Torah text itself, but rather, is an exchange of mutual love. Here, Moses speaks not only as leader, but also as friend and family member; finally, the intimacy between Moses and his people, only hinted at in Deuteronomy, finds its way to the surface.

When Moses was pleading for his life, he castigated God on account of his mother's suffering: "Shall my mother, Yocheved, to whom my life brought so much grief, suffer sorrow after my death?"[6] The concern seemed feigned, a last ditch appeal for Moses' own life. But as he prepared for the inevitable, his concern for his mother, not to mention his own family, reasserts its primacy. His mother, after all, will have lost all three of her children in the wilderness, to the service of God and the Israelites. She will live to enter the land, rabbinic tradition teaches, but without any of her kin.

Among the charges he makes to the new leader, Moses asked Joshua to care for his family:

> "You will have to carry a burden which proved too heavy for three [Moses and his siblings, Aaron and Miriam]. May God be with you! I implore you to take care of my mother, who has the terrible misfortune of losing all her children in her life-time. Now you are to be her son. Be kind to the poor proselyte (Tziporah, Moses' wife) and see that no evil is done her. In memory of our friendship treat my orphans, to whom it was not granted to be my successors, as members of your household."[7]

Realizing both his own loss—his sons were not chosen, and he must leave the family he loves—and the grief his family will surely feel, Moses acted as would any father: he attempted to ensure his family's well-being after his own death.

Finally, Moses had his own fears. By tradition, Moses' death was a sweet one: his soul was taken by a Divine kiss. But then what? Feeling lost and forsaken, he asked God about who would bury him, as he buried his brother, Aaron, and as the two of them buried Miriam years before. The Holy One promised to do so.[8] Moses merited such an honor, the Midrash says, because he remembered to find the bones of Joseph before the exodus, that they might be buried in the Land of Israel.[9] Such is the more personal eulogy the Rabbis give Moses in the Midrash; he is not only a man of Torah, a prophet of God, but also one who performs small deeds of loving-kindness that go unseen and uncredited by the public. No wonder we are told that even God weeps for Moses upon his death.[10] He was not simply a leader; he was a mensch, a decent human being.

As the written Torah ends, Moses is left buried in an unknown grave, his position given over to Joshua, his family mostly gone, his sons unblessed. He was a great prophet, the Torah teaches, and never again would the Israelite people know such a leader. The gift to us of the Midrash is that it gives us back the personal Moses alongside the Torah's portrayal of the public Moses. Too easily his life is bifurcated into seemingly unrelated public and private spheres. Without the Midrash, Moses' fight against death, his despair at leaving the world with his dreams unfulfilled, would be left untold. In truth, these private struggles do not detract from Moses' greatness. Rather, they fill out his life. His ability to lead his people stemmed not only from his role as lawgiver, but also from his personal relationships with his family, his love and concern for his people, and his wrestling with God. It is only with the Midrash's look at Moses' private life that we understand that the prophet who saw God face to face is also an ordinary human being, with loves and losses. It is of this man, who worried about his family and longed to see the Promised Land, that it is said, "Never again has there arisen in Israel a prophet like Moses" (Deut. 34:10). His greatness lay in his very humanness. In the hands of the rabbis, Moses' death comes alive, and Moses lives on.

RABBI SALLY J. PRIESAND

Epilogue

Looking Backward and Ahead

EARLY ON IN MY CAREER I discovered that both Isaac M. Wise and Stephen Wise were wise enough to understand the need for equality and to encourage full participation on the part of women in the secular world as well as the religious community. You may recall that Isaac Mayer Wise championed the right of women to have both voice and vote in congregational life. This is what he said: "[T]he principle of justice, and the law of God inherent in every human being, demand that woman be admitted to membership in the congregation, and be given equal rights with man; that her religious feelings be allowed scope for the sacred cause of Israel. We are ready to appear before any congregation in behalf of any woman wishing to become a member thereof, and to plead her cause."

Stephen Wise shared this commitment and applied it to the larger community. In 1915 he wrote, "The woman's movement rests upon the cardinal truth that, inasmuch as life is a sacred thing and personality inviolable, woman ought to be as free as is man to determine the content of life for herself. Woman must not have life marked out for her by custom or convention or expediency. . . . She must make and shape her own life, and she must no longer be expected to live in terms of relativity, in terms of dependence, in terms of complement."

In addition, in 1919 Stephen Wise wrote the following letter to a young woman in his congregation: "If you are really in earnest and wish to study for the ministry, there is no reason why you should not. The fact that no woman has served as rabbi is no reason why no woman should so serve. If you were my child, as in a sense you are, and felt you wished to enter the ministry, I should urge you to go on and prepare yourself with the conviction that opportunities for service would come to one eager to serve and possessed of the determination as you are to serve God and Israel through your vocation." When I read these words, I rather like to think that Isaac Mayer Wise and Stephen Wise would take pleasure in knowing that their vision has found fulfillment in our day and time.

I feel privileged to have participated in this pioneering effort, the complete ramifications of which remain as yet unknown. At the same time, I am well aware that the accomplishment is not mine alone. By a quirk of history, I was first, and since that time, many others have followed in my footsteps. I share the rabbinate with all of them and express my gratitude for their creativity, which so often energizes and inspires me.

It sounds corny to say that I love being a rabbi, but the truth is that I do, and I can't imagine doing anything else. In what other profession does one have the opportunity to touch the lives of other people in ways that are real and significant and often unknown?

The satisfaction I experience is due in large measure to the support and encouragement I have received from family and friends ever since the day nearly four decades ago when I announced that I wanted to be a rabbi, and is due most especially to the love and affection that my congregation showers on me. Every day I thank God for the privilege of being associated with Monmouth Reform Temple. Our creative partnership these last eighteen years has enriched my life in ways I never dreamed possible.

Among the many lessons my congregants have taught me, three are foremost in my mind, and I see reflected in them the gifts that feminism has given to all of us over the past thirty years. First, we have gained a broader understanding that the rabbi's primary task is to help other Jews become more responsible for their own Jewishness. In today's language, that is called empowerment, and nothing in my rabbinate gives me greater joy than to see my congregants study Torah, observe mitzvot, and do Judaism for themselves.

The Jew-by-choice who comes to the *bimah* for the first time to light Shabbat candles, family members gathered at the cemetery to conduct an unveiling ceremony for one of their beloved, the adult Hebrew student who sits in the sanctuary and proudly follows with her finger the words of the prayerbook, the engineer entrusted with the challenge of preparing a *D'var Torah*, the retiree who undertakes the mitzvah of *bikur cholim* (visiting the sick), the young adult who blows shofar, parents and children participating together in the task of *tikkun olam*—that is empowerment, and that remains our primary goal: to foster education, to promote observance, to encourage participation, to inspire commitment, to create a feeling of family. Not to be surrogate Jews, but to move away from the twin towers of hierarchy and power toward new opportunities for networking and partnership.

It is not our responsibility to be Jewish for the sake of the congregation, but to suggest ways in which all of us can be Jewish together. That idea is not unique to feminism, but the women's movement has served as catalyst, encouraging us to rethink previous models of leadership in which the rabbi maintained complete control and did everything for members of the congregation.

The second area in which we see the impact of feminism is

that of theology. Like most people, I grew up with the image of God as King—omnipotent and clearly male. My congregation has given me the opportunity, through experience and study, discussion and experimentation, to discover new models of Divinity, to know that God embodies characteristics both masculine and feminine, to fashion for myself, and hopefully for them, a meaningful theology that has been a source of strength, particularly in those moments of difficulty that are part of every life. Together, we have opened our hearts and our lives to greater spirituality. We are learning to talk to God and with God rather than about God, to enjoy that intimacy that comes when addressing God as "You." As a result, every member of our temple family, man and woman, young and old, parent and child, has the freedom to imagine God in any way he or she finds meaningful and comforting. The process has been enriching, and the possibilities for future growth are endless.

The third lesson I have learned from my congregation is this: success doesn't mean bigger. Twenty years ago, I thought the ultimate goal was to become rabbi of a large congregation; indeed, as the first woman to be ordained I thought it was my obligation. Our society teaches us in so many different ways that bigger is better, and within the context of the rabbinate, that if you don't continue to move up through the category system, you have somehow failed. Fortunately, for my own well-being, my congregation taught me to reject that notion.

Life is not measured by wealth or power, material possessions or fame. Life is counted in terms of goodness and growth. Someone once said that our purpose in living is not to get ahead of other people, but to get ahead of ourselves, always to play a better game of life. That is what success is all about. Have we done our best? Are we continuing to grow? Are we affected more deeply today by love and beauty and joy than we were yesterday? Are we more sensitive and compassionate toward others? Have we learned to overcome our fears and accept our failures? Have we triumphed over selfishness and bitterness, cruelty and hatred? Do we count our blessings in such a way that we make our blessings count? That's what success is. In the words of Albert Schweitzer, "The great secret of success is to go through life as a person who never gets used up. Grow into your ideas so that life can never rob you of them."

These, then, are the lessons I have learned as I look back over the past four decades. Empowerment is healthy for the Jewish people. Our renewed interest in theology makes us spiritually alive, and thus better able to be whole persons. And success doesn't mean bigger. As I look ahead, I am well aware that our journey is only just beginning.

I conclude with the words of Stephen Wise: "When nice and refined and timid people say to you, 'Remember to be like everybody else, don't attempt anything new, don't run the risk of seeming peculiar, don't dream of venturing upon novel courses whether in things great or small,' remember that there is a possible invasion of the soul's integrity that no person need endure. To the counsels of the timorous fling back the command to the brave—always do what you are afraid to do."

(This epilogue is adapted from remarks that Rabbi Priesand delivered on Founders' Day at Hebrew Union College–Jewish Institute of Religion in New York on March 17, 1992. The complete address can be found in A Treasury of Favorite Sermons by Leading American Rabbis, *ed. Sidney Greenberg [Northvale, N.J.: Jason Aronson, 1999].)*

Notes

Introduction

1 Gary P. Zola, "Twenty Years of Women in the Rabbinate," in *Women Rabbis: Exploration and Celebration*, ed. Gary P. Zola (Cincinnati: HUC–JIR Rabbinic Alumni Association Press, 1996), 2.

2 Alfred Gottschalk, "Who Shall Sojourn in the Tabernacle . . ." in Zola, ed., *Women Rabbis*, 20.

3 Ellen Lewis, "Luncheon Address, CCAR Convention 1991," in "Wisdom You Are My Sister," *CCAR Journal* (summer 1997): 16, 20.

4 Rachel Adler, *Engendering Judaism* (Philadeplphia: Jewish Publication Society, 1998), 38.

5 Abraham Geiger, "No Spiritual Minority," in Gunther Plaut, ed., *The Rise of Reform Judaism* (New York: World Union for Progressive Judaism, 1963), 253.

What You Need to Know to Use This Book

1 Naomi Goldenberg, *Changing of the Gods* (Boston: Beacon Press, 1979), 10, 13, 22.

2 Barry Holtz, *Back to the Sources* (New York: Summit, 1984), 180–181.

3 Mary Ann Tolbert, "Defining the Problem: The Bible and the Feminist Hermeneutics," *Semeia* 28 (1983): 22

Bereshit/Genesis

Bereshit · *Rabbi Lori Forman*

1 Women are obligated to fulfill these three mitzvot. *Mikveh* refers to the family

purity laws; *challah* refers to the obligation to remove a small piece of the dough from the *challah* to burn it as a reminder of the sacrifices when the Temple stood; and Shabbat refers to the obligation to light candles on Shabbat. These mitzvot are first mentioned in *Mishneh Shabbat* 2:6 as those whose transgression causes death in childbirth.

2 Genesis *Rabbah* 17:8.

3 Babylonian Talmud, *Eruvin* 18b; Genesis *Rabbah* 18:1.

4 See Adin Steinsaltz, *Biblical Images* (New York: Basic Books, 1984), 4–5.

5 See Nechama Aschkenasy, *Eve's Journey* (Philadelphia: University of Pennsylvania Press, 1986), 41.

Lech Lecha · *Rabbi Michal Shekel*

1 Or in some interpretations, Hagar encounters five different Divine messengers, four here and one in chapter 21. See Genesis *Rabbah* 45:7 and Exodus *Rabbah* 3:16.

2 See Genesis *Rabbah* 45:10. As translated in the Soncino edition: "God never condescended [*nizkak*] to hold converse with a woman save that righteous woman [Sarai]." This same point is repeated in Genesis *Rabbah* 20:6, 48:28 and 63:7. It is interesting that this midrash exempts Sarai, yet ignores the fact that God clearly does speak to another matriarch, Rebecca, in Gen. 25:23. This being the case, the objection to God's conversing with a woman falls apart.

3 See Gen. 15:2 and 15:8 where Abram questions God, resulting in the Covenant of the Pieces. See also Gen. 17:9–14 where *brit milah* (the covenant of circumcision) is given to Abram as an ever-present physical reminder.

4 In a later chapter, however, Adam also names Seth. Interestingly, we are not told who names Abel. Perhaps he did not survive because no one took responsibility for him.

5 Genesis 24:62. Genesis *Rabbah* 60:14 says that Isaac went to this location to get Hagar, the one who sat by the well.

6 According to midrash, Hagar is an Egyptian princess, who was given to Sarai in chapter 12. This would make her a princess before Sarai/Sarah becomes one!

Chaye Sarah · *Rabbi Rona Shapiro*

1 This idea is expressed throughout Soren Kierkegaard, *Fear and Trembling*, ed. and trans. Howard V. Hong and Edna H. Hong (Princeton, N.J.: Princeton University Press, 1983).

2 Carol Gilligan, *In A Different Voice: Psychological Theory and Women's Development* (Cambridge: Harvard University Press, 1982), 17.

Vayetze · *Rabbi Sandy Eisenberg Sasso*

1 Linda Clark, "A Sermon: Wrestling with Jacob's Angel" in *Image-Breaking/Image-Building*, ed. Linda Clark, Marian Ronan, and Eleanor Walker (New York: The Pilgrim Press, 1981).

2 *Midrash HaGadol*, cited in Louis Ginzberg, *The Legends of the Jews* (Philadelphia: Jewish Publication Society, 1968), I:197.

3 The Rabbis identify the descendants of Esau with Rome and with medieval Christianity.

4 *Eikha Rabbah P'tikhta, Midrash Rabbah* (New York: Soncino, 1983), 7:49.

Vayishlach · *Rabbi Lia Bass*

1 Genesis *Rabbah* 84:19.

2 The term *gezerah shavah* literally means "a comparable declaration," thus, learning from the appearance of the same word in two different places.

Vayeshev · *Rabbi Geela-Rayzel Raphael*

1 M. C. Astour, "Tamar the Hierodule," *Journal of Biblical Literature* (June 66): 85.

2 Louis Ginzberg, *Legends of the Jews* (Philadelphia: Jewish Publication Society, 1969), 2:34.

3 Astour, "Tamar the Hierodule," 190.

4 Ibid., 188.

5 Eugene Fisher, "Cultic Prostitution in the Ancient Near East? A Reassessment," *Biblical Theology Bulletin* 6 (June 76): 225.

6 Astour, "Tamar the Hierodule," 193.

7 Ginzberg, *Legends*, 2:37.

Miketz · *Rabbi Debra Judith Robbins*

1 Peggy Orenstein, *Schoolgirls: Young Women, Self-Esteem, and the Confidence Gap* (New York: Anchor Books/Doubleday, 1995), 280.

2 W. Gunther Plaut, *The Torah: A Modern Commentary* (New York: Union of American Hebrew Congregations, 1981) on Gen. 41:45. Also, Genesis *Rabbah* 89:2.

3 See Nachum M. Sarna, *Genesis*, JPS Torah Commentary (Philadelphia: Jewish Publication Society, 1989) on Gen. 41:45.

4 Judith S. Antonelli, *In the Image of God: A Feminist Commentary on the Torah* (Northvale, N.J.: Jason Aronson, 1995), 118.

5 Genesis *Rabbah* 90:4.

6 *Targum Yonatan, Sofrim* 21.

7 Robert Graves and Raphael Patai, *Hebrew Myths: The Book of Genesis* (New York: Greenwich House, 1983), 237.

8 Bill Moyers, *Genesis: A Living Conversation* (New York: Doubleday, 1996), 346.

9 According to Rav Chisdah, an uninterpreted dream is a bad thing because it could contain information that is harmful. By knowing the interpretation, one has the opportunity to change or influence the course of events.

10 Psalms 30:12, Jer. 31:13, Deut. 23:6.

11 Psalms 55:19, Isa. 35:10, I Sam. 14:45.

12 Isaiah 57:19, I Chron. 12:19, I Sam. 25:6.

13 My thanks to Danny Siegel for his translation of this passage and for connecting the Talmud passage to *tzedakah* and to the prayer of the traditional siddur.

14 *Midrash Hagadol* 48:1. Cited by Avivah Gottlieb Zornberg, *The Beginning of Desire: Reflections on Genesis* (New York: Image/Doubleday, 1996), 369.

15 Babylonian Talmud, *Berachot* 55b.

Vayigash · *Rabbi Shira Stern*

1 Rashi on 34:1.

2 Martin Buber, *I and Thou* (New York: Scribner, 1970), 67.

3 Ibid.

Vayechi · *Rabbi Barbara Rosman Penzner*

1 I have chosen to cite only four texts for this essay. Serach's legacy can be found in other rabbinic sources. Interestingly, she is also the source of much folklore, especially among the Jews of Isfahan, where a synagogue in her honor once stood, as well as a shrine that was a place of pilgrimage for Persian Jews.

2 *Midrash Hagadol* 45:26.

3 *Pirke de Rabbi Eliezar* 191–192.

4 *Mechilta Beshallah*, chapter 1.

5 *Pesikta de Rav Kahana* 11:13.

Shmot/Exodus

Shmot · *Rabbi Rebecca T. Alpert*

1 *Midrash Tanhuma* 2:6, edited by S. Buber, as quoted in Louis Ginzberg, *The Legends of the Jews* (Philadelphia: Jewish Publication Society, 1968), 5:423 n. 147.

2 See Marija Alseikaite Gimbutas, *The Civilization of the Goddess: The World of Old Europe*, ed. Joan Marler (San Francisco: HarperSanFrancisco, 1991).

3 *Zohar* 2, 12b.

4 Josephus, *Antiquities* 2, 11.1.

5 *Sefer VaYosha* 42–43, as quoted in Ginzberg, *Legends*, 2:294.

6 Ibid.

7 Ibid.

8 *Lekah*, Exod. 2:22, as quoted in Ginzberg, *Legends*, 5:412 n. 98.

9 Based on a poem by Hanna Tiferet Siegel, "Parshat Tziporah." Used by permission of the author.

10 Ginzberg, *Legends*, 6:136 n. 791.

Va-era · *Rabbi Karyn D. Kedar*

1 Chaim Stern, ed., *Gates of Forgiveness* (New York: CCAR Press, 1993), 24–27.

2 *Kavvanat Halev* (Jerusalem: Israel Movement for Progressive Judaism, 1989), 72.

Bo · *Rabbi Lucy H. F. Dinner*

1 Nahum M. Sarna, *Exodus*, JPS Torah Commentary (Philadelphia: Jewish Publication Society, 1991), 51.

2 Lawrence S. Kushner and Kerry M. Olitzky, *Sparks Beneath the Surface* (Northvale, N.J.: Jason Aronson, 1993), 80.

Beshalach · *Rabbi Sue Levi Elwell*

1 Phyllis Trible implies this detour in "Bringing Miriam Out of the Shadows," *Bible Review* (February 1989), 18, 20.

2 Drorah O'Donnell Setel, "Exodus," in Carol A. Newsom and Sharon H. Ringe, eds., *The Women's Bible Commentary* (Louisville, Ky.: Westminster/John Knox, 1992), 31.

3 Nahum M. Sarna, *Exodus*, JPS Torah Commentary (Philadelphia: Jewish Publication Society, 1991), 83, note 20, and *Mekilta* 10:74 ff.

4 Thanks to Ellen Frankel, *The Five Books of Miriam: A Woman's Commentary on the Torah* (New York: G.P. Putnam's Sons, 1996), 111, 311, for her reference to the work of Carol Meyers. See also Trible, "Bringing Miriam," 19.

5 *Mekilta* 10:89ff, Trible, "Bringing Miriam," 19–20, and Setel, "Exodus," 31.

6 *The Book of Legends: Sefer Ha-Aggadah: Legends from the Talmud and Midrash*, ed. Hayim Nahman Bialik and Yehoshua Hana Ravnitzky, trans. William G. Braude (New York: Schocken, 1992), 76:14.

7 Rashi on 17:10. See Leila Leah Bronner, *From Eve to Esther: Rabbinic Reconstructions of Biblical Women* (Louisville, Ky.: Westminster/John Knox, 1994), 169.

8 See Penina Adelman, *Miriam's Well: Rituals for Jewish Women around the Year* (Fresh Meadows, N.Y.: Biblio, 1986); Ellen Frankel, *Five Books of Miriam*; Tamara Cohen, Sue Levi Elwell, and Debbie Friedman, *The Journey Continues: The Ma'yan Haggadah* (New York: Ma'yan, 1999). See also CCAR *Haggadah* (New York: CCAR Press, forthcoming).

Yitro · *Rabbi Julie K. Gordon*

1 Charles B. Chavel, *Ramban (Nachmanides) Commentary on the Torah: Exodus* (New York: Shilo, 1973), 266. He is quoting Ibn Ezra and R'dak in *Sefer Hashorashim*, on the root *chayil*.

2 M. Rosenbaum and A. M. Silbermann, *Pentateuch with Targum Onkelos, Haftaroth and Rashi's Commentary: Exodus* (New York: Hebrew Publishing, 1930), 97.

3 Ibid., 99.

4 Judith Plaskow, *Standing Again at Sinai: Judaism from a Feminist Perspective* (San Francisco: Harper and Row, 1990).

Mishpatim · *Rabbi Nancy Fuchs-Kreimer*

1 Nehama Leibowitz, *Studies in Shemot (Exodus)* (Jerusalem: World Zionist Organization, Department for Torah Education and Culture in the Diaspora, 1976), 2:384.

2 Carol Gilligan, *In a Different Voice: Psychological Theory and Women's Development* (Cambridge: Harvard University Press, 1992).

Terumah · *Rabbi Sharon L. Sobel*

1 Pinchas Peli, *Torah Today: A Renewed Encounter with Scripture* (Washington, D.C.: B'nai Brith Books, 1987), 82.

2 Nehama Leibowitz, *Studies in Shemot (Exodus)*, part 2 (Jerusalem: World Zionist Organization, Department for Torah Education and Culture in the Diaspora, 1983), 468.

3 Ibid., 472.

Tetzaveh · *Rabbi Sara Paasche-Orlow*

1 Babylonian Talmud, *Yoma* 71b.

2 Jon D. Levinson, *Sinai and Zion: An Entry Into the Jewish Bible* (Minneapolis: Winston Press, 1985), 181.

3 Susan Grossman and Rivka Haut, eds., *Daughters of the King: Women and the Synagogue* (Philadelphia: Jewish Publication Society, 1992), 15.
4 Susan Starr Sered, *Women as Ritual Experts* (New York: Oxford University Press, 1992), 92.
5 As understood in Babylonian Talmud, *Menachot* 86b, "for thee and not for me."
6 Babylonian Talmud, *Shabbat* 22b.

Ki Tissa · *Rabbi Ellen Lippmann*

1 *Pirke de Rabbi Eliezar (The Chapters of Rabbi Eliezar the Great) according to the Text of the Manuscript Belonging to Abraham Epstein of Vienna*, trans. by Gerald Friedlander (New York: Sepher-Hermon, 1981), 354.
2 Ibid.
3 Ellen Frankel, *The Five Books of Miriam* (New York: G. P. Putnam's Sons, 1996), 137.
4 Samuel Berman, trans., *Midrash Tanhuma-Yelammedenu* (Hoboken, N.J.: KTAV, 1996), 598.
5 Exodus *Rabbah* 43:1.

Vayakhel · *Rabbi Nancy H. Wiener*

1 For a full discussion of the symbolism of bodily fluids in the priestly system, see Howard Eilberg-Schwartz, *The Savage in Judaism* (Bloomington: Indiana University Press, 1990).

Vayikra/Leviticus

Vayikra · *Rabbi Shoshana Gelfand*

1 Ramban, *Commentary on the Torah: Leviticus* (New York: Shilo, 1974), 3.
2 Martin Buber, *I and Thou* (New York: Scribner, 1970), 62.

Tzav · *Rabbi Claire Magidovitch Green*

1 A sense of what the rituals may have looked like may be obtained from a work such as *Illustrated Guide to Korbonos and Menochos* (Brooklyn: Torah Umesorah Publications, 1991), a work of romantic reconstruction rather than archaeology.
2 The term *terumat hadeshen* is talmudic, not biblical.

3   This reminds me of a scene from the 1968 MGM film, *Shoes of the Fisherman*. Anthony Quinn's character, the newly elected pope, finds himself overwhelmed by the trappings of the papacy. He takes off his regal papal vestments, slips out into the night dressed as a simple priest and, incognito, comes into touch with suffering souls to whom he ministers.

4   *Derech Eretz Zuta* 5, as quoted in Hayim Nachman Bialik and Yehoshua Hana Ravnitzky, eds., *Sefer Ha-aggadah* (Tel Aviv: Dvir, 1951), 552.

5   Nehama Leibowitz quotes this thirteenth century work, which lists and explains the 613 mitzvot, the traditional enumeration of the religious obligations in *Studies in Vayikra (Leviticus)* (Jerusalem: World Zionist Organization, Department for Torah Education and Culture in the Diaspora, 1980), 42.

6   "The perpetual fire on the altar expressed the devotion of the Israelite people to God by indicating that they were attendant upon God at all times in the sanctuary." Baruch A. Levine, *Leviticus*, JPS Torah Commentary (Philadelphia: Jewish Publication Society, 1989), 36.

7   "The literal translation of 'do not extinguish it,' can, according to Rabbi Schneur Zalman also be interpreted as 'you must extinguish the negative.' In other words, rid yourself of all negativism [in your personality] that prevents you from being consumed by a burning desire to be close to God" (Abraham Twerski, "Living Each Week," in *Vayikra Tzav* [http://www.anshe.org/Parashah/tzav5757.html]).

Tazria · *Rabbi Helaine Ettinger*

1   W. Gunther Plaut, ed., *The Torah: A Modern Commentary* (New York: Union of American Hebrew Congregations, 1981), 850.

2   Yaakov ben Yitzhak Ashkenazi, *Tz'enah Ur'enah: The Classic Anthology of Torah Lore and Midrashic Commentary*, trans. Miriam Stark Zakon (Jerusalem: Mesorah Publications, 1983), 2: 589.

3   Baruch A. Levine, *Leviticus*, JPS Torah Commentary (Philadelphia: Jewish Publication Society, 1989), 74.

4   I wish to acknowledge the help and insights I gained from studying this text with Anita Tamari and the other women of our Rosh Chodesh group in Israel: Rinah, Sharon, Jeri, Anne, Judith, and Susie. Our monthly celebrations and study sessions have enriched my appreciation of both Judaism and feminism immeasurably. At the same time, I wish to dedicate this interpretation to my children, Lyla, Yael, and Shai, whose births enabled me to appreciate my own connection to God and Humanity in new ways.

Metzorah · *Rabbi Laura Geller*

1 Rachel Adler argued this in her classic article, "Tumah and Taharah," in *First Jewish Catalogue*, ed. Michael and Sharon Strassfeld and Richard Siegel (Philadelphia: Jewish Publication Society, 1973), 167–171. She later changed her position in an article titled "In Your Blood Live: Re-visions of a Theology of Purity," first published in *Tikkun* 8, no. 1 (January/February 1993), 38–41, and reprinted in Debra Orenstein and Jane Litman, eds., *Lifecycles, V. 2: Jewish Women on Biblical Themes in Contemporary Life* (Woodstock, Vt.: Jewish Lights, 1997).

2 Carol Ochs, "Naso," in *Beginning the Journey*, ed. Emily Feigenson (New York: Women of Reform Judaism, 1997), 123–126.

3 Baruch Levine in his commentary on the Book of Leviticus includes dietary purity as a third way in which the categories of *taharah* and *tumah* continue until the present day. (*Leviticus*, JPS Torah Commentary [Philadelphia: JPS 1989], 220.)

4 Chaim Seidler-Feller in "Learn Torah With," Torah-by-Fax 4, no. 28 (May 2, 1998): 1.

5 Moses Isserles' gloss on *Shulchan Arukh* O.C. 88.

Acharei Mot · *Rabbi Dayle A. Friedman*

1 See, for example, Leviticus *Rabbah* 20:10, which portrays Nadav and Avihu as arrogant boasters, eager to assume power from the aging Moses and Aaron, or Leviticus *Rabbah* 12:1, where they are described as performing their rites while intoxicated. On the other hand, Leviticus *Rabbah* 12:2 suggests that the sanctuary has been made holy by virtue of the presence and sacrifice of these two righteous human beings.

2 Carol Staudacher, *Men and Grief: A Guide for Men Surviving the Death of a Loved One* (Oakland, Cailf.: New Harbinger, 1991), 14.

3 Ibid., 28.

4 Ibid., 36.

5 Deborah Tannen, *You Just Don't Understand: Men and Women in Conversation* (New York: Ballantine, 1990), 83.

6 M. Conway, C. Giannopoulos, and K. Stiefenhofer, "Response Styles to Sadness Are Related to Sex and Sex-role Orientation," cited in Daniel Canary et al., *Sex and Gender Differences in Personal Relationships* (New York: Guildford, 1997), 37.

7 Daena Goldsmith and Susan Dun, "Sex Differences and Similarities in the Communication of Social Support," cited in Julia T. Wood, *Gendered Lives: Communication, Gender and Culture* (Belmont, Calif.: Wadsworth, 1999), 203.

8 An example is found in Jer. 9:16, "So says the Eternal of hosts, reflect, and call for the mourning women, and they will come; and send for the skilled women, and they will come."

Emor · *Rabbi Valerie Lieber*

1 Julius Wellhausen, "Levites and Priests," *Anchor Bible Dictionary* 4 (New York: Doubleday, 1992).
2 Ibid.
3 Rashi, *The Pentateuch and Rashi's Commentary*, trans. Abraham Ben-Isaiah and Benjamin Sharfman (Brooklyn, N.Y.: S. S. & R, 1949), 246.

Behar · *Rabbinical Students Sharon Brous and Jill Hammer*

1 Regrettably, the text does not demand the freeing of non-Israelite slaves, who must remain with their masters as an inheritance (Lev. 25:44–46). This mars the egalitarian nature of the *yovel*. Still, *Parashat Behar* diminishes the power of slavery and supports the general principle of freedom and equality. In our day we can extend that principle to a wider community.
2 *Mekhilta Shabbeta* 1:103b; *Mekhilta d'Rabbi Shimon bar Yochai* 160.
3 Cf. Rashi on Exod. 21:7.
4 The Torah does not end slavery, and so one cannot make the claim that it entirely rejects the societal norms of the times. The Torah does, however, seek to mitigate slavery's effects in a way unique in the ancient world.
5 "Letter from a Birmingham Jail," in *I Have a Dream*, ed. James M. Washington (San Francisco: HarperCollins, 1992), 87.
6 According to F. Brown, S. R. Driver, and C. A. Briggs, the Hebrew *yovel* comes from the Phoenician *yaval*, "ram" (*Hebrew and English Lexicon of the Old Testament* [Oxford: Clarendon, 1951]), 385.
7 *Sifra Behar* 2:2.
8 R. Ephraim Lunchitz, in *Keli Yakar* on Deut. 31:12.

Bechukotai · *Rabbi Elizabeth Bolton*

1 Judith Plaskow, *Standing Again at Sinai: Judaism from a Feminist Perspective* (San Francisco: Harper and Row, 1990).
2 When chanted aloud during the weekly cycle of Torah readings, the curses are meant to be recited hurriedly and in a hushed voice.
3 Job 19:3. It is a common biblical device for numbers to stand in for certain timeframes or overall amounts.

4 Baruch A. Levine, *Leviticus*, JPS Torah Commentary (Philadelphia: Jewish Publication Society, 1989), 187.

5 Everett Fox, *The Five Books of Moses* (New York: Schocken, 1990), 632.

6 Ellen Frankel, *The Five Books of Miriam: A Women's Commentary on the Bible* (New York: G. P. Putnam's Sons, 1996), 191-2.

7 The midrash collection *Alphabet of Ben Sira* describes Lilith as Adam's first wife, who was banished from Eden for her rebellious nature.

8 See Dalia Ofer and Lenore J. Weitzman, eds., *Women in the Holocaust* (New Haven: Yale University Press, 1998); Julia Epstein and Lori Hope Lefkovitz, eds., *Shaping Losses: Cultural Memory and the Holocaust* (University of Illinois Press, forthcoming).

9 See Hayim Nahman Bialik and Yehoshua Ravnitzky, eds., *The Book of Legends/Sefer Ha-agadah: Legends from the Talmud and Midrash*, trans. William J. Braude (New York: Schocken, 1992), 537–574.

10 Leviticus *Rabbah* 25:5–6, quoted in Harvey Fields, *A Torah Commentary for Our Times* (New York: UAHC Press, 1991), 2:158.

11 Babylonian Talmud, *Kiddushin* 40b: "The Holy One brings suffering upon the righteous of the world in order that they may inherit the future world."

12 The song is widely anthologized. See Eleanor Gordon Mlotek, ed., *Mir Trogn A Gezang! The New Book of Yiddish Songs* (New York: Workmen's Circle Education Department, 1972), 190–91; poem by Hirsh Glik (1922–1944), music by Dmitri Pokrass.

Bamidbar/Numbers

Bamidbar · *Rabbi Sheryl Nosan*

1 This is reflected in numerous passages. For example the Bible offers no ritual to mark and celebrate the entrance of female babies into the covenant while it demands *brit milah* for male babies in Gen. 17:10–14. Narratives such as Gen. 29:31–30:24 celebrate the births of Jacob's sons and explain each boy's name while glossing over the delivery of a daughter and omitting the meaning of her name. Most dramatically, giving birth to a female rather than a male inexplicably renders a mother doubly ritually defiled, because the period of a woman's ritual defilement after birthing a girl is twice as long as the period after birthing a male, according to Lev. 12:2–5.

2 The concept of primogeniture was extremely important in the biblical world. The *reashit ono* (first fruit) of a man had special legal and social status (Gen.

49:3; Deut. 21:17); the *peter rechem* (breaker of the womb), or first child (if male) delivered by a woman, had special religious status, as reflected in Exod. 13:2, 12, and 15, as well as Exod. 34:19.

3 *Pidyon ha-ben* takes place on the weekday following the thirtieth day. Israel has minted special coins for *pidyon ha-ben*. Today, silver dollars are usually used in the United States.

4 See *Yoreh De'ah* 305:1, 23. Note that for the purposes of *pidyon ha-ben*, whether or not the son is the father's first-born is irrelevant.

5 See, for example, Anita Diamant, *The New Jewish Baby Book* (Woodstock, Vt.: Jewish Lights, 1994), 207–210. See also the *Reconstructionist Rabbinical Association Rabbi Manual* (Wyncote, Pa.: Reconstructionist Rabbinical Association, 1997), 33–45.

6 See, for example, *Rabbi's Manual* (New York: Central Conference of American Rabbis, 1988), 37.

7 I have created such blessings for men and women becoming parents. The blessings can be obtained from me by contacting the publisher.

Naso · *Rabbi Sarra Levine*

1 Translation from *Tanakh: A New Translation of the Holy Scriptures according to the Traditional Hebrew Text* (Philadelphia: Jewish Publication Society, 1985). The JPS edition notes that the meaning of the Hebrew is unclear.

2 Translation from Everett Fox, *The Five Books of Moses* (New York: Schocken, 1983).

3 Ibid.

Beha'alotecha · *Rabbi Ruth H. Sohn*

1 See, for example, *Sifrei Bemidbar* #106; *Mechilta d'Rabbi Ishmael, VaYassa Parashah* 5, Babylonian Talmud *Shabbat* 35a.

2 See Exod. 2:4–8; Exod. 15:20–21; Num. 12; 20:1; 26:59.

3 See for example, the ideas of G. Coats, W. R. Smith and M. Noth as discussed by Rita Burns, *Has the Lord Indeed Spoken Only through Moses? A Study of the Biblical Portrait of Miriam* (Atlanta: Scholars Press, 1987), 61–71.

4 Ibid., 51–61.

5 Ilana Pardes, *Countertraditions in the Bible: A Feminist Approach* (Cambridge: Harvard University Press, 1992), 10.

6 For example, *Sifrei Bemidbar* #99; *Tanhuma Tsav* 13; *Avot d'Rabbi Natan* A.9.

7 *Avot d'Rabbi Natan* A.9.

8 *Sifrei Bemidbar* #99.

9 For an insightful exploration of the rabbinic understanding of the relationship between body and spirit see Daniel Boyarin, *Carnal Israel* (Berkeley: University of California Press, 1993), especially 1–60.

Shelach-Lecha · *Rabbi Lisa A. Edwards*

1 According to a midrash on Num. 14:1 ("And all the congregation lifted up its
   voice, and the people cried that night"), that night was the ninth of Av, where-
   upon the Holy One said to them: "'You have wept a causeless weeping before
   Me. I shall therefore fix for you a permanent weeping for future generations.' At
   that hour it was decreed that the Temple should be destroyed and that Israel
   should be exiled among the nations" (Numbers *Rabbah* XVI.20).
2 The suggestion that it is men only is based, in part at least, on Num. 14:3, in
   which those complaining make reference to "our wives and children." If the
   women were also making complaints, they would not have said "our wives."
   Rashi is among those who does not believe the decree was against the women.
   Numbers 14:29–30 also suggests that only the "men perished according to
   God's decree."
3 See Judith Antonelli, *In the Image of God: A Feminist Commentary on the Torah* (Northvale, N.J.: Jason Aronson, 1995), 353.
4 Ibid., 353.
5 I am reminded of a verse from a wedding blessing by Sidney Greenberg: "May
   they never measure how much love or encouragement they offer; may they never
   count the times they forgive" (*Kol Haneshemah Shabbat Vehagim* [Wyncote, Pa.:
   Reconstructionist Press, 1994], 786).
6 *Megillah* 23b; *Sanhedrin* 2a.
7 Antonelli, *In the Image of God*, 354.
8 *Ruach acheret*, "a different spirit," is how God describes Caleb in Num. 14:24.

Korach · *Rabbi Elyse D. Frishman*

1 M. Scott Peck, *The Different Drum: Community Making and Peace* (New York: Simon
   and Schuster, 1987), 13–15.
2 Isabel Myers, *Manual: The Myers-Briggs Type Indicator* (Palo Alto, Calif.: Consulting
   Psychologists Press, 1962).

Chukkat · *Rabbi Audrey S. Pollack*

1 These are the words of Rabbi Yochanan in chapter 4, verse 7 of *Pesikta deRav
   Kahana*, trans. William G. Braude and Israel J. Kapstein (Philadelphia: Jewish
   Publication Society, 1975).

2 See Numbers *Rabbah* 19:5, which quotes Rabbi Joshua of Siknin on this matter. The other three *chukkot* are the laws concerning levirate marriage (although we are told "Thou shalt not uncover the nakedness of your brother's wife"); *shatnez* (forbidding the mixture of wool and linen in garments) (Deut. 22:11); and the law of the scapegoat (Lev. 16:26). *Midrash Rabbah: Numbers*, ed. H. Freedman and Maurice Simon (New York: Soncino, 1983), 755–756.

3 Ramban on Num. 19:17. See *Ramban (Nachmanides) Commentary on the Torah*, trans. Charles B. Chavel (New York: Shilo, 1971), 204–205.

4 Rashi on Num. 20:1. See *Chumash* with Rashi's Commentary, trans. A. M. Silbermann (Jerusalem: Routledge and Kegan Paul, 1934), 95b.

5 Rashi and Ramban's commentary on Num. 20:1–2 based on *Bavli Ta'anit* 9a (Silberman, trans., *Chumash*; Chaevl, trans., *Ramban*, 220).

6 *Mishnah Avot* 5:9. See *Mishnayot*, trans. Philip Blackman (New York: Judaica Press, 1963), 4:528.

7 *Tz'enah Ur'enah*, commentary on 20:1. See *Tz'enah Ur'enah* (New York: Mesorah, 1989), 769.

8 Louis Ginzberg, *The Legends of the Jews* (Philadelphia: Jewish Publication Society, 1946), 3:308.

9 *Tz'enah Ur'enah*, 2:769.

10 Alshich, commentary on Num. 20:1. See Nosson Scherman, *The Chumash: Stone Edition of the Artscroll Chumash* (New York: Mesorah, 1993), 843.

Balak · *Rabbi Diane Aronson Cohen*

1 Babylonian Talmud, *Ta'anit* 7a.
2 *Avot* 4:1.

Pinchas · *Rabbi Pamela Wax*

1 A fascinating look at inheritance in different cultures can be found in a chapter entitled "Inheritance," in James Hastings, ed., *Encyclopedia of Religion and Ethics* (New York: Charles Scribners' Sons, 1928), 7:295–311.

2 According to Jacob Milgrom, "The Karaites, in keeping with their strict adherence to Biblical law, interpret this literally. They apply it solely to the ancestor inheritance in the Holy Land but not to real estate elsewhere or to movable property, in which case daughters inherit equally with sons" (*Numbers*, JPS Torah Commentary [Philadelphia: Jewish Publication Society, 1990], 484).

3 References to some of these progressive rabbinic voices can be found in *Baba Batra* 109a, 110a-b, and 111a, and in the Palestinian Talmud, *Baba Batra* 8:1.

4 For further discussion, see Reuven Yaron, *Gifts in Contemplation of Death in Jewish*

and Roman Law (Oxford: Clarendon, 1960).

5 See, for example, *Mishnah Baba Batra* 8:5 which portrays the disdain that the Rabbis held for anyone who transgressed the biblical law of inheritance.

6 References to this document can be found in *Shulchan Arukh: Hoshen Mishpat* 281:7; *Eben Ha-ezer* 89:1; 108:3.

Matot · *Rabbi Stacy K. Offner*

1 Abraham Hasdai, Ben Hamelek Vehanazir (Barcelona: c. 1230), ch. 26.

2 Elizabeth Cady Stanton, *The Woman's Bible* (Seattle: Coalition Task Force on Women and Religion, 1974), 117.

3 M. Rosenbaum and A. M. Silbermann, eds., *Pentateuch and Rashi's Commentary* (Jerusalem: Silbermann, 1929), 144.

4 Carol Gilligan, *In a Different Voice* (Cambridge: Harvard University Press, 1982), 8.

Masa'ei · *Rabbi Hara E. Person*

1 Mary Douglas, *Purity and Danger* (New York: Routledge, 1966), 35.

2 Phyllis Bird, *Missing Persons and Mistaken Identities: Women and Gender in Ancient Israel* (Minneapolis: Fortress, 1997), 23.

3 See, for example, Gen. 6:22; Exod. 7:6; Exod. 12:28; Exod. 12:50.

4 See, for example, Gen. 42:20; Exod. 7:6; Exod. 12:28.

5 Jacob Milgrom, *Numbers*, JPS Torah Commentary (Philadelphia: Jewish Publication Society, 1989), 298.

6 Bird, *Missing Persons and Mistaken Identities*, 55.

Devarim/Deuteronomy

Va'etchanan · *Rabbi Rochelle Robins*

1 Deut. 11:9; 26:9; 15; 27:3; and 31:2.

2 Jeffrey H. Tigay, *Deuteronomy*, JPS Torah Commentary (Philadelphia: Jewish Publication Society, 1996), 438.

3 Ibid., 75.

4 See, for examples, Lev. 15:1–2 and 25, Lev. 15:1-2; Lam. 4:9.

5 The laws of family purity and *Niddah* (the menstruant woman who is forbidden to have sexual contact with her husband) are based on the following biblical citations: Lev. 15:19–33; 18:19; and 20:18. The *Arba'ah Turim* and the

Shulchan Arukh in the section of *Yoreh De'ah* are examples of rabbinic legal codes developed around the subject. For feminist analysis, see the essays in this book on the Leviticus sections.

6   Anne McClintock, *Imperial Leather: Race, Gender, and Sexuality in the Colonial Contest* (New York: Routledge, 1995), 23.

7   Ibid.

8   Pamela Gordon and Harold C. Washington, "Rape as a Military Metaphor in the Hebrew Bible" in *The Feminist Companion to the Latter Prophets*, ed. Athalya Brenner (Sheffield, England: Sheffield Academic Press, 1995), 308–09.

Shoftim · *Rabbi Susan Fendrick*

1   Babylonian Talmud, *Sotah* 46a.

2   See Judith Hauptman, *Rereading the Rabbis: A Woman's Voice* (Boulder, Colo.: Westview, 1999), regarding the way that rabbinic law of concern for women developed over time.

3   *Pirkei Avot* 5:26.

Ki Tetzey · *Rabbi Judith Gary Brown*

1   Two significant questions arise from the language of the text. First, why are three different terms—*ishah*, *na'arah*, and *betulah*—used for the girl/woman? Second, why is this a capital crime (and what does this imply)? With respect to the first question, the terms *na'arah* and *betulah* refer to a girl around the age of pubescence. The term *betulim* seems to mean "(signs of) virginity" or "evidence of pubescence." Maimonides, in his *Mishneh Torah* (*Hilkhot Na'arah Betulah* 3:2), specifies that *na'arah* means a girl between the age of twelve and twelve-and-a-half years of age. The term *ishah*, however, can mean either "woman" or "wife." In this regard, the opening phrase *Ki yikach ish ishah* technically means "If a man takes a woman/wife." So, perhaps, we are getting a glimpse of at what age daughters were married off in biblical society. The second question stems from the fact that the only case where prenuptial intercourse would be a capital crime is a case of adultery. Thus, the girl/woman would have to have been already betrothed at the time she has intercourse for this to be considered adultery. It seems then that this case reflects a scenario where the husband, after having sexual intercourse with his new wife, feels that she was not a virgin (presumably because there was no bleeding), and inquires and finds out that his wife was seen with another man in the period between their becoming betrothed and the marriage ceremony. In a capital case, it would be unheard of to base the whole case on a piece of evidence and not witnesses. This difficul-

ty in the text has led many to argue that the expression *hasimlah*, "the garment/cloth," meant "evidence" and the expression *ufarsu hasimlah*, "they spread the cloth,"was to be read as "they argued their case, with witnesses called by both sides, until the facts were 'as clear as a cloth.'" See Jeffrey H. Tigay, "Accusations of Premarital Unchastity" (excursus 20) in *Deuteronomy*, JPS Torah Commentary (Philadelphia: Jewish Publication Society, 1996), 476–77.

2   The Talmud cites scenarios for this occurrence and other possible scenarios. See ibid., 532.

3   *Pentateuch with Rashi's Commentary: Deuteronomy*, trans. M. Rosenbaum and A. M. Silbermann (New York: Hebrew Publishing, 1973), 110.

4   See David L. Lieber, "Divorce in the Bible," in *Encyclopaedia Judaica*, 6:123–25. A *minah* is a measure of silver equivalent to one hundred shekels, a shekel being between twenty and twenty-three grams of pure silver.

5   In fact, the Rabbis have been credited with elucidating a number of rights granted to the wife by the husband by virtue of marriage. For a list of these, see Shmuel Yerushalmi, *The Torah Anthology (Yalkut Me'am Lo'ez)*, trans. Rabbi Eliyahu Touger, Book 18 (New York: Moznayim, 1987), 37ff.

6   For a general discussion of the effects of patriarchal worldview on women's roles in biblical society, see Carole R. Fontaine, "The Abusive Bible: On the Use of Feminist Method in Pastoral Contexts," in *A Feminist Companion to Reading the Bible: Approaches, Methods and Strategies, Feminist Companion to the Bible*, vol. 11, ed. Athalya Brenner and Carole Fontaine (Sheffield, England: Sheffield Academic Press, 1997), 84–113.

Ki Tavo · *Rabbi Nancy Wechsler-Azen*

1   Genesis *Rabbah* 45:9 (*Midrash Rabbah*, trans. H. Freedman and Maurice Simon [New York: Soncino, 1983], 1:386–87).

Nitzavim · *Rabbi Miriam Carey Berkowitz*

1   Anita Diamant, *The New Jewish Baby Book* (Woodstock, Vt.: Jewish Lights, 1993), 87.

2   Tziporah, however, did circumcise her son with her own hands (Exod. 4:25).

3   See also *Midrash Rabbah* on Deut. 30:11–14, in which the Torah is available to all those who have the initiative to go out and learn, and the sluggard is chided for making excuses and missing the opportunity to learn Torah from a great teacher.

4   J. H. Hertz, *The Pentateuch and Haftorahs* (London: Soncino, 1981), 210.

Vayelech · *Rabbi Rosette Barron Haim*

1 *Pirke Avot* I:I.
2 Irving M. Bunim, *Ethics from Sinai* (New York: Philipp Feldheim, 1966), 21.
3 2 Kings 22:14–20.
4 *Targum*, 2 Kings 22:14.
5 *Midrash Tehillim* on Prov. 31:1.
6 Job 1:21.
7 Constance H. Buchanan, *Choosing to Lead: Women and the Crisis of American Values* (Boston: Beacon, 1996), 40.

V'zot Habrachah · *Rabbi Sandra J. Cohen*

1 Only the small tribe of Simeon is missing from his litany of blessing. Abraham Ibn Ezra, a medieval commentator, attributes this omission to a sin on Simeon's part back in the time of Jacob (Gen. 49:5) and, more recently, in the affair of Baal Peor (Num. 25:3), whereas the Ramban (Nachmanides) recalls that there are never more than twelve tribes listed, even in this last speech of Moses. Usually, the tribe of Levi, as a tribe without land, is omitted, or the two tribes of Joseph's sons, Ephraim and Manasseh, are counted as one. In this case, the small number of Simeonites, who will live mostly in cities within Judah's territory, are subsumed in Judah's blessing. But whether one agrees with Ibn Ezra or the Ramban, it is evident that there is not enough room for everyone. Either one can be cast out of the inheritance because of sin, or simply because there is not enough blessing for everyone.
2 Rashi on Deut. 34:8.
3 Deuteronomy *Rabbah* 11:10; cf. Louis Ginzberg, *The Legends of the Jews* (Philadelphia: Jewish Publication Society, 1939), 3:417ff.
4 *The Book of Legends: Sefer Ha-Aggadah*, eds. Hayim Nahman Bialik and Yehoshua Ravnitzky, trans. William G. Braude (New York: Schocken, 1992), 103.
5 Ibid., 104.
6 Louis Ginzberg, *The Legends of the Jews* (Philadelphia: Jewish Publication Society, 1956), 3:436.
7 Ibid., 6:153.
8 Bialik and Ravnitzky, eds., *Book of Legends*, 95.
9 Deuteronomy *Rabbah*, 11:7.
10 Bialik and Ravnitzky, eds., *Book of Legends*, 103.

Glossary

Adonai: The accepted pronunciation of YHVH, the four-letter name of God. It is not clear how those four letters were originally pronounced, since they are not vocalized in the Torah scroll. *See* **YHVH.**

Akedat Yitzhak: Literally, "the binding of Isaac." Refers to the story in Gen. 21, in which Abraham is called by God to bring his son Isaac up the mountain as an offering. At the last minute, Isaac is saved by Divine intervention.

Aliyah: The honor of being called up to the Torah for the blessings before and after its reading. Called "having an *aliyah*."

Aliyot: Plural of *aliyah*.

Bar mitzvah: A boy child's coming of age at thirteen, at which time he is permitted to have an *aliyah* and count in the *minyan*. Bar mitzvah also refers to the ceremony that acknowledges this milestone, as in, "I had a bar mitzvah."

Baraita: Literally, "outside." A rabbinic teaching from the first and second century C.E. that was not among those collected in the Mishnah by Rabbi Judah ha-Nasi.

Bat mitzvah: A girl child's coming of age, traditionally at twelve, but acknowledged in the liberal communities at thirteen. *Bat mitzvah* ceremonies began in the 1920s and exist now in almost all denominations in one form or another.

Bimah: The platform in the synagogue from where services are led. Usually, the rabbi and cantor stand on the *bimah*, as well as others who have service honors.

Bris: The Ashkenazic pronunciation of *brit. See* **Brit.**

Brit: Literally, "covenant." God makes a *brit* with many biblical characters. Today, we usually associate this word with the covenant of circumcision. See **Brit milah.**

Brit milah: Literally, "the covenant of circumcision." This ceremony is performed at eight days, when the foreskin of the infant boy is removed amid blessings and ritual. Circumcision was commanded to Abraham as a "sign" of the covenant for all males for all time.

Cantor: The person responsible for the musical portions of a prayer service.

Diaspora: Those places outside of the Land of Israel where Jews reside.

Etrog: The citron fruit taken and shaken on the holiday of Sukkot.

Halachah: The overall term for Jewish law, codified through the ages, since the Torah. Halachah is still evolving, in all the denominations.

Halachists: Experts in Halachah.

Haftarah: Sections of the Prophets read as an adjunct to the Saturday Torah reading. The *haftarah* of each week corresponds in theme to the weekly Torah reading. Plural is *haftarot.*

Havdalah: A ritual practiced on Saturday evening, after sunset, to separate the Sabbath from the regular weekdays, and to mark the official end of the Sabbath.

Kabbalah: Jewish mysticism developed throughout the ages but mostly associated with the system popularized in the thirteenth century C.E. in Safed.

Kabbalists: Those who practice Kabbalah.

Kashrut: The system of permitted and prohibited animals for eating. Presented in different sections of the Torah first, it is later refined and further defined by the Talmud.

Kedushah: Holiness. From the root *k-d-sh*, literally, "separate" or "sanctified."

Kehillah: The community.

Kipah: A head covering worn in prayer. Plural is *kipot.*

Kohen: A member of the highest priestly class who served in the desert Tabernacle and then in the Temple in Jerusalem. Some people still trace their lineage to the *kohanim* (pl.) of old, and these modern descendants receive the first *aliyah* in traditional synagogues as a sign of honor and respect. The infrequently used feminine form, *kohennet*, describes a woman of priestly descent.

Kol Ishah: The halachic prohibition against men hearing a woman's voice singing. Some interpret this more strictly to prohibit even hearing a woman give a lecture or speak loudly.

Kol Nidre: The opening prayer of the evening of Yom Kippur, for forgiveness of vows not kept.

Korban: The sacrifice; also, the sacrificial animal. Although individual animal sacrifices were recorded in the Torah as early as Noah, the communal system of sacrifice with all its ritual is described in Leviticus. The first Israelite communal sacrifice is understood to be the Paschal sacrifice in Exod. 12. Plural is *korbanot*.

Lashon hara: Literally, "evil/bad tongue"; any kind of slander, gossip, or the like. In traditional texts, any kind of talk about another person, either positive or negative, even passing seemingly "harmless" information, has the potential to become *lashon hara*.

Levites: Assistants to the priests, tracing their ancestry through Aaron. They were honored servants of the sacred rites in the desert Tabernacle and then in the Temple in Jerusalem. Those people who still trace their lineage to the Levites of old receive the second *aliyah* in a traditional synagogue. Called *leviim* in Hebrew.

Lulav: The branches taken and shaken as part of the Sukkot holiday.

Machpelah: The cave in Hebron where the patriarchs and matriarchs, all but Rachel, are buried. The story of its purchase by Abraham is found in Gen. 23.

Manna: The food provided to the Israelites during their forty years of wandering in the desert. Manna first appears in Exod. 16.

Menorah: The seven-branched candelabra used in the ancient biblical sanctuary and then later in the Temple in Jerusalem. This seven-branched *menorah* was adapted into a nine-branched *menorah* used only and specifically for the winter holiday of Chanukah.

Midrash: A rabbinic story, parable, or interpretation of biblical text. Comes from the root *d-r-sh,* "examine." These *midrashim* (pl.) help fill in gaps in the text, supply missing details or dialogue, and enliven the text with personal anecdotes. Early *midrashim* can be found in the Talmud, from the second century, but the first actual compendia were edited in the fifth and sixth centuries C.E. Modern "midrashim" are still being written today.

Midrashists: Those involved in the writing or creating of midrashim.

Mikveh: A pool of water composed partially of natural rainwater, built and filled to exact legal specifications. Immersion in a *mikveh* is meant to purify, renew, or change the status of people such as brides (and in some cases grooms), converts to Judaism, women after their monthly menstrual period, scribes, men before Shabbat, or even objects such as dishes. Separate *mikvaot* (pl.) are used to immerse corpses for final purification before burial.

Minyan: A quorum of ten needed for public prayers. In Orthodox services, only men are counted in the ten. In liberal services, either women or men or both together are counted in the ten.

Mishkan: The desert tabernacle erected by the Israelites after they left Egyptian slavery. The details of the building of the *mishkan* are in Exod. 25.

Mitzvah: A commandment from the Torah or later enacted by the Rabbis. Plural is *mitzvot.*

Niddah: The state of being in menstruation. It also refers to the woman herself when menstruating. In the traditional community there are very strict rules governing both the woman and those around her during that time.

Parashah: The weekly Torah portion. The Torah is divided into fifty-four portions, one to be read each week in the synagogue, on Mondays, Thursdays, and Saturdays. Plural is *parshiyot.*

Parnas: A respected community leader entrusted with the smooth running of the synagogue, and sometimes other communal institutions as well. Plural is *parnasim.*

Pidyon ha-ben: Redemption of the first-born, a ceremony practiced on the first-born male child, on his thirty-first day, to "release" him from servitude to the Temple.

Rosh Chodesh: The New Moon, celebrated monthly on the first day of the new Hebrew month.

Rosh Hashana: The Jewish New Year.

Seder: The ritualized service and dinner celebrated on the first two nights of Passover.

Shabbat: The Jewish Sabbath, beginning Friday at sundown and lasting until Saturday at sundown. Also known in the Ashkenazic pronunciation as *Shabbos.*

Shechinah: One of the names of God (though not found in the Torah) that has a feminine connotation, from the mystics. *Shechinah* is understood to be God's indwelling Presence as opposed to a more transcendent Presence.

Sheloshim: The thirty-day mourning period for close relatives following the burial.

Shivah: The intense seven-day mourning period immediately after the death of a close relative.

Sukkot: The fall Festival of Booths, during which Jews eat, and some sleep, in fragile huts for eight or seven days, depending on the community. The huts are reminders of the booths that the Jews lived in during the forty years of wandering in the desert.

Taharah: Literally, "purity." The state of being a person or object enters after immersion in the *mikveh.* In Temple times, persons in this state were able to participate in ritual activities. Also the ceremony of purification a corpse undergoes before burial. The purified person is then considered *tahor* (masc.) or *tehorah* (fem.).

Tallis: Ashkenazic pronunciation of *tallit.* Plural is *talleisim.*

Tallit: A prayer shawl worn during day time services and once a year at night on Yom Kippur. Women have begun making and wearing the *tallit* in recent times.

Talmud: The compilation of rabbinic law, which includes the Mishnah (legal decisions edited in the third century c.e.) and the Gemara (rabbinic discussions of those laws, edited in the sixth century c.e.). In the traditional community, the Talmud is authoritative on matters of daily life.

Tefillin: Phylacteries, or small leather boxes, attached with straps, which are worn on the head and arm each weekday morning as part of the worship. Traditionally only worn by men; many women are now taking on the donning of *tefillin*.

Trope: The system of cantillation, or the notes used for chanting the Torah, Haftarah, and Megillot.

Tumah: Literally "impurity." In Temple times, a person in this state was unable to participate in ritual activities. *Tumah* is contracted from contact with untouchable or unapproachable persons or objects, such as a corpse. The person who is impure is called *tamey* (masc.) or *temayah* (fem.).

Tzedakah: Alms for the poor, though literally, "righteousness." It is incumbent upon every Jew to give regular and cyclical *tzedakah*.

Tzitzit: Fringes to be worn on the four corners of a garment. The commandment to wear fringes appears twice in the Torah, in Num. 15:37 and Deut. 22:12.

Yarmulke: Yiddish for *kipah*, the skullcap worn in prayer to cover the head.

Yiddish: A Judeo-German dialect that was spoken by Jews throughout most of Eastern Europe.

Yeshiva: A full-time house of study of traditional texts. Plural is *yeshivot*.

YHVH: The four-letter Hebrew name of God, commonly pronounced "Adonai." Sometimes rendered as YHWH.

Yisrael: Israelites, any member of the Jewish people who does not trace their paternal ancestry to either *kohanim* (priests) or *leviim* (Levites).

Yom Kippur: The Day of Atonement, the most holy day of the Jewish calendar.

Bibliography and Suggested Further Reading

Torah Commentaries

Englemayer, Shammai, Joseph S. Ozarowski, and David M. Sofian. *Common Ground: The Weekly Torah Portion through the Eyes of a Conservative, Orthodox, and Reform Rabbi.* Northvale, N.J.: Jason Aronson, 1997.

Fields, Harvey J. *A Torah Commentary for Our Times.* 3 vols. New York: UAHC Press, 1990–1993.

Fox, Everett, ed. *The Five Books of Moses: Genesis, Exodus, Leviticus, Numbers, Deuteronomy: A New Translation with Introductions, Commentary, and Notes.* New York: Schocken, 1995.

Grishaver, Joel Lurie. *Learning Torah: A Self-Guided Journey through the Layers of Jewish Learning.* New York: UAHC Press, 1998.

Kushner, Lawrence S., and Kerry M. Olitzky. *Sparks beneath the Surface: A Spiritual Commentary on the Torah.* Northvale, N.J.: Jason Aronson, 1993.

Leibowitz, Nehama. *Studies in Bereshit (Genesis).* 4th ed. Jerusalem: World Zionist Organization, Department for Torah Education and Culture in the Diaspora, 1980.

———. *Studies in Shmot (Exodus).* 2 vols. Jerusalem: World Zionist Organization, Department for Torah Education and Culture in the Diaspora, 1980.

———. *Studies in Vayikra (Leviticus).* Jerusalem: World Zionist Organization, Department for Torah Education and Culture in the Diaspora, 1980.

————. *Studies in Bamidbar (Numbers)*. Rev. ed. Jerusalem: World Zionist Organization, Department for Torah Education and Culture in the Diaspora, 1982.

————. *Studies in Devarim (Deuteronomy)*. Jerusalem: World Zionist Organization, Department for Torah Education and Culture in the Diaspora, 1980.

Levine, Baruch A. *Leviticus*. The JPS Torah Commentary. Philadelphia: Jewish Publication Society, 1989.

Milgrom, Jacob. *Numbers*. The JPS Torah Commentary. Philadelphia: Jewish Publication Society, 1990.

Moyers, Bill D. *Genesis: A Living Conversation*. New York: Doubleday, 1997.

Peli, Pinchas. *Torah Today: A Renewed Encounter with Scripture*. Washington, D.C.: B'nai Brith Books, 1987.

Plaut, Gunther, ed. *The Torah: A Modern Commentary*. 12th ed. New York: UAHC Press, 1988.

Sarna, Nahum M. *Understanding Genesis*. New York: Schocken, 1970.

————. *Exploring Exodus: The Heritage of Biblical Israel*. New York: Schocken, 1987.

————. *Genesis*. The JPS Torah Commentary. Philadelphia: Jewish Publication Society, 1989.

————. *Exodus*. The JPS Torah Commentary. Philadelphia: Jewish Publication Society, 1991.

Steinsaltz, Adin, and Yehudit Keshet, trans. *Biblical Images*. Northvale, N.J.: Jason Aronson, 1994.

Tigray, Jeffrey H. *Deuteronomy*. The JPS Torah Commentary. Philadelphia: Jewish Publication Society, 1996.

Zakon, Miriam Stark, trans. *Tz'enah Ur'enah: The Classic Anthology of Torah Lore and Midrashic Commentary*. Jerusalem: Mesorah, 1983.

Zornberg, Avivah. *Genesis: The Beginning of Desire*. Philadelphia: Jewish Publication Society, 1995.

Bibliography and Suggested Further Reading

Midrash

Bialik, Hayyim Nahman, and Yehoshua Hana Ravnitzky, eds. William G. Braude, trans. *The Book of Legends/Sefer Ha-agadah: Legends from the Talmud and Midrash.* New York: Schocken, 1992.

Ginzberg, Louis. *The Legends of the Jews.* Philadelphia: Jewish Publication Society of America, 1909.

Women as Rabbis

Greenberg, Simon, ed. *The Ordination of Women as Rabbis: Studies and Responsa.* Moreshet Series: Studies in Jewish History, Literature, and Thought, vol. 14. New York: The Jewish Theological Seminary of America, 1988.

Nadell, Pamela Susan. *Women Who Would Be Rabbis: A History of Women's Ordination, 1889–1985.* Boston: Beacon, 1998.

Zola, Gary P., ed. *Women Rabbis: Exploration & Celebration: Papers Delivered at an Academic Conference Honoring Twenty Years of Women in the Rabbinate, 1972–1992.* Cincinnati: Hebrew Union College Press, 1996.

Women, Feminism, and Judaism

Adler, Rachel. *Engendering Judaism: An Inclusive Theology and Ethics.* Philadelphia: Jewish Publication Society, 1998.

Alpert, Rebecca. *Like Bread on the Seder Plate: Jewish Lesbians and the Transformation of Tradition.* New York: Columbia University Press, 1997.

Berrin, Susan, ed. *Celebrating the New Moon: A Rosh Chodesh Anthology.* Northvale, N.J.: Jason Aronson, 1996.

Cantor, Aviva. *Jewish Women, Jewish Men: The Legacy of Patriarchy in Jewish Life.* San Francisco: Harper and Row, 1995.

Davidman, Lynn, and Shelly Tenenbaum, eds. *Feminist Perspectives on Jewish Studies.* New Haven: Yale University Press, 1994.

Frankiel, Tamar. *The Voice of Sarah: Feminine Spirituality and Traditional Judaism.* San Francisco: Harper and Row, 1990.

Greenberg, Blu. *On Women and Judaism: A View from Tradition.* Philadelphia: Jewish Publication Society, 1981.

Heschel, Susannah, ed. *On Being a Jewish Feminist.* New York: Schocken, 1995.

Peskowitz, Miriam, and Laura Levitt, eds. *Judaism Since Gender.* New York: Routledge, 1997.

Plaskow, Judith. *Standing Again at Sinai: Judaism from a Feminist Perspective.* San Francisco: Harper and Row, 1990.

Plaskow, Judith, and Carole Christ. *Weaving the Visions: New Patterns in Feminist Spirituality.* San Francisco: HarperCollins, 1989.

Umansky, Ellen, and Diane Ashton, eds. *Four Centuries of Jewish Women's Spirituality: A Sourcebook.* Boston: Beacon, 1992.

Zolty, Shoshana Pantel. *"And All Your Children Shall Be Learned": Women and the Study of Torah in Jewish Law and History.* Northvale, N.J.: Jason Aronson, 1993.

Feminist Biblical Interpretation

Adler, Rachel. "In Your Blood, Live: Re-Visions of a Theology of Purity." *Tikkun* 8, no.1 (January/February 1993).

Antonelli, Judith S. *In the Image of God: A Feminist Commentary on the Torah.* Northvale, N.J.: Jason Aronson, 1997.

Bellis, Alice Ogden. *Helpmates, Harlots, and Heroes: Women's Stories in the Hebrew Bible.* Louisville: Westminster/John Knox, 1994.

Bird, Phyllis A. *Missing Persons and Mistaken Identities: Women and Gender in Ancient Israel.* Philadelphia: Fortress, 1997.

Brenner, Athalya, and Carole Fontaine, eds. *A Feminist Companion to Reading the Bible: Approaches, Methods and Strategies.* Feminist Companion to the Bible, vol. 11. Sheffield: Sheffield Academic Press, 1997.

Buchmann, Christina, and Celina Spiegel, eds. *Out of the Garden: Women Writers on the Bible.* New York: Fawcett Columbine, 1994.

Exum, J. Cheryl. *Fragmented Women: Feminist Subversions of Biblical Narratives.* Harrisburg, Pa.: Trinity Press International, 1993.

Feigenson, Emily, ed. *Beginning the Journey.* New York: Women of Reform Judaism, 1997.

Frankel, Ellen. *The Five Books of Miriam: A Woman's Commentary on the Torah.* New York: G. P. Putnam's Sons, 1996.

Goldstein, Elyse. *ReVisions: Seeing Torah through a Feminist Lens.* Woodstock, Vt.: Jewish Lights, 1998.

Meyers, Carol. *Discovering Eve: Ancient Israelite Women in Context.* New York: Oxford University Press, 1991.

Newsom, Carol A., and Sharon H. Ringe, eds. *The Women's Bible Commentary.* Louisville: Westminster/John Knox, 1992.

Orenstein, Debra, and Jane Rachel Litman, eds. *Lifecycles: Jewish Women on Biblical Themes in Contemporary Life.* Vol. 2. Woodstock, Vt.: Jewish Lights, 1997.

Pardes, Ilana. *Countertraditions in the Bible: A Feminist Approach.* Cambridge: Harvard University Press, 1992.

Schüssler Fiorenza, Elisabeth. *Bread Not Stone: The Challenge of Feminist Biblical Interpretation.* Boston: Beacon, 1995.

Trible, Phyllis. *Texts of Terror: Literary-Feminist Readings of Biblical Narratives.* Philadelphia: Fortress, 1984.

Female Biblical Characters

Bach, Alice, ed. *Women in the Hebrew Bible: A Reader.* New York: Routledge, 1998.

Bronner, Leila Leah. *From Eve to Esther: Rabbinic Reconstructions of Biblical Women.* Louisville: Westminster/John Knox, 1994.

Burns, Rita J. *Has the Lord Indeed Spoken Only Through Moses? A Study of the Biblical Portrait of Miriam.* Atlanta: Scholars Press, 1987.

Dame, Enid, et al., eds. *Which Lilith? Feminist Writers Re-Create the World's First Woman.* Northvale, N.J.: Jason Aronson, 1998.

Diamant, Anita. *The Red Tent.* New York: St. Martin's Press, 1997.

Hyman, Naomi Mara. *Biblical Women in the Midrash: A Sourcebook.* Northvale, N.J.: Jason Aronson, 1998.

Jeansonne, Sharon Pace. *The Women of Genesis: From Sarah to Potiphar's Wife.* Minneapolis: Fortress, 1990.

Koltuv, Barbara Black. *The Book of Lilith.* York Beach, Maine: Nicolas-Hays, 1987.

Labowitz, Shoni. *God, Sex, and Women of the Bible: Discovering Our Sensual, Spiritual Selves.* New York: Simon and Schuster, 1998.

Phillips, J. A. *Eve: The History of an Idea.* San Francisco: Harper and Row, 1984.

Rosen, Norma. *Biblical Women Unbound.* Philadelphia: Jewish Publication Society, 1996.

Teubal, Savina J. *Ancient Sisterhood: The Lost Traditions of Hagar and Sarah.* Athens, Ohio: Swallow Press and University of Ohio Press, 1997.

Thaw Ronson, Barbara L. *The Women of the Torah: Commentaries from the Talmud, Midrash, and Kabbalah.* Northvale, N.J.: Jason Aronson, 1998.

Zones, Jane Sprague, ed. *Taking the Fruit: Modern Women's Tales of the Bible.* Chico, Calif.: Women's Institute for Continuing Jewish Education, 1981.

On God, God Language, and the Goddess

Campbell, Joseph, and Charles Musès, eds. *In All Her Names: Explorations of the Feminine in Divinity.* San Francisco: HarperSanFrancisco, 1991.

Falk, Marcia. *The Book of Blessings.* San Francisco: HarperCollins, 1996.

Frymer-Kensky, Tikva. *In the Wake of the Goddess.* New York: Macmillan, 1992.

Goldenberg, Naomi R. *Changing of the Gods.* Boston: Beacon, 1979.

Gottlieb, Lynn. *She Who Dwells Within.* San Francisco: HarperSan Francisco, 1995.

Graves, Robert. *The White Goddess.* London: Faber and Faber, 1961.

Graves, Robert, and Raphael Patai. *Hebrew Myths: The Book of Genesis.* New York: Greenwich House, 1983.

Patai, Raphael. *The Hebrew Goddess.* Detroit: Wayne State University Press, 1990.

Plaskow, Judith. "Facing the Ambiguity of God." *Tikkun* 6, no. 5: p. 70.

Roundtable discussion. "If God Is God She Is Not Nice." *Journal of Feminist Studies in Religion* 5, no. 1 (spring 1989): pp. 103–117.

Stone, Merlin. *When God Was a Woman.* New York: Dial Press, 1976.

Weaver, Mary Jo. "Who Is the Goddess and Where Does She Get Us?" *Journal of Feminist Studies in Religion* 5, no. 1 (spring 1989): pp. 46–64.

———. "Can a Sexist Model Liberate Us? Ancient Near Eastern 'Fertility' Goddesses." *Journal of Feminist Studies in Religion* 5, no. 1 (spring 1989): pp. 65–76.

About the Contributors

Rabbi Rebecca T. Alpert was ordained from the Reconstructionist Rabbinical College in 1976 and is the codirector of the Women's Studies Program and Assistant Professor of Religion and Women's Studies at Temple University. She is the former dean of students at the Reconstructionist Rabbinical College. She is the coauthor with Jacob Staub of *Exploring Judaism: A Reconstructionist Approach*, author of *Like Bread on the Seder Plate: Jewish Lesbians and the Transformation of Tradition*, and editor of *Voices of the Religious Left: A Contemporary Sourcebook*.

"As a child, I knew I wanted to become a rabbi. In college, during my junior year in Israel, I read an article in *Newsweek* about a rabbinical student named Sally Priesand. I actually didn't know that women *couldn't* be rabbis until that moment. Priesand's story encouraged me to think more seriously again about my childhood dream. I entered rabbinical school in 1971 at the Reconstructionist Rabbinical College, and was among the first half dozen women to become rabbis in the United States. The intersection of feminism and Judaism became a great interest of mine, and despite the discouragement of various professors and mentors, I have spent much of my rabbinic and academic career writing about these issues. Later on, when I came out as a lesbian, I focused my writing and teaching on exploring how lesbian issues fit into a Jewish context as well."

Rabbi Lia Bass was ordained by The Jewish Theological Seminary of America in 1994. She is the first woman from Brazil to be ordained as a rabbi. Currently, Rabbi Bass serves as rabbi-in-residence at the Solomon Schechter Day School in Bergen County, New Jersey. Rabbi Bass is also a potter, and has great interest in Judaica as an expression of Jewish spirituality.

"I was a Hebrew/Torah teacher in a Jewish day school in Rio de Janeiro, as well as the Hillel director when I decided to become a rabbi. I was involved in many aspects of the Jewish community, yet the place I loved the most was the synagogue. Through the spirited leadership of Rabbi Nilton Bonder, I went to rabbinical school, but was unable to go back to my native Brazil."

Rabbi Miriam Carey Berkowitz (nee Carey M. Knight) was ordained in November of 1998, the youngest rabbi to finish the Machon Schechter program. She is assistant rabbi at the Park Avenue Synagogue in Manhattan, and enjoys ceramics and exercise in her free time. She grew up in Montreal, studied A-levels in England, and received a B.A. magna cum laude in International Relations from Harvard-Radcliffe in 1993. Having decided to become a rabbi, she spent a year at the Hebrew University of Jerusalem on a Wallenberg Fellowship, learning Hebrew, Talmud, and Bible with Nehama Leibowitz. She made aliyah in 1994 and was accepted at the Masorati (Conservative) Bet Midrash (Israeli rabbinical school), now called Machon Schechter. She has translated a book on mourning customs; worked at a children's home in Kiryat Gat; led High Holiday services in Boston and Vancouver; taught classes in Jerusalem on midrash, tefillah, and the laws of family purity; and interned as a hospital chaplain. She is married to Rabbi Matthew Berkowitz and the proud mother of Adir.

"I was inspired to become a rabbi thanks to the influence of Rabbi Sally Finestone at Harvard Hillel, a father who sang in the synagogue choir, and a grandfather who would not enter a house that had a 'Chanukah bush.' After being exposed to the riches of the Jewish heritage, I felt compelled to dedicate my life to passing on these treasures. Exposure to Israel and a passion for the Hebrew language completed the picture. Being a rabbi combines teaching, constant learning, spirituality, leadership, and counseling. It is a career that never leaves me bored and is, indeed, a calling. I owe great thanks to special teachers, including Professor Dov Zlotnick, Professor Ze'ev Falk, and Professor Judith Hauptman, and to my husband, Matthew, for constant support."

Rabbi Elizabeth Bolton was ordained from the Reconstructionist Rabbinical College in 1996, and initially pursued studies and a career in classical music. While at RRC, Liz filled many internships as student rabbi, cantor, and chaplain; was a founder of the Jewish Women's Studies Project, now Kolot: The Center for Jewish Women's and Gender Studies; and was founder/director of a rabbinical student choir, the RRC Api-Chorus. Liz is presently the rabbi of Congregation Beit Tikvah in Baltimore, Maryland, and is Director of Music and Liturgy for the Jewish Reconstructionist Federation.

"The challenge of claiming the rabbinate—indeed, claiming Judaism—as a lesbian has been more rewarding than I could have imagined. I feel the same way about parenting my two beautiful children, Doriya Leslie and Isaac Buddy, sleeping now as I finish my work late at night. May my response to these challenges continue to reflect the rabbinic dictum 'You are not called upon to complete the work, nor may you desist from it.' For the learning, the parenting, the teaching, and the singing, I continually offer thanks and blessings."

Rabbi Analia Bortz studied at the Beit Midrash LeLimudei Yahadut in Jerusalem and was ordained from the Seminario Rabinico Latinoamericano in Buenos Aires (Conservative) in 1994. She is married to Rabbi Mario Karpuj, and has two daughters, Tamar and Adina. She is the first South American female rabbi ordained in Jerusalem. She is also a physician (University of Buenos Aires, with a postgraduate in radiology). She has a Ph.D. in bioethics from the Catholic University of Chile. She now works as a full-time rabbi in the Comunidad Israelita and as a part-time physician at Van Buren's Hospital, both in Valparaiso, Chile, as well as a teacher of bioethics at the Medicine School, University of Chile.

"I decided to be a rabbi when I was eighteen years old, at the time I started to study medicine and saw that I wanted to help people not just with pills, but also with the spirit, the soul, and the love. I saw that the Jewish point of view has a lot to teach me. I thought about what it meant to be a woman rabbi, so as to participate in this vocation with another vision. I believe that if God gave the Torah to men and women, it means that we can appreciate the text in different ways. I take into account the words of Rabbi A. J. Heschel *[z"l]:* 'Medicine is Religion in acts, and Religion is Medicine in prayer.'"

Sharon Brous is a rabbinical student at The Jewish Theological Seminary of America, and is preparing to receive ordination in 2001. She began her rabbinical studies immediately after receiving her B.A. from Columbia University in 1995. Sharon has been working for many years to incorporate her love of Judaism and her interest in human and civil rights into her rabbinate. To that end, Sharon is working towards a master's degree in human rights at Columbia University while she concludes her studies at the seminary. She and her husband, David Light, live in Manhattan.

"My journey to the rabbinate has been thrilling at every juncture. In 1993, while studying in Israel, I was exposed, for the first time, to serious Jewish learning. I decided to become a rabbi after developing a deep passion for the study of traditional Jewish texts, and after being inspired by teachers who were able to successfully integrate their modern worldview and their love of Judaism. I also developed a strong sense that a career in the clergy would offer me the opportunity to teach and preach social justice, which I consider a fundamental component of the Jewish mission."

Rabbi Judith Gary Brown was ordained by the Reconstructionist Rabbinical College in 1986. Rabbi Brown has taught religion courses at Temple University and Villanova University. She was the managing editor of *The Reconstructionist,* and she worked as an editorial assistant on the *machzor* recently published in the *Kol Haneshamah* series of prayerbooks from the Reconstructionist Press. She is also a licensed veterinarian (University of Pennsylvania, 1992), and one of only two known people trained as both a rabbi and a veterinarian.

"My decision to become a rabbi was fostered out of two events in my life. First, my upbringing as an observant Conservative Jew did not answer the question 'Why?' that I so much needed to understand in order to make ritual observance meaningful. And second, my introduction to the writings of Mordecai Kaplan in college stimulated my 'relearning' of Judaism on an adult, intellectual level. I was motivated to become a rabbi so that I could teach generations of Jews the living and accessible expressions of Jewish tradition."

Rabbi Nina Beth Cardin was ordained from The Jewish Theological Seminary of America in 1988, as part of the first class of Conservative women rabbis. She is the Director of Jewish Life at the JCC of Greater Baltimore. In the years following graduation, she held several positions at JTS, including Assistant to the Vice-Chancellor for Administration and Advisor to Rabbinical Students in the Rabbinical School office. She served as editor of *Sh'ma,* and associate director of the National Center for Jewish Healing. Her books include *Out of the Depths I Call to You: A Book of Prayers for the Married Jewish Woman* (a translation and annotation of Italian Jewish women's prayers from the 1700s [Jason Aronson]), *Tears of Sorrow, Seeds of Hope: A Jewish Spiritual Companion for Infertility and Pregnancy Loss* (Jewish Lights), and *The Tapestry of Jewish Time: A Spiritual Guide to Holidays and Life Cycle Events* (Behrman House).

"Why did I choose to become a rabbi? Several answers, some mundane, some lofty, come close to the truth. I love the lure of the text. I love entering the worlds preserved and presented in our sacred literature, joining with all those who came before and all those who will come after. I love the texture of the rabbinic day: teaching, counseling, studying, planning, politicking, sharing, visiting. I am always awed and honored when people trust me with their secrets, their souls, their pain, and their dreams, all because I bear the honorable title, Rabbi. I love how it involves me, willy-nilly, in politics, community, private lives, public policy, the young and the old. And I love what some might consider its burden: the call to live a life constantly aware of the tradition, the people, and the God I am expected to represent. Perhaps it is this awareness of awareness that is the most precious gift of the rabbinate."

Rabbi Diane Aronson Cohen entered the rabbinate as a second career, after nearly twenty years raising children and working as a congregational volunteer. She was ordained by The Jewish Theological Seminary of America in 1993, and serves Temple Ohev Shalom in Colonia, New Jersey. She holds a B.A. in English literature from UCLA, an M.A. in education from the University of Judaism, and an M.A. from the seminary, where she was honored for her work in theology. She is active in a wide range of community organizations, both Jewish and secular, and has published articles and readings on prayer and Bible in a variety of anthologies and periodicals; in addition, she is a contributor to the forthcoming *chumash* being produced by United Synagogue. Her greatest concerns remain her children, Scott, Josh, Chuck, and Julie.

"Throughout my career, my focus has been on God and prayer. In my admissions essay, I spoke of seeking to bring the Jew and God closer together, and I find that in my teaching and my writing, this reconnecting continues to be my greatest concern. My sermons and Torah discussions stress finding ways to come closer to God and finding beauty in Jewish living. In the end, I guess it's all about reconnection: Jews and God, Jews and Torah, Jews and Israel, Jews and Jews."

Rabbi Sandra J. Cohen was ordained at Hebrew Union College–Jewish Institute of Religion in Cincinnati in 1995. After two years as an assistant rabbi at a large Reform temple, Rabbi Cohen now serves Temple Micah, a small synagogue in Denver. She is an active teacher in her community, offering Talmud and other text courses in a variety of settings, as well as serving as the dean of the community adult education program, the Denver Institute of Jewish Studies. She is the immediate past president of Seeking Common Ground, an organization that is dedicated to making peace, and that brings Denver, Israeli, and Palestinian girls together every summer toward that end. Rabbi Cohen also sits on the board of a variety of community organizations, ranging from CAJE of Colorado to the Colorado ACLU. She is married to attorney and musician Bennett Cohen, and they have one daughter, Shira.

"I decided to become a rabbi in college, realizing that such a path would bring together my love of learning and my desire to understand the text not as a foreign document, but rather as wisdom from our past that might speak to us today. Reading and striving to understand the ancient conversation between God and the Jewish people gives me a sense of connection with my community. As a rabbi, I am invited into people's lives often at extraordinary moments, and I am grateful for the chance to simply be there with them. My college professor, Dr. Calvin Roetzel, taught me that 'there is something about a Presence,' both human and divine. My rabbi, Howard Jaffe, modeled being that presence for me in my life. I thank both of them for helping me find a way of life so filled with meaning and joy."

Rabbi Cynthia A. Culpeper was ordained from The Jewish Theological Seminary of America in 1995. She first assumed the pulpit of Agudath Israel in Montgomery, Alabama, and now resides in Birmingham, serving as a community rabbi. In addition to teaching at Temple Beth El in Birmingham, she also teaches at the community Jewish day school and serves on several local Jewish, social action, and community relations boards.

"The five-year rabbinical program took me seven years to complete, and it wasn't until I started my penultimate year of study that I finally knew the rabbinate was the right direction for me. Serving as a rabbi has put me in contact with people hungry to learn more about our rich Jewish heritage, and I have enjoyed being a conduit for Jewish enrichment as much as I have enjoyed learning from the people with whom I come into contact."

Rabbi Lucy H.F. Dinner received her ordination from Hebrew Union College–Jewish Institute of Religion in 1988. She currently serves as the rabbi of Temple Beth Or in Raleigh, North Carolina. Despite warnings that "North Carolina will never accept a woman rabbi," Rabbi Dinner has been warmly received and led the congregation in a 50 percent growth in membership. Rabbi Dinner has written for the UAHC *Living Torah* publication and speaks about Jewish topics locally and nationally. She sits on the local Planned Parenthood Board and is active in community action. Nationally, Rabbi Dinner serves on the ARZA World Union North American Board, the UAHC Committee on the Jewish Family, the UAHC–CCAR Commission on Youth, and the Commission on Synagogue Affiliation.

"I grew up steeped in classical Reform Judaism, Southern style. I met my husband and found a profound love for living, celebrating, and teaching Judaism at the UAHC Henry S. Jacobs Camp in Utica, Mississippi. The combination of a family that emulated Jewish values through everyday experience and the embracing, spiritual life of Jacobs Camp inspired me to pursue the rabbinate."

Rabbi Lisa A. Edwards was ordained from Hebrew Union College–Jewish Institute of Religion in 1994 and has been the rabbi of Beth Chayim Chadashim (BCC) in Los Angeles since then. Founded in 1972, BCC was the world's first synagogue created by and for gay and lesbian Jews, and today is a community of gay, lesbian, bisexual, and transgender Jews, and their families and allies. Rabbi Edwards holds a Ph.D. in literature from the University of Iowa, where she wrote a dissertation titled "Restoring Voices: Traditional Jewish Sources in Post-Holocaust Jewish American Fiction." She and her partner, Tracy Moore (editor of *Lesbiot: Israeli Lesbians Talk about Sexuality, Feminism, Judaism and Their Lives* [Cassell]), had a *kiddushin* ceremony in 1995, on their tenth anniversary together, at which two Reform rabbis officiated.

"The combination of coming out as a lesbian and studying the Holocaust while living in a small, Midwestern, one synagogue town [Iowa City] inspired me to go to rabbinical school and to seek out a community that welcomed and honored diversity within Jewish tradition. My particular interests are Torah and liturgy, both of which I view through feminist lenses."

Rabbi Amy Eilberg was the first woman ordained as a Conservative rabbi by The Jewish Theological Seminary of America in 1985. She was a cofounder of the Bay Area Jewish Healing Center, where she directed the Center's Jewish Hospice Care Program. Nationally known as a leader of the Jewish healing movement, she lectures and writes on issues of Jewish spirituality and healing. She currently serves as a pastoral counselor in private practice in Palo Alto, California. She is married to Dr. Louis Newman and is the proud mother of one daughter, Penina Tova, and two stepsons, Etan and Jonah.

"I received my call to the rabbinate from my college rabbi, Al Axelrad, who took me out to lunch one day during my freshman year, after he had heard me lead Shabbat services. He looked me in the eye and said, 'You've got to be a rabbi.' He knew very well that at the time, 1972, the Conservative Movement was far from ready to even consider ordaining women. But I am grateful that Rabbi Al could imagine the rabbi that I was to become. It took twelve years before The Jewish Theological Seminary agreed to admit women, and then more years until I grew into the kind of rabbi I was meant to be. This work becomes more and more my life's work, and I'm sure I will continue to grow in it over the years."

Rabbi Sue Levi Elwell, Ph.D., was ordained and received a Master of Hebrew Letters degree from Hebrew Union College–Jewish Institute of Religion in 1986. She has served congregations in California and New Jersey, and has taught Jewish women's history and feminist spirituality to undergraduates and rabbinic students. Rabbi Elwell is the editor of the new CCAR *Haggadah,* and served as one of the editors of the acclaimed *The Journey Continues: The Ma'yan Haggadah.* The author of *The Jewish Women's Studies Guide* (University Press of America), she is editing, with colleagues Rebecca Alpert and Shirley Idelson, *Lesbian Rabbis: The First Generation* (Rutgers University Press). The founding director of the American Jewish Congress Feminist Center in Los Angeles, Rabbi Elwell served as the first rabbinic director of Ma'yan, the Jewish Women's Project of the Jewish Community Center on the Upper West Side in New York City. She currently serves as the associate director of the

Pennsylvania Council of the UAHC.

"I was born into an observant and deeply committed family of Reform Jews, and my earliest memories of synagogue are of warmth, beauty, and rich, powerful music. I remember my keen sense of injustice when I realized that the boys with whom I shared leadership of our local youth group had an option of further study and service that was closed to me; they entered a prerabbinic program at HUC when I went off to college. Years later, when I met Rabbi Sandy Sasso, I began to wonder whether the rabbinate would be a possibility for me, by then a serious feminist pregnant with my first child. Four years later, as I completed my doctorate and prepared to give birth to my second daughter, I entered HUC. I have been blessed with a rich and varied rabbinate."

Rabbi Rachel Esserman was ordained from the Reconstructionist Rabbinical College in 1998. Her book of poems, *I Stand by the River*, was published in 1998 by Keshet Press. Her writing has appeared in many publications, including *The Reconstructionist, Na'amat Women, Jewish Currents*, and *Sh'ma.*

"While always feeling Jewish at heart, it wasn't until I discovered Reconstructionism that I found a Judaism that allowed me to bring both my head and my heart into my religious practice. Learning that Judaism was an evolving religious civilization had a profound impact on me. For the first time, I was encouraged to struggle with tradition and to argue with the biblical text. My decision to become a rabbi was born of the desire to be an active part of that historical process."

Rabbi Helaine Ettinger was ordained by Hebrew Union College–Jewish Institute of Religion in New York in 1991. After serving as the rabbi to a congregation in Kinnelon, New Jersey, for five years, she moved with her family to Israel. There she has enjoyed becoming an active lay leader at Hod ve-Hadar Congregation in Kfar Saba. At Hod ve-Hadar she leads traditional and creative services, chants Torah, shares *Divrei Torah* in Hebrew, prepares students to become bar and bat mitzvah, develops children's activities, and serves as a resource to other members of the congregation. She is a teacher in the Masorti Movement's national program Bar/Bat Mitzvah for the Special Child, providing Jewish studies and enrichment for youth with developmental disabilities.

"My decision to become a rabbi was influenced by the female rabbinic students, now rabbis, I met during high school and college. I enjoy the fact that being a rabbi allows me to relate to people on multiple levels, for example, spiritually, emotionally, and educationally. It is a challenge to help weave all these human dimensions together into a cohesive Jewish whole. It is a privilege to share in other people's lives. This specific chapter grows out of my own struggle to balance the conflicting demands we all face as we try to integrate our personal and professional selves."

Rabbi Susan Fendrick was ordained from The Jewish Theological Seminary of America in 1995 and is Rabbi-in-Residence at Jewish Family & Life, a nonprofit and print Jewish publisher, where she is editor of *SocialAction.com* and JFL Books. She is vice-chair of the National Havurah Committee (NHC), and often teaches at NHC institutes and retreats; serves on the faculty in the area of bibliodrama for the Institute for Contemporary Midrash summer trainings; and is a frequent scholar-in-residence, teacher, and speaker for synagogues, *havurot*, and agencies throughout North America. She is the author of several published articles and essays, including an article for the journal *Living Text* on the use of bibliodrama to interpret non-narrative biblical passages. She is also at work on a book-length memoir about her family of Holocaust survivors.

"I began to consider the rabbinate at age nineteen, when I taught a year-long course on Jews and labor history for four children in a *havurah* bar/bat mitzvah program. My father, a first-generation American from a traditional Conservative background, first suggested it to me. At age twenty-eight, after pursuing independent Jewish learning in a variety of settings while working as a paralegal representing low-income tenants, and having considered careers in law and nurse-midwifery, I entered rabbinical school. I realized that it was the one thing about which I would otherwise always have wondered, 'What if?' I have no regrets."

Rabbi Lori Forman was ordained at The Jewish Theological Seminary of America in 1988 and is the Director of Jewish Resources for UJA–Federation of New York. She attended the University of California at Berkeley. Prior to coming to UJA–Federation, Lori held the position of National Interreligious Program Specialist for the American Jewish Committee. She is the coauthor of *Sacred Intentions: Daily Inspiration to Strengthen the Spirit, Based on Jewish Wisdom* and *Restful Reflections: Nighttime Inspiration to Calm the Soul, Based on Jewish Wisdom* (both Jewish Lights).

"I decided to enter the rabbinate as part of the first class of women at The Jewish Theological Seminary of America because I strongly felt women's voices needed to be added to the ranks of Jewish religious leaders. Today, almost twelve years after my ordination, I find that my particular contributions are minimal compared to the many ways I have changed through the experience of being a rabbi and interacting with my students. I hope that the journey continues and that I remain open to additional growth and new experiences."

Rabbi Dayle A. Friedman was ordained at Hebrew Union College–Jewish Institute of Religion in 1985, where she also earned master's degrees in Hebrew Literature and Jewish Communal Service. She is an adjunct faculty member at the Reconstructionist Rabbinical College, where she directs the Geriatric Chaplaincy Program and serves as a spiritual director. She is a consultant and author on aging, spirituality, and pastoral care and editor of *Jewish Pastoral Care: A Practical Handbook from Traditional and Contemporary Sources* (Jewish Lights). Rabbi Friedman holds an M.S.W. from the University of Southern California and a B.A. in Near Eastern and Judaic Studies from Brandeis University.

"I wanted to be a rabbi from the time I was seven years old, inspired by my childhood rabbi, Joseph Goldman, who was warm, inspiring, and engaging. I wanted to be on the *bimah*, too, singing, speaking, and praying. I imagined the rabbinate as an umbrella, beneath which I could find expression for my various ambitions: teacher, counselor, advocate, spiritual guide, scholar, and ritual leader. When I grew up, I hesitated to follow this long-held dream, fearful that as a woman, I would be denied my desire to serve the Jewish elderly. While training in social work and Jewish communal service, I read of the tragic death of June Milner *[z"l]*, a rabbinic student, and learned that she had served as student rabbi of a Jewish home for the aged. This news rekindled my rabbinic aspirations, and I not only enrolled in HUC–JIR's rabbinic program, but later held the same student post, which launched my geriatric chaplaincy career."

Rabbi Elyse D. Frishman was ordained from Hebrew Union College–Jewish Institute of Religion in New York in 1981. She is the spiritual leader for Congregation B'nai Jeshurun, The Barnert Temple in Franklin Lakes, New Jersey. Rabbi Frishman is nationally recognized as a leader in transforming Reform Jewish worship, and as a writer and editor of liturgy. She was recently appointed coeditor of the new Reform prayerbook. Rabbi Frishman has served on the CCAR Executive Board, the HUC–JIR Alumni Board, and as president of the Rockland County Board of Rabbis. She was a faculty member for Synagogue 2000, a cross-denominational program for synagogue transformation. Rabbi Frishman is married to Rabbi Daniel Freelander, the Director of Program for the Union of American Hebrew Congregations. They have three children, Adam, Jonah, and Devra.

"In the summer of 1975 at the UAHC Eisner Camp, following my junior year in college, I met women who were students at the Hebrew Union College seminary. This was the first time I learned that women could be rabbis. Friends convinced me to pursue the rabbinate. When considering my life's course, I discovered that the rabbinate offered opportunities in every area that appealed to me: ongoing study, teaching, counseling, creative thinking and programming, spiritual opportunity, and Jewish leadership. I'm struck by how naive I was then about the role of the rabbi; I viewed it so narrowly. Since then, I've come to appreciate how blessed I am by its offerings: the gift of community, the profound wisdom of Judaism, the challenge and reward of leadership."

Rabbi Nancy Fuchs-Kreimer was ordained from the Reconstructionist

Rabbinical School in 1982. She also earned a Ph.D. from Temple University in Jewish-Christian Relations. For the last fifteen years, she has been working at the Reconstructionist Rabbinical College, teaching about contemporary Jewish thought and about religions other than Judaism. While continuing to teach at the college, in July 1998 she began a new position as Rabbinic Director of the Jewish Identity Program of the Jewish Family and Children's Service of Greater Philadelphia. In that capacity, she works with the staff, board, and volunteers of the agency to bring a Jewish and spiritual dimension to their work. Nancy is also the author of *Parenting As a Spiritual Journey: Deepening Ordinary & Extraordinary Events into Sacred Occasions* (Jewish Lights).

"I first became interested in the rabbinate as a young child growing up in a Reconstructionist congregation. Although I have explored the academic study and teaching of religion and enjoy the freedom of thought and challenge of ideas, I keep returning to the rabbinate as a career in which I can most unabashedly merge my values, my spiritual passions, and my professional duties."

Rabbi Shoshana Gelfand was ordained at The Jewish Theological Seminary of America in 1993, where she studied as a Wexner Fellow. She is Director of Programs at the Wexner Heritage Foundation. She graduated magna cum laude from Bryn Mawr College and was a MacCracken Fellow at New York University. Rabbi Gelfand served as assistant rabbi at Congregation Anshe Emet in Chicago, and has also worked as scholar-in-residence at the JCC of Staten Island and Brandeis Bar Din Institute. She is currently involved in the Rabbinical Assembly as a member of the Committee on Jewish Law and Standards. She has also published articles in *The Journal of Synagogue Music, Masoret, Sh'ma,* and *The Jewish Spectator.*

"I originally came from a small Southern town in the Baptist Bible Belt and knew virtually nothing about Judaism. I had intended to study philosophy and music in college, but instead met an incredible professor, Dr. Samuel T. Lachs, who brought me to his *chavura* and sent me to study at JTS. I intended to go for a summer, but loved it so much that I stayed for rabbinical school."

Rabbi Laura Geller was ordained by Hebrew Union College–Jewish Institute of Religion in 1976, the third woman to be ordained in the Reform Movement. She was the first woman to become the senior rabbi of a major metropolitan congregation, Temple Emanuel of Beverly Hills, California. Prior to coming to Temple Emanuel, Rabbi Geller served for fourteen years as the Hillel director of the University of Southern California and for four years as the director of the American Jewish Congress, Pacific Southwest Region. While at Hillel, Rabbi Geller coorganized the award-winning 1984 conference "Illuminating the Unwritten Scroll: Women's Spirituality and Jewish Tradition." At the American Jewish Congress she cofounded the Los Angeles Jewish Feminist Center. Rabbi Geller has received many honors, including the ACLU of Southern California Award for Fostering Racial and Cultural Harmony and the California State Legislature Woman of the Year award.

"As an undergraduate at Brown University, I was influenced by two Protestant ministers who taught me through their example that spirituality and social justice enrich each other. Their example, along with wonderful professors of religious studies, challenged me to think about my own tradition. I went to Hebrew Union College as much to learn to be Jewish as to become a rabbi. Because my own undergraduate experience was so central in forming my spiritual identity, I chose to begin my career in Hillel, where I could work with other young people at such a crucial stage in their lives. As I grew older, I came to understand the need to create synagogues that could be centers of spirituality, community, and sources of *tikkun olam*, so I chose to go into congregational work."

Rabbi Elyse M. Goldstein was ordained at Hebrew Union College–Jewish Institute of Religion in 1983. She earned her B.A. in Judaic Studies and Sociology from Brandeis University, where she graduated summa cum laude and Phi Beta Kappa. Throughout her student years she served Temple Beth Or of the Deaf, where she became proficient in sign language and in serving the Jewish deaf. She is Rabbinic Director/Rosh Yeshiva of Kolel, The Adult Centre for Liberal Jewish Learning in Toronto, one of North America's only full-time liberal Jewish adult education centers, which she has directed since its inception. She is the author of *ReVisions: Seeing Torah through a Feminist Lens* (Jewish Lights), and many articles in both scholarly and popular journals. She is a nationally recognized specialist in teaching Torah to adults.

"I knew I wanted to be a rabbi from the day of my bat mitzvah on. Standing up there seemed the most natural thing in the world. It took me many years to discover this was an 'unusual' dream for a young woman. Jewish summer camp and youth group were both formative experiences in the development of my strong Jewish identity, and I credit the many charismatic and spiritual rabbis I met in camp, NFTY [the Reform youth movement], and at Brandeis for being my inspiration. I love being a rabbi, and have been blessed with wonderful rabbinic experiences."

Rabbi Julie K. Gordon, a native Minnesotan, was ordained from Hebrew Union College–Jewish Institute of Religion, New York City, in 1984. She is the Co-Senior Rabbi at the Temple of Aaron, a 1,400-family Conservative synagogue, with her husband, Rabbi Jonathan H. Ginsburg. She is the proud mother of their two children, Shoshana and Ari. Rabbi Gordon serves on the executive committee of the National United Jewish Community Rabbinic Cabinet, is 2000 Women's Campaign Chair of the St. Paul United Jewish Fund & Council, and is adjunct faculty at the College of St. Catherine, St. Paul, Minnesota. She also serves as the Jewish chaplain to the Veteran's Administration Medical Center in the Twin Cities.

"My spiritual journey to the rabbinate began in Albert Lea, Minnesota, a Jewish community of ten families and no synagogue. In the 1970s, when my Jewish identity was first forming, I identified with the liberal Conservative movement of Minneapolis-St. Paul encouraging women to fully participate in synagogue ritual. At that time, however, The Jewish Theological Seminary was not accepting women as rabbinical students, so I never considered the rabbinate as a career. When I met Laura Geller, the third woman accepted into HUC–JIR's rabbinical school, at a Hillel student conference, I identified with her spiritual path, immediately realizing I wanted to become a rabbi also. The rabbinate combines my desire to serve God, strengthen the Jewish people, and study Torah. I am dedicated to helping Jews find their spiritual connections within our wonderful tradition."

Rabbi Claire Magidovitch Green was ordained from the Reconstructionist Rabbinical College in 1988 and is rabbi at a residential senior center in suburban Philadelphia. She served as the first coordinator for the Coalition Against Jewish Domestic Violence of the Delaware Valley. The coalition, initiated by Jewish Women International, supports Shomerit Shalom Bayit, a telephone counseling service for Jewish victims of domestic violence, administered by Rabbi Green. Rabbi Green is a creator of meaningful ritual for couples and families who feel alienated from synagogue life. Rabbi Green lives in Huntingdon Valley, Pennsylvania, with her husband, Steven, and their sons, Daniel and Jacob.

"I never wanted my summer at UAHC Torah Corps camp to end. I was fifteen years old, studying and living with HUC–JIR professors and students in a community of shared commitment. My father *[z"l]*, a sabra, and brother were both ordained from HUC–JIR, the Reform seminary. Although I watched my father ordained in 1972 in the same class with Sally Priesand, the first woman ordained by a Jewish seminary, I credit my mother as the true inspiration for my vocation by her creating a warm Jewish environment at home. I want to translate the Jewish way of making meaning to those who feel that our culture is static and irrelevant."

Rabbi Rosette Barron Haim was ordained from Hebrew Union College–Jewish Institute of Religion in Cincinnati in 1988, and joined the staff of The Temple-Tifereth Israel in Cleveland, Ohio, in July of 1988. She has strengthened the areas of lifecycle and holiday celebrations and, among other things, serves as spiritual advisor to the Temple Young Associates, women's association, youth group, outreach programs, and the healing service. Rosie has raised the consciousness of the congregation to be more gender inclusive, and has introduced egalitarian language to the pulpit.

"I grew up in Galesburg, Illinois, and was 'turned on' to learning about Jewish life as a counselor at Olin-Sang-Ruby Union Institute Camp in Oconomowoc, Wisconsin. When I returned home from camp, I met student rabbi Dena Feingold, who was assigned to our community. A great inspiration and model for the possibility of becoming a rabbi, she was a strong influence in my decision. Another formative experience was spending my junior year in Israel, where, at the age of twenty, I became a bat mitzvah, with Rabbi David Forman officiating and serving as a practical advisor about the rabbinate. When I paused to examine the impact of these experiences and the things I enjoyed doing most, they all seemed to find expression in the career choice to become a rabbi. I have never regretted it!"

Jill Hammer is a rabbinical student at The Jewish Theological Seminary of America in New York and will be ordained in 2001. She received a Ph.D. in social psychology from the University of Connecticut in 1995 and a B.A. from Brandeis University in 1991. She has served as editor of *Living Text: The Journal of Contemporary Midrash,* and currently serves as an on-line editor for the Jewish Publication Society. She has published poems and stories, often midrashic, in journals such as *Lilith, Response, Kerem, Bridges, The Jewish Spectator,* and *The Jewish Women's Literary Annual,* and in Naomi Hyman's anthology, *Biblical Women in the Midrash: A Sourcebook* (Jason Aronson). Her own book of midrashim in short story form will be published by the Jewish Publication Society in 2001.

"I decided to become a rabbi while I was in graduate school pursuing my doctorate. At that time I was participating in a small university *havurah* that inspired me to imagine that I could be a rabbi. I chose to enter the rabbinate because Jewish ritual, study, creativity, and *tikkun olam* have become the focus of my life. I love living, teaching, and expanding Jewish text and tradition. Midrash, which I understand as the creative extension of Torah to express the truth of our lives, has become the focus of my rabbinate, and I hope to help other Jews connect to their own wells of revelatory insight."

Rabbi Karyn D. Kedar was ordained from Hebrew Union College–Jewish Institute of Religion in 1985. Immediately after ordination she immigrated to Israel and later became the first woman rabbi to serve in Jerusalem. After living and working in Israel for ten years, she returned to her native America and currently serves as the regional director of the Great Lakes Region of the Union of American Hebrew Congregations.

Rabbi Kedar's first book, *God Whispers: Stories of the Soul, Lessons of the Heart,* is published by Jewish Lights. She lives with her husband, Ezra, and their three children, Talia, Shiri, and Ilan, in the Chicago area.

"I dreamt of being a rabbi since age eight. When asked why, I simply answered that I wanted to know what rabbis knew. To this day I am in pursuit of knowledge that instructs the mind and inspires the soul."

Rabbi Sarra Levine was ordained from the Reconstructionist Rabbinical College in 1996. She is currently working on a Ph.D. in Talmud at New York University and teaching Talmud at RRC. Sarra is the cofounder and Rosh Yeshiva of Bat Kol: A Feminist House of Study, a feminist yeshiva that runs in Jerusalem. The yeshiva offers women from ages twenty through one hundred and twenty the opportunity to study Jewish texts through a feminist lens. Women from all over the world come together to explore what it means to be a Jewish feminist, and to create a Judaism that is truly inclusive.

"I chose the rabbinate after encountering many disenfranchised Jewish women who wished to be reconnected back into their Judaism, and could find no satisfying way of doing so. My dream was to open a feminist yeshiva where women could see themselves as integral in the process of building and maintaining Judaism."

Rabbi Valerie Lieber was ordained from Hebrew Union College–Jewish Institute of Religion in New York in 1995. Since that time, she has served as rabbi at Temple Beth Ahavath Sholom in Brooklyn, New York. Valerie has been active in the Women's Rabbinic Network, made up of women rabbis in the Reform movement, and serves as its treasurer. Some of the ideas in her essay are based on research done for her rabbinic thesis, "Under Every Leafy Tree: Harlotry in Biblical Law, Narrative and Prophecy."

"I decided to become a rabbi while a student at Swarthmore College because I wanted to make Judaism relevant for my generation of Jews. I was lucky enough to have met women rabbinic students while I was a teenager, so I never doubted that I could become one too."

Rabbi Ellen Lippmann was ordained from Hebrew Union College–Jewish Institute of Religion in 1991 and is Rabbi of Kolot Chayeinu/Voices of Our Lives, a progressive Jewish community in Brooklyn, New York. She also serves as the director of the Jewish Women's Program and of the library at the new 14th Street Y in Manhattan. Her writings, including several modern midrashim, have been published in various journals and collections. She is also known as an anti-hunger activist, having founded the soup kitchen at HUC–JIR in New York, served for five years as East Coast director of MAZON: A Jewish Response to Hunger and for three years as chair of Interfaith Voices Against Hunger, part of the New York City Coalition Against Hunger.

"I first decided to become a rabbi when I learned at the end of college that Sally Priesand had been ordained as the first woman rabbi. Who knew such miracles could happen! It took many years to get myself to the starting line, but once having arrived, I knew it to be the right decision, the answering of a call, I even venture to say. One of my greatest joys as a rabbi is the opportunity to teach and study Torah with others, adding our new layer of commentary to those we inherit."

Rabbi Sheryl Nosan, R.J.E., was ordained from the New York campus of Hebrew Union College–Jewish Institute of Religion in 1993. Sheryl was the first female rabbi to serve Congregation Har Zion in suburban Toronto. Sheryl also served a congregation in Teaneck, New Jersey, before taking a position as Rabbi-Educator in Congregation Beth Israel of San Diego. At each of her congregations, Sheryl has focused on Jewish education. Her ongoing studies include Bible and women's issues, as well as classical texts.

"I decided to become a rabbi during my college years when I realized that I wanted to continue learning and teaching that which I was most passionate about: Judaism. But that's not all. Growing up in a small town without a rabbi or a real religious school, I always felt that I missed out on Jewish learning. Later, I overcompensated by going to rabbinic school! My greatest Jewish influences were my parents. My father taught me to read Hebrew and my mother taught me to light candles and say blessings. I continue to treasure each Shabbat and holiday that I can spend with my parents, who were so influential in my becoming a rabbi."

Rabbi Stacy K. Offner was ordained from Hebrew Union College–Jewish Institute of Religion in 1984 and graduated from Kenyon College magna cum laude in 1977. She is the rabbi of Shir Tikvah Congregation in Minneapolis, where she has served since its founding in 1988. She has taught Jewish ethics at Hamline University for over ten years and sits on the ethics committee of Abbott Northwestern Hospital. She currently serves as chaplain of the Minnesota State Senate. Her articles on Judaism, feminism, and ethics have appeared in numerous publications. Offner lives in St. Paul with her partner, Nancy Abramson, and loves when her two adult stepchildren come home to visit.

"I first considered becoming a rabbi during my high school years when I was involved in a consciousness-raising group, along with the editor of this volume, Rabbi Elyse Goldstein. The exploration of Judaism and feminism that was unfolding at that time was a definite factor in my decision to enter the rabbinate, and continues to be a source of inspiration and challenge in my rabbinical work today."

Rabbi Sara Paasche-Orlow was ordained at The Jewish Theological Seminary of America in 1996. She is a cofounder of the Bavli Yerushalmi Project, a dialogue through text learning between Israeli and American Jews. She is currently working at the Jewish Life Network/Steinhardt Foundation as a program officer/educator focused on service and volunteerism as a gateway to Jewish identity and community building. She is the founder of a *havurah* that celebrates Sukkot and Shavuot in an agricultural setting. She co-edited a manual for Conservative rabbis on welcoming gay and lesbian Jews into congregational life. She is married to Dr. Michael Paasche-Orlow, and they have two children, Raziel and Lev.

"I was raised without any Jewish education and little Jewish cultural awareness. My mother's grandfather was ordained at The Jewish Theological Seminary. My father's mother is German, not Jewish, and was very active, along with her brothers, in the German resistance. I decided to go to rabbinical school during college with the wish to deepen my knowledge of Judaism, to take on the challenge of finding a full voice for women in Jewish life, and to work for social justice, following the legacy of my grandmother."

Rabbi Barbara Rosman Penzner was ordained from the Reconstructionist Rabbinical College in 1987. She has served in a number of congregational positions in the Boston area, and is currently rabbi of Temple Hillel B'nai Torah in West Roxbury. She has also worked with Combined Jewish Philanthropies, the Boston Federation, and on the Commission on Jewish Continuity, to create transformative Jewish educational experiences within congregations. It was that experience that led her to the Jerusalem Fellows program, a two-year fellowship in Israel with Jewish educators from all over the world. Rabbi Penzner served from 1996 to 1999 as president of the Reconstructionist Rabbinical Association, the national body of Reconstructionist rabbis.

"I decided to become a rabbi in 1980, having never met a woman rabbi before. The inspiration came to me on Simchat Torah, when someone handed me a Torah scroll for the very first time. Suddenly, I understood that the rabbinate was the life work I had been looking for. Several of my teachers guided me to RRC. It turned out to be a great choice, and I can't imagine a better life than to be a congregational rabbi and a mom. I am grateful to Dr. Marc Bregman of Hebrew Union College, Jerusalem, for sharing my passion for the midrash on Serach, and for pointing me to additional sources; and to my husband, Brian, who shares my love of learning and first introduced me to Serach from his own studies with Dr. Marc Brettler."

Rabbi Hara E. Person was ordained by Hebrew Union College–Jewish Institute of Religion in 1998. She has a B.A. from Amherst College and an M.A. in Fine Arts from New York University/International Center of Photography. She is editor of the UAHC Press and also of *click-onJudaism.com*, a website for Jews in their twenties and thirties. She is a co-editor of the newly revised *Introduction to Judaism: A Source Book* (UAHC Press). She lives in Brooklyn, New York, with her husband and two children.

"I am a first-generation Reform Jew, and was the first girl in my congregation to wear a tallit when I became bat mitzvah. I decided to become a rabbi when I was around eleven, because my rabbi was one of the only people I knew at that time who was proud to be Jewish and knowledgeable about Judaism. I changed my mind several times, and spent a while living in Israel and going to art school before I decided once again that I really did want to be a rabbi."

Rabbi Audrey S. Pollack received rabbinic ordination from Hebrew Union College–Jewish Institute of Religion in Cincinnati in 1994, and is the associate rabbi of Congregation Emanuel in Denver, Colorado. In addition to her congregational work, Rabbi Pollack writes feminist midrash and creative liturgy. Several of her feminist commentaries appear in *Beginning the Journey: A Women's Commentary on the Torah*, published by the Women of Reform Judaism. She is married to Phil Subeck, a social worker.

"I decided at a fairly young age, fourteen, that I wanted to become a rabbi. That I had not yet met a woman who was a rabbi was not an issue for me—as the oldest of three girls, I was raised by my parents to believe that I could do anything I wanted to do. When I was a teenager, my rabbis and cantor—Rabbi David Polish, Rabbi Peter Knobel, and Cantor Jeffrey Klepper—offered opportunities for the young adults of the synagogue to teach, lead services, and study. As I pursued my goal, I came to understand more and more that this was what God wanted me to do with my life: to become a rabbi was the best way that I could serve God and the Jewish people. As a congregational rabbi, my mission is to challenge people to discover what Judaism means for them, to encourage them to express it in their own lives, and to inspire them to have pride in their identity. My ambition is to create in our congregational community an atmosphere that nourishes growth and learning, on both an intellectual and a spiritual level. The synagogue is for me a home, a place of comfort, a place where we discover a Judaism that is deep and compelling."

Rabbi Sally J. Priesand was ordained as the first woman rabbi from Hebrew Union College–Jewish Institute of Religion in 1972, Cincinnati campus. Since 1981, she has served as rabbi of Monmouth Reform Temple in Tinton Falls, New Jersey. She has served on the board of trustees of the Union of American Hebrew Congregations and the executive board of the Central Conference of American Rabbis. Currently, she serves on the board of governors of Hebrew Union College–Jewish Institute of Religion and is Vice-President of the Rabbinic Alumni Association. She is the author of *Judaism and the New Woman* (Behrman House), and a contributor to *Women Rabbis: Exploration and Celebration* (HUC–JIR Rabbinic Alumni Association Press).

"At the age of sixteen, I decided I wanted to be a rabbi. It didn't seem to matter to me that there were no female rabbis. Fortunately, my parents gave me one of the greatest gifts that parents can give their children: the courage to dare and to dream. As a result, I never really doubted whether or not it was possible for a woman to be ordained. I am proud that today young girls grow up knowing they can be rabbis if they want to."

Rabbi Geela-Rayzel Raphael was ordained at the Reconstructionist Rabbinical College in 1997. She has also studied at Indiana University, Brandeis University, Pardes Institute, and the Hebrew University of Jerusalem. She is currently the rabbi at Leyv Ha-Ir Reconstructionist Congregation in Philadelphia. Rabbi Raphael is also a songwriter/liturgist and sings with MIRAJ, an a cappella trio, and Shabbat Unplugged, a rabbinically trained spiritual ensemble. "Bible Babes A-beltin'" is Raphael's recent recording.

"The rabbinate was just the logical step in my call to serve my people and the One who is beyond all. I worked eleven years in Hillel before taking the plunge at midlife to study an additional number of years at RRC. With Shechinah as my guide, I see my rabbinate as empowering others in their exploration of the prism called Judaism, midwifing souls to find their expression through art and intellect, and keeping in touch with the sacred on our life's journey. I have been inspired to the pulpit and the feminist transformation of Judaism by my ancestors and the trailblazers of this generation."

Rabbi Laura M. Rappaport was ordained from Hebrew Union College–Jewish Institute of Religion in 1988. She now lives in Boise, Idaho, dividing her time somewhat randomly among the following pursuits: serving as part-time rabbi of the Wood River Jewish Community of Sun Valley; offering her services as volunteer rabbi and *rebbetzin* to Congregation Ahavath Beth Israel of Boise (officially served by her husband, Rabbi Daniel Fink); freelance writing for *Boise Weekly;* teaching and preaching for Albertson College of Idaho and within the Episcopal Diocese of Idaho; and being mommy, teacher, chauffeur, and mediator to daughters, Tanya and Rosa.

"When I was five years old, my Sunday school teacher took us into the sanctuary and allowed us to touch the Torah scroll, and I cried. The awe, pride, and love that inspired my tears are an important part of how and why my life has taken its course. Throughout late childhood and well into my teenage years I was plagued with the same questions as so many others blossoming into full involvement with the world: Why am I here? What am I supposed to do? Where is meaning in this world so filled with death, despair, and tragedy? Can I possibly make a difference? The only place I could find serious discussion of these, my most pressing concerns, was in my Judaism, my synagogue, my Jewish books. I continue to be awed by the wisdom, the depth, and the emotional power of my beloved heritage. There is no greater joy or honor than to spend one's life engulfed in the work of learning and living Judaism and sharing its priceless gifts with others."

Rabbi Debra Judith Robbins was ordained at Hebrew Union College–Jewish Institute of Religion in Cincinnati in 1991, and received her Master of Hebrew Letters at HUC–JIR in Los Angeles. She is the associate rabbi at Temple Emanu-El in Dallas, Texas, and has been there since she was ordained. She has been developing and teaching a class about love, relationships, and Jewish values to teenagers for six years. She is the coordinator of adult Jewish learning at Temple Emanu-El, which includes Judaic and Hebrew classes, scholar-in-residence weekends, and retreats. She is also involved in the lay pastoral work of the Caring Congregation committee. She serves as chair of the ethics committee at Jewish Family Service as well as on the board. She is on the boards of AIDS Arms and Planned Parenthood, and is the rabbinical liaison to the Isaac Mayer Wise Academy. She has published an article, "The Sun, the Moon, and the Seasons: Ecological Implications of the Hebrew Calendar" in *Ecology & the Jewish Spirit: Where Nature and the Sacred Meet* (Jewish Lights), edited by Ellen Bernstein.

"I am married to Larry Scott Robbins, who is a graduate of the Erwin Daniels School of Jewish Communal Service at the Hebrew Union College in Los Angeles and is the director of resource development at United Way of Metropolitan Dallas. We are the proud parents of Samuel Norman Robbins, who is the first child to be born at a meeting of the Women's Rabbinic Network! (I received the call that he was born and that we would be able to adopt him while at the convention in La Jolla, March 2, 1998.) I was inspired to become a rabbi by my mother, Judith Tobias Robbins *[z"l]*, who died in 1974 when I was eleven years old. She was a creative educator, passionate Jew, and dedicated leader and volunteer at Temple Israel in Boston. My ordination has become her legacy and a true blessing in my life."

Rabbi Rochelle Robins was ordained at Hebrew Union College–Jewish Institute of Religion in 1998. She serves as the Jewish staff chaplain at the Hospital of the University of Pennsylvania. Rabbi Robins is a cofounder of Bat Kol: A Feminist House of Study, the first feminist yeshiva in Jerusalem, and serves as the organization's director.

465

"My first influence into the rabbinate was my father, Rabbi David Robins, who is also a graduate of HUC–JIR. There are numerous reasons why I decided to become a rabbi. I wanted to interact with the conversations in our tradition and in our community as a leader. I wanted to help build a safe place for gays and lesbians in the Jewish world. I wanted to express my social activism within the construct of what I considered to be Jewish ethics. While I have only given a few examples of my many dreams, the most powerful reason why I chose the rabbinate is also the most ambiguous: I knew in my heart this was the path I was meant to take. I still do not know where it will lead me in the long run or even tomorrow, yet I remain challenged and determined to continue to follow my heart in my life's work."

Rabbi Gila Colman Ruskin was ordained from Hebrew Union College–Jewish Institute of Religion in Cincinnati in 1983. She grew up in Detroit, Michigan, at Temple Beth El, and attended both Reform and Conservative religious school. Since 1983, she has been living in Baltimore with her husband, Paul, a geriatric psychiatrist, and her three children, Samuel, Shoshana, and Avital. She is a certified pastoral counselor. She currently teaches in two day schools (Conservative and Orthodox), and a wide variety of adult education programs and professional development courses for Jewish educators. She is the spiritual leader of Congregation Chevrei Tzedek, a unique participatory Conservative Congregation based on commitment to social action, adult education, and community davening and *Divrei Torah*. She is cofounder of the Baltimore Jewish Healing Network.

"I remember the moment on the *bimah* reading from the Torah at my bat mitzvah when I decided that I wanted to become a rabbi. The opportunities to empower Jews to become educated and active participants in fulfilling our covenant through study, ritual practice, Zionism, celebration, and building community have never ceased to excite me, despite the long hours, hard work, and juggling of family and profession. Guiding a class of children or adults through a text from our vast Jewish literature and encouraging them to make it their own by incorporating it into the way they lead their lives is what brings me the greatest fulfillment as a rabbi."

Rabbi Sandy Eisenberg Sasso was the first woman ordained from the Reconstructionist Rabbinical College in 1974. Rabbi Sasso was the first woman to serve a Conservative congregation. She became rabbi, along with her husband, Rabbi Dennis Sasso, of Congregation Beth-El Zedeck in Indianapolis in 1977. They are the first practicing rabbinical couple in world Jewish history. Rabbi Sasso was the first rabbi to become a mother, and Dennis and Sandy Sasso are the parents of David and Deborah Sasso. Rabbi Sasso has served as President of the Reconstructionist Rabbinical Association and Gleaner's Food Bank in Indianapolis as well as on numerous boards. She has written many articles on women and spirituality and has lectured nationally on women's spirituality and the religious imagination of children. Sandy Eisenberg Sasso is the author of award-winning children's books: *God's Paintbrush*; *In God's Name*; *A Prayer for the Earth: The Story of Naamah, Noah's Wife*; *But God Remembered: Stories of Women from Creation to the Promised Land*; *God in Between*; *For Heaven's Sake*; and *God Said Amen* (all Jewish Lights).

"I decided to become a rabbi when I was sixteen years old, following confirmation services at my congregation, Keneseth Israel in Philadelphia. The rabbis at the synagogue were encouraging and supportive. Rabbi Bertram Korn *[z"l]*, the senior rabbi, was my mentor and remained an important source of inspiration and support throughout seminary and during my early years in the rabbinate."

Rabbi Ilene Schneider, Ed.D., was ordained from the Reconstructionist Rabbinical College in 1976, and is the director of the Master of Arts in Education Program at Gratz College in Melrose Park, Pennsylvania. Dr. Schneider was one of the first six women rabbis in the United States. She earned her bachelor's degree from Simmons College and her master's and doctoral degrees in education from Temple University. She resides in Marlton, New Jersey, with her husband, Rabbi Gary M. Gans, and their sons, Natan and Ari.

"I was participating in a communal dinner on an Erev Shabbat in the autumn of 1969, my senior year of college, when one of my friends mentioned that the Reconstructionist movement had opened a rabbinical school the previous year. That chance comment opened before me a wealth of possibilities I'd never before considered. The decision I made that evening was one that helped me define who I was and how I could best serve the Jewish community."

Rabbi Rona Shapiro was ordained at The Jewish Theological Seminary of America in 1990. She also studied at the Pardes Institute in Jerusalem for two years and at the Drisha Institute in New York. Rona served as the executive director of Berkeley Hillel from 1990 to 1999, and now is director of education and outreach at Ma'yan: The Jewish Women's Project. She lives with her husband, David Franklin, and their daughter, Noa Rachel Shapiro-Franklin, in Brooklyn.

"During my time at Pardes, I was inspired by a sense of Jewish community knit together by Torah. I decided to dedicate my life to building such communities in America."

Rabbi Michal Shekel was ordained at Hebrew Union College–Jewish Institute of Religion in New York in 1990. She was in the first class of women accepted for rabbinical studies at The Jewish Theological Seminary of America in 1984. She is the author of numerous textbooks used in Jewish supplemental schools. In 1992, she became the first woman rabbi to lead services in post-Holocaust Germany (at the U.S. army base in Heidelberg). Having served congregations in New Jersey and Boston, she is currently the director of education at Temple Har Zion in Thornhill, Ontario.

"It took me a while to realize I wanted to be a rabbi. The seed was planted in my college days when I became increasingly involved in the Jewish community. The seed took root a number of years later. I was working in the field of news radio and becoming increasingly frustrated with the misguided sense of morality displayed in journalism. Those of us who were in the field chose it because we wanted to make a difference. Unfortunately, business and deadline pressures meant that ethical corners were often cut. There were other ways, moral ways, to make a difference in this world; I began to work in the Jewish community full time. Eventually, I came to the realization that if I truly wanted to serve the community, I would have to take on greater responsibilities personally, communally, and religiously. Becoming a rabbi was the manner in which I achieved taking on Divine commandments, personal responsibilities, and religious obligations."

Rabbi Beth J. Singer was ordained at Hebrew Union College–Jewish Institute of Religion in Cincinnati in 1989. She grew up in southern California and received a Bachelor of Arts in Women's Studies from Pomona College. She is a member of Phi Beta Kappa and graduated with honors. During her years at HUC–JIR, she and two other women founded a shelter for homeless women on the rabbinical school campus. Her spiritual home is Temple Beth Am in Seattle, where she currently shares the pulpit with her husband, Rabbi Jonathan Singer. Rabbi Beth Singer has given birth to three children and she has that number of birth stories.

"I grew up in an observant Reform Jewish home in which we celebrated Judaism daily at home and at Temple. With my father's encouragement, I began to consider the possibility of becoming a rabbi at the time I became a bat mitzvah. During my last week in high school, the class president handed each senior an index card and invited us to imagine where we thought we might be ten years after graduation. I wrote that I would be an ordained rabbi sharing a pulpit with my husband, and that we would be the parents of three children. My dreams have been realized!"

Rabbi Sharon L. Sobel was ordained from Hebrew Union College–Jewish Institute of Religion in May of 1989. She also holds a B.S. in Mass Communications, with concentrations in advertising/marketing and photography, from Boston University. From July 1989 to August 1995, Rabbi Sobel served as assistant rabbi at Holy Blossom Temple in Toronto. Since August 1995, she has served as rabbi of Temple Sinai in Stamford, Connecticut. Rabbi Sobel was the first female rabbi to serve a congregation in South Africa. As a student rabbi, she spent four and one-half months serving the Reform congregation in Pretoria (Temple Menorah), and assisting at the Reform synagogue in Johannesburg (Temple Emanu-Shalom) from May through October of 1987.

"Growing up as the daughter of a Reform rabbi, I was always involved in my father's synagogue in different ways. It was this involvement, as well as my parents' commitment to Judaism, that inspired me to become a rabbi."

Rabbi Ruth H. Sohn was ordained at Hebrew Union College–Jewish Institute of Religion in 1982. She currently teaches Jewish text study at Milken Community High School in Los Angeles, where she lives with her husband, Reuven Firestone, and their three children. Ruth's articles, biblical commentary, midrash, and poetry have appeared in various periodicals, prayerbooks, and books, including *Reading Ruth* (Ballantine), edited by Judith A. Kates and Gail Twersky Reimer, and *Kol Haneshama*, the Reconstructionist prayerbook.

"I started thinking about becoming a rabbi toward the end of my college studies in 1976. It was primarily my own renewed interest in Judaism and my growing desire to make accessible to others the richness of Jewish learning and practice that attracted me to the rabbinate and still informs my work as a rabbi. I love my work and continually feel renewed and challenged by my interactions with those I teach and our mutual encounter with Jewish texts."

Rabbi Julie Ringold Spitzer died in 1999 of ovarian cancer. Her essay was written in the months before her death, and edited posthumously by Rabbi Elyse Goldstein in memory of, and in deep respect for, Julie's life and work.

Rabbi Julie Ringold Spitzer was ordained at the Cincinnati campus of Hebrew Union College–Jewish Institute of Religion in 1985. She served as the regional director of the Union of American Hebrew Congregations Greater New York Council of Reform Synagogues. She was the first woman to serve in this position, and was the second woman to serve as regional director for any of the fourteen regions of the UAHC. She wrote and lectured widely on domestic violence in the Jewish community, and was involved in the community of ovarian cancer activists.

"I began to think seriously about the rabbinate in 1974, while an Eisendrath international exchange student in Israel. When a young man from my home congregation participated in the same trip a year earlier, and then announced his intention to become a rabbi, I reasoned, 'If he can do it, why can't I?'"

Rabbi Shira Stern was ordained at Hebrew Union College–Jewish Institute of Religion in New York in 1983, and spent fourteen years in the pulpit. She was named emerita of the Monroe Township Jewish Center, Monroe Township, New Jersey, when she retired. She created the Human Relations Commission in Monroe, was a member of the county and state Human Rights Commissions, and was a member of the Commission on Social Action of the Reform Movement for six years. She has taught two Jewish feminist courses at Rutgers University in New Brunswick, New Jersey. In addition to her political activism in the pro-choice movement, she has been widely featured in the print and television media on a variety of topics. She is currently a hospital and hospice chaplain, and the director of the Joint Chaplaincy Program for Middlesex County, New Jersey.

"I grew up on the periphery of the Jewish community as a girl in a 'conservadox' congregation, and realized as a teenager in the 1970s that I didn't have to stay upstairs in the women's section once a woman had been ordained. I became a rabbi to make an impact on my community on every level, from womb to tomb, wearing many hats and fulfilling a number of roles: counselor, teacher, cantor, storyteller, dreamer, and catalyst for change. My goal is twofold: to teach others to teach themselves, and to refine my own skills so that my learning continues."

Rabbi Pamela Wax was ordained from Hebrew Union College–Jewish Institute of Religion in New York in 1994. Her rabbinic thesis was titled "The Daughters of Tzelophehad Revisited: The Daughter in Jewish

Inheritance Law." After serving as Jewish chaplain at Goldwater Memorial Hospital in New York City for two and one-half years, Rabbi Wax currently serves as a congregational rabbi in North Adams, Massachusetts.

"Entering the rabbinate was my attempt to make a *havdalah* candle of my life, to weave together varied strands of self into a unified whole: the parts of me that were writer, counselor, political activist, teacher, liturgist, and passionate Jew. Having grown up in an unaffiliated Jewish household, Judaism was a very personal and often painful journey for me, though I ultimately viewed my outsider status as a strength when I entered the rabbinate. An advocate of outreach, I have taught numerous introduction to Judaism courses, which I consider one of my greatest contributions to the cause of Jewish continuity."

Rabbi Nancy Wechsler-Azen was ordained from Hebrew Union College–Jewish Institute of Religion, New York campus, in 1990. Her rabbinical thesis is titled "Rabbinic Attitudes toward Healing." She was the founding rabbi of Temple Kol Ami in Thornhill, Ontario. She has written and taught extensively on healing, Jewish spirituality, and feminism. She has published work in *Keeping Posted, Reform Judaism,* and is a writer for *Life-Lights* (Jewish Lights). She has served on the UAHC staff as assistant director with the Commission on Religious Living and taught for the National Center for Jewish Healing in New York City. Rabbi Wechsler-Azen has initiated healing programming in synagogues throughout America and Canada. She lives with her husband, Rabbi David Wechsler-Azen, and their son, Max, in the New York area.

"Primary influences in my decision to become a Jewish leader focus on my experiences as a camper, counselor, and songleader at the UAHC Camp Swig in Saratoga, California. My role models were rabbinical students who were also artists, lawyers, activists, dancers, and musicians. They demonstrated how spiritual vitality and creativity were intertwined. In the years of serving Jewish communities, my compassion and desire to create vibrant practice continues to deepen. For this I am grateful."

Rabbi Nancy H. Wiener was ordained at Hebrew Union College–Jewish Institute of Religion in 1990. She currently coordinates the Fieldwork Program at HUC–JIR in New York, and teaches courses in pastoral counseling. She also serves as the spiritual leader of the Pound Ridge Jewish Community in Pound Ridge, New York. Rabbi Wiener earned a doctor of ministry degree in Pastoral Counseling at HUC–JIR, and holds a master's degree in Jewish History from Columbia University. She has written *Beyond Breaking the Glass,* a book to help couples of all sexual orientations prepare for their liberal Jewish weddings. She has been published in *Reform Jewish Halakhah and Ethics, European Judaism,* and authored *And They Will Call Me: A Translation of Yiddish Poetry,1939–1945.* Rabbi Wiener was the first openly lesbian person to be hired as an administrator and faculty member at HUC–JIR.

"I contemplated becoming a rabbi earlier in my life, but opted for an academic path instead. Only during my final months at Columbia, immersed in the academic study of Jewish history, did I realize that my real passion was working with contemporary Jews, helping them appreciate their culture, their legacy, and their place within the chain of tradition. It was then that I made a commitment to become a rabbi."

Rabbi Elana Zaiman received her B.A. in Hebrew Literature from the University of Judaism in Los Angeles, and her M.A. in Judaic Studies, M.A. in Hebrew Literature, and rabbinical ordination from The Jewish Theological Seminary of America in New York in 1993. She also received her M.S.W. from Columbia University's School of Social Work. In the past, she has worked as program director and then acting director at Tufts University Hillel in Medford, Massachusetts, and program associate and associate scholar-in-residence at the Brandeis Bar Din Institute in California. Upon receiving her ordination in 1993, she spent five years as a rabbi at the Park Avenue Synagogue in Manhattan. Recently married and relocated to Seattle, Elana teaches adults and children in the Puget Sound region. She continues to conduct services and serve as scholar-in-residence for various communities.

"As a child, when not in synagogue, I would often conduct Shabbat services with my stuffed animals. I would place *kipot* on their heads, put *siddurim* in front of their faces, announce the pages, turn the pages, and then chant the service and deliver a brief *Devar Torah*. Clearly I was imitating my father the rabbi, and my grandfather the rabbi, but I believe that even at that age I was expressing my love for Judaism, for family and for community. Judaism was the place and the space where I felt comfortable. Judaism was the context that gave and continues to give my life meaning."

Notes

Notes

Notes

Notes

Notes

Notes

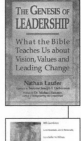

Pastoral Care Resources
LifeLights/™אורות החיים

LifeLights/™אורות החיים are inspirational, information-al booklets about challenges to our emotional and spiritual lives and how to deal with them. Offering help for wholeness and healing, each *LifeLight* is written from a uniquely Jewish spiritual perspective by a wise and caring soul—someone who knows the inner territory of grief, doubt, confusion and longing.

In addition to providing wise words to light a diffi-cult path, each *LifeLight* booklet provides suggestions for additional resources for reading. Many list organi-zations, Jewish and secular, that can provide help, along with information on how to contact them.

> "Invaluable for those needing comfort and
> instruction in times of difficulty and loss."
> **Rabbi David Wolpe,** Sinai Temple, Los Angeles, CA

> "Particularly useful for hospital visits and shiva calls—and
> they enable me to help at those times when I feel helpless."
> **Rabbi Sally Priesand,** Monmouth Reform Temple,
> Tinton Falls, NJ

Categories/Topics:

Health & Healing

Abortion and Judaism: Rabbinic Opinion and Jewish Law
Caring for Your Aging Parents
Caring for Yourself/When Someone Is Ill
Facing and Recovering from Surgery
Facing Cancer as a Family
Finding Spiritual Strength in Pain or Illness
Jewish Response to Dementia: Honoring Broken Tablets
Living with Cancer, One Day at a Time
Recognizing a Loved One's Addiction, and Providing Help
When Madness Comes Home: Living in the Shadow of a Loved One's Mental Illness

Loss / Grief / Death & Dying

Coping with the Death of a Spouse
From Death through Shiva: A Guide to Jewish Grieving Practices
Jewish Hospice: To Live, to Hope, to Heal
Making Sacred Choices at the End of Life
Mourning a Miscarriage
Taking the Time You Need to Mourn Your Loss
Talking to Children about Death
When Someone You Love Is Dying
When Someone You Love Needs Long-Term Care

Categories/Topics continued:

Judaism / Living a Jewish Life

Bar and Bat Mitzvah's Meaning: Preparing Spiritually with Your Child

Choosing a Congregation That Is Right for You

Considering Judaism: Choosing a Faith, Joining a People

Do Jews Believe in the Soul's Survival?

Exploring Judaism as an Adult

Jewish Meditation: How to Begin Your Practice

There's a Place for Us: Gays and Lesbians in the Jewish Community

To Meet Your Soul Mate, You Must Meet Your Soul

Yearning for God

Family Issues

Jewish Adoption: Unique Issues, Practical Solutions

Are You Being Hurt by Someone You Love? Domestic Abuse in the Jewish Community

Grandparenting Interfaith Grandchildren

Healing Estrangement in Your Family Relationships

Interfaith Families Making Jewish Choices

Jewish Approaches to Parenting Teens

Looking Back on Divorce and Letting Go

Parenting through a Divorce

Raising a Child with Special Needs

Talking to Your Children about God

Spiritual Care / Personal Growth

Bringing Your Sadness to God

Doing Teshuvah: Undoing Mistakes, Repairing Relationships and Finding Inner Peace

Easing the Burden of Stress

Finding a Way to Forgive

Finding the Help You Need: Psychotherapy, Pastoral Counseling, and the Promise of Spiritual Direction

Praying in Hard Times: The Soul's Imaginings

Surviving a Crisis or a Tragedy

Now available in hundreds of congregations, health-care facilities, funeral homes, colleges and military installations, these helpful, comforting resources can be uniquely presented in *LifeLights* display racks, available from Jewish Lights. **Each *LifeLight* topic is sold in packs of twelve for $9.95.** General discounts are available for quantity purchases.

Visit us online at **www.jewishlights.com** for a complete list of titles, authors, prices and ordering information, or call us at (802) 457-4000 or toll free at (800) 962-4544.

Congregation Resources

The Art of Public Prayer, 2nd Edition: Not for Clergy Only *By Lawrence A. Hoffman*
6 x 9, 272 pp, Quality PB, 978-1-893361-06-5 **$19.99** *(A SkyLight Paths book)*

Becoming a Congregation of Learners: Learning as a Key to Revitalizing
Congregational Life *By Isa Aron, PhD; Foreword by Rabbi Lawrence A. Hoffman*
6 x 9, 304 pp, Quality PB, 978-1-58023-089-6 **$19.95**

Finding a Spiritual Home: How a New Generation of Jews Can Transform the
American Synagogue *By Rabbi Sidney Schwarz*
6 x 9, 352 pp, Quality PB, 978-1-58023-185-5 **$19.95**

Jewish Pastoral Care, 2nd Edition: A Practical Handbook from Traditional &
Contemporary Sources *Edited by Rabbi Dayle A. Friedman*
6 x 9, 528 pp, HC, 978-1-58023-221-0 **$40.00**

Jewish Spiritual Direction: An Innovative Guide from Traditional and Contemporary
Sources *Edited by Rabbi Howard A. Addison and Barbara Eve Breitman*
6 x 9, 368 pp, HC, 978-1-58023-230-2 **$30.00**

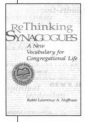

The Self-Renewing Congregation: Organizational Strategies for Revitalizing
Congregational Life *By Isa Aron, PhD; Foreword by Dr. Ron Wolfson*
6 x 9, 304 pp, Quality PB, 978-1-58023-166-4 **$19.95**

Spiritual Community: The Power to Restore Hope, Commitment and Joy
By Rabbi David A. Teutsch, PhD 5½ x 8½, 144 pp, HC, 978-1-58023-270-8 **$19.99**

The Spirituality of Welcoming: How to Transform Your Congregation into a
Sacred Community *By Dr. Ron Wolfson* 6 x 9, 224 pp, Quality PB, 978-1-58023-244-9 **$19.99**

Rethinking Synagogues: A New Vocabulary for Congregational Life
By Rabbi Lawrence A. Hoffman 6 x 9, 240 pp, Quality PB, 978-1-58023-248-7 **$19.99**

Children's Books

What You Will See Inside a Synagogue
By Rabbi Lawrence A. Hoffman and Dr. Ron Wolfson; Full-color photos by Bill Aron
A colorful, fun-to-read introduction that explains the ways and whys of Jewish
worship and religious life. 8½ x 10½, 32 pp, Full-color photos, Quality PB, 978-1-59473-256-0 **$8.99**
For ages 6 & up (A SkyLight Paths book)

The Kids' Fun Book of Jewish Time
By Emily Sper 9 x 7½, 24 pp, Full-color illus., HC, 978-1-58023-311-8 **$16.99**

In God's Hands
By Lawrence Kushner and Gary Schmidt 9 x 12, 32 pp, HC, 978-1-58023-224-1 **$16.99**

Because Nothing Looks Like God
By Lawrence and Karen Kushner
Introduces children to the possibilities of spiritual life.
11 x 8½, 32 pp, Full-color illus., HC, 978-1-58023-092-6 **$17.99** *For ages 4 & up*

Also Available: **Because Nothing Looks Like God Teacher's Guide**
8½ x 11, 22 pp, PB, 978-1-58023-140-4 **$6.95** *For ages 5–8*

Board Book Companions to *Because Nothing Looks Like God*
5 x 5, 24 pp, Full-color illus., SkyLight Paths Board Books *For ages 0–4*

What Does God Look Like? 978-1-893361-23-2 **$7.99**
How Does God Make Things Happen? 978-1-893361-24-9 **$7.95**
Where Is God? 978-1-893361-17-1 **$7.99**

The Book of Miracles: A Young Person's Guide to Jewish Spiritual Awareness
By Lawrence Kushner. All-new illustrations by the author
6 x 9, 96 pp, 2-color illus., HC, 978-1-879045-78-1 **$16.95** *For ages 9 and up*

In Our Image: God's First Creatures
By Nancy Sohn Swartz 9 x 12, 32 pp, Full-color illus., HC, 978-1-879045-99-6 **$16.95** *For ages 4 & up*

Also Available as a Board Book: **How Did the Animals Help God?**
5 x 5, 24 pp, Board, Full-color illus., 978-1-59473-044-3 **$7.99** *For ages 0–4 (A SkyLight Paths book)*

What Makes Someone a Jew?
By Lauren Seidman
Reflects the changing face of American Judaism.
10 x 8½, 32 pp, Full-color photos, Quality PB Original, 978-1-58023-321-7 **$8.99** *For ages 3–6*

Children's Books
by Sandy Eisenberg Sasso

Adam & Eve's First Sunset: God's New Day

Engaging new story explores fear and hope, faith and gratitude in ways that will delight kids and adults—inspiring us to bless each of God's days and nights.

9 x 12, 32 pp, Full-color illus., HC, 978-1-58023-177-0 **$17.95** *For ages 4 & up*

Also Available as a Board Book: Adam and Eve's New Day

5 x 5, 24 pp, Full-color illus., Board, 978-1-59473-205-8 **$7.99** *For ages 0–4 (A SkyLight Paths book)*

But God Remembered

Stories of Women from Creation to the Promised Land

Four different stories of women—Lillith, Serach, Bityah, and the Daughters of Z—teach us important values through their faith and actions.

9 x 12, 32 pp, Full-color illus., Quality PB, 978-1-58023-372-9 **$8.99**; HC, 978-1-879045-43-9 **$16.95** *For ages 8 & up*

Cain & Abel: Finding the Fruits of Peace

Shows children that we have the power to deal with anger in positive ways. Provides questions for kids and adults to explore together.

9 x 12, 32 pp, Full-color illus., HC, 978-1-58023-123-7 **$16.95** *For ages 5 & up*

God in Between

If you wanted to find God, where would you look? This magical, mythical tale teaches that God can be found where we are: within all of us and the relationships between us.

9 x 12, 32 pp, Full-color illus., HC, 978-1-879045-86-6 **$16.95** *For ages 4 & up*

God's Paintbrush: Special 10th Anniversary Edition

Wonderfully interactive, invites children of all faiths and backgrounds to encounter God through moments in their own lives. Provides questions adult and child can explore together.

11 x 8½, 32 pp, Full-color illus., HC, 978-1-58023-195-4 **$17.95** *For ages 4 & up*

Also Available: God's Paintbrush Teacher's Guide

8½ x 11, 32 pp, PB, 978-1-879045-57-6 **$8.95**

God's Paintbrush Celebration Kit

A Spiritual Activity Kit for Teachers and Students of All Faiths, All Backgrounds
Additional activity sheets available:

8-Student Activity Sheet Pack (40 sheets/5 sessions), 978-1-58023-058-2 **$19.95**

Single-Student Activity Sheet Pack (5 sessions), 978-1-58023-059-9 **$3.95**

In God's Name

Like an ancient myth in its poetic text and vibrant illustrations, this award-winning modern fable about the search for God's name celebrates the diversity and, at the same time, the unity of all people.

9 x 12, 32 pp, Full-color illus., HC, 978-1-879045-26-2 **$16.99** *For ages 4 & up*

Also Available as a Board Book: What Is God's Name?

5 x 5, 24 pp, Board, Full-color illus., 978-1-893361-10-2 **$7.99** *For ages 0–4 (A SkyLight Paths book)*

Also Available: In God's Name video and study guide

Computer animation, original music, and children's voices. 18 min. **$29.99**

Also Available in Spanish: El nombre de Dios

9 x 12, 32 pp, Full-color illus., HC, 978-1-893361-63-8 **$16.95** *(A SkyLight Paths book)*

Noah's Wife: The Story of Naamah

When God tells Noah to bring the animals of the world onto the ark, God also calls on Naamah, Noah's wife, to save each plant on Earth. Based on an ancient text.

9 x 12, 32 pp, Full-color illus., HC, 978-1-58023-134-3 **$16.95** *For ages 4 & up*

Also Available as a Board Book: Naamah, Noah's Wife

5 x 5, 24 pp, Full-color illus., Board, 978-1-893361-56-0 **$7.95** *For ages 0–4 (A SkyLight Paths book)*

For Heaven's Sake: Finding God in Unexpected Places

9 x 12, 32 pp, Full-color illus., HC, 978-1-58023-054-4 **$16.95** *For ages 4 & up*

God Said Amen: Finding the Answers to Our Prayers

9 x 12, 32 pp, Full-color illus., HC, 978-1-58023-080-3 **$16.95** *For ages 4 & up*

Theology/Philosophy

A Touch of the Sacred: A Theologian's Informal Guide to Jewish Belief
By Dr. Eugene B. Borowitz and Frances W. Schwartz Explores the musings from the
leading theologian of liberal Judaism. 6 x 9, 256 pp, HC, 978-1-58023-337-8 **$21.99**

Talking about God: Exploring the Meaning of Religious Life with
Kierkegaard, Buber, Tillich and Heschel *By Daniel F. Polish, PhD*
Examines the meaning of the human religious experience with the greatest theologians of modern times. 6 x 9, 160 pp, HC, 978-1-59473-230-0 **$21.99** *(A SkyLight Paths book)*

Jews & Judaism in the 21st Century: Human Responsibility, the
Presence of God, and the Future of the Covenant
Edited by Rabbi Edward Feinstein; Foreword by Paula E. Hyman
Five celebrated leaders in Judaism examine contemporary Jewish life.
6 x 9, 192 pp, HC, 978-1-58023-315-6 **$24.99**

Christians and Jews in Dialogue: Learning in the Presence of the Other
By Mary C. Boys and Sara S. Lee; Foreword by Dr. Dorothy Bass
6 x 9, 240 pp, HC, 978-1-59473-144-0 **$21.99** *(A SkyLight Paths book)*

The Death of Death: Resurrection and Immortality in Jewish Thought
By Neil Gillman 6 x 9, 336 pp, Quality PB, 978-1-58023-081-0 **$18.95**

Ethics of the Sages: Pirke Avot—Annotated & Explained
Translation & Annotation by Rabbi Rami Shapiro
5½ x 8½, 208 pp, Quality PB, 978-1-59473-207-2 **$16.99** *(A SkyLight Paths book)*

Hasidic Tales: Annotated & Explained
By Rabbi Rami Shapiro; Foreword by Andrew Harvey
5½ x 8½, 240 pp, Quality PB, 978-1-893361-86-7 **$16.95** *(A SkyLight Paths Book)*

A Heart of Many Rooms: Celebrating the Many Voices within Judaism
By David Hartman 6 x 9, 352 pp, Quality PB, 978-1-58023-156-5 **$19.95**

The Hebrew Prophets: Selections Annotated & Explained
Translation & Annotation by Rabbi Rami Shapiro; Foreword by Zalman M. Schachter-Shalomi
5½ x 8½, 224 pp, Quality PB, 978-1-59473-037-5 **$16.99** *(A SkyLight Paths book)*

A Jewish Understanding of the New Testament
By Rabbi Samuel Sandmel; Preface by Rabbi David Sandmel
5½ x 8½, 368 pp, Quality PB, 978-1-59473-048-1 **$19.99** *(A SkyLight Paths book)*

Keeping Faith with the Psalms: Deepen Your Relationship with God Using the Book
of Psalms *By Daniel F. Polish* 6 x 9, 320 pp, Quality PB, 978-1-58023-300-2 **$18.99**

A Living Covenant: The Innovative Spirit in Traditional Judaism
By David Hartman 6 x 9, 368 pp, Quality PB, 978-1-58023-011-7 **$20.00**

Love and Terror in the God Encounter
The Theological Legacy of Rabbi Joseph B. Soloveitchik
By David Hartman 6 x 9, 240 pp, Quality PB, 978-1-58023-176-3 **$19.95**

The Personhood of God: Biblical Theology, Human Faith and the Divine Image
By Dr. Yochanan Muffs; Foreword by Dr. David Hartman 6 x 9, 240 pp, HC, 978-1-58023-265-4 **$24.99**

Traces of God: Seeing God in Torah, History and Everyday Life
By Neil Gillman 6 x 9, 240 pp, HC, 978-1-58023-249-4 **$21.99**

We Jews and Jesus: Exploring Theological Differences for Mutual Understanding
By Rabbi Samuel Sandmel; Preface by Rabbi David Sandmel
6 x 9, 176 pp, Quality PB, 978-1-59473-208-9 **$16.99** *(A SkyLight Paths book)*

Your Word Is Fire: The Hasidic Masters on Contemplative Prayer
Edited and translated by Arthur Green and Barry W. Holtz
6 x 9, 160 pp, Quality PB, 978-1-879045-25-5 **$15.95**

I Am Jewish
Personal Reflections Inspired by the Last Words of Daniel Pearl
Almost 150 Jews—both famous and not—from all walks of life, from all around
the world, write about many aspects of their Judaism.
Edited by Judea and Ruth Pearl
6 x 9, 304 pp, Deluxe PB w/flaps, 978-1-58023-259-3 **$18.99**
Download a free copy of the *I Am Jewish Teacher's Guide* at our website:
www.jewishlights.com

Theology/Philosophy/The Way Into... Series

The Way Into... series offers an accessible and highly usable "guided tour" of the Jewish faith, people, history and beliefs—in total, an introduction to Judaism that will enable you to understand and interact with the sacred texts of the Jewish tradition. Each volume is written by a leading contemporary scholar and teacher, and explores one key aspect of Judaism. *The Way Into...* series enables all readers to achieve a real sense of Jewish cultural literacy through guided study.

The Way Into Encountering God in Judaism
By Neil Gillman
For everyone who wants to understand how Jews have encountered God throughout history and today.
6 x 9, 240 pp, Quality PB, 978-1-58023-199-2 **$18.99**; HC, 978-1-58023-025-4 **$21.95**
Also Available: **The Jewish Approach to God:** A Brief Introduction for Christians
By Neil Gillman
5½ x 8½, 192 pp, Quality PB, 978-1-58023-190-9 **$16.95**

The Way Into Jewish Mystical Tradition
By Lawrence Kushner
Allows readers to interact directly with the sacred mystical text of the Jewish tradition. An accessible introduction to the concepts of Jewish mysticism, their religious and spiritual significance and how they relate to life today.
6 x 9, 224 pp, Quality PB, 978-1-58023-200-5 **$18.99**; HC, 978-1-58023-029-2 **$21.95**

The Way Into Jewish Prayer
By Lawrence A. Hoffman
Opens the door to 3,000 years of Jewish prayer, making available all anyone needs to feel at home in the Jewish way of communicating with God.
6 x 9, 208 pp, Quality PB, 978-1-58023-201-2 **$18.99**

Also Available: **The Way Into Jewish Prayer Teacher's Guide**
By Rabbi Jennifer Ossakow Goldsmith
8½ x 11, 42 pp, PB, 978-1-58023-345-3 **$8.99**
Visit our website to download a free copy.

The Way Into Judaism and the Environment
By Jeremy Benstein
Explores the ways in which Judaism contributes to contemporary social-environmental issues, the extent to which Judaism is part of the problem and how it can be part of the solution.
6 x 9, 288 pp, HC, 978-1-58023-268-5 **$24.99**

The Way Into *Tikkun Olam* (Repairing the World)
By Elliot N. Dorff
An accessible introduction to the Jewish concept of the individual's responsibility to care for others and repair the world.
6 x 9, 320 pp, HC, 978-1-58023-269-2 **$24.99**; 304 pp, Quality PB, 978-1-58023-328-6 **$18.99**

The Way Into Torah
By Norman J. Cohen
Helps guide in the exploration of the origins and development of Torah, explains why it should be studied and how to do it.
6 x 9, 176 pp, Quality PB, 978-1-58023-198-5 **$16.99**

The Way Into the Varieties of Jewishness
By Sylvia Barack Fishman, PhD
Explores the religious and historical understanding of what it has meant to be Jewish from ancient times to the present controversy over "Who is a Jew?"
6 x 9, 288 pp, HC, 978-1-58023-030-8 **$24.99**

Current Events/History

A Dream of Zion: American Jews Reflect on Why Israel Matters to Them
Edited by Rabbi Jeffrey K. Salkin Explores what Jewish people in America have to say about Israel. 6 x 9, 304 pp, HC, 978-1-58023-340-8 **$24.99**
Also Available: **A Dream of Zion Teacher's Guide** 8½ x 11, 18 pp, PB, 978-1-58023-356-9 **$8.99**

The Jewish Connection to Israel, the Promised Land: A Brief Introduction for Christians *By Rabbi Eugene Korn, PhD* 5½ x 8½, 192 pp, Quality PB, 978-1-58023-318-7 **$14.99**

The Story of the Jews: A 4,000-Year Adventure—A Graphic History Book
Written & illustrated by Stan Mack 6 x 9, 288 pp, illus., Quality PB, 978-1-58023-155-8 **$16.99**

Hannah Senesh: Her Life and Diary, the First Complete Edition
By Hannah Senesh; Foreword by Marge Piercy; Preface by Eitan Senesh
6 x 9, 368 pp, Quality PB, 978-1-58023-342-2 **$19.99**; 352 pp, HC, 978-1-58023-212-8 **$24.99**

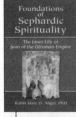

The Ethiopian Jews of Israel: Personal Stories of Life in the Promised Land *By Len Lyons, PhD; Foreword by Alan Dershowitz; Photographs by Ilan Ossendryver* Recounts, through photographs and words, stories of Ethiopian Jews.
10½ x 10, 240 pp, 100 full-color photos, HC, 978-1-58023-323-1 **$34.99**

Foundations of Sephardic Spirituality: The Inner Life of Jews of the Ottoman Empire
By Rabbi Marc D. Angel, PhD 6 x 9, 224 pp, HC, 978-1-58023-243-2 **$24.99**

Judaism and Justice: The Jewish Passion to Repair the World
By Rabbi Sidney Schwarz 6 x 9, 352 pp, Quality PB, 978-1-58023-353-8 **$19.99**

Ecology/Environment

A Wild Faith: Jewish Ways into Wilderness, Wilderness Ways into Judaism
By Rabbi Mike Comins; Foreword by Nigel Savage
Offers ways to enliven and deepen your spiritual life through wilderness experience.
6 x 9, 240 pp, Quality PB, 978-1-58023-316-3 **$16.99**

Ecology & the Jewish Spirit: Where Nature & the Sacred Meet
Edited by Ellen Bernstein 6 x 9, 288 pp, Quality PB, 978-1-58023-082-7 **$18.99**

Torah of the Earth: Exploring 4,000 Years of Ecology in Jewish Thought
Vol. 1: Biblical Israel: One Land, One People; Rabbinic Judaism: One People, Many Lands
Vol. 2: Zionism: One Land, Two Peoples; Eco-Judaism: One Earth, Many Peoples
Edited by Arthur Waskow Vol. 1: 6 x 9, 272 pp, Quality PB, 978-1-58023-086-5 **$19.95**
Vol. 2: 6 x 9, 336 pp, Quality PB, 978-1-58023-087-2 **$19.95**

The Way Into Judaism and the Environment
By Jeremy Benstein 6 x 9, 224 pp, HC, 978-1-58023-268-5 **$24.99**

Grief/Healing

Healing and the Jewish Imagination: Spiritual and Practical Perspectives on Judaism and Health *Edited by Rabbi William Cutter, PhD*
Explores Judaism for comfort in times of illness and perspectives on suffering.
6 x 9, 240 pp, HC, 978-1-58023-314-9 **$24.99**

Grief in Our Seasons: A Mourner's Kaddish Companion *By Rabbi Kerry M. Olitzky*
4½ x 6½, 448 pp, Quality PB, 978-1-879045-55-2 **$15.95**

Healing of Soul, Healing of Body: Spiritual Leaders Unfold the Strength & Solace in Psalms *Edited by Rabbi Simkha Y. Weintraub, CSW*
6 x 9, 128 pp, 2-color illus. text, Quality PB, 978-1-879045-31-6 **$14.99**

Mourning & Mitzvah, 2nd Edition: A Guided Journal for Walking the Mourner's Path through Grief to Healing *By Anne Brener, LCSW*
7½ x 9, 304 pp, Quality PB, 978-1-58023-113-8 **$19.99**

Tears of Sorrow, Seeds of Hope, 2nd Edition: A Jewish Spiritual Companion for Infertility and Pregnancy Loss *By Rabbi Nina Beth Cardin*
6 x 9, 208 pp, Quality PB, 978-1-58023-233-3 **$18.99**

A Time to Mourn, a Time to Comfort, 2nd Edition: A Guide to Jewish Bereavement *By Dr. Ron Wolfson*
7 x 9, 384 pp, Quality PB, 978-1-58023-253-1 **$19.99**

When a Grandparent Dies: A Kid's Own Remembering Workbook for Dealing with Shiva and the Year Beyond *By Nechama Liss-Levinson, PhD*
8 x 10, 48 pp, 2-color text, HC, 978-1-879045-44-6 **$15.95** *For ages 7–13*

Meditation

The Handbook of Jewish Meditation Practices
A Guide for Enriching the Sabbath and Other Days of Your Life
By Rabbi David A. Cooper Easy-to-learn meditation techniques.
6 x 9, 208 pp, Quality PB, 978-1-58023-102-2 **$16.95**

Discovering Jewish Meditation: Instruction & Guidance for Learning an Ancient
Spiritual Practice *By Nan Fink Gefen*
6 x 9, 208 pp, Quality PB, 978-1-58023-067-4 **$16.95**

A Heart of Stillness: A Complete Guide to Learning the Art of Meditation
By David A. Cooper 5½ x 8½, 272 pp, Quality PB, 978-1-893361-03-4 **$16.95** *(A SkyLight Paths book)*

Meditation from the Heart of Judaism: Today's Teachers Share Their Practices,
Techniques, and Faith *Edited by Avram Davis*
6 x 9, 256 pp, Quality PB, 978-1-58023-049-0 **$16.95**

Silence, Simplicity & Solitude: A Complete Guide to Spiritual Retreat at Home
By David A. Cooper 5½ x 8½, 336 pp, Quality PB, 978-1-893361-04-1 **$16.95**
(A SkyLight Paths book)

Ritual/Sacred Practice

The Jewish Dream Book: The Key to Opening the Inner Meaning of
Your Dreams *By Vanessa L. Ochs with Elizabeth Ochs; Full-color illus. by Kristina Swarner*
Instructions for how modern people can perform ancient Jewish dream practices
and dream interpretations drawn from the Jewish wisdom tradition.
8 x 8, 128 pp, Full-color illus., Deluxe PB w/flaps, 978-1-58023-132-9 **$16.95**

God in Your Body: Kabbalah, Mindfulness and Embodied Spiritual Practice
By Jay Michaelson
The first comprehensive treatment of the body in Jewish spiritual practice and an
essential guide to the sacred.
6 x 9, 288 pp, Quality PB, 978-1-58023-304-0 **$18.99**

The Book of Jewish Sacred Practices: CLAL's Guide to Everyday & Holiday
Rituals & Blessings *Edited by Rabbi Irwin Kula and Vanessa L. Ochs, PhD*
6 x 9, 368 pp, Quality PB, 978-1-58023-152-7 **$18.95**

Jewish Ritual: A Brief Introduction for Christians
By Rabbi Kerry M. Olitzky and Rabbi Daniel Judson
5½ x 8½, 144 pp, Quality PB, 978-1-58023-210-4 **$14.99**

The Rituals & Practices of a Jewish Life: A Handbook for Personal Spiritual
Renewal *Edited by Rabbi Kerry M. Olitzky and Rabbi Daniel Judson*
6 x 9, 272 pp, illus., Quality PB, 978-1-58023-169-5 **$18.95**

The Sacred Art of Lovingkindness: Preparing to Practice
By Rabbi Rami Shapiro 5½ x 8½, 176 pp, Quality PB, 978-1-59473-151-8 **$16.99**
(A SkyLight Paths book)

Science Fiction/Mystery & Detective Fiction

Mystery Midrash: An Anthology of Jewish Mystery & Detective Fiction
Edited by Lawrence W. Raphael; Preface by Joel Siegel
6 x 9, 304 pp, Quality PB, 978-1-58023-055-1 **$16.95**

Criminal Kabbalah: An Intriguing Anthology of Jewish Mystery & Detective Fiction
Edited by Lawrence W. Raphael; Foreword by Laurie R. King
6 x 9, 256 pp, Quality PB, 978-1-58023-109-1 **$16.95**

Wandering Stars: An Anthology of Jewish Fantasy & Science Fiction
Edited by Jack Dann; Introduction by Isaac Asimov
6 x 9, 272 pp, Quality PB, 978-1-58023-005-6 **$18.99**

More Wandering Stars: An Anthology of Outstanding Stories of Jewish Fantasy and
Science Fiction *Edited by Jack Dann; Introduction by Isaac Asimov*
6 x 9, 192 pp, Quality PB, 978-1-58023-063-6 **$16.95**

Spirituality/Lawrence Kushner

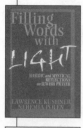

Filling Words with Light: Hasidic and Mystical Reflections on Jewish Prayer
By Lawrence Kushner and Nehemia Polen
5½ x 8½, 176 pp, Quality PB, 978-1-58023-238-8 **$16.99**; HC, 978-1-58023-216-6 **$21.99**

The Book of Letters: A Mystical Hebrew Alphabet
Popular HC Edition, 6 x 9, 80 pp, 2-color text, 978-1-879045-00-2 **$24.95**
Collector's Limited Edition, 9 x 12, 80 pp, gold foil embossed pages, w/limited edition silkscreened
print, 978-1-879045-04-0 **$349.00**

The Book of Miracles: A Young Person's Guide to Jewish Spiritual Awareness
6 x 9, 96 pp, 2-color illus., HC, 978-1-879045-78-1 **$16.95** *For ages 9 and up*

The Book of Words: Talking Spiritual Life, Living Spiritual Talk
6 x 9, 160 pp, Quality PB, 978-1-58023-020-9 **$16.95**

Eyes Remade for Wonder: A Lawrence Kushner Reader *Introduction by Thomas Moore*
6 x 9, 240 pp, Quality PB, 978-1-58023-042-1 **$18.95**

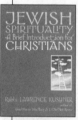

God Was in This Place & I, i Did Not Know: Finding Self, Spirituality and
Ultimate Meaning 6 x 9, 192 pp, Quality PB, 978-1-879045-33-0 **$16.95**

Honey from the Rock: An Introduction to Jewish Mysticism
6 x 9, 176 pp, Quality PB, 978-1-58023-073-5 **$16.95**

Invisible Lines of Connection: Sacred Stories of the Ordinary
5½ x 8½, 160 pp, Quality PB, 978-1-879045-98-9 **$15.95**

Jewish Spirituality—A Brief Introduction for Christians
5½ x 8½, 112 pp, Quality PB, 978-1-58023-150-3 **$12.95**

The River of Light: Jewish Mystical Awareness
6 x 9, 192 pp, Quality PB, 978-1-58023-096-4 **$16.95**

The Way Into Jewish Mystical Tradition
6 x 9, 224 pp, Quality PB, 978-1-58023-200-5 **$18.99**; HC, 978-1-58023-029-2 **$21.95**

Spirituality/Prayer

My People's Passover Haggadah: Traditional Texts, Modern Commentaries
Edited by Rabbi Lawrence A. Hoffman, PhD, and David Arnow, PhD Diverse commentaries
on the traditional Passover Haggadah—in two volumes! Vol. 1: 7 x 10, 304 pp, HC
978-1-58023-354-5 **$24.99** Vol. 2: 7 x 10, 320 pp, HC, 978-1-58023-346-0 **$24.99**

Witnesses to the One: The Spiritual History of the *Sh'ma* By Rabbi Joseph B.
Meszler; Foreword by Rabbi Elyse Goldstein 6 x 9, 176 pp, HC, 978-1-58023-309-5 **$19.99**

My People's Prayer Book Series

Traditional Prayers, Modern Commentaries *Edited by Rabbi Lawrence A. Hoffman*
Provides diverse and exciting commentary to the traditional liturgy, helping modern
men and women find new wisdom in Jewish prayer, and bring liturgy into their lives.
Each book includes Hebrew text, modern translation, and commentaries from all
perspectives of the Jewish world.

Vol. 1—The *Sh'ma* and Its Blessings
7 x 10, 168 pp, HC, 978-1-879045-79-8 **$24.99**
Vol. 2—The *Amidah*
7 x 10, 240 pp, HC, 978-1-879045-80-4 **$24.95**
Vol. 3—*P'sukei D'zimrah* (Morning Psalms)
7 x 10, 240 pp, HC, 978-1-879045-81-1 **$24.95**
Vol. 4—*Seder K'riat Hatorah* (The Torah Service)
7 x 10, 264 pp, HC, 978-1-879045-82-8 **$23.95**
Vol. 5—*Birkhot Hashachar* (Morning Blessings)
7 x 10, 240 pp, HC, 978-1-879045-83-5 **$24.95**
Vol. 6—*Tachanun* and Concluding Prayers
7 x 10, 240 pp, HC, 978-1-879045-84-2 **$24.95**
Vol. 7—Shabbat at Home
7 x 10, 240 pp, HC, 978-1-879045-85-9 **$24.95**
Vol. 8—*Kabbalat Shabbat* (Welcoming Shabbat in the Synagogue)
7 x 10, 240 pp, HC, 978-1-58023-121-3 **$24.99**
Vol. 9—Welcoming the Night: *Minchah* and *Ma'ariv* (Afternoon and
Evening Prayer) 7 x 10, 272 pp, HC, 978-1-58023-262-3 **$24.99**
Vol. 10—Shabbat Morning: *Shacharit* and *Musaf* (Morning and
Additional Services) 7 x 10, 240 pp, HC, 978-1-58023-240-1 **$24.99**

Spirituality

Journeys to a Jewish Life: Inspiring Stories from the Spiritual Journeys of American Jews *By Paula Amann*
Examines the soul treks of Jews lost and found. 6 x 9, 208 pp, HC, 978-1-58023-317-0 **$19.99**

The Adventures of Rabbi Harvey: A Graphic Novel of Jewish Wisdom and Wit in the Wild West *By Steve Sheinkin*
Jewish and American folktales combine in this witty and original graphic novel collection. Creatively retold and set on the western frontier of the 1870s.
6 x 9, 144 pp, Full-color illus., Quality PB, 978-1-58023-310-1 **$16.99**
Also Available: **The Adventures of Rabbi Harvey Teacher's Guide**
8½ x 11, 32 pp, PB, 978-1-58023-326-2 **$8.99**

Ethics of the Sages: *Pirke Avot—Annotated & Explained*
Translation and Annotation by Rabbi Rami Shapiro
5½ x 8½, 192 pp, Quality PB, 978-1-59473-207-2 **$16.99** *(A SkyLight Paths book)*

A Book of Life: Embracing Judaism as a Spiritual Practice
By Michael Strassfeld 6 x 9, 528 pp, Quality PB, 978-1-58023-247-0 **$19.99**

Meaning and Mitzvah: Daily Practices for Reclaiming Judaism through Prayer, God, Torah, Hebrew, Mitzvot and Peoplehood *By Rabbi Goldie Milgram*
7 x 9, 336 pp, Quality PB, 978-1-58023-256-2 **$19.99**

The Soul of the Story: Meetings with Remarkable People
By Rabbi David Zeller 6 x 9, 288 pp, HC, 978-1-58023-272-2 **$21.99**

Aleph-Bet Yoga: Embodying the Hebrew Letters for Physical and Spiritual Well-Being
By Steven A. Rapp. Foreword by Tamar Frankiel, PhD and Judy Greenfeld. Preface by Hart Lazer.
7 x 10, 128 pp, b/w photos, Quality PB, Layflat binding, 978-1-58023-162-6 **$16.95**

Does the Soul Survive? A Jewish Journey to Belief in Afterlife, Past Lives & Living with Purpose *By Rabbi Elie Kaplan Spitz; Foreword by Brian L. Weiss, MD*
6 x 9, 288 pp, Quality PB, 978-1-58023-165-7 **$16.99**

First Steps to a New Jewish Spirit: Reb Zalman's Guide to Recapturing the Intimacy & Ecstasy in Your Relationship with God *By Rabbi Zalman M. Schachter-Shalomi with Donald Gropman* 6 x 9, 144 pp, Quality PB, 978-1-58023-182-4 **$16.95**

God in Our Relationships: Spirituality between People from the Teachings of Martin Buber *By Rabbi Dennis S. Ross* 5½ x 8½, 160 pp, Quality PB, 978-1-58023-147-3 **$16.95**

Judaism, Physics and God: Searching for Sacred Metaphors in a Post-Einstein World
By Rabbi David W. Nelson 6 x 9, 368 pp, Quality PB, inc. reader's discussion guide, 978-1-58023-306-4 **$18.99**;
HC, 352 pp, 978-1-58023-252-4 **$24.99**

The Jewish Lights Spirituality Handbook: A Guide to Understanding, Exploring & Living a Spiritual Life *Edited by Stuart M. Matlins*
What exactly is "Jewish" about spirituality? How do I make it a part of my life? Fifty of today's foremost spiritual leaders share their ideas and experience with us.
6 x 9, 456 pp, Quality PB, 978-1-58023-093-3 **$19.99**

Bringing the Psalms to Life: How to Understand and Use the Book of Psalms
By Daniel F. Polish 6 x 9, 208 pp, Quality PB, 978-1-58023-157-2 **$16.95**;
HC, 978-1-58023-077-3 **$21.95**

God & the Big Bang: Discovering Harmony between Science & Spirituality
By Daniel C. Matt 6 x 9, 216 pp, Quality PB, 978-1-879045-89-7 **$16.99**

Minding the Temple of the Soul: Balancing Body, Mind, and Spirit through Traditional Jewish Prayer, Movement, and Meditation *By Tamar Frankiel, PhD, and Judy Greenfeld*
7 x 10, 184 pp, illus., Quality PB, 978-1-879045-64-4 **$16.95**
Audiotape of the Blessings and Meditations: 60 min. **$9.95**
Videotape of the Movements and Meditations: 46 min. **$20.00**

One God Clapping: The Spiritual Path of a Zen Rabbi *By Alan Lew with Sherril Jaffe*
5½ x 8½, 336 pp, Quality PB, 978-1-58023-115-2 **$16.95**

There Is No Messiah ... and You're It: The Stunning Transformation of Judaism's Most Provocative Idea *By Rabbi Robert N. Levine, DD*
6 x 9, 192 pp, Quality PB, 978-1-58023-255-5 **$16.99**

These Are the Words: A Vocabulary of Jewish Spiritual Life
By Arthur Green 6 x 9, 304 pp, Quality PB, 978-1-58023-107-7 **$18.95**

Holidays/Holy Days

Rosh Hashanah Readings: Inspiration, Information and Contemplation

Yom Kippur Readings: Inspiration, Information and Contemplation

Edited by Rabbi Dov Peretz Elkins with Section Introductions from Arthur Green's These Are the Words

An extraordinary collection of readings, prayers and insights that enable the modern worshiper to enter into the spirit of the High Holy Days in a personal and powerful way, permitting the meaning of the Jewish New Year to enter the heart.

RHR: 6 x 9, 400 pp, HC, 978-1-58023-239-5 **$24.99**

YKR: 6 x 9, 368 pp, HC, 978-1-58023-271-5 **$24.99**

Jewish Holidays: A Brief Introduction for Christians
By Rabbi Kerry M. Olitzky and Rabbi Daniel Judson
5½ x 8½, 144 pp, Quality PB, 978-1-58023-302-6 **$16.99**

Reclaiming Judaism as a Spiritual Practice: Holy Days and Shabbat
By Rabbi Goldie Milgram
7 x 9, 272 pp, Quality PB, 978-1-58023-205-0 **$19.99**

7th Heaven: Celebrating Shabbat with Rebbe Nachman of Breslov
By Moshe Mykoff with the Breslov Research Institute
5⅛ x 8¼, 224 pp, Deluxe PB w/flaps, 978-1-58023-175-6 **$18.95**

Shabbat, 2nd Edition: The Family Guide to Preparing for and Celebrating the Sabbath
By Dr. Ron Wolfson 7 x 9, 320 pp, illus., Quality PB, 978-1-58023-164-0 **$19.99**

Hanukkah, 2nd Edition: The Family Guide to Spiritual Celebration
By Dr. Ron Wolfson. Edited by Joel Lurie Grishaver.
7 x 9, 240 pp, illus., Quality PB, 978-1-58023-122-0 **$18.95**

The Jewish Family Fun Book, 2nd Edition: Holiday Projects, Everyday Activities, and Travel Ideas with Jewish Themes *By Danielle Dardashti and Roni Sarig. Illus. by Avi Katz.*
6 x 9, 304 pp, 70+ b/w illus. & diagrams, Quality PB, 978-1-58023-333-0 **$18.99**

The Jewish Lights Book of Fun Classroom Activities: Simple and Seasonal Projects for Teachers and Students *By Danielle Dardashti and Roni Sarig*
6 x 9, 240 pp, Quality PB, 978-1-58023-206-7 **$19.99**

Passover

My People's Passover Haggadah
Traditional Texts, Modern Commentaries
Edited by Rabbi Lawrence A. Hoffman, PhD, and David Arnow, PhD
A diverse and exciting collection of commentaries on the traditional Passover Haggadah—in two volumes!
Vol. 1: 7 x 10, 304 pp, HC, 978-1-58023-354-5 **$24.99**
Vol. 2: 7 x 10, 320 pp, HC, 978-1-58023-346-0 **$24.99**

Leading the Passover Journey
The Seder's Meaning Revealed, the Haggadah's Story Retold
By Rabbi Nathan Laufer
Uncovers the hidden meaning of the Seder's rituals and customs.
6 x 9, 224 pp, HC, 978-1-58023-211-1 **$24.99**

The Women's Passover Companion: Women's Reflections on the Festival of Freedom
Edited by Rabbi Sharon Cohen Anisfeld, Tara Mohr, and Catherine Spector
6 x 9, 352 pp, Quality PB, 978-1-58023-231-9 **$19.99**

The Women's Seder Sourcebook: Rituals & Readings for Use at the Passover Seder
Edited by Rabbi Sharon Cohen Anisfeld, Tara Mohr, and Catherine Spector
6 x 9, 384 pp, Quality PB, 978-1-58023-232-6 **$19.99**

Creating Lively Passover Seders: A Sourcebook of Engaging Tales, Texts & Activities
By David Arnow, PhD 7 x 9, 416 pp, Quality PB, 978-1-58023-184-8 **$24.99**

Passover, 2nd Edition: The Family Guide to Spiritual Celebration
By Dr. Ron Wolfson with Joel Lurie Grishaver 7 x 9, 352 pp, Quality PB, 978-1-58023-174-9 **$19.95**

Life Cycle
Marriage / Parenting / Family / Aging

The New Jewish Baby Album: Creating and Celebrating the Beginning of a Spiritual Life—A Jewish Lights Companion
By the Editors at Jewish Lights. Foreword by Anita Diamant. Preface by Rabbi Sandy Eisenberg Sasso.
A spiritual keepsake that will be treasured for generations. More than just a memory book, *shows you how—and why it's important*—to create a Jewish home and a Jewish life. 8 x 10, 64 pp, Deluxe Padded HC, Full-color illus., 978-1-58023-138-1 **$19.95**

The Jewish Pregnancy Book: A Resource for the Soul, Body & Mind during Pregnancy, Birth & the First Three Months
By Sandy Falk, MD, and Rabbi Daniel Judson, with Steven A. Rapp
Includes medical information, prayers and rituals for each stage of pregnancy, from a liberal Jewish perspective. 7 x 10, 208 pp, Quality PB, b/w photos, 978-1-58023-178-7 **$16.95**

Celebrating Your New Jewish Daughter: Creating Jewish Ways to Welcome Baby Girls into the Covenant—New and Traditional Ceremonies *By Debra Nussbaum Cohen; Foreword by Rabbi Sandy Eisenberg Sasso* 6 x 9, 272 pp, Quality PB, 978-1-58023-090-2 **$18.95**

The New Jewish Baby Book, 2nd Edition: Names, Ceremonies & Customs—A Guide for Today's Families *By Anita Diamant* 6 x 9, 336 pp, Quality PB, 978-1-58023-251-7 **$19.99**

Parenting as a Spiritual Journey: Deepening Ordinary and Extraordinary Events into Sacred Occasions *By Rabbi Nancy Fuchs-Kreimer*
6 x 9, 224 pp, Quality PB, 978-1-58023-016-2 **$16.95**

Parenting Jewish Teens: A Guide for the Perplexed
By Joanne Doades
Explores the questions and issues that shape the world in which today's Jewish teenagers live.
6 x 9, 200 pp, Quality PB, 978-1-58023-305-7 **$16.99**

Judaism for Two: A Spiritual Guide for Strengthening and Celebrating Your Loving Relationship *By Rabbi Nancy Fuchs-Kreimer and Rabbi Nancy H. Wiener; Foreword by Rabbi Elliot N. Dorff* Addresses the ways Jewish teachings can enhance and strengthen committed relationships. 6 x 9, 224 pp, Quality PB, 978-1-58023-254-8 **$16.99**

Embracing the Covenant: Converts to Judaism Talk About Why & How
By Rabbi Allan Berkowitz and Patti Moskovitz 6 x 9, 192 pp, Quality PB, 978-1-879045-50-7 **$16.95**

The Guide to Jewish Interfaith Family Life: An InterfaithFamily.com Handbook
Edited by Ronnie Friedland and Edmund Case 6 x 9, 384 pp, Quality PB, 978-1-58023-153-4 **$18.95**

Introducing My Faith and My Community
The Jewish Outreach Institute Guide for the Christian in a Jewish Interfaith Relationship
By Rabbi Kerry M. Olitzky 6 x 9, 176 pp, Quality PB, 978-1-58023-192-3 **$16.99**

Making a Successful Jewish Interfaith Marriage: The Jewish Outreach Institute Guide to Opportunities, Challenges and Resources *By Rabbi Kerry M. Olitzky with Joan Peterson Littman*
6 x 9, 176 pp, Quality PB, 978-1-58023-170-1 **$16.95**

The Creative Jewish Wedding Book: A Hands-On Guide to New & Old Traditions, Ceremonies & Celebrations *By Gabrielle Kaplan-Mayer*
9 x 9, 288 pp, b/w photos, Quality PB, 978-1-58023-194-7 **$19.99**

Divorce Is a Mitzvah: A Practical Guide to Finding Wholeness and Holiness When Your Marriage Dies *By Rabbi Perry Netter; Afterword by Rabbi Laura Geller.*
6 x 9, 224 pp, Quality PB, 978-1-58023-172-5 **$16.95**

A Heart of Wisdom: Making the Jewish Journey from Midlife through the Elder Years
Edited by Susan Berrin; Foreword by Harold Kushner
6 x 9, 384 pp, Quality PB, 978-1-58023-051-3 **$18.95**

So That Your Values Live On: Ethical Wills and How to Prepare Them
Edited by Jack Riemer and Nathaniel Stampfer
6 x 9, 272 pp, Quality PB, 978-1-879045-34-7 **$18.99**

Inspiration

Happiness and the Human Spirit: The Spirituality of Becoming the Best You Can Be *By Abraham J. Twerski, MD*
Shows you that true happiness is attainable once you stop looking outside yourself for the source.   6 x 9, 176 pp, HC, 978-1-58023-343-9 **$19.99**

The Bridge to Forgiveness: Stories and Prayers for Finding God and Restoring Wholeness *By Rabbi Karyn D. Kedar*
Examines how forgiveness can be the bridge that connects us to wholeness and peace.
6 x 9, 176 pp, HC, 978-1-58023-324-8 **$19.99**

God's To-Do List: 103 Ways to Be an Angel and Do God's Work on Earth
By Dr. Ron Wolfson 6 x 9, 150 pp, Quality PB, 978-1-58023-301-9 **$16.99**

God in All Moments: Mystical & Practical Spiritual Wisdom from Hasidic Masters
Edited and translated by Or N. Rose with Ebn D. Leader
5½ x 8½, 192 pp, Quality PB, 978-1-58023-186-2 **$16.95**

Our Dance with God: Finding Prayer, Perspective and Meaning in the Stories of Our Lives *By Karyn D. Kedar* 6 x 9, 176 pp, Quality PB, 978-1-58023-202-9 **$16.99**
Also Available: **The Dance of the Dolphin** (HC edition of *Our Dance with God*)
6 x 9, 176 pp, HC, 978-1-58023-154-1 **$19.95**

The Empty Chair: Finding Hope and Joy—Timeless Wisdom from a Hasidic Master, Rebbe Nachman of Breslov *Adapted by Moshe Mykoff and the Breslov Research Institute*
4 x 6, 128 pp, 2-color text, Deluxe PB w/flaps, 978-1-879045-67-5 **$9.99**

The Gentle Weapon: Prayers for Everyday and Not-So-Everyday Moments—Timeless Wisdom from the Teachings of the Hasidic Master, Rebbe Nachman of Breslov
Adapted by Moshe Mykoff and S. C. Mizrahi, together with the Breslov Research Institute
4 x 6, 144 pp, 2-color text, Deluxe PB w/flaps, 978-1-58023-022-3 **$9.99**

God Whispers: Stories of the Soul, Lessons of the Heart *By Karyn D. Kedar*
6 x 9, 176 pp, Quality PB, 978-1-58023-088-9 **$15.95**

Restful Reflections: Nighttime Inspiration to Calm the Soul, Based on Jewish Wisdom
By Rabbi Kerry M. Olitzky & Rabbi Lori Forman 4½ x 6½, 448 pp, Quality PB, 978-1-58023-091-9 **$15.95**

Sacred Intentions: Daily Inspiration to Strengthen the Spirit, Based on Jewish Wisdom
By Rabbi Kerry M. Olitzky and Rabbi Lori Forman 4½ x 6½, 448 pp, Quality PB, 978-1-58023-061-2 **$15.95**

Kabbalah/Mysticism/Enneagram

Awakening to Kabbalah: The Guiding Light of Spiritual Fulfillment
By Rav Michael Laitman, PhD 6 x 9, 192 pp, HC, 978-1-58023-264-7 **$21.99**

Seek My Face: A Jewish Mystical Theology *By Arthur Green*
6 x 9, 304 pp, Quality PB, 978-1-58023-130-5 **$19.95**

Zohar: Annotated & Explained
Translation and annotation by Daniel C. Matt; Foreword by Andrew Harvey
5½ x 8½, 176 pp, Quality PB, 978-1-893361-51-5 **$15.99**   *(A SkyLight Paths book)*

Ehyeh: A Kabbalah for Tomorrow
By Arthur Green 6 x 9, 224 pp, Quality PB, 978-1-58023-213-5 **$16.99**

The Flame of the Heart: Prayers of a Chasidic Mystic *By Reb Noson of Breslov. Translated by David Sears with the Breslov Research Institute* 5 x 7¼, 160 pp, Quality PB, 978-1-58023-246-3 **$15.99**

The Gift of Kabbalah: Discovering the Secrets of Heaven, Renewing Your Life on Earth
By Tamar Frankiel, PhD 6 x 9, 256 pp, Quality PB, 978-1-58023-141-1 **$16.95;**
HC, 978-1-58023-108-4 **$21.95**

Kabbalah: A Brief Introduction for Christians
By Tamar Frankiel, PhD 5½ x 8½, 208 pp, Quality PB, 978-1-58023-303-3 **$16.99**

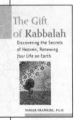

The Lost Princess and Other Kabbalistic Tales of Rebbe Nachman of Breslov
The Seven Beggars and Other Kabbalistic Tales of Rebbe Nachman of Breslov
Translated by Rabbi Aryeh Kaplan; Preface by Rabbi Chaim Kramer
Lost Princess: 6 x 9, 400 pp, Quality PB, 978-1-58023-217-3 **$18.99**
Seven Beggars: 6 x 9, 192 pp, Quality PB, 978-1-58023-250-0 **$16.99**

See also *The Way Into Jewish Mystical Tradition* in Spirituality / The Way Into... Series

Spirituality/Women's Interest

The Quotable Jewish Woman: Wisdom, Inspiration & Humor from the Mind & Heart
Edited and compiled by Elaine Bernstein Partnow
6 x 9, 496 pp, Quality PB, 978-1-58023-236-4 **$19.99**; HC, 978-1-58023-193-0 **$29.99**

The Divine Feminine in Biblical Wisdom Literature: Selections Annotated &
Explained *Translated and Annotated by Rabbi Rami Shapiro*
5½ x 8½, 240 pp, Quality PB, 978-1-59473-109-9 **$16.99** *(A SkyLight Paths book)*

The Women's Haftarah Commentary: New Insights from Women Rabbis on the
54 Weekly Haftarah Portions, the 5 Megillot & Special Shabbatot
Edited by Rabbi Elyse Goldstein 6 x 9, 560 pp, Quality PB, 978-1-58023-371-2 **$19.99**

New Jewish Feminism: Probing the Past, Forging the Future
Edited by Rabbi Elyse Goldstein; Foreword by Anita Diamant
6 x 9, 350 pp (est), HC, 978-1-58023-359-0 **$24.99**

See Holidays for *The Women's Passover Companion: Women's Reflections
on the Festival of Freedom* and *The Women's Seder Sourcebook: Rituals &
Readings for Use at the Passover Seder.* Also see Bar/Bat Mitzvah for *The
JGirl's Guide: The Young Jewish Woman's Handbook for Coming of Age.*

Spirituality / Crafts
(from SkyLight Paths, our sister imprint)

The Knitting Way: A Guide to Spiritual Self-Discovery
By Linda Skolnick and Janice MacDaniels
Shows how to use the practice of knitting to strengthen our spiritual selves.
7 x 9, 240 pp, Quality PB, 978-1-59473-079-5 **$16.99**

The Quilting Path: A Guide to Spiritual Self-Discovery through Fabric,
Thread and Kabbalah *By Louise Silk*
Explores how to cultivate personal growth through quilt making.
7 x 9, 192 pp, Quality PB, 978-1-59473-206-5 **$16.99**

The Painting Path: Embodying Spiritual Discovery through Yoga, Brush
and Color *By Linda Novick; Foreword by Richard Segalman*
Explores the divine connection you can experience through art.
7 x 9, 208 pp, 8-page full-color insert, Quality PB, 978-1-59473-226-3 **$18.99**

The Scrapbooking Journey: A Hands-On Guide to Spiritual Discovery
By Cory Richardson-Lauve; Foreword by Stacy Julian
Reveals how this craft can become a practice used to deepen and shape your life.
7 x 9, 176 pp, 8-page full-color insert, b/w photos, Quality PB, 978-1-59473-216-4 **$18.99**

Travel

Israel—A Spiritual Travel Guide, 2nd Edition
A Companion for the Modern Jewish Pilgrim
By Rabbi Lawrence A. Hoffman 4¾ x 10, 256 pp, Quality PB, illus., 978-1-58023-261-6 **$18.99**
Also Available: **The Israel Mission Leader's Guide** 978-1-58023-085-8 **$4.95**

12-Step

100 Blessings Every Day: Daily Twelve Step Recovery Affirmations, Exercises for
Personal Growth & Renewal Reflecting Seasons of the Jewish Year
By Rabbi Kerry M. Olitzky; Foreword by Rabbi Neil Gillman
4½ x 6½, 432 pp, Quality PB, 978-1-879045-30-9 **$16.99**

Recovery from Codependence: A Jewish Twelve Steps Guide to Healing Your Soul
By Rabbi Kerry M. Olitzky 6 x 9, 160 pp, Quality PB, 978-1-879045-32-3 **$13.95**

Twelve Jewish Steps to Recovery: A Personal Guide to Turning from Alcoholism &
Other Addictions—Drugs, Food, Gambling, Sex ...
By Rabbi Kerry M. Olitzky and Stuart A. Copans, MD; Preface by Abraham J. Twerski, MD
6 x 9, 144 pp, Quality PB, 978-1-879045-09-5 **$15.99**

About Jewish Lights

People of all faiths and backgrounds yearn for books that attract, engage, educate, and spiritually inspire.

Our principal goal is to stimulate thought and help all people learn about who the Jewish People are, where they come from, and what the future can be made to hold. While people of our diverse Jewish heritage are the primary audience, our books speak to people in the Christian world as well and will broaden their understanding of Judaism and the roots of their own faith.

We bring to you authors who are at the forefront of spiritual thought and experience. While each has something different to say, they all say it in a voice that you can hear.

Our books are designed to welcome you and then to engage, stimulate, and inspire. We judge our success not only by whether or not our books are beautiful and commercially successful, but by whether or not they make a difference in your life.

For your information and convenience, at the back of this book we have provided a list of other Jewish Lights books you might find interesting and useful. They cover all the categories of your life:

Bar/Bat Mitzvah	Life Cycle
Bible Study / Midrash	Meditation
Children's Books	Parenting
Congregation Resources	Prayer
Current Events / History	Ritual / Sacred Practice
Ecology/ Environment	Spirituality
Fiction: Mystery, Science Fiction	Theology / Philosophy
Grief / Healing	Travel
Holidays / Holy Days	12-Step
Inspiration	Women's Interest
Kabbalah / Mysticism / Enneagram	

Stuart M. Matlins, Publisher

Or phone, fax, mail or e-mail to: **JEWISH LIGHTS Publishing**
Sunset Farm Offices, Route 4 • P.O. Box 237 • Woodstock, Vermont 05091
Tel: (802) 457-4000 • Fax: (802) 457-4004 • www.jewishlights.com
Credit card orders: (800) 962-4544 (8:30AM–5:30PM ET Monday–Friday)
Generous discounts on quantity orders. SATISFACTION GUARANTEED. Prices subject to change.

For more information about each book, visit our website at www.jewishlights.com